AMBIGUOUS
ORDER

AMBIGUOUS ORDER

Military Forces in African States

HERBERT M. HOWE

LYNNE
RIENNER
PUBLISHERS

BOULDER
LONDON

Paperback edition published in the United States of America in 2005 by
Lynne Rienner Publishers, Inc.
1800 30th Street, Boulder, Colorado 80301
www.rienner.com

and in the United Kingdom by
Lynne Rienner Publishers, Inc.
3 Henrietta Street, Covent Garden, London WC2E 8LU

Published in hardcover in 2001.

ISBN 1-58826-315-0 (pbk. : alk. paper)

Printed and bound in the United States of America

The paper used in this publication meets the requirements
of the American National Standard for Permanence of
Paper for Printed Library Materials Z39.48-1992.

5 4 3 2

Dedicated to my parents,
Professors Herbert and Evelyn Howe,
Who encouraged my interest in the world
And whatever writing skills I possess.
I wish them many more happy years.

CONTENTS

Acknowledgments   ix

1 Introduction: Changing Security Patterns in Sub-Saharan Africa   1

2 The Roots and Results of African Military Unprofessionalism   27

3 Africa's Ongoing Security Predicament   73

4 ECOMOG and Regional Peacekeeping   129

5 Executive Outcomes and Private Security   187

6 ACRI: U.S. Support of African Military Professionalism   243

7 Conclusion: Toward Restoring the Civil-Military Divide   269

List of Acronyms and Abbreviations   293
Bibliography   297
Index   307
About the Book   316

ACKNOWLEDGMENTS

I first became interested in African military conflicts during my Peace Corps service in Nigeria. The Biafran war, a secessionist attempt by eastern Nigeria, killed about a million civilians between 1967 and early 1970.

I returned to Africa in the mid-1970s to study the liberation wars in southern Africa. As a freelance correspondent for the *Philadelphia Inquirer,* I traveled throughout Zimbabwe (then Rhodesia), where I met both insurgents and foreign soldiers, or "mercenaries." Subsequently, study at the University of Wisconsin, the Fletcher School of Law and Diplomacy, and Harvard University provided me with a deeper background to what I had witnessed during my travels. Among the many professors who assisted me were Kenneth Dike, Clarence Clyde Ferguson, Steven Feierman, Martin Kilson, Robert Meagher, W. Scott Thompson, and John Willis.

Teaching at Georgetown University in Washington since 1984 has afforded me access to a wide range of experts on Africa. A very incomplete listing of those who generously have contributed to my understanding of Africa includes Ambassadors Chester Crocker, Ibrahim Gambari, John Leigh, Marshall McCallie, Donald McHenry, and Mamadou Seck and Professors Anthony Arend, George Ayitteh, Pauline Baker, Michael Brown, William Foltz, Eboe Hutchful, Gilbert Khadiagala, Carol Lancaster, René Lemarchand, Peter Lewis, Robin Luckham, John McNeill, Marina Ottaway, Will Reno, George Shambaugh, Tim Sisk, John Spence, Steven Stedman, and William Zartman. My thanks also go to Rudy Atallah, Zainab Bangura, Walt Barrows, John Bayley, Doug Brooks, John Cronin, Margaret Culbert, Dumiso Dabengwa, Frederick Ehrenreich, Carl Ek, J. 'Kayode Fayemi,

Scott Fisher, Janet Fleischman, Chris Fomunyoh, Connie Freeman, Michael Grunberg, Emmanuel Gyimah-Boladi, Rusty Higgs, E. J. Hoogendorn, Paul Kamara, Karen Kwiatkowski, Kathleen List, Terrence Lyons, Tony Marley, Stacy Marsh, Susan Mashkes, Bernie McCabe, Steven Metz, Paul Moorcraft, Ibrahim Mwani, Abel-Fatau Musah, Kevin O'Brien, 'Funmi Olonisakin, Joseph Opala, Philip Parham, Khareen Pech, Arnold Quainoo, Les Rudman, Bert Sachse, Joseph Sala, Barry Schutz, Bryant Shaw, Joseph Smaldone, Chris Smith, Patrick Smith, Charles Snyder, Tim Spicer, William Stoakley, Bill Thom, Michael Thomas, Alex Vines, Margaret Vogt, Dunstan Wai, Ibrahim Wani, Steve Weigert, Rocklyn Williams, Brian Wolfe, and Jim Woods. Special appreciation goes to Walter Barrows, Thomas Ofcansky, Ambassador Andrew Steigman, James Woods, and Jennifer Windsor. Despite this assistance, any mistakes remaining in this work are mine alone.

The School of Foreign Service at Georgetown facilitated my work as a visiting research fellow in spring 1999 at the Centre for Defence Studies, King's College, the University of London. Amnesty International, the Campaign for Democracy and Development, and the Global Coalition for Africa also assisted my research overseas. Students in my African Military Conflict and Resolution class provided a stimulating sounding board for various topics. Students and staff members who were especially helpful include Alissa Chase, Veronique Dozier, Michelle Gavin, Manjiv Jayakumar, Kerri Ann Lack, Meg O'Brien, Will Schlickenmaier, and Jennifer Smith. The staff at Lynne Rienner Publishers supplied greatly appreciated wisdom and tolerance. The reference librarians at Georgetown's Lauinger Library unfailingly assisted me. Evelyn and Charles Payson provided me with a home away from home in Wisconsin.

Several points about my research require mentioning. I limited my focus to ECOMOG, Executive Outcomes, and the African Crisis Response Intitiative as recent examples of regional, private, and Western-assisted security. Due to space constraints, I did not examine several other examples, which, fortunately, other scholars are currently examining.

I traveled to Liberia to observe ECOMOG in 1995 and then to Sierra Leone the following year to gather material about Executive Outcomes. Many of those who assisted me did so only on the condition that they remain anonymous; although I cannot identify them, I am truly grateful for their assistance. I must emphasize my appreciation of soldiers in ECOMOG. While I continue to be critical of ECOMOG's overall record, the Nigerian-led force has saved the lives of numerous West Africans who otherwise would have been victims of war. And although I give some limited praise to private security forces, in large part because of their record—especially when compared with other groups—in Sierra Leone, I hope that Africa will develop its own highly professional militaries, independent of reliance on foreign help.

My strongest hope for this book is that, in whatever small way, it will encourage debate about how Africa may attain greater security and avoid the scourge of war.

I

INTRODUCTION:
CHANGING SECURITY PATTERNS
IN SUB-SAHARAN AFRICA

U nprecedented domestic and regional security threats are challenging many sub-Saharan African states. The region's balance of military power between state and insurgency appears to be shifting often in
favor of the latter, and African states are deploying their forces beyond
their borders more frequently. An arc of conflict runs from the Horn of
Africa down to southern Africa. Ethiopia and Eritrea have engaged in
an especially destructive conventional conflict with weaponry new to
Africa. The exceptionally brutal "low-intensity" insurgencies in Liberia
and Sierra Leone have destabilized parts of West Africa, while the military free-for-all in Congo* has formed the geographic center of an inter-
locked series of conflicts and instability stretching from Chad and
Sudan in the north to Angola and Zimbabwe in the south in what is
termed Africa's "first world war."[1] The low-intensity nature of most
African conflicts—decentralized insurgent groups having few fixed
bases or targetable economic-military assets, while wielding low-cost
but effective weaponry and engaging in often indiscriminate brutality
against civilians—poses exceptional problems for conventionally
trained militaries.

Responsibility for security, but not the power to achieve it, has
devolved increasingly from the West and the United Nations to individual states and regional organizations. United Nations Secretary-General
Kofi Annan reflected this when he stated that the UN "does not have . . .

---

*In May 1997, Zaire became the Democratic Republic of Congo, which I refer
to as Congo (not to be confused with the Republic of Congo, or Congo-
Brazzaville) throughout this book.

the institutional capacity to conduct military enforcement measures. . . . Under present conditions, *ad hoc* Member States' coalitions of the willing offer the most effective deterrent to aggression or to the escalation or spread of an ongoing conflict."[2] "African solutions for African problems" is the prevailing mantra about security on the continent. But many African nations lack adequate security capability, either to defend their own territorial integrity or to participate effectively in the conditions suggested by Secretary-General Annan.

This book assumes that the political nature of the state strongly influences military professionalism—a concept that includes both military capabilities and political responsibility to the state[3]—and that competent and loyal militaries can safeguard political and economic development. Max Weber cited the monopoly of military coercion as a defining characteristic of the post-1648 state system,[4] and Martin van Creveld writes that "the first duty of any social entity is to protect the lives of its members. Either modern states cope with low-intensity conflict, or else they will disappear."[5] Provision of effective security allows peaceful development and validates the state to its citizenry.

Personal rule, sub-Saharan Africa's predominant governing method since independence, has often weakened military professionalism. The civil-military divide has been breached by civilians attempting to manipulate military affairs and by military officers who pursue political control of the state. The resultant weaker militaries increasingly threaten state legitimacy in the post–Cold War era.

In the pages that follow I identify three military strategies that African states are using to address the threats to their present existence. The strategies are regional intervention forces, private security companies, and Western-sponsored upgrades of state militaries—and I argue that they are likely to fail unless African states emphasize indigenous military professionalism. Most academic works examine African armed forces as political actors, but few works have assessed *military* behavior and potential.[6] This book focuses on military capabilities and examines these armed forces' political responsibility primarily in relationship to military operations and their conduct toward the civilian population.

This book also examines several security dilemmas that African states and their supporters face. The first and most important involves the tension between military capabilities and political responsibility. Africa has had some ninety military coups since 1963, and many rulers believe that their political survival depends on emphasizing military loyalty at the expense of capability; thus, some rulers have debilitated their own security forces in an effort to preserve political power. The result is weak militaries that cannot address the often growing domestic and regional threats to fragile regimes.

Generalizing about some forty-five differing states poses obvious difficulties. Although Cassandra-like observers may point dramatically to "failing" or "collapsed" states as indicating "new barbarians" or a "coming anarchy"[7] (Sierra Leone and Somalia), Africa also boasts countries that have negotiated inclusive peace settlements of their previous conflicts (South Africa and Mozambique) and those whose economic growth rates rank among the world's best (Uganda and Ghana). Furthermore, each state's security situation can change quickly (Sierra Leone). Some states have had little or no insurgency activity since independence (Botswana and Ivory Coast) and have few worries about any shifting of security balances. Militaries in some states have refrained from seizing power (Senegal and Zambia).

This book maintains that many African militaries lack significant technical skills, but it acknowledges that: First, military capabilities are relative—that is, an African military only needs to be mediocre by first world standards when facing manifestly incompetent opponents; Second, there are the African militaries that appear competent and loyal, for instance, those of Senegal, Ghana, and Botswana; Third, even unprofessional militaries have professional officers who excel in military skills and who avoid political involvement. Nigeria's military, which this book singles out as often acting unprofessionally during the 1980s and 1990s, at least once had numerous capable officers who preferred that partisan politics and the military remain separate. And, finally, once-capable militaries can "reprofessionalize" under a determined head of state. President Olusegun Obasanjo of Nigeria began pursuing this goal following his election in mid-1999.

All the same, many ill-prepared African states face security threats beyond their capabilities, given that some African states are little more than juridical entities.[8] In recent history, the colonial rulers and then the superpowers had helped to prop up these states before 1990, thus postponing the states' regimes' need to develop their own capable militaries. By the mid-1980s, two factors—parasitic personal rulers who had denied basic political and human rights (while often emasculating their states' militaries) and unfavorable shifts in exported commodities and imported oil prices—had further weakened African regimes. Writers began using such labels as "lame leviathans" and such adjectives as "enfeebled," "quasi," or "vacuous" to describe any given African state.[9] "Globalization," the growing influence of powerful international government and private organizations, has helped to shift the military balance of power toward the insurgents since 1990. Foreign-instigated economic and political reforms, accompanied by drops in foreign aid, usually weakened regime control whereas the largely unregulated mineral, arms, and mercenary markets, on balance, have assisted rebel groups.

Increasing donor demands for African democratization and economic reform further debilitated some governments' effective authority following the Cold War. Dropoffs in foreign military and economic assistance reduced the availability of patronage with which leaders could purchase domestic support and security. Less foreign support also attenuated the possibility of non-African military intervention that would protect regimes from domestic or foreign enemies.

The end of superpower rivalry has proved empowering for insurgents in several respects and has dramatically changed the nature of African conflict. During the Cold War, foreign supporters usually linked their material support to groups exhibiting acceptable ideological or political agendas; Warsaw Pact nations often being the primary suppliers to African rebellions. Now, after the collapse of the Soviet Union and the demobilization or shrinking of non-African militaries, such cash-strapped nations as Bulgaria sell equipment to insurgents without political preconditions.

Insurgents now enjoy greater freedom of action. Mary Kaldor describes the current "new wars" as a mixture of war, wide-scale human rights abuses, and organized crime.[10] Since 1990, the attacks on noncombatants and relief agencies, the use of child-soldiers, and the targeting of economic resources (often to pay for readily available weaponry) has surged. The availability of weapons has escalated the number of armed participants, especially poorly trained militias and insurgent groups, and contributed to the militarization of African political discourse. Adding to the volatile mix are skilled demobilized soldiers from South Africa and Eastern Europe.

Many African states now lack the military resources to halt the shift of the coercive balance. Somalia, Liberia, and Sierra Leone were three examples during the 1990s of countries having virtually no national military to face growing armed opposition. From 1960 to 1990, insurgencies and invasions overthrew only two sub-Saharan African states (Chad and Uganda); during the 1990s, however, armed force, exclusive of coups, toppled at least six governments.

Regional geopolitical rivalries appear to be spreading rapidly as African states increasingly disregard concepts of national sovereignty. Shrinking Western strategic interest and the corresponding lack of patronage undermine some regimes while encouraging expansionist tendencies in others. Some of the militarily more capable states, notably Uganda and Angola, are projecting their forces into neighboring countries, especially in southern and central Africa, often to destabilize the existing authority. Specific reasons for this include economic aggrandizement, preemptive self-defense, greater availability of long-range weapons systems, the growth of armed participants, and the personalities of various leaders. I suggest that "military mercantilism"—a regime's regional use of its military for financial gain—as a growing cause of African conflict. Weakened states and regional conflicts are closely linked because fragile states often attract external intervention, either to protect or overthrow the existing regime.

Some twenty-five major conflicts since 1960 have sapped Africa's already limited human, political, and economic infrastructure.[11] Africa's wars have killed more than 7 million people and created about 19 million refugees. In terms of physical destruction, money diverted from developmental budgets, and soaring defense spending, the economic toll has proven staggering. The effects of war linger long after the fighting: devastated infrastructure and generations of poorly educated and violence-prone youths will hamper economic investment and development in the near future. These military conflicts could lead to what *Africa Confidential* terms "a massive restructuring of the continent's international system, which will strengthen some states and maybe obliterate others."[12]

The human toll, horrific in its own right, contributes to political instability. Ninety percent of all deaths have been innocent civilians. Rapes, assaults, and robberies—almost certainly results of war—scar vast numbers of civilians. Sierra Leone's Revolutionary United Front (RUF) has inflicted amputations and mutilations on perhaps 20,000 civilians. Human Rights Watch writes that Sierra Leone's conflict also has seen

> men, women and children, probably numbering in the thousands . . . abducted by the [rebel] AFRC/RUF for use as combatants, forced laborers, or sexual slaves. Women have been actively targeted through sexual violence, including rape and sexual slavery. Children have been targets of killings and violence and are forcibly recruited as soldiers.[13]

Furthermore, fighting often increases the risk of disease. As part of the overall damage to public health, conflicts disrupt access to medical treatment and to food and suitable water. Two years of fighting in Congo alone may have killed close to two million people, and the

International Rescue Committee notes that "the overwhelming majority" of these deaths "are attributable to preventable diseases and malnu-
trition."[14] Some belligerent forces deliberately target medical facilities
for destruction. Recent wars have significantly contributed to the spread
of AIDS and other diseases.[15] For example, 92 percent of Sierra Leone's
rebels have tested positive for sexually transmitted diseases.[16] UN and
regional peacekeeping forces have also contributed to the spread of
AIDS.[17]

Refugees created by the conflicts not only reflect existing political
problems but also create new ones, draining as they do recipient states
of resources and sometimes posing serious security threats. Several of
the post–Cold War conflicts have generated very many refugees:
Liberia's war, for instance, sent over a million refugees into neighboring states, and Somalia's conflict spilled about a million refugees into
Kenya and Ethiopia.[18] Refugees themselves may join fighting groups
(Rwandan Tutsis in Uganda accounted for 20 percent of Yoweri
Museveni's National Resistance Army during the 1980s) and occasionally form emigré armies: Tanzania and Uganda sheltered armed groups
that overthrew, or helped overthrow, two governments. Tanzania, along
with Ugandan dissidents, toppled Idi Amin's regime in Uganda in 1979,
and Uganda helped Rwandan exiles to overthrow the Hutu government
in 1994. The armed Hutu refugees in Zaire (now the Democratic
Republic of the Congo) became the pretext for an invasion of Zaire by
the Tutsi-dominated government of Rwanda and by Uganda, Rwanda's
close ally—an invasion that helped to topple the government of Sese
Seko Mobutu.

Brutal conflict can aggravate the initial causes of the fighting and
destroy the possibility of a common loyalty to a country with ethnically
diverse societies (Rwanda and Burundi, for instance, have ongoing cycles
of retributive internal violence).[19] In addition, domestic conflict can
quickly spread to other fragile states: Liberia's fighting helped to spark
Sierra Leone's war (1991 to present), encouraged coups in Gambia (1994)
and Sierra Leone (1992, 1996, 1997), played an indirect role in a failed
coup attempt in Guinea (1996), and created a serious refugee situation in
all of Liberia's neighboring states. Some wars, notably that in Congo during the late 1990s, can intensify neighboring conflicts.[20] Attacks in
Namibia by the Caprivi Liberation Army in August 1999 apparently were
sponsored by Jonas Savimbi's UNITA in retaliation for Namibia's support
of Laurent Kabila's Congo government—a major opponent of UNITA.

Conflict may also undercut the legitimacy of traditional authority and thus increase the difficulty of postconflict political development; heavily armed youngsters challenged the authority of the clan elders in Somalia during the early 1990s, for example. And conflict has reversed potential transitions to democratization in Rwanda and Angola.

The increased availability of weaponry is another long-lasting effect (as well as a cause) of conflict and has contributed to the militarization of political discourse. Thirty years of war have seen Africa import some 10 million automatic assault rifles and innumerable other weapons, many of which have remained in circulation long after the initial hostilities ended. The longed-for ending of the Cold War and apartheid released large weapon supplies from conflict areas, notably in Ethiopia, South Africa, Angola, and Mozambique. In the late 1980s Mozambique, a nation of some 16 million people, had about 1 million AK-47s in *private* hands (the price, as low as $5 for each rifle, proved an especially attractive feature). Antipersonnel land mines in their random destructiveness also hurt future economic development.[21]

Although "collapsed states" are not exclusively a post–Cold War phenomenon, the problem of African state survival has deepened and spread since 1989.[22] Some nations have instituted impressive reforms that augur well for long-term development; South Africa, Uganda, Ghana, Mali, and Mozambique are some of Africa's tentative success stories. Yet conflicts in Somalia, Liberia, Sierra Leone, Rwanda, and both Congos have destroyed economic infrastructure, inflicted massive human suffering, weakened hopes for a cohesive national identity within these countries, and often spread into neighboring countries. Surprisingly, some of Africa's poorest states have engaged in protracted wars. Rwanda has had troops in Congo since 1997, and Ethiopia and Eritrea plunged into a disastrous, conventional border conflict that wiped out most of their previous economic gains.

The World Bank predicted a 3.8-percent median growth rate for sub-Saharan Africa in 1998, down from 4.5 percent in 1997. While numerous factors, such as fluctuating commodity prices, also affect growth levels, conflict appears especially important. Noting this growth decline, the *Economist* suggests that

> the biggest threat to Africa now comes from war. . . . War now consumes Africa from the Horn to Namibia. Nearly a third of sub-Saharan Africa's 42 countries are embroiled in international or civil wars . . . at least 13 have sent troops to neighbors' wars. Other countries are plagued by gangs of armed criminals, who can be as disruptive as political rebels.[23]

Salim Ahmed Salim, secretary-general of the Organization of African Unity (OAU), draws a strong link between peace and growth: "There is a clear recognition among leaders that as long as there is conflict, all the talk about economic development will remain just that, talk. And as long as this conflict remains so widespread, the outside world will just not care about Africa."[24]

Africa's post-1990 security situation shares some strong characteristics with other world regions. Much of Chapter 3 examines four of these commonalities: the Cold War's ending and the resulting negative effects on existing problems, the changing nature of insurgency warfare, the disinclination of the international community to intervene militarily, and the promises and pitfalls of greater regional security responsibility.

African and other third world conflicts can threaten some Western interests. They can pull Western states into costly and dangerous efforts at "peacekeeping," "peace enforcement," or "nation building" in areas seemingly unimportant to the West, and such interventions are financially costly. The Somalia intervention cost the United States about $1.5 billion, mostly between December 1992 and December 1993. Peacekeeping and "operations other than war" (OOTW) can lessen Western military readiness.[25] Damaged economic and educational infrastructure hurts international economic development, worsening public health standards raise the possibility of pandemic diseases, and increased migration to Western countries can inflame nativist sentiments. Collapsed states allow a power vacuum into which forces threatening to international stability, such as terrorism, arms and drug trafficking, and money laundering, can quickly enter and spread.[26] If unchecked, the violent death of an "unimportant" state can create worrisome precedents for battlefield conduct in future conflicts. Michael Brown maintains that "the international community . . . will find its distinctions and norms hard to sustain in the long run if it allows them to be trampled in ethnic conflicts in which civilians are attacked deliberately and systematically. So the breakup of a state, even a small one, also has implications for international law and order."[27] On the other hand, professional African militaries would lessen the need for outside forces and could assist UN and other peacekeeping missions.

Can African Militaries Strengthen African States?

Some critics argue that African militaries are unprofessional, irrelevant, or dangerous and that a "military solution" is oxymoronic. Other observers suggest that militaries have the potential to contribute to state stability. This section examines these varying positions.

Unprofessional Militaries

African security forces may worsen, rather than cure, the problem of instability. Many of Africa's militaries are unprofessional, lacking both technical expertise for combat and political responsibility to the state.[28] Samuel Decalo characterizes most African militaries as technologically limited, each with "a handful of mutually competitive officers of different ranks seething with a variety of corporate, ethnic, and personal differences."[29] Since professionalism is a central focus of this book, I give it considerable attention below.

The "unprofessional" argument assumes that national political structures and values help determine a force's character and that Africa's prevailing system of personal, rather than institutional, rule has proven incompatible with military professionalism. Armed forces that are neither militarily competent nor politically responsible threaten national development.

Professionalism usually requires an *institutionalized* system of stable and widely accepted political values that exist independent of a specific regime. Implicit is the distinction between the state (ongoing) and the regime (temporary). In other words, the values and interests of the state, including the military, claim precedence over any other temporarily powerful group or leader. This resembles Max Weber's distinction between "rational-legal" and "charismatic" authority as well as Huntington's definition of political modernization.[30] The primacy of civic (inclusive) versus ethnic (or other subgroup) nationalism is implicit within the institutionalization argument.[31]

Groups within most institutionalized political systems have both rights and responsibilities—Weber's "fixed and official jurisdictional areas, which are generally ordered by rules."[32] This horizontal distribution of power ensures that each government agency enjoys some functional autonomy and that no one branch of government controls the distribution of state resources.

Military professionalism is a two-way street. Civilian and military officials agree not to cross the divide into each others' affairs. The armed forces enjoy considerable jurisdiction in military matters: they determine selection and promotion of personnel using their own merit criteria, and they implement policies of command and control, manpower, firepower, intelligence, communications, and logistics. The balancing of power among government agencies and between the govern-

ment and the public specifically helps to check unpopular military
incursions into foreign lands (opposition to France's rule in Algeria and
to U.S. intervention in Vietnam are two major examples).

The professional military's political responsibility requires it to
accept state control and to subsume such subnational loyalties as ethnicity, regionalism, and ideology.[33] The military accomplishes this with its
own internal system of responsibility. Officers and enlisted men accept
the rank structure and abjure using their coercive capabilities for subnational or individual gain (ethnic coups, private business ventures, or
human rights violations being three possibilities). Professional forces
also accept that civilian oversight can assist military efficiency.

Africa has had predominantly personalist political systems since
independence, and such regimes have often sustained unprofessional militaries. Robert Jackson and Carl Rosberg, while noting significant differences among personal rulers, wrote in the early 1980s that "politics in
most black African states do not conform to an institutionalized system. .
. the new African statesman was a personal ruler more than a constitutional and institutional one."[34] Most contemporary scholars of the African
state concur with this view: Michael Bratton and Nicolas van de Walle
conclude that "authority is entirely personalized, shaped by the ruler's
preferences rather than any codified system of laws."[35] The long list of
examples of rulers who typified a *l'état, c'est moi* deportment include
Siaka Stevens of Sierra Leone, Mobutu Sese Seko of Zaire, Jean-Bedel
Bokassa of the Central African Republic, and Samuel Doe of Liberia.[36]
The primacy of personal (and corporate), instead of state, interests has
been the military's "prime characteristic," according to Decalo.[37]

Personalist political systems diverge markedly from institutional
ones because the rulers have greater freedom to advance the short-term
interests of the regime, including security, at the expense of developing
long-term state institutions.[38] A ruler's control of the state's resources
provides maximum patronage powers and prevents the growth of functionally autonomous power centers whose expertise could promote
national development; rulers sometimes even turn to foreign collaborators rather than sanction indigenous capability. Bratton and van de
Walle observe this distinction between regime survival and national
needs when they write that personal rulers "selectively distribute favors
and material benefits to loyal followers who are not citizens of the polity so much as the ruler's clients."[39] The resultant uncertainty can bolster
a ruler's power by maximizing public dependence on one-man rule and
the state's patronage capabilities. Personalist African rulers since the

mid-1990s have deployed their militaries into neighboring countries without having to seek parliamentary or public acquiescence.

These leaders reverse Huntington's argument that institutionalization can create stability. Rather than increase the coherence of state institutions as a source of strength, these and other rulers construe state (including military) and private-sector development as threats to their rule and deny them functional autonomy. ("There is no such thing as a definite sphere of authority and of competence," writes Weber about charismatic systems.)[40] Such rulers contradict realist assumptions about the primacy of the state and the salience of national interest. Plundering of state resources and emasculation of the military by rentier governments has resulted from this emphasis upon the regime versus the state. Unprofessional militaries beholden to regimes rather than to states have exacted an economic toll upon national development. Jacques de Barrin wrote about the abusive Ugandan military in the mid-1980s and how it "came to undermine the very state which built it up and relied upon it."[41] Some rulers have gone so far as to voluntarily surrender aspects of national sovereignty by inviting foreign firms to assume important state or parastatal responsibilities; the hiring of private security or mining companies as substitutes for local capability are two such examples.

Several, especially southern African, countries have militaries that were linked historically during the liberation struggle to the political parties now in power. Examples include Mozambique's armed forces with Front for the Liberation of Mozambique (FRELIMO), Zimbabwe's with Zimbabwean African National Union (ZANU), and Namibia's with South West African People's Organization (SWAPO). Despite postindependence integration of some nonparty officers and enlistees, the bulk of the top officers retain membership in, and a long identity with, the prevailing party. None of these three militaries has staged coup attempts, but loyalty may be restricted more to the ruler and/or party rather than to the state.

Personal rule in Africa and its denial of functionally autonomous power for the military has hurt the armed forces' professionalism. Personalist leaders see the combination of technical expertise and political loyalty as a security dilemma because the autonomy that military competence requires impinges upon a ruler's desire for personal control. This is the first security dilemma discussed in this book; countries with personal rule rarely have both loyal *and* competent forces. Faced with this tension between two major components of military professionalism, personalist rulers subvert the armed forces for their own political survival (and usually financial gain). Their frequent crossing of the civil-military divide eliminates an army's politically disinterested ethos and almost always weakens its military capabilities.

Denial of a military's functional autonomy allows a ruler (who may be a military officer himself) to select, promote, reassign, and cashier personnel on the basis of subnational loyalties, most notably ethnicity, rather than merit. Africa's rulers have often stripped the militaries of operational competence while proffering various patronage rewards to personnel to ensure their allegiance. Christopher Clapham notes that basing selection and promotion on (usually ethnic) patron-client relationships hurts effective military capabilities: "The patron-client structures which form the common currency of African social organisation are particularly ill-adapted to the needs of large and disciplined military forces."[42]

Manipulation by personal rulers often includes parallel forces (e.g., presidential guards, state-sponsored militias, indigenous security companies, mercenary groups), which peripheralize the national militaries by siphoning off supplies, soldiers, responsibilities, and prestige. Such forces usually answer only to the ruler, function as a counterweight to the established military, and serve only his personal interests.

"Privatization of security" is generally used to describe corporate (or "mercenary") military involvement in Africa. Yet, as Clapham notes, the term can just as readily be applied to the hijacking of the national security forces by an unrepresentative government for its own gain.[43] I contend that much of Africa's military structures have some private aspect, whether to push rulers' personal or subnational desires or to seek financial gain. Many personalist rulers have reconfigured their forces to match their regimes'—rather than the states'—ethnic, regional, or religious loyalties. National security, which should protect all citizens of the state, becomes a partisan or entrepreneurial force. To alleviate anger in the often enfeebled officer corps, personalist rulers often exacerbate the zero-sum relationship of the regime versus state by allowing, and sometimes encouraging, the soldiers to appropriate military funding (especially by equipment procurement practices) or to intrude into the civilian economy by granting significant economic rights, such as search and seizure authorizations. Sometimes this privatization becomes overtly commercial, as when the regime grants commercial licenses to active-duty officers or when officers transfer soldiers and material from the country's military into their own private security firms. Several African militaries, including Zimbabwe's and Congo's, have recently followed a long-standing international practice of establishing commercial companies that often have little to do with national defense.[44]

Peripheralization and privatization damage Africa's security in many ways. Parallel forces can exacerbate social divisions: they are usually ethnically based and they use force, or at least its threat, to pursue the personal policies of their commander. By answering directly to their presidents, the forces are even less accountable than the national militaries. Parallel groups create divisions and competition between themselves and national militaries as they compete for resources, personnel, and status. State-sponsored militias usually have poorer human rights records than the national army and, by increasing the number of armed and often poorly trained fighters, may increase the nation's insecurity. Profit seeking, when accompanied by nonaccountability, may well encourage human rights abuses and perhaps even the perpetuation of conflict.

Military rulers themselves are often to blame for the lack of professionalism: surprisingly, "securocrat" rule has lessened defensive capabilities. Political administration and personal business matters attract the attention of officers in military regimes and weaken such mundane and relatively unrewarding security capabilities as training and discipline. Military budgets after a coup have often risen, but more money has not brought greater efficiency, the army's unquestioned authority encouraging unmonitored and unnecessary spending. The hope of some scholars during the 1960s that praetorian militaries could become capable modernizers of backward states, as in Kemal Ataturk's Turkey, has rarely been realized.[45]

Various actors, such as civilian political leaders, subnational groups, and ambitious military officers, cross the civil-military divide but the results are similar: political militaries in Africa often cannot redress the coercive balance and assist peaceful development.

The Irrelevance of Military Solutions

The second limitation of military contributions to peaceful settlements in Africa is that battlefield victories rarely deal with the underlying social, economic, and political causes of conflict or the peaceful means of conflict resolution. In other words, armed force addresses the effects rather than the cause of conflict. "The longer-term answer to managing conflicts," notes Timothy Sisk, "is to improve the capacity of African institutions at regional, sub-regional, national and local levels to manage tensions and mediate disputes without recourse to violence and

armed insurrection."[46] Donald Snow adds that "the best form of counterinsurgency is good government."[47] Finally, military victories by
themselves may exacerbate resentment from the losers and raise the
possibility of continued opposition.

The Danger of Military Solutions

A third limitation is that a capable military defense of an intolerable status quo *is* clearly undesirable: it hamstrings development while bottling
a discontent that later might explode violently. Various African rulers
have disavowed common democratic standards, including the distinction between the interests of the ruler versus the interests of the common good and the state as an impersonal mediator between conflicting
parties. The racist states of southern Africa, as well as Mobutu's Zaire
and Haile Mariam Mengistu's Ethiopia, were clearly unrepresentative
and unusually repressive. Strong military capabilities lessen the willingness of such governments to engage in peaceful diplomacy.

The nature of some African governments, notably those that define
"security" as regime or minority stability only, may not justify their
defense. Africa's putative wave of democratization has receded, and
personal rule, which had been Africa's predominant and unrepresentative mode of government for its first thirty years of independence, has
continued. Additionally, some regimes appear to have institutionalized
illegality. Bayart, Ellis, and Hibou worry about a growing "criminalization of the *state* in Africa" [emphasis added] whereby unaccountable
rulers are privatizing the state, and sometimes the security forces, for
their own economic gain.[48]

This introduces the second security dilemma, a choice between sovereignty and legitimacy. Stability, per se, is not an unalloyed ideal, and
coups, rebel movements, or subversion by neighboring states can provide a welcome cleansing of kleptocratic and repressive regimes. Few
people mourned the overthrow of Uganda's Idi Amin. Yet the OAU in
its 1963 charter forbids interference in the internal affairs of fellow
African states, fearing that any precedent, regardless of the target's
legitimacy, could spark a series of attacks and counterattacks that would
set African development back.

The third security dilemma focuses on the tension between a state's
domestic and regional policies and how outside, especially Western,
states should respond. A government may implement needed economic
reforms but pursue an aggressive regional policy that includes invasion
of its neighbors. Several reformist African states commended by

President Clinton in 1997 as constituting an "African renaissance" have received U.S. military assistance to protect their domestic reforms, but they have concurrently mounted military attacks on their neighbors, Rwanda and Uganda being two such examples. A closely related problem is that military assistance may inadvertently destabilize the recipient by increasing fears and military buildups by its neighbors.[49] Sometimes a government that practices deplorable domestic policies may play a constructive role regionally by dispatching peacekeepers to troubled states, perhaps to offset international criticism of its internal policies. The Babangida and Abacha governments in Nigeria during the 1990s were manifestly undemocratic and kleptocratic toward their citizenry but they also provided massive support to the Economic Community of West African States Ceasefire Monitoring Group (ECO-MOG), a regional peacekeeping force in Liberia and then Sierra Leone.

The Case for Military Contributions to Stability

African militaries can contribute to lasting stability, despite possible limitations. Military professionalism in the third world has recently received sharpened interest as a key component of development. Britain's Department for International Development (DFID) has made military reform a top priority, but as Secretary of State for International Development Clare Short acknowledges, "Development organisations have in the past tended to shy away from the issue of security sector reform."[50] The World Bank's Post-Conflict Unit states its increasing belief that "the state of a country's security has a major impact on the Bank's ability to respond to the country's needs."[51] And Michael Ignatieff writes that "more than development, more than aid or emergency relief, more than peacekeepers, these societies need states, with professional armies under the command of trained leaders."[52]

National forces have lacked professionalism partly because the political rulers have not encouraged such professionalism. I posit that militaries often reflect national political values and that a more representative and less personalist political system could elevate a military's capability and loyalty by encouraging transparency, meritocracy, and accountability.

Furthermore, professionalism is relative. Some unprofessional state militaries have significantly violated human rights, but some insurgencies have established a worse record—especially during this post–Cold War era of less control by foreign patrons.[53] Even relatively professional militaries, when compared to irregular forces, usually exercise greater selectivity in personnel recruitment, pay more attention to the restrained use of force, and are more accountable to the general public for their deeds—for example, discerning between combatants and noncombatants, legitimate and illegitimate targets, and civilized and brutish treatment of prisoners.

The absence of a professional force encourages subnational groups to look after their own defense. Citizens face greater threats from such nonstate actors who make local rather than national appeals, provide little or no training in proper military conduct during hostilities, lack established enforcement mechanisms against members who mistreat innocent civilians, and exhibit less vulnerability than states to international criticism. Factions may lower conduct from controlled *bellum hostile* (warfare restricted by standards) to uncontrolled *bellum romanum* (slaughter, or unrestricted warfare).[54] Some ECOMOG officers and enlistees stole significant resources from Liberia and Sierra Leone and committed some human rights abuses, but their malfeasance appears limited when compared to violations perpetrated by the rebel groups.

Peaceful conflict resolution may well be "the longer-term answer" to conflicts, as Sisk notes. But conflicts often require military muscle to stop immediate human rights violations and create a "mutually hurting stalemate" that forces the combatants to talk peacefully.[55] Rwanda's 1994 genocide saw the Rwandan government and civilian militias kill some 700,000 Rwandan civilians within a two-month period. An international study group concluded that "in retrospect, a capable force of 5,000 troops inserted during April 7–21 could have significantly squelched the violence, prevented its spread from the capital to the countryside, and removed the RPF's [Rwandan Patriotic Front's] pretext for renewing its fight with the RGF [Rwandan Government Forces]."[56]

A few analysts believe that thorough prosecution of wars provides for a more lasting peace than many of the attempts to end conflicts peacefully. Edward Luttwak writes that "an unpleasant truth often overlooked is that although war is a great evil, it does have a great virtue: it can resolve political conflicts and lead to peace," whereas well-meaning relief aid and cease fires often prolong the conflict by allowing combatants to rebuild their capability.[57] This view has its African proponents.[58] Some military victories have helped to create greater stability and national integration: Nigeria's defeat of Biafran secession, as well as a commendable reconciliation policy toward the rebels, largely dissolved further thoughts of an independent eastern Nigeria. The Rwanda

Patriotic Front's defeat of the Hutu *génocidaires* saved innumerable lives and ushered in a period, perhaps tentative, of greater peace.[59]

Some African regimes (such as contemporary Congo or Cameroon) are clearly undemocratic and repressive, and therefore probably not deserving of any military assistance, but other governments (such as present-day Nigeria and Uganda) have attempted desirable reforms, thus obviating clearly objectionable insurgencies. Sometimes an unproductive or unrepresentative status quo is preferable to the insurgent alternative. Sierra Leone's RUF has committed gross acts against Sierra Leonean civilians, and its insurgency (along with a brief stay in power) has damaged the country far more than the basically inept, and often corrupt, national government of Ahmed Kabbah.

Finally, those professional militaries that demonstrate loyalty to the state, rather than only to a specific regime, assist countries experiencing an interregnum between authoritarianism and a hoped-for democracy. Alexis de Tocqueville noted that "the most perilous moment for a bad government is one when it seeks to mend its ways,"[60] and a powerful umpire can facilitate the peaceful transition.

Three Approaches

African governments have been experimenting with three approaches to internal security: regional intervention forces, private security companies, and Western attempts to assist military professionalism. Each of these offers some hope of protecting African stability and development. I hypothesize that a variety of military and political factors—especially the unwillingness of many governments to encourage the development of professional militaries—have prevented these options from offering significant relief. This book studies how these experiments could be improved and whether political democratization may help develop both a military's technical capabilities and its political loyalty.

Regional and private (mercenary) military groupings are two dramatically different alternatives for state security. Multinational forces have become the preferred form of intervention during the post-Cold War period, and regional groupings offer several hypothetical advantages over nonregional units: greater knowledge of the region, acceptance, commitment, and more suitable military capabilities. ECOMOG, created initially from five West African militaries, became the first third world peacekeeping force after the end of the Cold War, and its considerable commitment of eight years in Liberia (1990–1998) and more than two years in Sierra Leone (1997–2000) provides important lessons for regional peacekeeping.

Mercenary companies were a sometimes dominant military power in Europe prior to the 1700s, despite widespread criticism. Machiavelli counseled his prince that private soldiers were either incompetent or disloyal.[61] But with a decline in state military capability, security theoreticians and futurists suggest that private security could regain some of its historical importance. Martin van Creveld believes that "the spread of sporadic, small-scale war will cause regular armed forces themselves to change form, shrink in size, and wither away. As they do, much of the day-to-day burden of defending society against the threat of low-intensity conflict will be transferred to the booming security business; and indeed the time may come when the organizations that comprise that business will, like the *condottieri* of old, take over the state."[62]

Private security companies (PSCs) form a part of the much larger wave of global "privatization" that has reshaped thinking about foreign policy as well as erstwhile government functions (e.g., postal service, utilities, public health). Western governments since 1945, but especially since 1990, have increasingly permitted or even encouraged such private actors as relief agencies, businesses, and retired statesmen to assume responsibilities that states had once monopolized.[63] Privatization assumes lower costs, less state responsibility or accountability, and greater efficiency.[64]

Private security companies are growing worldwide, and Executive Outcomes, while unique in some ways, and defunct by early 1999, nonetheless illustrates many of the significant attractions as well as the clear limitations of private security. Executive Outcomes, a South African-based private army, helped local forces to counter insurgencies in Angola (1993–1996) and Sierra Leone (1995–1997). Executive Outcomes no longer functions, but numerous other companies, both African and non-African, have acquired a wide range of contracts.

But restructuring existing African forces into multinational forces or supplementing them with private security will prove insufficient. National forces will remain the basic military unit in Africa, even as many of them are unable to maintain essential skills and discipline. This ineptitude multiplies when they are combined into regional forces to which they bring a jumble of doctrines, equipment, and languages. Upgrading of national militaries is a *sine qua non* of African security, but achieving it presents serious problems.

The U.S.-proposed Africa Crisis Response Initiative (ACRI) is an effort to increase Africa's level of military professionalism, beginning with national battalions. ACRI, initially proposed in 1997, has become the first-ever attempt to provide Western funding and training for an interoperable third-world peacekeeping capacity. Its training and much of its equipment is standardized so that battalions from the participating states can quickly unite into a single force when needed. Any success of ACRI and other Western initiatives could relieve some of the political pressure on the West and the UN to intervene in unfamiliar or relatively unimportant crises.

Structure of the Book

In examining the security effects of colonialism and then personal rule, Chapter 2 discusses why African states cannot rely on their national militaries to redress the balance of power. The chapter also examines the tension between efficiency and loyalty and why military rule has often reduced security capabilities.

Chapter 3 briefly examines some causes of African conflicts and discusses why the balance of military power is shifting against many African states and why Africa cannot depend on Western states or the United Nations for military intervention.

Chapter 4 examines multinational African military forces, the first external defense option for redressing the military balance. Regional military groupings have several hypothetical advantages over nonregional interveners, and this chapter assesses whether ECOMOG has demonstrated the groupings' validity. The chapter stresses the need of multinational units for already-professional national forces and maintains that personal rule in West Africa during the 1980s had debilitated most of ECOMOG's contingents.

Chapter 5 looks at the burgeoning private security field and whether Executive Outcomes's experiences in Angola and Sierra Leone disprove Machiavelli's concerns about the competence and loyalty of mercenaries. It then argues that military capabilities and political responsibility to the state are not the only two criteria for evaluating PSCs because these companies have contributed to the privatization of state resources by self-seeking African officials. The privatization and commercialization of security by African officials is a largely unexamined phenomenon that is helping to entrench personal rule governments and, perhaps, to prolong conflicts.

Chapter 6 uses ACRI to assess whether foreign training programs, the third external security option, can professionalize African militaries significantly enough for them to help redress the power balance. The domestic versus regional dilemma arises here because ACRI has provided training and some equipment to Uganda, which later destabilized the neighboring countries of Congo and Sudan. It is argued here that foreign attempts at professionalization will have limited success, at best.

The final chapter offers judgments about the three foreign attempts to assist African military professionalism and suggests that just as authoritarian states have encouraged militaries to be unprofessional, more democratic regimes could assist the military capabilities and the political loyalty of their national forces. Yet, the fourth security dilemma arises here: can democratization, which hopes to encourage stability, become a domestically and regionally destabilizing force?

Notes

1. Susan Rice, U.S. Assistant Secretary of State for Africa, quoted by Marina Ottaway, "Post-Imperial Africa at War," p. 202.

2. Quoted by Mark Malan, "The Crisis In External Response," in Cilliers and Mason, *Peace, Profit, or Plunder?* p. 46.

3. The very rich, but generally dated, literature on African civil-military relations includes Samuel Decalo, *Coups and Army Rule in Africa;* Ruth First, *Power in Africa;* Samuel P. Huntington, *The Soldier and the State: The Theory and Politics of Civil-Military Relations;* Kenneth W. Grundy, *Conflicting Images of the Military in Africa,* and Claude E. Welch, Jr., ed., *Soldier and State in Africa: A Comparative Analysis of Military Intervention and Political Change.* Single-nation studies include Robin Luckham, *The Nigerian Military,* and Thomas Cox, *Civil Military Relations in Sierra Leone.* The U.S. Department of Defense–commissioned country handbooks, produced initially by The American University and later by the Library of Congress, include a national security chapter.

4. Max Weber, *The Theory of Social and Economic Organization,* p. 154.

5. Martin van Creveld, *The Transformation of War,* p. 224.

6. For example, Samuel Decalo, *Coups and Army Rule in Africa.*

7. Paul Richards coins the term "new barbarians," which he critically considers a "Malthus-with-guns" perspective on post-1990 conflicts. Richards puts Robert Kaplan and Martin van Creveld into this school. Paul Richards, *Fighting for the Rain Forest,* pp. xiv, xvii; Robert Kaplan, "The Coming Anarchy."

8. Robert Jackson and Carl Rosberg, *Personal Rule in Black Africa.*

9. Thomas Callaghy, "The State As Lame Leviathan: The Patrimonial Administrative State in Africa," *The African State in Transition* (London: Macmillan, 1987); Victor Azarya and Naomi Chazan, "Disengagement From the State in Africa." Robert Jackson and Carl Rosberg, "The Marginality Of

African States," in Carter and O'Meara, eds., *African Independence: The First Twenty–Five Years*. Chabal and Daloz, *Africa Works*, p. 1. Michael Bratton and Nicolas van de Walle examine the economic aspect: "State elites in Africa have sought political power primarily to obtain and defend economic benefits, to the point that they have blocked private accumulation by independent groups in society, thus undermining the entire project of economic development." Bratton and van de Walle, *Democratic Experiments In Africa*, p. 47. Joel Migdal argues along the same lines in *Strong Societies and Weak States*. See also William Reno, *Warlord Politics and African States*.

10. Mary Kaldor, *New and Old Wars: Organized Violence in a Global Era* (Cambridge, Mass.: Polity, 1999).

11. These are estimates obtained from U.S. government officials and relief agencies. The figure includes internally displaced as well as external refugees. The statistics may be too conservative. Jakkie Cilliers, writing in the mid-1990s, mentions "35 major armed conflicts, which together have taken the lives of almost ten million people" and which, along with drought and disease, "have given the continent a refugee population currently estimated at 26 million people." Jakkie Cilliers, "Security and Transition in South Africa," in Diamond and Plattner, eds., *Civil-Military Relations and Democracy*.

12. "Emerging Maps: Africa Scrambles For Africa," *Africa Confidential* 40,1, (January 8, 1999), p. 1.

13. Human Rights Watch, "Sierra Leone. Sowing Terror: Atrocities Against Civilians In Sierra Leone," July 1998, p. 4.

14. "New Evidence Reveals Staggering Loss of Life in Eastern Congo: 1.7 Million Dead in 22-Month War." Press release, International Rescue Committee. Http://www.theirc.org.

15. The *New York Times,* writing about AIDS in Rwanda, notes that "the [Rwandan] upheaval broke down social taboos against promiscuity and the ever-present threat of violence made it harder to persuade people to worry about a disease that takes years to show up. . . . Even if arrested now, the epidemic will take the life of 1 person out of 10 in the next decade." *New York Times,* "Ravaged by War and Massacre, Rwanda Faces Scourge of AIDS," May 28, 1998. Refugee flows create serious disease problems that can rapidly move beyond the refugee population.

16. "A War Against Women," *Washington Post,* April 11, 2000.

17. "HIV/AIDS: UN Peacekeepers Spread Disease," *Los Angeles Times,* January 7, 2000. The UN now sponsors a Civil Military Alliance to Combat HIV and AIDS to lessen the AIDS spread by its soldiers.

18. The Rwandan genocide, within a single twenty-four-hour period in 1994, forced 250,000 panicked civilians into Burundi, Uganda, Tanzania, and Zaire.

19. Some countries have adopted policies of remarkable tolerance that lessen postconflict violence. Reconciliation policies help lower tensions and the chances for more conflict. The Nigerian government in 1970 welcomed the defeated "Biafrans" back into Nigeria and worked to prevent retribution against the Ibos. The majority governments in Zimbabwe and South Africa adopted reconciliation policies that defused much suspicion and anger, South Africa's Truth and Reconciliation Commission being a major example.

20. Referring to Congo, Assistant Secretary of State for Africa Susan Rice testified that a "political vacuum in the heart of Africa is a perfect setting not only for various state and non-state actors to replenish themselves and rebuild strength but an attractive venue for [anti-American] groups." She cites Libya's and Sudan's involvement in the war and then speculates that the conflict has "contribute[d] both to the intensity and possibly the duration of the Angolan civil war . . . [and] has the potential to adversely affect Burundi's peace process," as well as assisting armed Rwandan Hutus who "are a tremendously destabilizing factor for the entire Great Lakes region." "Central African Conflict and Its Implications for Africa and for the Future of U.S. Policy Goals and Strategies," Statement before the Senate Foreign Relations Committee, Subcommittee on African Affairs.

21. Antipersonnel mines can divert large amounts of money to the victims and prevent them from contributing to national development (Angola probably has over 10 million land mines still buried and the highest percentage per capita of quadriplegics in the world). Mine-infested territory reduces the amount of arable land. Removal exacts both human and financial costs: some common mines cost $2 to produce but $1,000 to remove from the ground.

22. William Zartman defines collapsed states as those "where the structure, authority (legitimate power), law, and political order have fallen apart . . . the phenomenon is historic and worldwide . . . but nowhere are there more examples than in contemporary Africa." I. William Zartman, "Introduction: Posing the Problem Of State Collapse," in *Collapsed States: The Disintegration and Restoration Of Legitimate Authority,* p. 1.

23. "A Continent Goes to War," *The Economist,* October 3, 1998, p. 47. The World Bank's chief of the Africa region's Capacity Building Division states that "it is becoming clear that the first order of business is to restore stability over an increasingly fragmented political and administrative environment." Mamadou Dia, "Indigenous Management Practices: Lessons for Africa's Management in the '90s," in Ismail Serageldin and June Taboroff, eds., *Culture and Development in Africa* (Washington, D.C.: World Bank, 1994), p. 171.

24. "Africa Ills: Insights on Cure but Avoiding the Medicine," *New York Times,* February 10, 1996, p. 6.

25. Militaries traditionally have trained soldiers for offensive combat operations, rather than OOTW, which detract from the military's primary mission and often require different doctrines and tactics. The U.S. Army in 1999 believed, according to the *Washington Post,* that "the strain of peacekeeping is so great that two of its 10 divisions are unready for war." "Army's Unready Divisions" Budget Feint or Fact?" *Washington Post,* November 15, 1999. Also see Stephen J. Cimbala, "Military Persuasion and the American Way of War," *Strategic Review,* Fall, 1994, quoted in "Army SOF: Right Tool for OOTW," *Special Warfare* (10,3) Summer 1997, p. 4. Peacekeeping's inherent restraint upon military force can create psychological distress among soldiers who cannot stop wide-scale human rights abuse. "Price of Waging Peace: Romeo Dallaire's Collapse Symbolizes a New Type of Stress Afflicting Soldiers," *National Post* (Canada), July 15, 2000.

26. This book notes that foreign states have entered Congo for personal

and political reasons. One of the more worrisome possibilities is that of North Korea's providing troops and training to the Kabila government in return for what London's *Sunday Telegraph* terms "access to the country's largest uranium mine, "Alarm over North Korea's Secret Deal for Congo Uranium," *Sunday Telegraph,* January 16, 2000.

27. Michael Brown, "Introduction," *The International Dimensions Of Internal Conflict,* p. 9.

28. Samuel Huntington defines expertise as "the basis of objective standards of professional competence for separating the profession from laymen and measuring the relative competence of members of the profession." Samuel P. Huntington, *The Soldier and the State,* p. 8.

Welch underlines the "'modern' organizational characteristics . . . centralization, discipline, hierarchy, communications, and *esprit de corps.*" Claude Welch, "The Roots and Implications Of Military Intervention," *Soldier and State in Africa,* p. 38.

"The principal *responsibility* of the military officer is to the state," notes Huntington, and the state is the "single recognized source of legitimate authority over the military forces." Huntington, *The Soldier and the State,* p. 16 [emphasis added]. Huntington also lists corporate identity as an element of professionalism.

Few militaries anywhere are fully technically expert and politically responsible, yet, as William Gutteridge notes, professionalism's ideal criteria provide valuable "guidelines and reference points" for evaluating security forces. William Gutteridge, *Military Regimes in Africa,* p. 27.

29. Samuel Decalo, *Coups and Army Rule in Africa,* pp. 14–15.

30. Rational authority rests "on a belief in the 'legality' of patterns of normative rules and the right of those elevated to authority under such rules to issue commands whereas charismatic authority depends on devotion to the specific and exceptional sanctity, heroism or exemplary character of an individual person." Max Weber, "The Pure Types of Legitimate Authority," in S. N. Eisenstadt, ed., *Max Weber on Charisma and Nation-Building,* p. 46.

Huntington describes political modernization as "the rationalization of authority: the replacement of a large number of traditional, religious, familial, and ethnic political authorities by a singular, secular, national political authority. . . . It means national integration and the centralization or accumulation of power." Samuel P. Huntington, "Political Modernization: America vs. Europe," p. 378.

31. Civic nationalism is "based on equal and universal citizenship rights within a territory [and] depends on a supporting framework of laws . . . as well as effective institutions. Ethnic nationalism, in contrast, depends not on institutions, but on culture." Jack Snyder, "Nationalism and the Crisis of the Post-Soviet State," in Michael E. Brown, ed., *Ethnic Conflict and International Security* (Princeton: Princeton University Press, 1993), p. 86.

32. Eisenstadt, *Max Weber,* p. 66.

33. Institutionalized militaries can appear very "political" when discussing defense budgets with civilian authorities, but they agree not to enter purely civilian matters and to accept final civilian authority.

34. Jackson and Rosberg, *Personal Rule in Black Africa,* pp. 1, 16. The

authors note important differences within the inclusive "personal rule" label by distinguishing among "prince" (Senegal's accomodationist Leopold Senghor), "prophet" (Ghana's messianic Kwame Nkrumah), "autocrat" (Côte d'Ivoire's managerial Félix Houphouët-Boigny), and "tyrant"(Uganda's despotic Idi Amin). The differences within personal rule helped to shape the national militaries.

35. Bratton and van de Walle, *Democratic Experiments in Africa,* p. 61. Chabal and Daloz write that "what all African states share is a generalized system of patrimonialism. . . . The state in sub-Saharan Africa has not been institutionalized, in that it has not become structurally differentiated from society and an acute degree of apparent disorder, as evidenced by a high level of governmental and administrative inefficiency, a lack of institutionalization, a general disregard for the rules of the formal political and economic sectors. . . . To focus on political elites is thus to highlight the ways in which power is personalized and how legitimacy continues primarily to rest on practices of redistribution." Chabal and Daloz, *Africa Works,* pp. xix, 2. See also Bratton and van de Walle, *Democratic Experiments in Africa,* pp. 61–96.

36. Writing in the mid-1970s about Africa's "military cliques," Decalo observed that their "overriding preoccupation [is] with personal and corporate aggrandizement" and that the military fragments "only *indirectly* and *secondarily* along ethnic, class or ideological lines . . . [but] is primarily a consequence of the eruption of competing personal ambitions." Decalo, 1976, *Coups and Army Rule in Africa,* p. 24.

37. Decalo, *Coups and Army Rule in Africa,* p. 24. Examples in the 1990s include the massive misappropriation of state resources by military officers in Sierra Leone and Nigeria and reported multiple cases of corruption in Uganda.

38. "In African political systems," as Peter Lock notes, "the distinction between state and government has little tradition. Security means in the first place, regime security." Peter Lock, "Africa, Military Downsizing and the Growth in the Security Industry," in Cilliers and Mason, eds., *Peace, Profit or Plunder?* p. 24.

Hastings K. Banda, former president of Malawi, reflected that "nothing is not my business in this country: everything is my business, everything. The state of education, the state of our economy, the state of our agriculture, the state of our transport, everything is my business." Banda, quoted in Bratton and van de Walle, *Democratic Experiments in Africa.*

39. Ibid., p. 61.

40. Eisenstadt, *Max Weber,* p. 50.

41. Jacques de Barrin, "Behind the Facade of Uganda's Democracy," *Manchester Guardian Weekly,* July 22, 1984, quoted in Chazan et al., *Politics and Society in Contemporary Africa,* p. 60. Van de Walle writes that "surveys of businesspeople consistently reveal that public sector failures in most countries of the [African] region constitute a major obstacle to private-sector activity . . . roadblocks . . . appear to have no function other than to provide income to underpaid officers; but they raise the costs of commerce, sometimes substantially so." Nicolas van de Walle, "Africa and the World Economy," in Harbeson and Rothchild, eds., *Africa in World Politics,* p. 268.

42. Christopher Clapham, "African Security Systems: Privatization and the Scope For Mercenary Conflict," in Mills and Stremlau, eds., *The Privatisation of Security in Africa* (Johannesburg: South African Institute of International Affairs, 1999), p. 37.

43. Ibid., p. 24.

44. Chapter 4 of this book examines this growing practice. For an global overview, see "Soldiers In Business," *New York Times,* September 27, 1999.

45. L. W. Pye, "Armies In the Process Of Political Modernization," in J. J. Johnson, ed., *The Role of the Military in Underdeveloped Countries.* Nicole Ball noted in 1989 that the "modernizing characteristics ascribed to the military frequently lacked substance. In other instances, the modernizing attributes can be shown to have existed in particular countries at specific points in time but they cannot be assured to exist continuously." Nicole Ball, *Security and Economy in the Third World,* p. 17. Exceptions to this rule could be presidents Jerry Rawlings of Ghana and Yoweri Musevini of Uganda.

46. Timothy Sisk, "Institutional Capacity-Building for African Conflict Management," in Smock and Crocker, *African Conflict Resolution,* p. 104.

47. Donald M. Snow, *Uncivil Wars,* p. 84.

48. Jean-François Bayart, Stephen Ellis, and Beatrice Hibou, *The Criminalization of the State in Africa.*

49. Writers sometimes refer to this problem as *"the* security dilemma." See Alan Collins, *The Security Dilemma and the End of the Cold War.*

50. Clare Short, "Recent British Initiatives," March 1999. Http://www.dfid.gov.uk

51. Post-Conflict Unit, "Security, Poverty Reduction & Sustainable Development. Challenges for the New Millennium." The World Bank, September 1999, p. v.

52. Michael Ignatieff, *The Warrior's Honor,* pp. 159–160.

53. Notable exceptions exist. Paul Kagame's Rwandan Patriotic Front (RPF) *may* have acted responsibly toward civilians. Philip Gourevitch writes that "what most vividly impressed observers in the waning days of the genocide was the overall restraint of this rebel army, even as its soldiers were finding their ancestral villages, and their own families, annihilated." Philip Gourevitch, *We Wish to Inform You,* p. 219. Other observers believe that the RPF was responsible only when compared to the *génocidaires* and that the RPF committed serious human rights abuses in Rwanda and then Zaire as it searched for young Hutu men.

54. Ignatieff, *Warrior's Honor,* pp. 148–149.

55. Term from I. W. Zartman, *Ripe for Resolution: Conflict and Intervention in Africa* (New York: Oxford University Press, 1985).

56. Scott Feil, *Could Five Thousand Peacekeepers Have Saved 500,000 Rwandans?* p. 2. General Roméo Dallaire, the UN's military commander in Rwanda, was the first to assert that five thousand professional soldiers could have stopped the genocide from occuring. Gourevitch writes about Dallaire's conclusion that "no military analyst whom I've heard of has ever questioned his judgement, and a great many have confirmed it." Gourevitch, *We Wish to Inform You,* p. 150.

57. Edward Luttwak, "Give War a Chance," *Foreign Affairs.*

58. Ali Mazrui asks about Rwanda and other conflictual countries, "Are we witnessing the colonial state being washed clean with buckets of blood? Are these [conflicts] . . . birth pangs of a new African political order wanting to be born?" Ali Mazrui, "Conflict As a Retreat From Modernity," in *Conflict in Africa* (London: J.B. Tauris, 1995), Oliver Furley, ed., p. 22.

Steven Kavuma, Uganda's Defense Minister, told the *Washington Post* in 1999 that the fighting was "the destruction of the old order and the creation of a new order. There is no way we could have jumped from colonialism to just broad, peaceful Africa. Much of this [fighting] was inevitable. It will take time." "New African Leaders Turn on One Another," *Washington Post,* September 2, 1999.

59. The RPF committed its own, more limited, atrocities against real or suspected *génocidaires* in mid–1994.

60. Alexis de Tocqueville, *The Old Regime and the French Revolution,* p. 176.

61. Niccolò Machiavelli, *The Prince,* pp. 44, 46.

62. Van Creveld, *Transformation of War,* p. 207.

Alvin and Heidi Toffler ask: "Why not, when nations have already lost the monopoly of violence, consider creating volunteer mercenary forces organized by private corporations to fight wars on a contract-fee basis for the United Nations, the *condottieri* of yesterday armed with some of the weapons . . . of tomorrow?" Alvin and Heidi Toffler, *War and Anti-War: Survival At the Dawn of the 21st Century,* p. 273.

63. The number of UN-accredited nongovernment organizations (NGOs) has risen from forty-one in 1948 to over 1,500 at present, and NGOs provided some $10 billion of international aid in 1997. Many relief agencies have assumed functions once firmly held by donor states. Some private foundations and religious groups have entered political diplomacy. The San Egidio community, a Vatican lay organization, supervised Mozambique's negotiations that ended a civil war, which, directly and indirectly, had killed about a million people.

64. John D. Donahue characterizes the potential advantages as "unencumbered administrative flexibility and concentrated decision-making authority that allows for the fastest technical adaptation and the greatest devotion to cost control." John D. Donahue, *The Privatization Decision,* p. 216. Donahue notes that "privatization is not only an inelegant term; it is also lamentably imprecise," Donahue, *The Privatization Decision,* p. 5. For example, it may refer either to a government's divesting itself of parastatals or to the government's contracting out for services often previously supplied by the government.

2

THE ROOTS AND RESULTS OF AFRICAN MILITARY UNPROFESSIONALISM

A frica needs military forces that demonstrate both technical capabilities and political responsibility to the state. But developing and maintaining military professionalism require time and an exacting mix of political, social, and economic factors: Samuel Huntington suggests as prerequisites an existing nation-state, a system of democratic structures and ideals, a single and widely accepted authority over the armed forces, and a minimal level of technology and urbanization.[1] Charles Tilly and Huntington note how an external military threat has historically galvanized more efficient states and their militaries.[2]

Most African states lack most of these prerequisites, which helps to explain their often unprofessional militaries. Their boundaries, inherited from the colonial era, incorporate such variegated ethnic, regional, linguistic, and religious differences that few African countries can be labeled as nation-states. Colonial rulers did not encourage democratic political institutions or African-based economic development. Illiteracy continues to plague African states, especially those countries that are suffering prolonged conflict. Colonial rule further lessened hopes for professionalism when it crossed the civil-military divide by establishing ethnic recruiting criteria and by deploying forces domestically. Both policies contributed to the forces' politicization.

But after independence, many African authoritarian regimes crossed the civil-military divide further when they deliberately created or condoned unprofessional militaries. This could initially appear counterintuitive: unpopular governments would presumably seek competent soldiers or police to offset the governments' lack of public legitimacy. Yet, personalist rulers since independence have feared their militaries' armed might and so developed strategies of controlling the military.

Sensing a tension between military capabilities and political loyalty to the regime, these rulers often emphasized the armed forces' allegiance at the expense of operational effectiveness. Loyalty appeared more important than efficiency, given the domestic occurrence of postindependence coups and the regional absence of external threats.

These personal rulers employed five tactics that aided their short-term political survival at the expense of long-term institutionalization. They continued the colonial habit of employing subnational, and especially ethnic, criteria to recruit soldiers. The rulers also initiated or greatly expanded military corruption, especially by permitting conflicts of military-political-economic interest, as a means of co-opting the officer corps. Leaders created personally loyal, parallel militaries as counterweights to the national armed forces. Many, especially francophone, states could also rely on foreign protection. Finally, many presidents continued the colonial tradition of domestic deployment of the armed forces for partisan political reasons.

These five strategies of military control politicized and weakened the armed forces, while arguably lessening the frequency of military coups.[3] These unprofessional security units constitute a major reason why many African states today are losing the military balance of power to domestic insurgencies and to some regionally aggressive states.

This chapter focuses on these strategies, especially during the personal rule era, and especially on how they affected (1) the Nigerian military, given its later dominance of ECOMOG and (2) the Sierra Leonean, Liberian, and Angolan forces, whose unprofessionalism required the entry of multinational or private security forces.

The Colonial Era

Most colonial military forces displayed some professional traits of political responsibility and military capability.[4] Colonial administrators, for their part, exemplified Weber's rational-legal rather than charismatic approach. They were foreign civil servants for whom using the security forces for personal gain would have contravened previous training and jeopardized future government employment.

They rarely, if ever, crossed the civil-military dividing line by challenging civilian rule. Officers, especially from Britain and France, were steeped in the tradition of military acceptance of civilian control (the French military had gained *la grande muette* label). No colonial army in sub-Saharan Africa between 1880 and 1960 staged a military coup. As for technical capabilities, the European forces possessed security skills and equipment that far exceeded those of African groups. As a result of the above, writes Clapham, "colonial armies scored very highly on the effectiveness scale."[5]

But what colonial authorities achieved in the short run, namely competent security, they helped to damage in the long run. Colonial militaries do bear some responsibility for Africa's presently inadequate levels of professionalism: they secured only the relatively short-run interests of the colonial regime rather than those of the African country. Africa had relatively few national militaries during colonialism: the French and the British formed regional military organizations, notably the regionally recruited *Tirailleurs Sénégalais*[6] of French West Africa, the Royal West African Frontier Force (RWAFF), and the King's African Rifles (KAR). Only at independence in the early 1960s did many countries acquire their own forces. Colonially controlled forces kept the peace by protecting national borders and by suppressing domestic unrest. Yet, by failing to develop an indigenous and professional officer corps, the forces laid the groundwork for future unprofessional militaries. The lack of national militaries and the lack of local officer corps paralleled colonialism's failure to encourage national political identities and political institutions in their African territories. And, as described below, colonialism's ethnic recruitment and its use of its soldiers for domestic political purposes set a deleterious precedent of politicized armies.

Ethnic Recruitment

Ethnic selection and promotion usually hurt national security by decreasing public acceptance of the military (and government). This in turn reduces the talent pool from which the armed forces can draw. An ethnically defined force may also adopt an "us against them" attitude that leads to its mistreatment of the civilian population. Ethnic selection works against a common identity by placing and supporting an exclusive subnationalism above an inclusive nationalism. It also lowers political acceptance of the state by groups excluded from the military, and raises their fears of state-sponsored repression.

Colonial authorities both unintentionally and intentionally "ethnicized" African militaries.[7] The Europeans who held most officer positions during the colonial era acted on behalf of their minority regime, rather than the desires of the country. This was especially true in Kenya, Angola, and Mozambique, as well as Rhodesia and South Africa.

Africans undoubtedly perceived these officers as armed ethnic representatives of repressive regimes or, as Decalo terms the armies, "essentially mercenary forces of repression."[8]

Colonial authorities often deliberately selected soldiers from
indigenous minority ethnic groups, from "more martial" groups, or
from rural areas that had cooperated with the colonialization.[9] The
minority Tutsi of Rwanda and Burundi dominated the militaries in those
two Hutu-majority states. The British in Uganda, while favoring the
southern Baganda kingdom politically, selected most of its soldiers
from the more "warlike" north, especially from the Acholi area.
Enlisted men in colonial Ghana (formerly the Gold Coast) hailed exclusively from the Northern Territories Protectorate, which formed but
one-third of the country. Colonial authorities granted a disproportionate
number of positions to minority groups, largely to undercut the strength
of indigenous majority independence movements, and they recruited
rural inhabitants to reduce the chances that the enlistees would be
swayed by the urban-based doctrines of nationalism.

Colonial powers increasingly accepted African officer candidates
during the 1950s. But the British RWAFF and KAR, especially, did not
promote from among their largely rural and often illiterate enlistees,
emphasizing instead formal educational achievements often found
among ethnic groups not previously represented in the military. For
example, in Nigeria southern Ibos gained many of the initial officer
positions during the 1950s, but many of the often long-serving enlistees
in the Nigerian army were of northern origin. This two-tiered policy
intensified ethnic rivalries.

Domestic Deployment

Militaries traditionally have been created and configured for external
defense rather than for internal coercion. Security analysts note that
militaries owe some of their strength to their outward focus. "External
military missions are the most conducive to healthy patterns of civil-
military relations," writes Michael Desch, whereas "nonmilitary, internal missions often engender various pathologies."[10] Deployment inside
African countries (which varied over time and among the European
powers) hurt a force's future professionalism by setting undesirable
precedents—lowering the division between civilian and military autonomy, weakening the force's unity, diminishing its acceptance by society
as an unbiased national defender, and reducing its external capabilities.

Cost-conscious colonial administrators sometimes employed their
militaries, which were essentially armies of occupation, as police.[11] For

example, the Force Publique was the Belgian Congo's major police force for many years.[12] Ghana's military was the internal policing unit between 1945 and the country's independence in 1957. In Liberia (never a colony but ruled by a small settler elite with standard colonial administrative practices), the Liberian Frontier Force served the same dual role.

Even though domestic operations would hurt military professionalism more in the postcolonial period than during colonialism, several undesirable aspects did stem from colonial rule. Local enforcement of unpopular policies (tax collection, for one) greatly reduced security forces' popularity. Catherine Coquery-Vidrovitch, in writing of equatorial Africa in the early twentieth century, said that "auxiliary troops sacked and terrorized villages, beat up or murdered recalcitrants and seized hostages. . . . People became terrified of the *commandant;* they fled and rebelled."[13] The often obscene practices of the early Force Publique, which included cutting off hands and burning villages to enforce production of rubber quotas, help to explain the Force's depending on slaves to fill the enlisted ranks.

Bryant Shaw writes about how domestic deployment changed a military's structure and discipline. The Force Publique had a "centripetal" wish to have full contingents remain together for training, discipline, quick deployment, and common identity. Yet the civilians' "centrifugal" desire was to have the Force geographically dispersed as small police units. As a result, "the short term demands of local occupation," concludes Shaw, "preempted and subverted the long term need for a coherent, professional armed force."[14] The Belgian Congo's territorial administrators often used the local military units for their own economic pursuits and created precedents for later military corruption and thievery: "Some of the worst tendencies of the present-day FAZ [Forces Armées Zaïroises]," noted Roger Glickson and Joshua Sinai, "are traceable to the early organization and practices of the Belgian colonial force."[15] Most colonial forces restricted corruption, but the enlistees in the Liberian Frontier Force (the forerunner to the Armed Forces of Liberia), for example, were expected to supplement their inadequate pay by relying on local communities—a policy that led to abuse of the civilian population.

Lack of Urgency

Fear of invasion has traditionally encouraged states to develop professional militaries: the Napoleonic Wars accelerated Europe's military capabilities and, specifically, the creation of professional officer corps.[16] Writing about contemporary international threats, Michael Desch argues that a "state facing a traditional, external challenge . . . [will] grant the military substantial autonomy in the narrow military realm in return for complete political loyalty."[17]

Peaceful African interstate relations, colonialism's access to European militaries, and colonialism's assumption that it would continue indefinitely slowed the development of indigenous African national militaries.[18] That African states rarely faced outside armies over the past 100 years obviated the need for capable defense forces. Indeed, the Berlin Conference of 1884–1885 established Africa's boundaries in part to avoid *European* conflict in Africa. The absence of antagonisms in Europe after 1918 among the major colonial powers—Britain, France, Portugal, and Belgium—and the weak military capabilities of the colonies meant that colonial states in Africa did not fight each other.

The general absence of fighting in the region after World War I lessened counterinsurgency capabilities in low-intensity conflicts. The British in Kenya initially assumed that their conventional forces could quickly dispose of the "Mau-Mau." But it took innovative counterinsurgency (COIN) tactics, and specifically the use of "pseudo" units, to defeat the often unskilled but courageous rebels.[19] Other white minority–run countries, including Rhodesia and South Africa, would create powerful COIN forces.

Colonial powers had military resources other than the national military in a specific colony. They could deploy regionally recruited French West African or KAR units: for example, Ugandan soldiers (including Idi Amin) in the KAR helped to quell the Mau-Mau rebellion in Kenya during the mid-1950s. France or Britain could deploy metropolitan forces to combat serious internal threats, the British sending in regular army units, such as the Lancashire Fusiliers, to combat Kenya's Land Freedom Army (or Mau-Mau). These powers could also transfer their African units among colonies, if necessary. Most African independence movements had no armed wings: most violence occurred in those few colonies with significant white settlement. In such countries as Kenya, Rhodesia, Angola, and Mozambique, as well as South Africa,[20] white settlers constituted military units whose loyalty to white colonial rule was unquestioned.[21]

Colonial metropoles, at least up to World War II, had felt little need to prepare a first generation of African military leaders.[22] The absence of threats from other African states, especially after 1918, slowed the development of an indigenous officer class. And since relatively few independence movements had gained a national following, colonial authorities could thus fairly assume a long future for colonialism—and they undoubtedly feared that militarily skilled Africans would later assist whatever independence movements did exist.

World Wars I and II did see a major use of African troops, in Africa and elsewhere. The Tirailleurs Sénégalais had nearly 200,000 men in Europe during each of these wars, and about 15 percent of that number were killed. The KAR sent thousands of anglophone Africans to Burma, North Africa, and Madagascar.

Yet the effects on African military professionalism were limited. British colonial officers virtually monopolized "African" officer corps until, and often after, independence, as a few examples show. "Africanization of the Sierra Leonean military forces was practically nonexistent throughout the 1950s," notes Tom Cox;[23] and the departing British appointed the first African major only in August 1960. The Belgian Congo's Force Publique of 24,000 soldiers had no Africans of higher rank than its three sergeant-majors at independence in 1960. The Tirailleurs Sénégalais had only twenty-eight African officers in 1946, and that number would decline:"There were actually fewer African officers in 1954 than there had been in 1946," writes Myron Echenberg.[24] France does deserve credit, however, for Africanizing its colonial officer corps faster than other European powers.[25]

Most commissioned officers and many noncommissioned officers (NCOs) in the Nigerian military by 1960 were still British. Fifty British officers and two recently commissioned African officers (one of them Idi Amin) headed Uganda's military at independence.[26] Belgium accepted Congolese into its military secondary school beginning only in 1958, two years before the Belgian Congo's independence. "At this rate, it would have taken generations to completely Africanize the [Zairian] military," note Glickson and Sinai.[27] Belgium recruited the first Rwandans for the proposed Garde National in 1959, a year before independence.

The overall lack of urgency discouraged a "best that you can be" selection criterion for colonial soldiers until shortly before independence. "The ideal colonial soldier was supposed to be illiterate, uncontaminated by mission education, from a remote area, physically tough, and politically unsophisticated," writes Charles Snyder.[28]

Colonial powers generally did not emphasize indigenous officer selection and training, even as independence became a greater possibility. Foreign officers often assumed that they would continue to staff much of the military during a prolonged transition following formal independence. The Belgian commander of the Force Publique at independence told his Congolese soldiers and NCOs that "before independence equals after independence," that is, Belgians would continue to command the Force Publique. Such arrogance, as will be seen, helped spark violent reactions. For Africa generally, the absence of African officers who could pass on to successive generations their corporate pride and political responsibility would hurt later indigenous military professionalism.[29]

Following World War II, Britain and France considered greatly expanding their African militaries; after all, both countries had suffered grievous manpower losses. But, as Chester Crocker notes, various factors, such as the importance of strategic interests elsewhere, the financial costs, and the need to deploy a large number of skilled officers and NCOs away from Europe, determined otherwise.[30]

The white-ruled states of southern Africa, and especially South Africa, stood as an exception to the above, since they had always felt a strong need to maintain superior military forces. Feeling threatened by the Africans they were trying to subjugate, the whites created security forces based on European standards and equipment, to which they enjoyed easy access, but which they adapted to African requirements. This professionalism would later contribute to the success of Executive Outcomes and other mercenary operations.

The South African Defence Force (SADF) began in 1912 but its organizational antecedents started much earlier. Starting in the late 1700s South African forces had fought blacks in the "Kaffir" and then the Zulu wars. The Great Trek (1836–1852) impressed the *laager* metaphor upon the minority Afrikaners: that a well-armed and united minority could withstand a larger but less united and poorly armed force.[31]

The Boer War (1899–1902) pitted the Afrikaner whites against the British government and English South Africans. Although heavily outnumbered and outgunned, the embattled Afrikaners developed effective guerrilla tactics that exacted a heavy toll on the eventually successful British. The war intensified the Afrikaners' belief that they needed an effective military to survive in an often antagonistic environment. Subsequently, the SADF's prolonged contact at the officer level with first world (especially British) militaries and its combat in both World Wars and Korea provided experiences unique among African forces.[32]

This absence of an external threat against most other states eliminated any ongoing need for colonial rulers to draw on large numbers of Africans and to give them command responsibilities. The lack of an indigenous officer corps prevented any chance for a strong sense of national, rather than ethnic or regional, identity to develop over time. The absence of an external menace also discouraged the often cash-strapped colonies from developing secondary strategic considerations, including greater training by the metropole, regional training exercises, reserve military forces, ground and air transportation, maintenance capability, and interior road building.

The Postindependence Era: Personal Rule

The ethnicization of the militaries, their domestic deployment, and the lack of foreign threats all served colonialism well. The European officers ensured loyalty, potential opposition was divided, and use of the national army (rather than a police force) for domestic purposes reduced the financial costs of security. But these three factors, along with the rise of military corruption and parallel security forces, also ensured that African militaries would lack political loyalty and military efficiency after independence.

The existence of armed forces posed a mixed blessing for Africa's incoming rulers. Armies helped symbolize the nation's independence, offered employment possibilities to the newly franchised citizens, and could provide security to the government, but they also represented a potential threat. All in all, no ruler abolished his country's military upon independence, and, indeed, military budgets often soared in the mid-1960s.

Personal rulers at independence saw a need for political loyalty rather than military efficiency, which rulers often distrusted. Michael Schatzberg wrote of Mobutu that "one of the things he fears most is an effective military establishment."[33] These rulers exercised strong executive control over their security forces. For example, Mobutu personally controlled his armed forces and most of the police units.[34] Moreover, many officer corps initially had included only a few Africans; most of them came from the same ethnic or geographic region and could feel pulled more by allegiance to ethnicity, personality, or religion than to nationalism.

The post-1960 rise of authoritarian personal rule made the interests of new regimes and rulers, rather than those of their states, paramount: rulers sacrificed possible long-run institutionalization for short-run political expediency. As President Kwame Nkrumah of Ghana had suggested, "Seek ye first the political kingdom and everything else shall be added unto you,"[35] and political competition for the all-important state resources quickly became a zero-sum game. The absence of institutionalized agreements allowed civilian leaders to cross the civil-military divide, something which colonial administrators had not done. This intrusion debilitated both military capabilities and political responsibility of many African militaries.[36]

Siaka Stevens of Sierra Leone exemplified the crossing of the civil-military divide when he largely erased a major criterion of professionalism: the partition between civilian and military affairs. "I had long, long ago thought that the army is no longer a foreign army," he recalled upon his retirement. "The army and police being an integral part of the administration, let them be represented, so I brought them in. . . . We want to make one unit in the country."[37]

Stevens's actual intention was to place them under the control of his All Peoples Congress (APC) party. Retired Col. Ambrose Genda remembers that under Stevens "the army was no longer looking for volunteers who wanted to make the military a career. It was enlisting relatives and friends of members of the APC. So the loyalty of the soldier, which was to the country during colonial times, shifted to the political party."[38] And party informants in the army soon created a destructive atmosphere of suspicion. Sierra Leone's Albert Margai, who ruled from 1964 to 1967, had championed his fellow Mendes in government and in the rapidly Africanizing Republic of Sierra Leonean Military Force (RSLMF). Stevens, who followed Margai and ruled for the next seventeen years, stripped power from the parliament and judiciary, stole large amounts from the treasury, and increased his control over the armed forces.[39]

Countervailing institutional civilian control over the military of Sierra Leone and other countries was often absent in personal-rule systems. Neither government nor private groups exercised any critical oversight, and private profiteering at the expense of national security was the result. The British government in 1999 looked back upon the RSLMF and concluded that

> the Sierra Leonean Ministry of Defence has played a weak and ineffective role ever since independence in 1961. It has operated under the direct control of the chief executive. . . . Budgetary and policy decisions have been taken directly between the President and the Chief of Defence Staff and even individual army commanders . . . there has never been any effective internal or external audit or control over procurement . . . [the officers have] placed their soldiers largely outside the reach of the police and courts. The results have been a wide range of human rights abuses, financial misallocation and outright corruption, and unpublished crimes against their fellow citizens. . . . The Army becomes a law unto itself.[40]

Criticism of using a national institution for group or personal gain is easy to voice, but these rulers faced a dilemma of damned if you do and damned if you don't. The political ethos of state helps determine the extent of military professionalism, and colonialism had left behind neither nation-states nor adequate, African-led, professional militaries. The result was that African officers often demonstrated their coup capabilities after 1963.

Short-term political survival was a strong incentive for the rulers to compromise military autonomy. Yet such actions had longer-term consequences. In Sierra Leone's case, a weak RSLMF would later facilitate the growth of the Revolutionary United Front (RUF) through the RSLMF's technical incompetence and its absence of strong loyalty to the state.

African rulers continued colonialism's subnational (especially ethnic) recruitment while tolerating—or encouraging—military corruption and creating parallel security units as counterweights to the existing armed forces. These leaders also followed colonialism's example of using soldiers for domestic partisan political purposes. A continuing lack of urgency, aided by the possibility of foreign support to threatened states and by international assumptions about sovereignty, allowed regimes to stress political loyalty at the expense of military competence. By 1989, when the military balance of power began changing, there was a prevalence of unprofessional forces that could not defend their countries.

Subnational Favoritism

Personal rule and ethnicization of militaries have been closely linked. Crawford Young has noted that "the very nature of personal autocracy led rulers to build armies according to an ethnic security map."[41] The absence of accepted national institutions proved a double-edged sword: it heightened political uncertainty as it allowed the rulers to intrude into the armed forces' selection and recruitment process.

Perceived threats to the regime (as well as the requirements of patron-client relationships) strongly encouraged ethnic recruitment; already apprehensive rulers usually narrowed the ethnic base of their own security forces.[42] Eboe Hutchful laments that "in many African armies and security forces, informal links and structures of power based on such factors as ethnic, family and political connections, count for much more than formal hierarchy and lines of command."[43]

Military ethnicization thus continued. Whites continued to monopolize the senior ranks in the forces of South Africa, Namibia, Angola, Mozambique, and former Rhodesia. Samuel Doe ethnicized the Armed Forces of Liberia by appointing fellow Krahn (a group that comprised only 4 percent of Liberia's population) to top positions. Siaka Stevens removed most of the RSLMF's most capable officers and replaced them with his fellow (and less threatening) Limba tribesmen. Siad Barre transformed the Somali armed services into a Maraheen faction, especially when the United States withdrew its support at the Cold War's end. Schatzberg wrote about Zaire that "the more Mobutu's political and psychological insecurity has grown, the more he has relied on ethnic quotas in the military."[44] Some rulers, notably Julius Nyerere of Tanzania, commendably bucked this trend, but ethnic and other subnational identifications continue as important selection criteria in many states.[45]

In late 1982, the new Mugabe government of Zimbabwe created the Fifth Brigade, ostensibly to root out several hundred armed ZAPU dissidents in Matabeleland, home of the minority Ndebele. But the brigade, which was composed of ethnic Shona, operated as a group of armed thugs pursuing an anti-Ndebele policy, rather than as a unit of the national army. Brigade commanders reportedly told their soldiers at rallies that "all Ndebeles are dissidents."[46] The unit killed perhaps two thousand Ndebele civilians by mid-1983 and an additional two thousand by the end of its Matabeland operation in 1987. The brigade intensified animosity between Zimbabwe's two main ethnic groups, as many Ndebele saw the Fifth Brigade's campaign "as a war fought not against dissidents but against the Ndeblele and ZAPU."[47]

When extreme ethnicization of the military was difficult, given the relative smallness of the ruler's group or probable backlash from the existing officer corps, a ruler might empower a paramilitary force into which he would place his own kinsmen. Barrows notes that in Gabon of the 1980s, "the Presidential Guard is considerably more capable than the army."[48] Kenya's General Services Unit was "a virtually all-Kikuyu hit-squad" during the 1960s and 1970s, as described by Decalo.[49]

Ethnic tensions sometimes had racial overtones after independence. Many rulers displayed ambivalence about replacing the European officer corps, given the desire for efficiency and order during the political transition. The politically expedient need to "Africanize" the armed forces saw a rapid insertion at independence of young Africans into the officer ranks, but not a concomitant acceptance by their white superior officers. Following Lieutenant General Janssen's "before independence equals after independence" dictum, the Congo's Force Publique mutinied—an action that triggered the Congo's civil wars of 1960–1964. In 1964, whites still dominated the officer corps of Kenya, Uganda, and Tanzania, a fact that helped to trigger coup attempts in those countries by young African officers who sought rapid promotion and better pay. Dismissal of white officers also provided a blank slate for the first African rulers. Nkrumah's 1961 sacking of all British military personnel "destroyed an apolitical safeguard and exposed the military to [Nkrumah's] political manipulation," according to Thomas Ofcansky.[50]

Ethnicization of the military has not slackened in many countries and will likely continue as long as Africa continues to have personalized political rule: as the foundation of their officer corps, President Biya of Cameroon has his Beti, President Eyadema of Togo has his Kabre, and President Moi of Kenya has his Kalenjin.[51] As late as 1990, Sudan presented an extreme example in which every officer, in that ethnically diverse state, was reportedly northern, Muslim, and Arab. Gourevitch notes that in pre-1994 Rwanda "members of the armed forces were forbidden to marry Tutsis and it went without saying that they were not supposed to be Tutsis themselves."[52]

The effect of unrealistic expectations and the lack of experience was quickly noticeable shortly after the independence of any number of new states and established precedents for the future. In the Nigerian and other militaries, "there was little difference in age and experience between officers at the upper and lower levels of the hierarchy,"[53] a fact that lessened respect for, and obedience to, superior officers. Rapid promotions in the early 1960s afforded insufficient time for adequate officer education or the fostering of personal ties within the unit, and it created an assumption of continued fast promotions. Idi Amin was a notable example of such rapid promotion: within ten years he rose from effendi (a rank between a noncommissioned and a commissioned officer) to general. And an often overlooked result of the rapid "Africanization" of the officer corps was the long-lasting harm done to the vital noncommissioned officer body.[54] Ethnic identity became a genie that would not return to the bottle. Jomo Kenyatta removed many of the primarily Kamba officers corps and replaced them with his Kikuyu tribesmen. His successor, Daniel Arap Moi, then replaced many of the Kikuyu officers with his own Kalenjin—an action that helped precipitate a 1982 coup attempt by junior Kikuyu and Luo officers.

Military coups disposed of experienced personnel, fractured existing command-and-control structures, and begat future coups. Ethnic replacement of the military's command by coup often became self-perpetuating, as the first ethnic coups provided license for such future actions by other groups.[55] Amin's Uganda offers an extreme example of how coups lowered force standards. Amin's 1971 coup helped "a number of laborers, drivers and bodyguards [to] become high-ranking officers, although they had little or no military training."[56] Whereas the pre-Amin military in Uganda was largely Acholi, Amin rapidly staffed his army with West Nile groups (e.g., Kakwa, Lugbara, Madi). Indeed, under Amin's rule, his favored Ugandans would kill Acholi officers and then assume the rank of the dead officers. Similarly, after Samuel Doe's 1980 coup in Liberia, "the personnel and the recruiting standards of the officer corps completely changed."[57] Both repressive and incompetent, Doe increasingly staffed the Armed Forces of Liberia with his fellow minority Krahn, who then brutalized the Mano and Gio ethnic groups. Not surprisingly, Charles Taylor's 1989 invasion from Côte d'Ivoire drew massive support from those two groups. And as for Nigeria, Robin Luckham notes that "once the army was in power its vaunted unity began to crumble."[58] This was especially true about the frequent coups, or coup attempts, by junior officers.[59]

Nepotism was another feature of subnational recruitment to the military force, when immediate family members came to occupy top security positions. Equatorial Guinea presents an extreme case where, as Decalo notes, Macías Nguema's "bloody tyranny . . . was sustained throughout its lengthy interregnum by an incredible military mafioso of cousins, nephews, uncles and relatives by marriage."[60] Brig. Julius Maada Bio of Sierra Leone remembers, "These [Sierra Leonean] officers didn't have to take exams or take orders from superiors. You couldn't criticize them, even if you outranked them. They'd respond, 'Do you know who I am?'"[61]

Corruption

Corruption among postindependence military and civilian rulers undermined professionalism (and revealed the lack of loyalty to the state) by wasting defense money on irrelevant equipment, focusing officers' attention on private financial endeavors, and dividing already fractious militaries more deeply. Regarding this corruption, Decalo wrote that "the glue binding military elites to civilian authority is pecuniary self-interest."[62] Kenneth Kaunda of Zambia, as well as Kenyatta and Moi of Kenya, overlooked any possible conflict-of-interest dilemmas and provided large farms at minimal prices to officers and encouraged others to engage in retail trade.

Procurement practices by African militaries, a rarely examined subject, have severely hamstrung military capabilities. While professional militaries employ rational threat assessments to determine purchase decisions, even the most professional militaries make questionable purchases (e.g., overpriced toilet seats for the U.S. military). But the often dramatic unwillingness of African governments to control military purchasing—accompanied by the lack of public oversight—sharpened the potential for serious waste. The exclusion of an informed civic society from decisionmaking prevented oversight of military doctrine, personnel issues, and procurement. Furthermore, military regimes prevented any legislative oversight or other monitoring from within the government, and they sometimes acted against civilian investigators or critics.

Nigeria's procurement policies are important, given the large size of its military establishment (78,000 in 2000) and its leading regional military role (significant intervention in Liberia and Sierra Leone, as well as various other peacekeeping and training missions). Corruption in Nigeria has been commonplace for several decades: officers have benefited from the "backhander" (or kickback), which supplied a percentage (usually about 20 percent) of the total cost to officers who assisted with a sale. One example is from the 1970s, when Nigerian officers reportedly received $3.6 million from Lockheed Corporation when they purchased six Hercules C-130 transport planes worth $45 million.[63]

Procurement favored large-scale items (the backhander being greater) over training and replacement materiel and, as such, this practice often disregarded threat assessments. Corrupt procurement practices "overconventionalized" the Nigerian military and weakened its ability to contain low-intensity conflicts. During the 1970s and 1980s, Nigeria purchased 150 Vickers MK3 and fifty T-55 main battle tanks, various MiG and Alpha fighter jets (designed to counter enemy air power), and Roland surface-to-air missiles, yet the primary threat was from low-intensity, ground-based conflict. No neighbor of Nigeria possessed any significant mechanized army or jet fighter capability, so what the country needed was light and highly mobile infantry, given the region's low-intensity conflicts and Nigeria's desire to assist in regional peacekeeping. Yet the government stopped a nascent airborne capability in the early 1980s, and it declined U.S. offers to provide riverine training—an especially important priority for Nigeria with its oil-rich delta. A U.S. officer familiar with the negotiations suggests that "there wasn't enough money to skim off" as an explanation for the programs' demise.[64] But the Nigerian regime's fear of an operationally competent but politically divided military also is a highly plausible explanation.

Efforts at procurement of costly sophisticated equipment did not consider the continent's relatively low educational and technical standards. Billy J. Dudley writes that "most African armies, owing to lack of technical skills, a relatively low level of education, inexperience deriving from the escalation of numbers and the sometimes over-rapid indigenisation of the officer corps were incapable of using the sophisticated products of the modern armaments industry."[65]

Nigeria has produced a remarkably well-educated population but still faces a mismatch between weapons systems and available operators. Maj. Gen. George Innih, Nigeria's quartermaster general and chief procurement officer of the army during the early 1980s, noted that in the previous decade the country's military had "tried to introduce the latest and most technologically advanced equipment into its military inventory without giving due consideration to the other geopolitical and social influences as well as, especially, the country's technological base."[66] The military never obtained the required number of mechanics or storage-maintenance areas to service its new equipment properly. A Nigerian study of army preparedness noted "disconcerting" results, which included below-acceptable levels of combat arms, training, mobility, and maintenance and logistics support that "was either grossly inadequate or in some cases virtually non-existent."[67] In Nigeria by 1992, "training and maintenance deficiencies in the air force resulted in high loss of aircraft and pilots."[68]

Nigeria does not stand alone in its paucity of trained technical personnel. Ghana has substantial peacekeeping experience and important operational training facilities, for example, a jungle warfare training school at Achiasi.[69] But as Thomas Ofcansky writes about Ghana in 1995, almost forty years after independence, "servicing of all types of equipment has been extremely poor, largely because of inadequate maintenance capabilities. As a result, foreign military advisors or technicians perform all major maintenance tasks."[70]

Service-determined, rather than joint force–coordinated, purchases have worked against standardization and regularity of supply. At least until the 1980s, Nigeria's military lacked a joint-services group to coordinate and prioritize purchases.[71] Since each service had wide autonomy in purchasing equipment, more individual officers financially benefited. Fayemi notes that Nigeria's military once had 194 types of ammunition of sixty-two makes from fourteen countries and that it possessed planes from Czechoslovakia, Britain, France, Italy, Germany, the

United States, and the Soviet Union. Supply diversification can offer some, notably political, advantages, but it also results in higher unit pricing, only limited rebates from bulk purchasing, shortages of equipment, and difficulties in maintenance.

Nigeria's Operation Seadog in 1985 indicated how poorly regulated (and often corrupt) procurement weakens military capabilities. Maj. Gen. Abdullahi Mamman recalls that

> Operation Seadog has gone a long way to illustrate to us how uncoordinated the procurement system is in our services. We had ships from the Navy that could not communicate with each other; there was no way the three services could initially communicate with each other as each service has different communication sets operating on different frequencies. For example, the air force could not communicate with the ground forces they were supporting.[72]

Seadog was Nigeria's first joint-training exercise since the end of the Biafran war, fifteen years earlier.[73]

Corruption occurs in ways other than in procurement. Presidential appointments provided some officers with a license for larceny, since a personal-rule state contains few independent authorities. Jimi Peters writes that Nigeria's President Babangida "ensured that only those he considered loyal were appointed to key military and political positions."[74] These officers now had a certain carte blanche; not only did they have access to state funds but enjoyed a de facto immunity from prosecution. "Even where these activities became public knowledge," writes Peters, "the government did not prosecute anyone, thus giving the impression that they had public backing."[75] Many officers quickly began using their offices for personal gain, knowing that future reshufflings were unpredictable but likely.

Various governments, especially in Mobutu's Zaire, tried to buy military support by allowing their officers varying levels of *chasse gardée* (private reserve) for personal gain. Such governments tolerated—or perhaps could not control—officers sometimes pocketing a percentage of their own soldiers' wages. British and U.S. officials believe that various levels of Nigerian officers take up to 50 percent of a soldier's pay before the rightful beneficiary receives it.[76] This has worsened troop behavior toward civilians, with soldiers extorting money and food—sometimes out of necessity. Such pilfering became tragically evident with some ECOMOG forces, especially Nigeria's, in Liberia and Sierra Leone.

To sidetrack possible discontent among enlistees, many of whom receive pay only erratically from their superiors, several governments extended the rentier concept and permitted the lower ranks to extort money from the citizenry. Schatzberg comments upon this in Mobutu's Zaire, and Decalo writes of Uganda in the late 1960s that "in the countryside . . . the army moved as though in feudal domains. Corruption, embezzlement, petty theft, smuggling, and general rowdiness by army elements remained outside the scope of the government or the police.[77]

Some military corruption occurs when the regime refuses to pay the military. Soldiers will sell their equipment or begin smuggling to provide for their own welfare. These actions can destabilize domestic or regional politics. Guinea-Bissau's military was strapped for cash in the mid-1990s and therefore started smuggling guns and land mines to the neighboring Casamance separatist movement in Senegal (the army also exported marijuana).[78]

Parallel Forces

Rulers' trepidations about khaki-clad loyalty has often prompted the creation of parallel security forces, usually ethnically based, as counterweights. These forces are a variant of private security organizations because they primarily protect the ruler and his regime, rather than defending the nation. Among these forces were Kwame Nkrumah's President's Own Guard Regiment (POGR) in Ghana, Siaka Stevens's Special Security Division in Sierra Leone, Mobutu Sese Seko's Division Speciale Presidentielle, Sani Abacha's Special Bodyguard Service in Nigeria, and Juvénal Habyarimana's Presidential Guard in Rwanda.[79] Popular nicknames for these unpopular forces indicate that citizens realized how their rulers had personalized security forces. Steven's SSD was known as "Siaka Stevens's Dogs," and a Kenyan unit popularly became "Moi's Old Men."

As already noted, ethnically based parallel forces gained remarkable strength (Kenya's General Services Unit, which was "capable of defeating the entire army by itself," put down the Kenyan air force's attempted coup in 1982).[80] Increasingly in the 1990s, rulers created their own combat militias, such as Interahamwe ("those who work together") in Rwanda, rather than relying exclusively on the often less trustworthy national military.

These presidential-political units generally proved counterproductive to the state because they prospered at the expense of the army, thus working against greater professionalism. Parallel forces angered the existing national forces because of the presidents' implicit vote of no confidence, the groups' freedom from the military's normal chain of command, and their first choice in equipment. The military's resentment of presidential security formations sometimes influenced coups: Ghanaian coup leaders, for example, cited the dislike of the POGR as a major justification for toppling Nkrumah. Col. A. A. Afrifa recalls that "we were also aware that members of the President's Own Guard Regiment were receiving kingly treatment. Their pay was way higher and it was an open fact that they possessed better equipment. The men who had been transferred from the Regular Army no longer owed any allegiance and loyalty to the Chief of Defence Staff, but to Kwame Nkrumah."[81] Again, however, it is easy to understand why African rulers employ parallel forces: they certainly complicate coup planning and sometimes stifle actual attempts, as Moi's GSU did in 1982.

Parallel forces may also discourage professional capabilities in the regular militaries. The *Economist* Intelligence Unit writes of "an uneasy relationship" between Sudan's national military and the Peoples' Defense Force (PDF), "not only because ill-trained conscripts to the PDF are often a liability on the battlefield but also because they act as informers for the NIF [National Islamic Front government]."[82] Presidential or party units, by providing seemingly trusted security, do not encourage rulers to improve the military capabilities or social representativeness of the national military. Furthermore, unaccountable, parallel forces have engaged in blatant corruption. Stephen Ellis notes that in Chad "the Presidential Guard and its Zaghawa associates are actively engaged in operations best described as predation,"[83] and Western observers believe that Guinea's Presidential Guard may be involved in smuggling diamonds out of Sierra Leone.[84]

Rulers have sometimes selected foreign specialists, who symbolized international support and had no ties to subnational groups. A U.S. Senate staff report in 1982 noted Mobutu's preference for foreign military help that was "more prestigious and reliable, less expensive, and far less challenging to his leadership" than a local force and "has a symbolic value which far exceeds the actual number of foreign personnel involved. The 'tripwire' presence of these personnel represents the assurance of foreign intervention during a crisis."[85] French personnel ran several intelligence bureaus for West African rulers in the 1970s and 1980s, and Ethiopia's Mengistu used East German advisors for his intelligence service. President Omar Bongo in Gabon employed his "Corsican mafia" as a counterweight to his potentially disloyal military. And rulers sometimes hired foreigners as personal bodyguards.

Domestic Deployment

The desire to contain political discontent in a noninstitutionalized state drove some African politicians to invoke Thomas Hobbes ("When nothing else is turned up, clubs are trumps") and call upon the military for domestic repression. Their civilian-ordered domestic deployment, along with other forms of crossing the civil-military divide, encouraged a sometimes reticent military to become a partisan actor. The resulting coups and embezzlement further undermined the military's political responsibility and technical expertise.

Competitive politics insinuated themselves into various militaries soon after their nations' independence, and Luckham, among others, argues that the intrusion of politics undermined a nascent military professionalism. The domestic use of the national military forces against election protestors in western Nigeria in 1964 and against the Kabaka of Buganda in Uganda in 1966 encouraged a perception of those militaries as political actors. In the mid-1980s, the regularity of SADF deployment into restive black townships inside South Africa triggered a similar, bitter view and further lowered public regard. The Kenyan military participated in fund-raising and political campaign activities for President Moi's Kenya African National Union party in 1983, following an abortive coup attempt the previous year. Perhaps not surprisingly, the Kenyan military became known as the "presidential army."[86]

Relatively few militaries anywhere appreciate deployment at home because it creates internal divisions, demands new responsibilities,[87] and may lead an unprofessional military to challenge the existing state. For example, Obote's domestic use of an Amin-led army against the Kabaka of Buganda later backfired once the army realized its power in a weak state: in 1971 Amin overthrew Obote.

Some African officers did oppose the politicizing trend. Luckham states that "political pressures on the army and antagonism towards the political authorities within [the Nigerian military] grew in proportion to its role in terms of internal security rather than external defense."[88] In Uganda, the competition among civilian politicians for military support was so intense that the main entrance to the army headquarters had a sign stating, "Politicians Not Allowed."[89]

Civilian rulers probably did not realize initially that by crossing the divide, they could be hit by military traffic. Initially, African militaries rarely sought political duties—after all, no military coups occurred between 1957 and the beginning of 1963.[90] But once ordered or induced by civilian politicians into domestic politics, the military forces could transform themselves into powerful actors pursuing their own ends.

Politicized militaries quickly realized their power to intimidate or to overthrow governments. For instance, even though the 1964 military coup in Uganda failed, the government quickly boosted military salaries by up to 300 percent. "The army witnessed the government's timidity under pressure," remarks Decalo.[91] A spiraling relationship developed: crossing of the line by one party (military or civilian) often spurred a corresponding reaction from the affected party. Disgust with civilian politics, anger at being given unfamiliar political tasks, and, increasingly, desire for group or personal gain contributed to the militaries' staging of some seventy-five coups by the mid-1980s.

Lack of Urgency

Africa's refraining from frequent interstate conflict[92] and its ability to garner foreign military support reduced the need to develop capable militaries and allowed regimes to structure their militaries for political loyalty.

Political opposition to invasions by the Organization of African Unity (OAU) and the superpowers had had a major stabilizing effect. And, if faced by especially serious domestic or foreign threats, African states could often call upon professional forces, usually from the colonial metropole, that posed no security threat to the regime (the inability of most African states to project military force any sizable distance was another, but often overlooked, explanation for the lack of invasions). Schatzberg wrote of the former Zaire that "it matters little to Mobutu if his armed forces are able to repel an invasion. He knows if his regime should face serious difficulty he can always call on his friends in the West for succor. Shaba I and Shaba II [invasions by former Zairois residing in Angola] demonstrated that."[93]

The OAU was created in 1963 by African nations seeking a collective African voice to discourage armed neocolonialism or subversion among themselves. These states were especially troubled by the ongoing "Congo crisis," in which the mineral-rich province of Katanga attempted to secede shortly after Congo's independence in July 1960. Union Minière, a Belgian mineral firm, had actively supported Katanga's secessionist attempt, even to the point of funding European and African mercenaries.

Subsequent foreign military involvement in Katanga by the UN, United States, Soviet Union, white-ruled states of southern Africa, and several mercenary groups threatened not only to divide the Congo but also to stifle African nations' newly won independence. Also, many

OAU members feared subversion of the existing state system by Africa's more revolutionary leaders. Kwame Nkrumah of Ghana, for example, had been supporting and training rebel groups opposed to several West African regimes. The OAU's 1963 charter implicitly acknowledged these various threats by calling for the inviolability of national borders and denouncing any uninvited interference in a member state's internal affairs. The OAU's strongly held position undoubtedly lessened unwanted foreign interference, until recently, in Africa's domestic politics. The white-governed countries remained the exceptions to the OAU policy, the organization creating a liberation fund to finance military campaigns against white rule.

African and non-African leaders accepted the concept of *uti possidetis* (literally, "as you possess"), which also served to lessen interstate hostilities.[94] Whereas "self-determination" had had some revolutionary overtones during colonialism, independent Africa applied the concept only to the existing state structure, believing that a redrawing of boundaries could pose more problems than solutions. Therefore African states, often with outside help, defeated all secessionist attempts, such as Katanga in Zaire and Biafra in Nigeria.

Relatively few African states were invaded between 1960 and 1990,[95] and during the Cold War, the Soviet Union, France, Britain, and the United States rarely, if ever, supported invasions of African states.[96] Outside forces could criticize, but not overthrow, authoritarian or even genocidal rulers. Thus, African leaders at the 1979 OAU summit lambasted Tanzania for entering Uganda and overthrowing the undeniably evil Idi Amin, whose regime had killed at least 400,000 Ugandans in eight years.[97] Olusegun Obasanjo, Nigeria's widely respected president, castigated the invasion as "a dangerous precedent of unimaginable consequences."[98]

States especially attractive to the United States, the Soviet Union, or their allies could rely on foreign patronage and intervention when needed: these two countries alone supplied $20 billion worth of military hardware during the Cold War.[99] The West intervened militarily several times in the former Zaire (1964, 1977–1978, for example),[100] and the Soviet Union dispatched massive amounts of weaponry to, and sometimes helped finance Cuban troops in, Ethiopia and Angola, roughly between 1975 and 1990. Each of these intercessions protected, rather than restructured, the existing national boundaries—the possibility of intervention or increased military aid probably helped discourage some insurgencies.

However, many francophone states relied on French military intervention to protect against domestic threats. France continued its close ties with former colonies after independence, far more so than other metropoles.[101] The Entente Agreement of 1959 and subsequent agreements "secured for France a virtual monopoly of external military assistance to the Council of Entente countries, legitimated the continued presence of French armed forces on their soil and served as justification for occasional direct military interventions," according to Joe Smaldone.[102] During the 1970s and 1980s France had some nine thousand troops in five, mostly West African, bases and another four thousand in southern France, who could arrive in West Africa within forty-eight hours. French troops intervened some twenty times between 1960 and the mid-1990s. Under Valery Giscard d'Estaing's administration, France became known as "NATO's gendarme in Africa,"[103] and François Mitterand once described the French military as the "Cuba of the West."[104] French military support, as Decalo and others note, discouraged coup attempts by often unprofessional forces.[105]

Regimes also hired ad hoc collections of mercenaries, sometimes to provide combat capability that the rulers had not allowed their own forces to acquire. Nigeria employed Egyptian and European pilots against Biafra, which itself had hired a motley group of Europeans. Mobutu called on mercenaries at various occasions because he had deliberately diminished the capabilities of his Forces Armées Zaïroises (FAZ). Perhaps a thousand British, South African, French, and U.S. mercenaries fought for the Rhodesian minority government.

Mercenaries exhibited a mixed degree of professionalism, but their effect was largely negative: numerous political drawbacks outweighed their technical contributions. Foreigners fighting for pay weakens the political legitimacy of their employers. Mercenaries generally undermined chances for long-run military professionalism (as did presidential guards), serving as a vote of no confidence, operating outside the existing command structure, and having privileged access to equipment.

This relative security of the Cold War era permitted African rulers to concentrate on the military's political loyalty and to disregard military efficiency. The lack of maintenance, even upon expensive pieces of equipment, became especially widespread. Frederick Ehrenreich notes that in Liberia, in 1985, "vehicle operational readiness was reported to be extremely low and the tactical battalions were considered to be practically immobile."[106] Even well-regarded forces displayed dramatic deficiencies. A 1988 Ghanaian government commission reported that the operational state of readiness of the Army was so low that none of the Infantry brigades could quickly launch either a fully equipped battalion or even a company into action, not least since less than 10 per cent of their respective transport fleets were operational owing to lack of tyres and spare parts. Equipment was often obsolete or unserviceable . . . however, the problems of the Army paled besides those of the two smaller services [the Air Force and Navy].[107]

Other Factors

African rulers' fears of coups prompted them to curtail operational capabilities, whether by restricting ammunition (Sierra Leone's Siaka Stevens limited each soldier to one bullet yearly), fuel, spare parts, or training expertise (Mobutu deliberately employed trainers from a range of countries to limit coordination between units). Rulers often encouraged competition or jealousy among services and officers. They removed officers who appeared untrustworthy (or too competent), played the regular militaries off against other armed groups, such as presidential guards or mercenaries, and placed specific constraints on operational capabilities. The condoning, and sometimes encouraging, of procurement corruption also lowered military capabilities, as the Nigerian case will illustrate. Very few African militaries have any significant special operational capability, given rulers' fears of capable units.[108]

Decalo observes about Uganda's Milton Obote that

using classic "divide and rule" tactics, he appointed different foreign military missions to each battalion, scrambled operational channels of command, played off the police against the army (and later set up two elite paramilitary structures), encouraged personal infighting between his main military "proteges," and removed from operational control of troops officers who appeared [politically] unreliable or too authoritative.[109]

Ideology sometimes provided a counterweight to external military influence. After Nkrumah dismissed British officers in 1961, he placed in all units political commissars who preached the philosophy of Nkrumah's political party and watched for "neocolonial" sentiments among the officers. Political party memberships became a requirement for officers in some militaries, and, as previously noted, political nonalignment cramped the technical efficiency of some militaries.[110]

Have armies whose roots lie in the ideologically based liberation struggles of southern Africa exhibited a superior amount of political responsibility and technical competence? The verdict is mixed. Annette Seegers writes that in "most SADC [Southern African Development Community] countries, civil-military relations were shaped by guerrilla struggles and insurrections. Marxist-Leninist lines of thinking emphasized civilian-political supremacy, enforced by political parties over military organizations. Post-struggle experiences did not upset civil-military stability."[111] The militaries in Angola, Mozambique, Zimbabwe, Namibia, and South Africa have attempted few, if any, coups.

Yet two caveats are necessary. First, a change in regime has not tested the military's loyalty to the state, as opposed to just the regime; none of the above states has witnessed a transition of government since independence. Second, although ideology probably has aided the armed forces' loyalty to the government, it has not encouraged superior military capabilities. Mozambique is a particular case in point. Decalo wrote in 1989 that "the often unruly and undisciplined Mozambican forces all along retained their original ethnic/regional cleavages, *pro forma* exploited their base-zones by extracting illegal payments from farmers . . . [and suffered from] low pay, poor terms of service, ethnic tensions and charges of favoritism, inadequate military facilities and materials, unpopular development tasks, no home leave, and inept and brutal commanding officers."[112] Western defense analysts agree that Mozambique's armed forces remained largely unprofessional throughout the 1990s.[113]

The Anomaly of South Africa

The white-commanded SADF was an exception to the above examples. It physically represented apartheid, was ethnically recruited, and was sometimes deployed domestically, but it retained a functional autonomy highly unusual in Africa during the 1970s and 1980s.

The modern SADF has had the advantage of time to develop a professional officer corps. The force's long-standing British heritage of "the technical subordination of the military to civil political authority" was supplemented by various South African statutes that barred its soldiers from any partisan political activity. For example, SADF personnel could not belong to any political party.[114]

White society in South Africa provided many of Huntington's criteria for professional militaries. It was a very small nation-state, allowed a quasi-democratic system (for whites only), enjoyed significant authority over its security forces,[115] and possessed more than minimal levels of technology and education. White civilians and officers respected the civil-military divide, in part because they benefited from the status quo and because their being the ethnic minority required a united instrument of defense. Philip Frankel terms the ex-SADF as "highly professional" in its political relations with the civilian government,[116] and most observers, regardless of political sentiment, agree that the SADF had military capabilities unique to sub-Saharan Africa.

The whites, who constituted about 15 percent of the total South African population, displayed considerable political unity on security matters during much of the twentieth century. They saw a strong security force as a necessary protector against the vast majority's aspirations. The constricted democratic system allowed the whites to organize politically and to compete for political office, and in the eyes of many white soldiers, this added to the legitimacy of the state and obviated any need for physical violence.

The SADF enjoyed functional autonomy in return for its subordination to civilian rule. Civilian leaders rarely, if ever, transferred or cashiered officers for political reasons. The absence of political interference in military matters after the 1950s led to less factionalism in the SADF and therefore less incentive for officers to intrude into government affairs. The SADF's later allegiance during President F. W. de Klerk's contentious policy of moving toward majority rule revealed the force's ingrained sense of political loyalty to the state—despite the widespread personal opposition to de Klerk's reforms by many white SADF personnel.[117]

Whites enjoyed remarkable employment possibilities, due to their relatively small numbers, their enforced prevention of black social mobility, and their technologically developed economy and education system. Such an economy meant that potential officers saw a military career largely as an end in itself rather than as a means to political or economic power. And a growing sense of urgency after 1960 prompted the whites to augment their already daunting security forces. For instance, South Africa's demographics encouraged security planners to increase the training of black personnel.

International opposition to South Africa's apartheid policies encouraged a massive increase in the SADF's self-reliance: the government created the parastatal Armscor in 1963, shortly after the United States instituted a limited arms embargo, and by the mid-1980s Armscor claimed to have made South Africa 80-percent self-sufficient in weaponry. And some SADF special operations officers developed their knowledge of covert weapons networks: such skills would later contribute to the success of Executive Outcomes.

The SADF's light infantry and special operations units developed "force multiplier" capabilities, that is, a small group of highly-trained personnel could have a disproportionate effect upon a conflict. The Reconnaissance Commandos, the Parachute Battalion, the 32 Battalion, and the largely Namibian Koevoet paramilitary force honed their skills during some fifteen years of destabilizing neighboring states that permitted South African armed opposition groups to operate. Such SADF units gained the considerable, albeit usually grudging, respect of most observers.

Military Rule

The ascendency of the armed forces as political actors reduced their professionalism. Officers often imitated civilian rulers by emasculating their own militaries through corruption, especially in procurement practices, and through the restructuring of military units and assignment of personnel.[118] Not surprisingly, African conflicts up to 1990 revealed the mediocre military capabilities of these forces and illustrated why various states have examined multinational forces, private security organizations, and Western aid in upgrading local professionalism.

Military officers sometimes vitiated whatever countervailing influences upon the military had previously existed. The U.S. Institute of Peace notes that in Ghana "the military takeover of government result[ed] in further role contraction for the civilian staff [in the Defence Ministry] and assumption by the military of direct control of budgeting, allocation, accounting, and procurement functions."[119]

Political reassignments of officers provided mixed benefits— maybe aiding security in some cases by thwarting some coups and rendering officers beholden to their patrons, but often raising resentment within the ranks.[120] The rapid turnover of officers encouraged indiscipline and reduced esprit de corps. Efficiency and innovation suffered as remaining officers grew more cautious about offering advice, especially if it was adverse. Jimi Peters notes that the politicization of the Nigerian military had driven dispirited professional officers to resign.[121] Nigeria, which was Africa's leading regional military during much of the 1990s, suffered especially from an exceptionally large number of forced retirements that resulted from coup threats. Politically inspired retirements "liquidated the senior ranks of [the Nigerian military's] professional cadre. The remaining officer corps became understandably reticent . . . to give professional military advice necessary for the improvement of the organization."[122] For example, the air force alone lost over thirty officers with the rank of air commodore or above after a failed coup in April 1990.

Opportunities for wealth and political status diverted the attention of numerous officers from the comparatively mundane and time-consuming needs of running a military. The Strategic Studies Institute of the U.S. Army War College contends that "during the decades of military rule, the Nigerian armed forces have lost nearly all semblance of professionalism and become thoroughly corrupted. Senior officers all become immensely rich through theft, while junior officers and enlisted men live in poverty."[123] Lt. Gen. Salihu Ibrahim, an army chief of staff under President (and General) Babangida, remarked that among Nigerian officers "it was an open secret that some officers preferred political appointments over and above regimental appointments no matter the relevance of such appointments to their career prospects."[124]

Nigerian officers conducted what the *Daily Mail and Guardian* termed "one of the swiftest lootings of the national treasury by any military administration."[125] A senior incoming official in 1999 lamented that "soldiers are queueing up to award themselves contracts at every ministry. The foreign currency reserves have just evaporated. By the time it's over I suspect there'll be very little in the bank. It's very irresponsible but par for the course with the military."[126]

President Obasanjo in his 1999 inaugural address spoke about how this switch in officers' occupation had damaged the Nigerian armed forces' professionalism.

> The incursion of the military into government has been a disaster for our country. The *espirit de corps* among military personnel has been destroyed. Professionalism has been lost. Most youths go into the military now not to pursue a noble career but with the sole intention of taking part in coups and to be appointed as military administrators of states and chairmen of task forces. As a retired officer, my heart bleeds to see the degradation in the proficiency of the military.[127]

Officers in several countries were able to hold political, military, and private commercial positions simultaneously—with the obvious attendant possibilities for conflict of interest. That senior officers retained their rank while serving in political positions discouraged ambitious junior officers from excelling.

Corruption not only weakened technical capabilities but also created internal divisions. In Nigeria, as J. 'Kayode Fayemi writes, it "led to serious disagreements *among* senior officers and served as part-justification for some coups d'état" [emphasis added].[128] Coup-inspired, political promotions frustrated those officers who were passed over and probably reinforced separate ethnic identities. Some professional officers reportedly became disenchanted with their own military and quietly resigned, others being cashiered by insecure regimes.

The Ugandan People's Defence Force (UPDF) has suffered from some fourteen years of corruption and incompetence. Its present officers gained a reputation for effectiveness as guerrilla leaders when, in 1986, their National Resistance Army became the first insurgency to overthrow a sub-Saharan government. But more than a decade after Yoweri Museveni's rise to power, the UPDF's corruption has corroded its military capabilities.[129]

The nonaccountability inherent in personal rule is largely to blame. Gen. Salim Saleh is President Museveni's half-brother and a hero of the guerrilla struggle, two attributes that apparently allow him to engage in blatant corruption. A U.S. State Department official underlines the role of personalism when stating that "Saleh no longer holds a formal position but far more important than a paper relationship is his relationship with his brother [Musevini]."[130] Saleh had been implicated in several scandals, but he continued to hold important defense positions. He was retired in 1989 due to accusations of conflict of interest, and then became a military advisor to the president in 1996, but allegations of questionable helicopter procurement and attempts to buy a soon-to-be-privatized state bank forced his second retirement. Saleh, despite being officially relieved of other duties in 1999 because of a banking scandal, handles all foreign military procurement for the UPDF and he easily crosses the military-commercial divide.

In 1999 alone, accusations of corruption focused upon the questionable procurement of MiG-21 planes, T-54/55 tanks (sixty-two of which were inoperable),[131] helicopters, and rations past their safety dates. In 1996 the Ugandan military had paid premium prices for Belarussian helicopters, which needed major overhauls before they could become operational, and several leading Ugandan officials reportedly got significant kickbacks in return for paying the inflated prices. The Museveni government did not take any legal action for several years until September 1999, when press revelations forced it to do so. These apparent instances of corruption fit a continuing pattern of illegality. For example, the military's theft of foreign relief supplies in western Uganda in June 1997 forced President Museveni to replace the UPDF's entire western command, and several observers believe that officers' skimming of enlistees' pay is common.

Such corruption has chipped away at military capabilities by distracting officers from their primary function of providing military security, spending valuable foreign exchange on wasteful or irrelevant military equipment, and lowering the morale of the underpaid enlistees. The corruption helps to explain why the UPDF has proved incapable of defeating the widely hated Lord's Resistance Army in northern Uganda. Finally, by mid-1999 international donors had begun to threaten aid reductions if military corruption continued.

Operational weakness is the upshot of all the above factors. Officers in several sub-Saharan militaries sometimes opposed military campaigns because they knew the severe weaknesses of their own forces and feared the personal consequences of any defeat. Fayemi writes that in Nigeria "the fear of loss of prestige and privileges following from military unpreparedness was enough disincentive to any military option the few times the subject [of external deployment] was broached."[132] The bias against operational effectiveness and specialized units, as well as the military's tolerance of corruption, would later haunt Nigeria in its actions in Liberia and Sierra Leone (as detailed in Chapter 4).

Nigeria's case of political intrusion weakening combat capabilities was fairly typical elsewhere. Charles Snyder wrote about Zaire that "reports of nonpayment of salaries, lack of provisions, and poor logistical management are chronic. Frequent rotation of key personnel to avoid political activities encourages divisiveness in leader relationships. Consequently, the army was utterly ineffective against Katangan guerillas in the 1977 and 1978 Shaba invasions."[133]

Thomas Callaghy notes much of the same, reporting that most Zairian senior and mid-level officers fled during the 1978 fighting, leaving area defense to junior officers and NCOs. One explanation for these flight-not-fight officers is that Mobutu had purged his army of some 250 officers in early 1997 following possible coup plotting.

Amin's Ugandan military was equally helpless (or hapless) when it fought Tanzania in 1979. Anthony Clayton states that "unpaid in many units, demoralized and lacking ammunition, [it] generally offered weak resistance. . . . Being either untrained or poorly trained, the Ugandans opted to fight around or from within their wheeled armoured personnel carriers, so making themselves targets for encirclement and Tanzanian anti-tank weaponry."[134]

Commenting on contemporary Sierra Leone, Desmond Davies writes that "this lack of professionalism allowed the RUF to make significant military advances against government forces."[135] One study notes that "Sierra Leone was incapable of fighting a war. The army's young soldiers fought with rusty, out-of-date weapons and insufficient ammunition. They lacked radios, boots and uniforms, field kitchens, and elementary medical care. . . . [The senior officers were] beneficiaries of the patronage process, had no military experience and were incapable of exercising command."[136]

Expansion of militaries at the beginning of hostilities usually undermines military capabilities. Defense budgets do not rise proportionately with the growth of personnel, and most African militaries have a distinct shortage of NCOs for training new recruits. African regimes at war are forced to hire mostly unemployed (or unemployable) and poorly educated young men. The Forces Armées Rwandaises, which Gerald Prunier describes as "rather professional and disciplined" prior to combat in the early 1990s,[137] expanded from 5,200 in October 1990 to 50,000 in mid-1992. Most of the new recruits sought "an opportunity to eat, drink, and loot since pay was minimal and irregular. The volunteers were mostly landless peasants, urban unemployed and even some former drifters. They had little or no education."[138]

The Sierra Leonean military grew from about 4,000 in 1990 to 12,000 by 1993, responding to the threat of the several-hundred-strong RUF, and was forced to hire almost any man who applied. A soldier received six weeks of basic training from an overstretched NCO staff and then was sent to the front. Julius Maada-Bio, Sierra Leone's president in the mid-1990s, was a platoon commander in late 1991 and early 1992 with ECOMOG. As a platoon commander, he normally would have commanded about forty soldiers. But widespread desertion by colonels and majors saw Maada-Bio assume command of a few companies—some 400 men. Maada-Bio relates that before one battle, 200 out of 600 Sierra Leonean soldiers deserted.[139]

The Sierra Leonean government lacked the money to pay for this threefold increase in often undisciplined soldiers, many of whom harassed civilians and stole their property. Some also covertly assisted the RUF by providing intelligence and weaponry, and thus gained the sobriquet of "sobels"—soldiers by day and rebels by night. Sierra Leone's subsequent rulers failed to improve military competence and the army increasingly became an active security problem.[140]

Military rule in sub-Saharan Africa has not promoted state security or political development.[141] The early hopes of Lucien Pye, Samuel Huntington, and others for politically modernizing militaries did not materialize. Cleavages within their armies forced numerous regimes to "devote considerably more time and effort to consolidating and warding off alternate challenges to their authority than to providing the country with purposeful leadership," writes Decalo.[142] Surges in military spending, especially on equipment and salaries for loyal ethnically-based units, siphoned government spending and foreign exchange from more economically productive endeavors.

This lack of professionalism in many African armies by the end of the 1980s appears to validate Decalo's assertion that

> African armies have rarely been cohesive, nontribal, Westernized, or even complex organizational structures. . . . many African armies bear little resemblance to a modern complex organizational model and are instead a coterie of distinct armed camps owing primary clientalist allegiance to a handful of mutually competitive officers of different ranks seething with a variety of corporate, ethnic, and personal differences.[143]

African Military Capabilities

The shift in the coercive balance in the early 1990s, as shown by the growth of collapsed or threatened states, strongly suggested a need for capable African militaries. But the military legacies of the colonial and the personal-rule era continued, and many African militaries, despite the best intentions and dedication of numerous skilled officers, remained clearly unprofessional. Even when noting that capabilities are relative (a "mediocre" military can defeat an even less capable opponent), Western analysts generally believe that "Africa's standing armies have generally been minuscule, their weapons inferior, and their training and facilities outmoded. The mission of preserving internal order has always predominated."[144]

A report commissioned by the U.S. Defense Department notes, inter alia, that only seven out of forty-six sub-Saharan militaries are "capable of deploying without significant augmentation an equipped, professional battalion for a multinational peace or humanitarian operation," that nine states have "strong officer corps (experienced, trained, and professional)," that only six of the forty-two militaries can "perform engineering tasks such as construction, bridging, and water provision," that no sub-Saharan states can "provide sustained transportation of personnel and equipment to a peace or humanitarian operation," and that only two states have any "significant naval capability."[145]

Western observers have underscored Africa's logistical, communications, and multilateral difficulties. "The pandemic shortage of skilled manpower and managerial leadership within African armies is felt most severely in the logistical area," writes Charles Snyder,[146] and Walter Barrows notes that "mobility in combat is among the most difficult military capacities to acquire and the majority of African states will master it only slowly, if at all."[147] When the United States, the Soviet Union, and other powers transferred major military items to African nations, they also supplied maintenance packages. Once the foreigners departed (or, in the case of the Soviet Union, ceased to exist), some African states were left with camouflaged "white elephants." Hence Mozambique, the possessor of, among other equipment, forty-four MiG-21s, did not "have one plane that flies or one boat that floats" in 1996.[148] Zambian critics in the armed forces maintained in early 1999 that only seven out of twenty T-59 tanks were serviceable, and, according to a Zambian air force officer in 1999, that all of the twelve MiG-21 interceptors "are in Israel for repairs since 1992."[149]

The irregularity of full salary payments leads to corruption and low morale in the military. Glickson and Sinai noted about Zaire's military that "a considerable portion of military equipment is not operational [in the early 1990s], primarily as a result of a shortage of spare parts, poor maintenance, and theft [and the major cause is] the low irregular pay that soldiers receive, resulting in the theft and sale of spare parts and even basic equipment to supplement their meager salaries."[150] In 2000, the London *Sunday Telegraph* noted that even UN peacekeeping payments could be irregular. Nigerian troops had not been paid in four months "as their government has pocketed UN contributions intended for the soldiers...the Nigerian government is the worst abuser of the system."[151]

Political fears of large troop deployments and militaries' lack of functioning equipment restricted field training exercises, as already noted in Nigeria's case. Other countries have also gone some fifteen years without conducting large-scale exercises. A Zambian officer told the *Post of Zambia* that "the Zambian army has never conducted a major military training exercise where a self-critique would have been done as to its efficiency in relation to the neighboring countries. The last exercise was in 1972."[152]

An increasing threat to the cohesiveness of Africa's national militaries is AIDS, which is depleting the ranks of experienced personnel. The armed forces probably have a higher AIDS incidence rate than the rest of society, since soldiers are often based away from their regular sexual partners and because they have enough money to hire prostitutes. Definitive HIV/AIDS incidence rates are lacking for Africa, but U.S.

defense specialists believe that between 8 and 60 percent of African militaries are HIV-positive. The South African National Defence Force reportedly has HIV-rates of about 14 percent with some units having rates up to 40 percent.[153] While the Nigerian military has an overall level of about 13 percent, its units that served in ECOMOG have decidedly higher levels.[154]

As already noted, sub-Saharan African states lack effective, multilateral intervention capability. Another Defense Department study concluded that African militaries have "virtually nonexistent" capability to lead successful peace-keeping operations and that "no African country has the capability to lift heavy equipment by air," although "several African militaries" can provide "well-trained, well-equipped troops."[155] Language is also an often overlooked problem, especially for multinational forces: for example, poor communication among invading Rwandans and Tanzanians and their local Zairian allies hurt operational efficiency. Several commanders reportedly ordered Zairian rebels to bury over 200 cases of ammunition and weaponry, but the insurgents confused "bury" with "burn."[156]

Interstate cooperation, such as joint training and exercises and adoption of compatible equipment, can foster military professionalism as well as multilateral capability. But this occurs only sporadically. The OAU has hesitated to become involved in military affairs, even though article 20 of its charter seemingly allows it a role in defense operations in Africa. The OAU demurred on Kwame Nkrumah's call during the 1960s for an all-Africa high command because, inter alia, such a force would drain African states of scarce military resources and possibly be directed against some other OAU members.[157] OAU intervention in Chad (1977–1982) incorporated both failed mediation efforts and the creation of a military force that lacked either a clear mandate or requisite military capabilities.[158] The OAU refused any significant military role in subsequent conflicts.

The OAU could have done little else, given its poor staffing and funding.[159] After all, the OAU is a voluntary rather than a command organization, and its consensual nature and very limited resources preclude an activist stance. John Ostheimer had concluded in the mid-1980s that "the OAU is unable to finance even its more limited present activities, much less deal with expanded functions."[160]

In the end, many African officials preferred to emphasize their existing military links to their former colonial metropole, this being most noticeable in former French colonies. Ostheimer noted that "most of the Francophone states have close ties to France that may be costly for them to forgo. For example, defence links with France have a measure of reliability that would be hard to replace with inter-African alliances."[161] French troops have intervened to save governments in Gabon, Chad, Mauritania, Zaire, Central African Republic, Senegal, and Togo.

By the late 1980s, whatever cooperation that occurred was largely reactive and situational—such as Zimbabwe's entering Mozambique to protect the FRELIMO government against the RENAMO insurgency during much of the 1980s—or else low-key, consisting of a few training teams or small joint exercises.[162] This situation joined the factors discussed above in contributing to Africa's growing security crisis in the 1990s and beyond.

Notes

1. Samuel P. Huntington, *The Soldier and the State*, pp. 32–39.
2. Charles Tilly, *The Formation of National States in Western Europe*, and Huntington, *The Soldier and the State*.
3. Presidential guards sometimes led coups, however. A recent example of this occurred in Niger in April 1999 when a member of the guard assassinated President Ibrahim Mainassara Barre.
4. Interestingly, Clapham writes that these militaries "had the organisational and technological capacity to generate the confidence trick on which the maintenance of security classically depends: they were powerful, because they were believed to be powerful." "African Security Systems: Privatisation and the Scope for Mercenary Conflict," in Greg Mills and John Stremlau, eds., *The Privatisation of Security in Africa* (Johannesburg: The South African Institute of International Affairs), p. 26.
5. Ibid.
6. The Tirailleurs Sénégalais was a misnomer: the unit comprised Africans from all over French West Africa. Myron Echenberg, *Colonial Conscripts*.
7. Colonial powers recruited Africans rather than using metropolitan troops. African troops cost less, demonstrated a willingness and local knowledge, and politically were more expendable in terms of combat casualties.
8. Samuel Decalo, *Coups and Army Rule in Africa*, p. 6.
9. Both French and British authorities held these views, and Echenberg writes that "as late as the 1950s, officers were repeating the homilies . . . regarding 'warlike races.'" Echenberg, *Colonial Conscripts*, p. 15.
10. Michael Desch, "Threat Environments and Military Missions," in Diamond and Plattner, eds., *Civil-Military Relations and Democracy*, p. 13.
11. "Colonial troops served quasi-police functions. Their primary role was domestic, not international, despite their extensive manpower contributions during the two World Wars. Colonial armies existed primarily to suppress tax riots and ethnic conflict." Claude Welch, "Pretorianism In West Africa," p. 219.

12. A good history of the Force Publique is Bryant Shaw's "Force Publique, Force Unique: The Military in the Belgian Congo, 1914–1939," Ph.D. diss., University of Wisconsin, 1984.

13. Catherine Coquery-Vidrovitch, "French Black Africa," *Cambridge History of Africa,* vol. 7 (Cambridge: Cambridge University Press, 1986), p. 338.

14. Shaw, "Force Publique," p. 333.

15. Roger Glickson and Joshua Sinai, "National Security," in Meditz and Merrill, eds., *Zaire: Country Handbook,* p. 283.

16. Huntington writes that "only in the Napoleonic Wars did officers begin to acquire a specialized technique to distinguish themselves from laymen and begin to develop the standards, values, and organization inherent in that technique. . . . Prior to 1800 there was no such thing as a professional officer corps. In 1900 such bodies existed in virtually all major [European] countries." *The Soldier and the State,* p. 19.

17. Europeans created the national militaries; there were no militaries existing before colonialism whose jurisdiction coincided with the new state boundaries. This meant, among other things, the lack of an existing structure, an officer class, or an accepted military ethos that included loyalty to the colonially created state.

18. There was limited fighting against German outposts in Africa during World War I. Germany's defeat and the transfer of its colonies to other nations (Britain and France, primarily) facilitated peaceful relations among the colonies.

19. "Pseudo" units impersonate and infiltrate the enemy by adopting their tactics, clothing, and weaponry. The British used them successfully in Malaya during the early 1950s and shortly thereafter in Kenya. Ian Henderson and Philip Goodhart, *Man Hunt in Kenya.* The Rhodesian government created the Selous Scouts, based partly on the Malaya-Kenya model.

20. Colonies with significant white populations usually had all-white military units (e.g., Kenya's Kenya Regiment, Rhodesia's Rhodesian Light Infantry). A study of the Kenya Regiment is Guy Campbell's *The Charging Buffalo.*

21. France's Army of Africa was made up of *colons* from North African colonies, and the Kenya Regiment was an all-white unit that served against the Mau-Mau.

22. Portugal represented an extreme case, given Lisbon's assumptions into the late 1960s that it had entered its second 300-year period of domination of Lusophone Africa.

23. Thomas Cox, *Civil-Military Relations in Sierra Leone,* p. 27.

24. Echenberg, *Colonial Conscripts,* p. 117.

25. Gutteridge records that France in the 1950s made "a much more deliberate effort than the British to assimilate African military personnel by the use of training methods normally employed in France and by setting up special schools for officers and NCOs both in France and West Africa." William Gutteridge, *Military Regimes in Africa,* p. 46.

26. British rule in Kenya created the first "effendi" (Warrant Officer) in 1956 and an officer candidate school in 1958.

27. Glickson and Sinai, "National Security," in Meditz and Merrill, eds., *Zaire: Country Handbook*, p. 285.

28. Charles Snyder, "African Ground Forces," in Arlinghaus and Baker, eds., *African Armies: Evolution and Capabilities*, p. 114.
Col. A. A. Afrifa of Ghana writes that "the British army did not at first attract the most able of our men . . . [seemingly] only the failures in our society joined the army . . . [and] put on the white man's uniform." A. A. Afrifa, *The Ghana Coup*, p. 93.

29. An alternative view says that the British and French created small but highly professional African officer corps. A reader of this manuscript, who wishes to remain anonymous, writes that "professionalism in the KAR and RWAFF formed the foundations of these [professional] units. Most post-independence militaries would be hard-pressed to match this high degree of professionalism. Kenyan officers...trace their unit's heritage back to colonial times with pride." Private correspondence, January 2000.

30. Chester Crocker, "Military Dependence: The Colonial Legacy in Africa," *Journal of Modern African Studies*. For example, Crocker writes that in Britain in the early 1950s, "after years of clamor for a great African army, the Tory government scrapped plans to raise a single additional West African division on grounds of cost and the requirement for 1,200 British cadres to train and lead the force." Crocker, p. 178.

31. In 1838, a small group of Afrikaners encamped near the Buffalo River defeated a much larger group of Zulu warriors in what became known as the Battle of Blood [formerly Buffalo] River. Akin to pioneers in the American West, they circled their wagons and held off a much larger force. The circle, or *laager*, became a potent political metaphor for the power of a small but fully unified group against a much larger, but less organized, force.

32. The regional RWAFF, KAR, and forces of French West and Equatorial Africa did serve in World War II, although few Africans held leadership or command positions. In the 1950s Ethiopia sent a contingent to Korea.

33. Schatzberg, *The Dialects*, p. 66.

34. "The President directly commands both the FAZ [Forces Armées Zaïroises] and the GDN [Gendarmie Nationale] in his capacity as commander-in-chief of the armed forces," Schatzberg, *The Dialectics*, p. 55.

35. Nkrumah quoted by B. J. Dudley, "Decolonization and the Problems of Independence," in Michael Crowder, ed., *Cambridge History of Africa*, vol. 8 (Cambridge: Cambridge University Press, 1984), p. 52.

36. Welch holds that "political interference in the internal affairs of the army"... [was] "the most significant factor to create antagonism between military and civilian leaders." Claude Welch, "A Comparative Analysis of Military Intervention and Political Change," *Soldier and the State in Africa*, p. 33.

37. "Extracts from an Interview with President Siaka Stevens," *West Africa*, September 9, 1985, pp. 1848–1849.

38. "Sierra Leone: A Complex Case," *West Africa*, March 1–14, 1999, p. 122.

39. Cox's *Civil-Military Relations in Sierra Leone* is the best study of the Sierra Leone military during the country's first decade of independence.

40. "Sierra Leone Security Sector Programme (SISEP): Project

Memorandum and Framework, Final Version, DFID-WNAD," May 1999, pp. 23, 35.

41. Crawford Young, quoted in Michael Bratton and Nicolas van de Walle, *Democratic Experiments in Africa,* p. 216.

42. Some rulers continued the colonial assumptions of "martial races." Gnassingbé Eyadema has packed Togo's officer corps with his own Kabre ethnic group and, reminiscent of the former colonialists, Eyadema states that northerners "are more courageous than the people of the south," who "fear being killed." "'Big Man' Holds Rule in Togo," *Washington Post,* July 12, 1998.

43. Eboe Hutchful, "Understanding the African Security Crisis," in Musah and Fayemi, eds., *Mercenaries. An African Security Dilemma,* p. 212.

44. Schatzberg, *The Dialectics,* p. 66.

45. The British in Tanzania had obtained up to a third of the KAR from Hehe and Kuria. President Nyerere actively sought a broader cross section for the Tanzanian Peoples' Defence Force officer corps.

46. Catholic Commission for Justice and Peace in Zimbabwe, "Report on the 1980s Disturbance in Matabeleland and the Midlands," March 1997. Http://www.mg.co.za/mg/Zim/Zimreport.

47. Ibid.

48. Walter Barrows, "Changing Military Capabilities in Black Africa," in Foltz and Bienen, eds., *Arms and the African. Military Influences on Africa's International Relations,* p. 106.

49. Samuel Decalo, "Modalities of Civil-Military Stability in Africa," *Journal of Modern African Studies,* p. 562.

50. Thomas Ofcansky, "National Security," in Sandra Meditz, ed., *Ghana: Country Handbook* (Washington, D.C.: Library of Congress, 1995), p. 269.

51. *Africa Confidential* probably overstated the case when it wrote in 1995 that the Kenyan army "is now Kalenjin at the bottom, Kalenjin at the middle, and Kalenjin at the top." "Presidential Army," *Africa Confidential,* April 28, 1995, p. 2.

52. Philip Gourevitch, *We Wish to Inform You,* p. 69.

53. Robin Luckham, *The Nigerian Military,* p. 3.

54. Frederick Ehrenreich notes that "a side effect of the rapid production of African officers was a lasting shortage, which became acute in several areas of the experienced senior NCOs and technical personnel who had been the backbone of the colonial forces. It took much less time to turn NCOs into officers to produce their replacements." "National Security," in Harold Nelson, ed., *Kenya: Country Handbook* (Washington, D.C.: American University Press, 1984), pp. 248–249.

55. In Uganda, Geoffrey Binaisa, Amin's successor, allowed the minister of defence, Yoweri Museveni, to recruit from Museveni's southwest region. Subsequent anger at this policy soon caused a coup that restored Milton Obote as president.

56. Ofcansky. "National Security," in Rita M. Byrnes, ed., *Uganda: Area Handbook,* p. 202. Ironically, Amin invoked military professionalism in his first presidential address. "I am not a politician but a professional soldier. I am,

therefore, a man of few words, and I have been brief throughout my professional career." David Lamb, "The Ghost of Idi Amin," *The Africans,* p. 77.

57. Ehrenreich, *Liberia,* 268.

58. Luckham, *The Nigerian Military,* p. 177.

59. Charles Snyder writes that such coups "tend to sweep away authority
or effectiveness that exists in an army's chain of command." Snyder, "African
Ground Forces," p. 120.

60. Decalo, *The Stable Minority: Civilian Rule in Africa,* 1998, p. 564.

61. Joseph Momoh relaxed the ammunition process only slightly. Julius
Maada-Bio recalls that soldiers had to account for every round they fired by
turning in the empty shell casings. Maada-Bio claims that possession of any
bullets without official approval constituted a treasonous offense. Interview,
September 1999.

62. Decalo, "Modalities of Civil-Military Stability in Africa," *Journal of
Modern African Studies,* p. 574.

63. J. 'Kayode Fayemi, *Threats to Military Expenditure and National
Security: Analysis of Trends in Post Civil War Defence Planning in Nigeria—
1970-1990.* Ph.D. dissertation, War Studies Department, King's College,
University of London, 1993.

64. Interview with U.S. State Department official, October 1999.

65. B. J. Dudley, "Decolonization and Problems of Independence,"
Cambridge History of Africa, p. 93.

66. Maj. Gen. George Innih, "The Procurement Process," in T. A.
Imobighe, ed., *Nigerian Defence and Security: Issues and Options for Policy,*
p. 39, quoted in Fayemi, "Threats, Military Expenditure and National Security:
Analysis of Trends in Post Civil War Defence Planning in Nigeria—
1970–1990," Ph.D. diss., University of London, 1993.

67. Peters, *The Nigerian Military,* p. 180.

68. Joseph Smaldone, "National Security," *Nigeria: Country Handbook*
(Washington, D.C.: Library of Congress, 1992), p. 282.

69. Ghana participated in UN peacekeeping operations in Cambodia,
Croatia, Western Sahara, Iraq/Kuwait, Rwanda, and Lebanon during the late
1980s and early 1990s.

70. Ofcansky, *Ghana,* p. 277.

71. "Joint Headquarters . . . always complained about its powerlessness to
make the services co-ordinate their plans and weapons procurement plans."
Peters, *The Nigerian Military,* p. 179. Nigeria established the Training and
Doctrine Command (TRADOC) in 1984.

72. Fayemi, "Threats," p. 252.

73. Again, Nigeria's experience approximated that of other states that
have paid scant attention to training. For example, newspaper reports in 1999
stated that the Zambian military had last conducted a major training exercise in
1972.

74. Peters, *The Nigerian Military,* p. 215. Ibrahim Babangida seized control of Nigeria in August 1985 in a military coup.

75. Ibid.

76. Interviews, London and Washington, 1999.

77. Schatzberg, *The Dialectics of Oppression,* pp. 52–70.

78. President João Vieira had had acrimonious relations with his military dating back to his overthrow of Luiz Cabral in 1980. In the mid-1990s Vieira executed several soldiers suspected of attempting a coup, refused to appoint a chief of staff, threatened large-scale demobilization, and cut the military budget. Brig. Ansumane Mane led a rebellion against President Vieira that brought in an ECOMOG force of Senegalese and Guinean troops in the late 1990s.

79. Abacha's SBS caused considerable resentment and pushed Nigeria's respected Maj. Gen. Chris Alli to retire in protest. The unit reported to the chief of special staff in the president's office and bypassed the regular chain of command. The major who commanded the SBS gave commands to army generals and had North Koreans and Libyans—not the usual trainers of Nigeria's army—to train the SBS.

80. Samuel Decalo, *The Stable Minority,* p. 237.

81. Afrifa, *The Ghana Coup,* p. 100.

82. *Economist* Intelligence Unit, *Sudan, Country Profile, 1998–1999,* p. 11.

83. Bayart, Ellis, and Hibou, "From Kleptocracy to the Felonious State?" *The Criminalization of the State in Africa,* p. 21.

84. Interviews with U.S. State Department and private security employees, Washington, D.C., October 1998.

85. "Zaire: A Staff Report to the Committee on Foreign Relations." United States Senate, July 1982, p. 5.

86. "Presidential Army," *Africa Confidential,* April 28, 1995, p. 2.

87. A military doubling as a police force has to have domestic and foreign intelligence capabilities, police and military training, and different types of equipment.

88. Luckham, *The Nigerian Military,* p. 202. Luckham also notes that "commitment to internal security destroyed the army's impartial political image" and that "police-type operations, whether in Nigeria or in the Congo, tended to blur the line between professional political matters and to strengthen the military antipathy toward politicians." Luckham, pp. 249, 248.

89. Decalo, *Coups and Army Rule,* p. 205.

90. Many Africanists initially discounted such a possibility. As Claude Welch reflected in the mid-1970s, "It seemed as though the new countries of post-colonial Africa would escape the dreary round of coup and counter-coup typical of Latin America, the Middle East, and Southeast Asia." "The Roots and Implications of Military Intervention," *Soldier and State in Africa,* p. 2.

91. Decalo, *Coups and Army Rule,* p. 203.

92. This surprised many observers. Jeffrey Herbst notes that Africa has had little interstate conflict." Jeffrey Herbst, "War and State in Africa," *International Security* 14, no. 4, Spring 1990. Various factors at independence suggested frequent interstate conflict: the imposed arbitrary borders, the lack of regional ethos and cooperation, the OAU's military or legal inability to enforce its noninterference demands, the lack of defensive ability of some African states, and the sometimes strong ideological/personal differences could invite cross-border hostilities. Definite international condemnation of interstate conflict and the military inability of most African states to mount a sustained invasion further explain the lack of interstate conflict. The regionally aggressive

former white-run states of Rhodesia (now Zimbabwe) and South Africa were the major exceptions.

93. Schatzberg, *The Dialectics of Oppression*, p. 68.

94. This acceptance contrasted with statements at preindependence conferences that had lambasted "the artificial frontiers drawn by the imperialist powers to divide the peoples of Africa" and called for "the abolition or adjustment of such frontiers at an early date." Quoted by Crawford Young in "Self-Determination and the African State System," in Deng and Zartman, eds., *Conflict Resolution in Africa*, p. 327.

95. Exceptions included Somalia's intervention in Ethiopia's Ogaden (1976–1977), anti-Mobutu rebels invasion of Zaire from Angola in 1977 and 1978, Tanzania's overthrow of Amin in 1979, Libyan troops' incursion into Chad at various times during the 1970s and 1980s, and South Africa's repeated incursions into Angola during the 1980s. Robert Denard, a French mercenary, successfully invaded the Comoros twice.

96. "Moscow sought change, but only change within the existing pattern of states created by the legacy of empire." Mark Katz, "Collapsed Empires," *Managing Global Chaos,* p. 31. African sensitivity to non-African challenge of the status quo was apparent following France's two interventions against governments in Gabon in 1964 and the Central African Republic in 1979.

97. Uganda had invaded Tanzania's Kagera Salient in late 1978 in pursuit of armed Ugandan rebels. Nyerere used Amin's limited incursion as a pretext for invasion of Uganda and the overthrow of Amin.

98. Obasanjo, quoted in Colin Legum, ed., *Africa Contemporary Record: Annual Survey and Documents, 1979–1980,* p. A62.

99. Clapham notes that "on almost every occasion when state security in Africa has been threatened, usually by domestic and much more seldom by external opposition, the external factor [of intervention] has been critical." Christopher Clapham, "African Security Systems: Privatisation and the Scope for Mercenary Conflict," in Mills and Stremlau, eds., *The Privatisation of Security in Africa,* p. 37.

100. "These invasions in 1977–1978, highlighted the political and military weakness of the Mobutu regime, and only foreign intervention kept the Zairian state intact." Glickson and Sinai, "National Security," p. 278.

101. Britain rarely intervened to protect governments. The major exception being its dispatching the Royal Marine Commandos to stop coup attempts in 1964 against the Tanzanian, Ugandan, and Kenyan governments. It has occasionally sent small Special Air Service (SAS) units to assist threatened governments. A recent example of significant involvement—perhaps as many as 80 soldiers—occurred during Great Britain's "Operation Palliser" in Sierra Leone in mid-2000.

102. Joseph Smaldone, "National Security," in Robert E. Handloff, ed., *Ivory Coast: Country Handbook,* p. 198. Alain Rouvez in 1993 estimated French troop presence as follows: Djibouti (3,500–4,000), Senegal (1,250), Chad (1,000), Central African Republic (1,300), Côte d'Ivoire (500), and Gabon (500). He briefly describes French motives for the various interventions. Alain Rouvez, "French, British and Belgian Military Involvement," *Disconsolate Empires,* pp. 33, 54.

103. Admittedly, this is a questionable label, given France's ambivalent

NATO history. For example, it resigned from NATO's integrated military command structure in 1966.

104. Rouvez, *Disconsolate Empires,* p. 54.

105. "Internal military conspiracies are utterly foolhardy since any gains will be automatically reversed by superior force of arms." Decalo, "Modalities of Civil-Military Stability," p. 568.

106. Frederick Ehrenreich, "National Security," in Harold D. Nelson, ed., *Liberia: Country Handbook* (Washington, D.C.: American University Press, 1985), p. 273.

107. Eboe Hutchful, "Military Policy and Reform," *Journal of Modern African Studies,* p. 269.

108. Interviews with U.S. Department of Defense officials, September and October 1999.

109. Decalo, *Coups and Army Rule in Africa,* p. 205.

110. Nigeria's diversifying of its foreign procurement did reduce dependence on a single source but created some major logistical difficulties. Glickson and Sinai write of Zaire that "by expanding and diversifying the sources of military assistance, Mobutu hoped to reduce Zaire's reliance on any source of aid . . . [yet] it produced a kaleidoscope of military education that at times made it difficult for officers in the same unit to interact effectively. It also created pockets of competing pressure groups that believed that their source of training was superior to the others." Glickson and Sinai, "National Security," p. 290.

111. Annette Seegers, "SADC's Political and Security Dimensions (circa 2000): South Africa's Experience." Paper prepared for the U.S. State Department conference on New Directions in the Southern African Development Community, Meridian International Centre, Washington, D.C., December 10, 1999.

112. Decalo, "Modalities of Civil-Military Stability in Africa," *Journal of Modern African Studies,* p. 560. See also Herbert Howe, "Mozambique: Military Weakness Led to Cease-fire with S. Africa," *Christian Science Monitor,* October 18, 1984. Morale in Guinea- Bissau's Peoples' Revolutionary Armed Forces plummeted after independence: perhaps 90 percent of the armed forces joined a military putsch against the president in 1998. See "Guinea-Bissau: "Human Rights in War and Peace," Amnesty International Report, AFR, July 1999, p. 7.

113. Interviews in Maputo, Mozambique, 1995, and Britain and the United States, 1998–1999.

114. Philip H. Frankel, *Praetoria's Pretorians: Civil-Military Relations in South Africa,* p. xvi.

115. Civilian oversight declined during the 1980s as the SADF and other security units planned and conducted operations outside public or parliamentary scrutiny.

116. Frankel, *Pretoria's Pretorians,* pp. xvii, 1–2.

117. See Herbert M. Howe, "The South African Defence Force and Political Reform," *Journal of Modern African Studies,* 1994.

118. Officers proved to be as corrupt as their civilian counterparts. President Mobutu stole over $5 billion from Zaire; President Doe siphoned off impressive amounts from Liberia's smaller treasury; and various Nigerian rulers in mufti profited enormously.

119. David R. Smock, ed., "Creative Approaches to Managing Conflict in Africa," p. 12.

120. A. A. Afrifa provides an example of bitterness following Nkrumah's dismissal of Ghana's chief of defence staff and his deputy. *The Ghana Coup,* esp. p. 99.

121. Peters, *The Nigerian Military,* p. 215.

122. Fayemi, "Threats," p. 302.

123. Kent Hughes Butts and Steven Metz, "Armies and Democracy in the New Africa: Lessons From Nigeria and South Africa," p. v.

124. Peters, *The Nigerian Military,* p. 224.

125. "Military Left Nigerian Coffers Dry," *Daily Mail and Guardian,* May 25, 1999. Http://www.mg.co.za/mg/news/99May2/25may-nigeria.html

126. Ibid.

127. Http://www.internews.org/nigeria/politics/politics~franset.html
A reported anecdote about President Obasanjo's son reveals the political, rather than military, motivations of entering officers. *Africa Confidential* reports that Obasanjo "asked his son at the Command and Staff College, how many of his fellow officers saw the army as a route to political power. 'Nine out of every ten,' came the reply." "Soldier Go, Soldier Come," *Africa Confidential,* March 5, 1999, p. 1.

128. Fayemi, "Threats," p. 252.

129. "The Ugandan army is not the fighting force it used to be. It once enjoyed a reputation for discipline and respecting human rights, but its officers have long since grown corrupt, its troops incompetent and rather good at running away." "Uganda. A Dirty War that Can't Be Won." *Economist,* October 4, 1997.
Some observers believe that the exiled Rwandan Tutsis, who constituted a significant percentage of the UPDF in the 1980s, were among Uganda's best soldiers and that their subsequent departure for Rwanda after 1990 weakened the UPDF.

130. Interview, October 1999.

131. Some of the food in forty-two railway cars of a 1999 South African food shipment was deemed unfit for consumption, yet the Ugandan military paid for the shipment. A repairer of military vehicles grossly overcharged the Ministry of Defense, which did not object to the inflated charges. Interviews, U.S. State Department officials, October 1999.

132. Fayemi, "Threats," p. 190.

133. Snyder, "African Ground Forces," p. 131.

134. Anthony Clayton, *Frontiersmen: Warfare in Africa Since 1950,* p. 107.

135. Desmond Davies, "Sierra Leone: A Complex Case," *West Africa,* March 1–14, 1999, p. 122.

136. "Analytical Study of Irregular Warfare in Sierra Leone and Liberia," SAIC, September 30, 1998, p. 1–12. Report of a conference done for the U.S. Defense Intelligence Agency.

137. Prunier, *The Rwanda Crisis,* p. 113.

138. Ibid.

139. Interview, September 1999.

140. In chronological order, Valentine Strasser, Julius Maada Bio, and

Ahmed Tejan Kabbah. Junior officer anger was a major reason for the military discontent that ousted President Momoh in 1992. Maada Bio then pushed aside Strasser in 1996.

141. Decalo concludes that "there is little empirical validity to contentions that most African military regimes even aim at radical socioeconomic change, the reduction of corruption, or economic development." Decalo, *Coups and Army Rule,* p. 32. See also Decalo, *Civil-Military Relations,* p. 43.

142. Decalo, *Coups and Army Rule,* p. 15.

143. Ibid., pp. 14–15.

144. Snyder, "African Ground Forces," p. 115.

145. Defense Forecasts International (DFI), "African Capabilities for Peace Operations," prepared for OSD/ISA/Africa Region, October 17, 1997, pp. 6–8, 10.

146. Snyder, "African Ground Forces," p. 119.

147. Walter Barrows, "Changing Military Capabilities In Black Africa," in Foltz and Bienen, *Arms and the African,* p. 113.

148. Interview with Western defense attaché, July 1996.

149. "Angola Worries Zambia Army, ZAF," *Post of Zambia,* March 9, 1999. Http://www.africanews.org/central/zambia/stories
The Military Balance, 1999–2000 notes about the MiG-21s that "8 [of the 12 are] undergoing refurbishment," p. 279.

150. Glickson and Sinai, "National Security," p. 300.

151. "Nigerian Troops in Sierra Leone Are Kept Waiting for Wages," *London Sunday Telegraph,* July 18, 2000.

152. *The Post of Zambia.*

153. "Army Tries to Build a Dyke Against Its Sea of Troubles," *Business Day,* April 3, 2000.

154. Interview, April 2000.

155. DFI, "Practical Steps to Enhance African Capabilities for Peace Operations: The U.S. Role." Executive Briefing. Defense Forecasts International for OSD/ISA/African Region, January 1997, p. 10.

156. Ibid.

157. "Congo Now in War of Words," *USA Today,* May 27, 1997, p. 9A.

158. These leaders feared that self-proclaimed radical states (i.e., Ghana, Guinea, and Mali) would control the force and use it to spread their ideology. Nkrumah was already supporting several guerrilla groups against neighboring black states. The news weekly, *West Africa,* may have issued the first call for a continental force, "African Fire Brigade," *West Africa,* February 15, 1964, p. 169. A positive view of Nkrumah's proposal is T. A. Imobighe, "An African High Command: The Search for a Feasible Strategy of Continental Defence," *African Affairs,* 79, April 1980.

159. The OAU sent a peacekeeping force of Nigerian, Senegalese, and Zairian soldiers to Chad in late 1981 to serve as a buffer between the government of Goukouni Oueddei and the rival force led by Hissene Habré. Habré's forces effectively skirted the inter-African force and seized power in June 1982. "The inability of the OAU to impose or police a settlement on the ground in Chad was apparent." Naomi Chazan et al., *Politics and Society in Contemporary Africa,* p. 381.

160. An excellent look at the OAU and African conflict during the Cold War is William Foltz, "The Organization of African Unity and the Resolution of Africa's Conflict," in Deng and Zartman, *Conflict Resolution in Africa.*

161. John M. Ostheimer, "Cooperation Among African States," *African Security Issues: Sovereignty, Stability, and Solidarity* (Boulder, Colo.: Westview, 1984), p. 161.

162. Ibid., p. 166.

163. The white-ruled states of southern Africa had cooperated extensively during the 1970s. South Africa provided Rhodesia with several thousand ground troops (who the South African government misleadingly identified as policemen), pilots, and mechanics, as well as equipment and foreign exchange. These two states assisted Portuguese-ruled Mozambique, and South Africa helped Portuguese-held Angola.

3

AFRICA'S ONGOING
SECURITY PREDICAMENT

T he lack of adequate security did not alarm many African regimes
before 1989, as the previous chapter notes. But the changing nature
of conflict on the continent is presently shifting the balance of coercion
away from domestic rulers in a growing number of states and toward
insurgencies and regionally opportunistic states. Personal rulers in several states, including Zimbabwe, Uganda, Angola, and Namibia, have
involved their countries in unpopular regional fighting. Although
besieged states and their citizens increasingly need protection, some
events—the end of the Cold War and the now unpopular foreign intervention into Somalia, especially—ensure that African regimes cannot
rely on international intercession.

African Security and the Causes of Conflicts

"African security" defies neat classifications. Sub-Saharan Africa
includes forty-five states with often strong historical and cultural differences. This diversity poses a problem for a survey of the subcontinent,
especially when trying to distinguish dramatic aberrations from more
mundane norms. Differences in region and time add two more crucial
variables. Some regions have improved their stability—most notably,
southern Africa (at least, until the late 1990s)—whereas others, including sections of West Africa, appear locked in a pattern of conflict.[1]
Although the shift in the balance of coercion has generally helped insurgents, some states (especially in central and southern Africa) may be
gaining military strength as they engage in cross-border operations.

Moreover, a country's security situation can change quickly.

Between 1995 and 2000, Sierra Leone went from a civil war to democratic elections and relative peace, to a military coup, a stepping-back
into increased violence, and then a shaky cease-fire and peace settlement, which disintegrated again into widespread violence. Much of the
world initially hailed and supported Africa's "new leaders," who had
introduced stability and nascent economic growth into their countries,
as the vanguard of an "African renaissance."[2] Yet by late 1998, most of
these leaders were fighting destructive interstate conflicts that ended
and then often reversed previous economic gains. Even southern Africa,
a region largely at peace by the mid-1990s, sent combat forces into the
Congo conflict by the late 1990s, and Angola had sunk again into full-
scale domestic warfare.

"Security," in Africa and elsewhere, has an evolving definition.
Some writers, especially recently, have broadly defined it. Caroline
Thomas, for example, refers to "the whole range of a state's dimensions
. . . nation-building, the search for secure systems of food, health,
money and trade."[3] I take a more traditional approach, defining security
in terms of military capabilities that can be marshaled to defend an
established government.

There are some general characteristics to African security. Sub-
Saharan Africa appears manifestly less secure than it did at independence when, as Peter Lock notes, "the state was basically in full control
of any weapons on its territories."[4] Today, about a third of Africa's
states are in domestic or regional combat (or both), and private citizens
and a growing number of state and private groups have millions of
weapons. Much of the fighting is of low intensity.[5] Groups that are
decentralized and difficult to identify possess cheap but effective
weaponry and often brutalize civilian populations. And Africa's conflicts are increasingly being waged in cities, not just in rural areas.

The size and strength of African armed forces vary considerably.[6]
Twenty-one militaries number fewer than ten thousand soldiers, whereas some four forces have more than eighty thousand.[7] The army predominates in all of the militaries, and several nations have little or no
air and naval capability. However, some states, especially in southern
Africa, have demonstrated their airlift prowess in regional conflicts
(Angola being the prime example). Some militaries possess significant
manpower and equipment (order of battle), yet their operational quality
is often suspect (a major contention of this book is that few African militaries have significant military capabilities). Yet strength is relative,
and a mediocre military can triumph over an even less competent force.
Those regimes that gained power through military conflict often have

the more capable fighting forces: Angola, Zimbabwe, Uganda, Ethiopia, and Eritrea, for example.

Most African conflicts since independence have been intrastate, generally featuring an ethnic or regional group opposing an existing regime.[8] But African wars are increasingly presenting strong interstate aspects: invasion, direct or indirect support for insurgents, and armed intervention on behalf of the threatened regime from outside the country.[9] African, rather than Western, states have become the major interveners (a later section of this chapter examines these and other new aspects of African wars).[10]

Since 1990, factions engaging in low-intensity conflict in Africa have posed increasingly severe problems for counterinsurgency planners. Rebels can tap into widespread public disillusionment or anger directed at a string of unaccountable, personal rulers. They can press-gang child soldiers to swell their ranks, if necessary, and rarely suffer from international retribution. Rebels are often highly self-sufficient, purchasing readily available weaponry and living off the land. Thus, they prove less controllable by outside forces than were those in previous insurgencies. They can divide and subdivide into splinter groups, lessening the chances for successful comprehensive negotiations; the attraction of personal gain may lessen their desire for political negotiations. They are poorly trained and therefore often unpredictable: Donald Snow writes that the major characteristic of the new insurgencies "is the apparent absence of clear military objectives that can be translated into coherent strategies and tactics."[11] They do not engage in fixed-position combat (and wear no uniforms), and can shift alliances quickly, given their lack of ideology. Factions often target any valuable resource or population without needing to obey established codes of conduct, and may use drugs to induce extreme behavior. And they are increasingly engaged in urban warfare.

This last point frustrated the United States and the UN in Somalia and ECOMOG in Sierra Leone and, given Africa's rapid urbanization, will increasingly bedevil state or foreign intervention forces. Recent urban battlefields include Mogadishu (Somalia), Brazzaville (Congo-Brazzaville), Bangui (Central African Republic), Huambo (Angola), Kigali (Rwanda), Freetown (Sierra Leone), Bujumburua (Burundi), and Monrovia (Liberia). Maj. Gen. Timothy Shelpidi, ECOMOG's force commander in Sierra Leone during 1998, notes some of the specific difficulties of urban counterinsurgency: "The streets in downtown Freetown are generally narrow and this made manoeuvering difficult. . . . Rebel snipers used buildings and high-rise structures to fire at ECO-

MOG. This made dislodging them very hard [including the problems of ricochets and of hitting civilians] but we made sure not to destroy everything that moved."[12]

Urban fighting produces especially troublesome political problems, including an often higher number of casualties (military and civilian) and more economic destruction.

A full discussion of the causes of African conflict is not possible here, but certainly colonialism planted several of the seeds for postindependence conflicts.[13] Some eighty years of foreign rule, from roughly 1885 to 1965, saw, inter alia, (1) the creation of arbitrary borders that enclosed a wide range of ethnic, religious, and economic groups; (2) the presence of personal-rule oligarchies and "divide-and-rule" policies that encouraged conflicting subnationalisms along ethnic, religious, or regional lines rather than the development of integrative national political cultures; and (3) the centralization in the state of most necessary functions that when combined with oligarchy, focused intense competition for control of the state and its resources, while disavowing common democratic standards. Colonialism created or encouraged many of these trends; Africa's first generation of political leaders and the Cold War often reinforced them.

Ethnicity's appeal has proven surprisingly tenacious.[14] "For most Africans sub-national ethnicity is a moral good and an important object of social as well as political identity," note Robert Jackson and Carl Rosberg.[15] Yet opportunistic leaders manipulate these deeply felt loyalties to advance their personal agendas. Ethnic rivalries, especially when overlaid with religious, regional, and economic differences, have provoked widespread suffering during the past thirty-five years. David Welsh writes that "collapse of the state in Somalia, virtual implosion of the state in Liberia, horrific genocide in Rwanda, endemic conflict in Burundi, a seemingly never-ending civil war in Sudan, and the failure of either democratic or military regimes in Nigeria all appear to point to a massive failure to cope with ethnicity."[16]

The weak nature of the African state has abetted conflict. By the late 1990s, several "sovereign" entities were factions of narrowing private interests and clearly lacked control of basic government functions as well as widespread public legitimacy. As such, they constituted states in name only. "In large swathes of sub-Saharan Africa, the capacity to execute any form of policy has quite simply evaporated," write Bayart, Ellis, and Hibou [17] This decline in governing capability, caused by a mix of subnational rivalries, military unprofessionalism, and widespread state corruption, has encouraged nonstate actors to assert them-selves and challenge state capability.

The loss of state control has increased domestic and regional con-flict. "Wars are raging because many states have become hollow enti-ties," as Marina Ottaway notes. "Governments cannot exercise basic control over their territories."[18] Effective authority increasingly devolves to the states' peripheries, and incompetent or ethnicized mili-taries encourage subnational groups to create means of self-protection. Weak or collapsed states encourage intervention by other states for a range of reasons that include protecting of the latters' citizens, prevent-ing the spread of regional conflict, or profiting from the seizure of their weakened neighbor's assets.

Contradictory Effects of the End of the Cold War

The security of African states has deteriorated since 1989 as insurgents have frequently gained relative power and as some states militarily infringe upon their neighbors' sovereignty. Diminished foreign patron-age, a basic change in the nature of African conflict, and the previously examined unaccountable system of personal rule have proved the three major causes.

The Cold War did destabilize various states. Driven by strategic rather than normative considerations, the superpowers supplied finan-cial support and military hardware, which sometimes intensified cleav-ages and prolonged conflicts.[19] Richard Grimmett estimates that Soviet military aid to sub-Saharan Africa totaled $18.9 billion in the period from 1981 to 1988, whereas the U.S. figure was just below $1 billion.[20] The Soviet Union's assistance to Ethiopia and Angola ratcheted up the existing conflicts' destructiveness. The U.S. "Reagan Doctrine," with its military assistance to noncommunist insurgencies, produced smaller but still similar effects. The weaponry, especially small arms and mines, continues to threaten African security.[21]

Yet the Cold War's demise did not strengthen Africa's overall secu-rity.[22] Instead, it often has tipped local balances of power away from the state and toward insurgent organizations. Like Hobbes's Leviathan—a strong government that could defeat any challenges to its domestic peace—the Cold War had a stabilizing effect, albeit one that varied among regions and states.[23] Superpower support to threatened govern-ments relieved those states of the need to use scarce foreign exchange

for weapon purchases. Superpower influence at times moderated particularly bellicose rulers and insurgencies and often maintained the political status quo with political and material support. As will be noted, the
United States and the Soviet Union refused military support to regimes
contemplating invasion of neighboring states.[24] The superpowers feared
being dragged into local conflicts that did not affect their own national
interests. And a common opposition to colonialism and white racism
helped unify African states against a perceived common foe.

Governments could call upon foreign military assistance during the
Cold War, and this undoubtedly dampened the aspirations of some
potential insurgents or invaders. For example, France deployed troops
from its African bases at least seven times during the 1970s and 1980s
to defend client regimes. Several Western nations, including the United
States, Belgium, and France, militarily assisted Zaire's Mobutu to repel
ex-Zairois who invaded Shaba province in 1977 and 1978.[25] Zaire's
"failed army" would have been swept aside without this help.

The ending of the Cold War helped to destabilize many former personalist states as patronage levels declined.[26] William Reno writes that
in "Africa as a whole donors and creditors [now] provide less money
and make more demands."[27] The United States and other nations
stopped assisting anticommunist regimes, which curtailed those states'
domestic patronage powers, and increasingly conditioned their foreign
assistance upon economic and political liberalization. Drops in economic and political aid had a security effect because they lessened rulers'
legitimacy.

Donor demands for structural adjustment, including deep cuts in the
bureaucratic ranks and strict budgetary controls, a lessening of food
subsidies, a greater private-sector role, and an overall push for political
democratization, have placed additional pressure on personal-rule
regimes and removed some elite support. Stephen Stedman writes that
"economic conditionality cut at the heart of the patrimonial state."[28]
Some donors, such as Japan and the Netherlands, now link their foreign
aid to reductions in military spending by the recipients. This trend
toward tying aid to domestic reforms began before 1990, but it greatly
intensified with the Cold War's conclusion.

These reforms, desirable in the long term, sometimes introduce
short-term instability that can threaten the measures and, as Stedman
writes, "simultaneous economic and political liberalization may result
in the failure of both."[29] Democratization has sometimes inadvertently
increased conflict when disappointed losers resort to major violence.[30]
Jeffrey Herbst writes of Africa that "the wave of [democratic] transi-

tions across the continent has produced a cohort of former rulers who have become accustomed to power and, even out of power, control significant numbers of soldiers and weapons. The potential for destabilization is obvious."[31]

Rwanda offers the bloodiest example. Hutus who resented President Juvénal Habyarimana's acquiescence in such reforms, which granted significant concessions to the Tutsi minority, apparently killed their fellow Hutu leader. They then embarked on an anti-Tutsi genocide during which the murder rate was at least three times faster than in the Nazi death camps of World War II.[32] Other examples of violent backlash to democratic inroads include Jonas Savimbi restarting the Angolan conflict in 1992 following preliminary election returns that suggested his defeat, and the three major presidential candidates in Congo-Brazzaville creating their own armies in the early 1990s. Denis Sassou-Nguesso, the once and now current president of Congo-Brazzaville, employed his own militia and the Angolan armed forces in 1997 to overthrow Pascal Lissouba, to whom Sassou-Nguesso had lost in a democratic election.

The demise of the Cold War helped to change the nature of African conflict and to tilt the balance of coercion against many regimes.[33] Heightened weapons availability and the expansion of armed actors, the ethnic and economic (rather than ideological) strategy of some insurgencies and leaders, and the targeting of noncombatant populations have threatened regime stability.

Regionally, cross-border combat operations have increased during the 1990s. As examples, the late 1990s saw an unprecedented seven states fighting in one country (Congo), a multinational force (ECO-MOG) fighting in two countries, and a host of smaller and mostly bilateral operations (Angola in Congo-Brazzaville and South Africa and Botswana in Lesotho). Contributing factors include economic aggrandizement, a partial redefinition of sovereignty, greater availability of long-range weaponry, and the self-serving personalities of various leaders.

Factors Intensifying Domestic Conflicts

Guns: Cheap, Available, and Deadly

The Cold War and then its cessation facilitated the dumping of large amounts of military equipment and trained personnel upon the world market.[34] Significant amounts of the vast firepower supplied by the United States, the Soviet Union, and China now circulate among Africa's domestic and regional conflicts. Several states built formidable arsenals before 1989. Oil and diamond-rich Angola spent many billions of dollars on a wide range of weaponry: in 1987 alone, its MPLA (Popular Movement For the Liberation of Angola) government purchased $2.7 billion worth at concessionary prices. Somalia spent $1 billion on arms between 1975 and 1985. Some estimates place the number of weapons at 500,000 in Mogadishu, a city of one million, that is, one gun for every two people!

The weapons trade has changed tremendously since the Cold War, when the primarily state-to-state transfers involved high-maintenance equipment (e.g., jet fighters, transport planes, armored personnel carriers, tanks) that was easily traceable. But between 1988 and 1995 such official transfers in sub-Saharan Africa declined from $4.27 billion to $270 million.[35]

At the same time, gray (commercial) and black (illegal) small-arms sales jumped tremendously.[36] Unlike the more visible state-to-state transfers of large equipment, the illegal movement of small arms is much harder to measure, monitor, and trace back to the source. The rise in small-arms trafficking is very worrisome.[37] Christopher Smith writes that "increasingly, these weapons are being made available to and are being acquired by a range of sub-state actors . . . the impact and social cost of light weapons proliferation has greatly increased since the superpowers withdrew their patronage to developing countries following the collapse of the Soviet Union."[38] Estimates vary about aggregate totals of small arms, but private groups and individuals in sub-Saharan Africa probably hold over 5 million such weapons.

Eastern European countries and China in particular have few, if any, ideological compunctions about whom they sell to in this post–Cold War period.[39] Domestic economic and political pressure, rather, encourage major export initiatives.

Bulgaria is a significant example, given the importance of weaponry to its economy, its determination to export about 80 percent of its production (about 10 percent of its foreign exchange comes from arm sales), and the widespread use in Africa of Bulgarian arms. The end of the Cold War saw much of that country's production capability go unused, with many workers losing their jobs and staging strikes while the country lost vital foreign exchange. Competing Bulgarian political parties came to use the drop in arms industry employment as a political football.

The Bulgarian government responded by intensifying its willingness to sell weaponry to any buyers, including opposing sides in the same conflict and pariah states and factions under arms embargoes by the UN and other organizations. Bulgaria obviously cared little about the buyers' use of the weaponry. The former director of Kintex, the state's arms-trading company, declared that he had "no idea where the weapons went, and anyway it's not my problem."[40] Bulgaria has supplied the MPLA government and Jonas Savimbi's UNITA in Angola as well as the Burundian armed forces and the Hutu-dominated former Rwandan military, even though international arms embargoes had been placed upon these last three forces. Bulgaria has also served as a center of both legal and illegal arms brokering and transshipment.

Aggressive export techniques have paid dividends. By 1995, Bulgaria's arms industry had erased the job cuts of the early 1990s and was employing 500,000 people—despite the country's overall 12-percent unemployment. The Arms Project of Human Rights Watch states that weapons exports "helped keep the economy afloat by bringing in hard currency."[41] At least one Bulgarian company, Arsenal, exports the majority of its products to Africa.

Insurgencies can easily obtain cheap, durable, and effective firepower. One country can supply both sides in a conflict: for instance, some intelligence analysts believe that up to three hundred private Ukrainian citizens have assisted Sierra Leone's RUF—while, at the same time, the Ukrainian government sells MI-24 attack helicopters to the Sierra Leonean government. Also states, parastatals, or individual soldiers sell redundant weaponry: groups in the Niger Delta opposed to the Nigerian government have reportedly obtained guns from ECO-MOG soldiers returning from Sierra Leone.[42]

A leading purveyor is Victor Bout, a former Soviet air force officer, whose aviation business owns about 70 military planes and helicopters. Bout has "a stranglehold on sanctions-busting aerial freight," claims a Western intelligence officer, and the *Financial Times* notes that "each time he [Bout] is subjected to scrutiny, he moves his freight operations elsewhere."[43] He has conducted his operations from the United Arab Emirates, South Africa, Belgium, Liberia, Swaziland, and the Central African Republic.

Well-intentioned demobilizations of soldiers, often at the request of foreign governments or institutions, can free weaponry for use elsewhere. Such was the case in Uganda: the World Bank's request for partial demobilization resulted in Uganda's giving the surplus weaponry to the Rwandan Patriotic Front, which was based in exile inside Uganda.

Gerald Prunier writes that "this quite important source of equipment was what enabled the RPF to rearm" between August 1993 and April 1994. He concludes that "the World Bank contributed unwittingly to the RPF victory in the Rwandese civil war."[44]

Africa's diminished strategic importance and the disappearance of the Warsaw Pact alliance has resulted in fewer grants of weaponry to African states and insurgencies since 1990. But private merchants are replacing these official sources, and this mutation adds to Africa's insecurity, as will be noted.

Africa also has a nascent but growing arms industry. South Africa is among the world's top ten arms exporters and has supplied weaponry to opposing forces in the Congo campaign.[45] As well, some six sub-Saharan states can manufacture small arms.[46] Other countries overhaul, or "remanufacture," military equipment, Eritrea being a prime example. Increased capability in ammunition production also lessens the potential external influence of embargoes. Kenya's Eldoret plant is presently capable of producing 20 million 7.62mm NATO-standard rounds annually, and Nigeria has manufactured all the small rounds needed by ECOMOG. Sudan's Military Industry Corporation produces ammunition, land mines, and small arms. Uganda's National Enterprise Corporation, built with aid from China, produces small arms and ammunition and perhaps land mines. Some African states, notably Nigeria, Uganda, and Angola, host air charter companies that can provide airlift capability for cross-border operations.[47] This wider availability of sources sometimes helps undermine whatever control over violence Western states or African security forces may have had.

Technological changes often assist the insurgent. The reduced weight and simplicity of today's small arms allows child soldiers, some as young as eight years old, to carry and operate weaponry. Nonlethal technology, especially communications, also helps to level the playing field between state and insurgent, and the growing willingness of states to assist rebels provides an important conduit of technology. Rassemblement Congolaise Pour la Démocratie rebels reportedly use Ugandan-supplied iridium satellite phones as well as other communications gear that allows eavesdropping on government phone and radio messages.[48] Faction leaders now employ sophisticated but inexpensive communications to reach the outside world: Liberia's Charles Taylor used satellite phones to promote his rebel cause over the BBC World Service, and Joseph Kony of Uganda's Lord's Resistance Army utilizes the Internet to publish his "Ten Point Program."[49]

A sobering point is that conflicts do not require sophisticated weaponry to inflict havoc. The Rwandan *génocidaires,* using little more than machetes, killed at a much faster rate than did the Third Reich's death camps.

Africa's porous borders and unmonitored airports allow multiple transport routes for the weaponry. UNITA has used a number of African countries as transit points for its weapons and fuel deliveries, the most probable nations being South Africa, Namibia, Mozambique, Zambia, Uganda, Congo, Burkina Faso, Côte d'Ivoire, Congo-Brazzaville, and Togo. The case of South Africa vividly illustrates the lack of monitoring: South Africa in 1997 had thirty-six "international" airports, most of which did not have adequate air traffic control or regular police, customs, or immigration monitoring. Most African countries lack adequate means of detecting and then interdicting these flights.

Growing Number of Combatants

Heightened weapons availability has allowed the arming of more ill-trained factions, many of which include child soldiers. The Liberian conflict involved some seven armed factions, as well as ECOMOG. Congo-Brazzaville's three leading politicians, including President Lissouba, each had its own private army between 1993 and 1997, and the president could also call upon the nation's military.

This expansion tilts the coercive balance by pitting more combatants against the state, causing more destruction, and by reducing foreign desire to insert peacekeepers. More armed groups, especially when lacking a major political *raison d'être,* complicate the problems of obtaining peaceful settlements. The appearance of modern weaponry in the hands of one disputant often prompts a similar response from its opponents and raises the militarization of political discourse.[50] Kathi Austin notes that "logic dictates that those who can provide arms or security rise more quickly to the top. More moderate political leaders pursue the military option just to keep up."[51] The expanded number of combatants also poses postconflict difficulties, including banditry, greater financial costs of demobilization, and integration of child soldiers back into society.

Disaffected, usually urbanized African youths have posed a low-level security problem for several generations. Algeria's *hittiste,* Nigeria's *rarray,* and East Africa's *bayaye* are young males with scant education and job possibilities who usually enter a life of petty crime. Child soldiers have long assisted armed political movements, including the Mulele rebellion (Congo in the 1960s), Biafra's secession (Nigeria in the 1960s), ZAPU and ZANU's liberation struggle (Zimbabwe in the 1970s), and the National Resistance Army (Uganda in the 1980s).

But previous rebellions usually did not coerce children to join and did exercise control over the youths, especially if the insurgents depended on superpower support; neither the United States nor the Soviet Union wanted to be associated with press-ganged, hyperviolent youth. Changes in population (Africa's increasing majority of citizens under the age of 16), demography (growing urbanization), combat (undermining the unarmed power of "traditional" rulers), and culture (Paul Richards and others noting the growing prevalence of video violence that encourages unemployed youths to join insurgent or bandit groups) are possible societal explanations for the increase in child soldiers.[52]

Human rights groups estimate that Africa has more than 120,000 underage soldiers.[53] The Liberian conflict had about 18,000 fighters under the age of seventeen.[54] Various sources estimate that 7,500 children have fought in Sierra Leone's war.[55] The expanding use of child soldiers arguably reflects the movement away from broader societal interests by those insurgencies willing to place in battle society's more vulnerable members.

The new phenomenon of children who are often coerced enlarges the manpower pool while perhaps supplying superior soldiers,[56] drugs and videos stimulating these youths to perform exceptionally violent deeds. The potential for social advancement that violence offers in rural communities sometimes appeals to relatively alienated youth. Richards and others see often little control over these "soldiers" and believe that the childrens' quasi-anarchic behavior lessens the hopes for successful negotiations:

> Rebel commanders in Liberia and Sierra Leone seemingly retained little control over the tiger they had chosen to ride. . . . The long-protracted peace negotiations in Liberia and the continuation of fighting in Sierra Leone is probably best explained not by the intransigence of rebel leaders but the internal incoherence of their movements.[57]

The loss of state coercive power and the wider availability of weaponry has encouraged the rulers to privatize security beyond the traditional presidential guards—either by creating their personal militias or else by aiding locally based forces. Comfort Ero believes that "militia groups will continue to grow and serve as alternatives to state armies and police forces." Ero and other writers refer to the "militianization" of African conflict.[58] These paramilitaries sometimes have significant numbers: Rwanda's Interahamwe numbers perhaps 15,000 men. Several governments sponsor collections of militias: Kabila's Congo, for example, assists the Mayi-Mayi (which itself is a grouping of several local militias), the Interahamwe, the former Rwandan military, the Défenses Civiles Populaires in Katanga Province, and the Burundian Forces Pour la Defénse de la Démocratie. The Angolan government has distributed about a million weapons to its civil defence forces, and Uganda has armed its much smaller Local Defence Units. Congo-Brazzaville represented the extreme case of security peripheralization: the country had no real military in 1999, and different factions and Sassou-Nguesso's Cobra militia provided whatever security did exist.

Governments sometimes encourage local forces in order to save money, reduce casualties, and provide plausible deniability. These groups also have greater knowledge of local conditions as well as greater desire to fight to settle long-standing grievances. ECOMOG provided arms, ammunition, intelligence, and free transit to factions in Liberia, in part because these local fighters knew the topography, terrain, languages, and customs far better than the foreign multinational force. The National Islamic Front government in Sudan has sponsored various militias, including some that fight against each other (e.g., Riek Machar's South Sudan Defence Force, Paulino Matiep's South Sudan Unity Movement/Army). Extremist elements within the Rwandan military created the "zero network" and the Amasasu (Bullets) paramilitary groupings during the early 1990s. These local forces have low operating costs and offer the government deniability for controversial, and often unpopular, actions.

Paramilitaries, whether controlled directly by the regime or operating largely autonomously, can aid the coercive shift against their employer. Juan Linz notes that a government "is faced with a serious loss of legitimacy . . . when [it] allows organized groups with paramilitary discipline whose purpose is to use force for political ends to emerge in the society. Such groups are likely to become more and more autonomous, [and] to develop their own ideology and purposes."[59]

Paramilitaries usually lack discipline, have less training in universally recognized rules of war, and sometimes must live off the land. Prunier describes numerous Rwandan Interahamwe and Impuzamugambi as a "a lumpenproletariat of street boys, rag-pickers, car-washers, and homeless unemployed. For these people the genocide was the best thing that could ever happen to them."[60] In other words, the economy of war is better than no economy at all. Weak control of these groups, which Kaldor contrasts with that of Cold War guerrilla movements, allows wide-scale pillaging and human rights abuses.[61]

The abuse of civilians, a frequent result of government irregular forces, can assist insurgent recruitment and support. For example, Namibia's Special Field Force (SFF), composed mostly of unemployed guerrilla fighters, mounted security sweeps of the Caprivi Strip in search of Caprivi Liberation Army supporters in mid-1999.[62] SFF tactics increased resentment of the government and sent several thousand Caprivians into exile. Having been created from a sense of desperation by governments, these groups not only receive less training and status but are placed too quickly into combat.

Several results of the use of these groups contradict their purposes. The mutiny, such as occurred with the Pfumo re Vhanu irregulars in Zimbabwe-Rhodesia in 1979, is probably more common than in national militaries.[63] As noted below, ECOMOG's military support of various Liberian factions probably prolonged the war and led to several factions turning against their benefactor when their goals became different.

Encouragement of neighboring groups to fight each other also complicates future settlements. Describing how this factor affects southern Sudanese militias, Human Rights Watch suggests that "because it pits southerners against each other and neighbor against neighbor, it makes the likelihood of establishing a lasting peace remote."[64] Local militias that receive military support may seek political and economic concessions in order to acquiesce in peace settlements: one of the Mayi-Mayi spokesmen remarked in late 1999 that "the war is not over. It will go on as long as we are not part of the peace process."[65] Arming loosely controlled groups also aids future banditry. Weapons that the Angolan government provided to about 1 million citizens in Luanda in 1992 added to what Human Rights Watch terms "a significant rise in armed crime and banditry."[66] And retrieval of these weapons following a conflict can prove difficult.

Mercenaries (the subject of Chapter 5) add to Africa's pool of combatants. The Warsaw Pact's demise, the resulting Western military downsizing, and the end of South African apartheid all encouraged major manpower demobilizations and, as examined below, the enlargement of mercenary activity. Up to a thousand ex-SADF personnel have served in African conflicts (including Angola, the two Congos, Uganda, and Sierra Leone), sometimes as infantry "ground pounders," but more often as "force multipliers" whose advising, training, flying, and communications/technical skills multiply local capabilities. As with the paramilitaries and factions, they may add to the number of usually ill-disciplined combatants.

Finally, combatants from a concluded, or even continuing, conflict may join a newer cause. Rwandan Interahamwe by the late 1990s were fighting for Laurent Kabila's Congo, Jonas Savimbi's UNITA, the Allied Democratic Forces (a Ugandan insurgent group), and with some of the factions in Congo-Brazzaville.

The Resurgence of Ethnic Conflict

As a corollary to Hobbes's Leviathan, the weakening of African state control—caused by a mix of personal rule, unfavorable commodity prices, the departure of superpower patronage and protection, and the imposition of foreign conditions—sometimes induces ethnic and regional challenges to reassert themselves.[67] Frances Deng writes that

> it can be credibly argued that the gist of these internal conflicts is that the ethnic pieces that were put together by the colonial glue, and reinforced by the old world order, are now pulling apart and reasserting their autonomy or independence. Old identities, undermined and rendered dormant by the structures and values of the nation-state system are reemerging and redefining the standards of participation, distribution and legitimacy.[68]

Weakened state structures, including the security forces, have pushed both rulers and local groups to seek their own self-defense. Jack Snyder writes that ethnic nationalism "predominates when institutions collapse, when existing institutions are not fulfilling people's basic needs and when satisfactory alternative structures are not readily available."[69] Ethnic groups' arming themselves for greater security convinces other groups to follow suit and thus swells the number of non-state armed actors. Nigeria by mid-2000 was increasingly witnessing this phenomenon.[70]

This post–Cold War "unleashed ethnicity" argument helps to explain some, but not all, of Africa's conflicts; rarely has it been the major cause. Examples of this might include Liberia, Somalia, and Sudan. As the United States effectively ceased supporting Liberia's Samuel Doe, a member of the Krahn ethnic group, Doe increasingly "ethnicized" his government with greater numbers of Krahn. When Charles Taylor subsequently invaded Liberia, he deliberately sought and secured support from anti-Krahn groups (and Taylor did not rely on ethnic appeals for his support), most of Liberia's six factions having a distinct ethnic identity. In Somalia, a decline in U.S. support to Siad Barre saw the Somali president increasingly invoke Marehan ethnic appeals. For Sudan, the demise of Soviet patronage hastened the downfall of Ethiopia's Mengistu, whose military aid had encouraged various southern Sudanese rebel groups to remain united in the Sudanese Peoples' Liberation Army (SPLA). The SPLA divided after Mengistu's aid ended, and Riek Machar's Nasir faction (later the South Sudan Independence Movement/Army) began combat operations against its former ally, the SPLA's largest faction led by John Garang. Yet some insurgencies, such as Sierra Leone's RUF, feature only a weak ethnic causality.

Economic Motivations

Insurgencies increasingly feature more of an economic rather than a political-ideological focus.[71] The collapse of communism was more than the destruction of a political system, it also underlined both the demise of communism's international ideological appeal and the end of the Warsaw Pact's tying of arms to ideological correctness.

The pragmatic need for concessionary foreign assistance, as well as sometimes genuine beliefs, had prompted most third world rebel groups to claim an ideological base during the Cold War. Weaponry, money, and ideology granted the superpowers some influence over the insurgencies, and the local leaders had significant control over their troops.

Insurgencies backed by the superpowers established a strong philosophical underpinning during the Cold War. This was so especially in southern Africa.[72] Most of the guerrilla movements approximated Mao Tse-Tung's classic three stages of guerrilla warfare and advocated the development of a political base before the beginning of military operations. The movements sought to gain the voluntary loyalty of the citizenry and not use physical coercion against civilians. Raymond Copson notes that

> most of Africa's major resistance groups . . . tried to make it clear that they were political movements with respectable political objectives and not mere warrior bands. The political platforms of resistance movements were authored by the leaders, who had come to maturity in a post-war, post-independence intellectual environment and perceived themselves as working on behalf of the higher ideals found in that environment. In framing their objectives, they drew from the storehouse of modern political concepts—from Western democratic principles to Marxist dreams of leading the proletariat to a classless society.[73]

The fading of communism as an ideology to rally opposition created what Kaldor terms "the narrowing space for substantive political differences."[74] Snow's and Eboe Hutchful's descriptions, however, are in contrast to Copson's. Snow notes that "there is no common center of gravity to which the combatants' appeal. . . . The conflicts seem, indeed, to be a new breed of internal war," and Hutchful believes that "unlike the earlier liberation wars, this form of rebellion is typically initiated and led by an obscure and nihilistic leader, sometimes with no political organization or political agenda."[75]

Economic gain appears increasingly enticing as control of the state becomes less attractive. Bayart and others see "the economic logic of predation" as more important than political, ethnic, or regional considerations in several African conflicts.[76] Nkrumah's advice of "seek ye first the political kingdom and everything else shall come unto you" is less persuasive when the "kingdom" suffers from less foreign patronage than before, from the rise of foreign economic and political conditions, and from the legacy of *rentier* rulers who have depleted the country's resources. Economic opportunities rather than ideology attract and then retain guerrillas. The reduction in often free military equipment from the superpowers has contributed to this economic imperative, as factions seize their nation's resources to purchase weaponry. Examples include Charles Taylor's NPFL in Liberia and Foday Sankoh's RUF in Sierra Leone.[77]

The RUF held onto most of Sierra Leone's diamond-producing areas from 1998 through mid-2000 and moved about $70 million dollars of diamonds through Burkina Faso and Liberia annually for eventual sale in Europe and South Africa.[78] Diamond revenue purchased increasingly potent firepower, as well as mercenary troops and advisors, some of whom knew Sierra Leone well from prior work with Executive Outcomes. As noted below, government-aligned forces may also benefit from prolonging, rather than winning, violent conflicts.

Jonas Savimbi and his UNITA ran what *Africa Confidential* terms "the world's largest diamond smuggling operation between late 1992 and the beginning of 1998."[79] UNITA accounted for 75 to 90 percent of Angola's total diamond production and reportedly employed 100,000 miners in 1996.[80] "Significant quantities" have been traded to Angolan government officials, apparently for fuel, weapons, or intelligence.[81] Bayart, Ellis, and Hibou see "a direct relation between strategies of war or armed struggle and the sale or distribution of drugs, for example in Liberia and Sierra Leone, or to a lesser extent in Chad, Rwanda, and Burundi."[82]

The importance of this shift toward economic gain is multifaceted. Financially driven groups may likely prolong a conflict to exploit resource areas rather than to compete (and risk losing) in elections. Economic gains, along with Africa's poverty, protection of ethnic groups, and the easy availability of weaponry, encourage a multiplicity of factions to enter a conflict. The pursuit of resources and the decline of ideology have encouraged greater mistreatment of the civilian population. Writing about the worldwide "new insurgency," Donald Snow observes that "without a clearly articulated political goal there is little if any political framework to limit the extent and nature of the violence, as in Sierra Leone. The 'rebellion' . . . has no reason to appeal politically to the population in the areas in which it is active; its 'strategy' is marauding terror of the subject population."[83] The *New York Times* suggests the relationship between financial motivation and violence toward civilians: "Diamond money transformed UNITA into a far more ferocious military organization than it had been while receiving support from either the CIA or the South African government."[84] Seemingly anarchic viciousness does get political results, however, by further delegitimizing a government and its security forces.

A growing number of warlords may prefer the economic benefits of sole administration and exploitation of profitable areas, rather than the political demands of running a poorly developed and divided country. "In an increasing number of cases," notes Christopher Clapham, "insurgents found it easier just to capture the trading networks on which states had depended, and use them for their own purposes."[85] Indeed, Clapham wonders whether insurgent leaders in devastated countries ask "whether such states were worth capturing at all."[86] Peter Lock acknowledges that some insurgent leaders do not primarily seek control of "an exhausted territorial nation-state" but that they may gain certain international advantages by securing de jure rule.[87] Other observers believe that insurgent rulers do seek national political power but must first secure economic resources to purchase weaponry and political loyalty.

West Africa offers several examples of the ascendancy of personal, especially economic, aggrandizement over political or ideological goals. William Reno demonstrates that some of the Liberian factions between 1990 and 1996 were "warlord" armies seeking the economic status quo rather than possible governmental power.[88] Ibrahim Abdullah describes Sierra Leone's RUF as being a lumpen movement of "largely unemployed and unemployable youth" that "does not share any of the essential [revolutionary] characteristics of ideology, organization, and discipline."[89] Abdullah goes beyond just Sierra Leone's nonideological RUF when he writes that "it is this lack of a clear-cut programme, the wanton use of violence for the sake of violence, and the absence of a well-articulated ideology which disqualifies such second-independence movements as a vehicle for progressive change in Africa."[90]

The potential for economic gain can weaken military capabilities and sometimes encourages both sides of a conflict to prolong fighting. Angola's defense minister acknowledged that senior officials made large profits, the Angolan equivalent of kickbacks from weapons purchases (a pro-government newspaper reported senior officers receiving $320 million in commissions). And the *Guardian Weekly* reports that "lower down the line of command, soldiers are selling fuel, weapons and even uniforms to UNITA."[91] Clapham writes about Angola, "where both the 'national government' of the MPLA and the 'rebel forces' of Savimbi were essentially concerned with creaming resources from the oil sector on the one hand, and from diamonds on the other."[92] Global Witness, the London-based human rights organization, claims that President dos Santos controls a company that possesses a $720 million contract to supply his Angolan armed forces over a five-year period. Heike Behrend notes that the Ugandan government's struggle against the Lord's Resistance Army "became a business which was more profitable than peace. They [the government and the rebels] thus developed an interest in keeping the war going, and extending it to other areas, such as Rwanda or Zaire."[93]

The goal of economic power, especially when combined with the easy availability of weapons, may have encouraged a multiplicity of factions in several conflicts. Zimbabwean and Congolese officers have formed Osleg Private, Ltd., a mineral company to market Congolese diamonds, and as Chapter 4 notes, some observers fear that the pursuit of profits may persuade Zimbabwe to keep its forces in Congo. Somali factions fight for economic control in specific geographic areas—especially sea ports and the trade in the drug qat (and, previously, the resources of relief groups). And repatriation of cash by partisans abroad has helped fuel conflicts in Rwanda, Ethiopia, and Eritrea.

The increased abandonment of political principles for economic gain is also reflected among international arms suppliers—many of whom, admittedly, had few principles to begin with. Eastern European countries will now sell to most parties, even opponents in the same conflict. Russia—either the state or private companies—apparently has sold MiG/Su aircraft to both Ethiopia and Eritrea during 1998 and 1999. In Eastern Europe, arms dealers work with governments to procure or deliver the weapons.[94] The growth of private suppliers lessens political considerations and, according to the U.S. Defense Intelligence Agency, "is a troubling development, because the independent dealers are motivated strictly by profit, will sell to anyone, and care little about the consequences."[95] Weapons suppliers are entering into and assisting in other criminal activities in Africa: the U.S. State Department reports that "gun runners and drug peddlers in southern Africa are beginning to pool their resources to maximize profits."[96] Non-African states, as well, have at times destabilized African countries for economic gain. Belgium assisted the breakaway, mineral-rich Katanga Province in Congo during the early 1960s, and France may have supported Denis Sassou-Nguesso's overthrow of the Congo-Brazzaville government in order for French companies to gain valuable oil concessions.

Targeting of Noncombatants

Civilians have never been immune from armed groups, but insurgents during the 1990s have increasingly targeted civilians. Snow writes that the first consequence of "new internal wars" is that they "involve *higher levels of atrocity and inhumanity* and that they are also less controllable from the outside [emphasis in the original]."[97]

Few, if any, of Africa's current rebellions even try to live up to "the higher ideals" mentioned by Copson. Unrestrained by superpower influences, Sierra Leone's RUF conducts aptly named military campaigns, such as "No Living Thing," in which its recruits have amputated limbs of perhaps 30,000 civilians, raped women, and press-ganged child soldiers.[98] Uganda's Lord's Resistance Army has gained a reputation similar to the RUF's. Each of Liberia's factions between 1990 and 1996 committed grievous human rights violations, which sometimes included cannibalism, against the civilian population.

Insurgents have often brutalized African society, and the growth of such activity has coincided with the end of the Cold War. The insurgents' need to abide by international standards of war has lessened as their own ability to purchase weaponry from ideologically disinterested sources has increased. Rebels no longer need to rely on foreign states that might refuse to assist politically embarrassing clients. African governments or insurgencies during the Cold War that did not depend on Western or communist support were more likely to target civilians as a matter of policy; Amin's Uganda (then increasingly supported by Libya) and the South African-supported RENAMO in Mozambique were two examples. On the other hand, FRELIMO in the Mozambique of the 1960s and 1970s, ZIPRA and ZANLA in the Rhodesia of the 1970s, and Umkhonto we Sizwe in the South Africa of the 1970s and 1980s did not inflict massive suffering upon innocents and sometimes faced their patrons' anger when they did attack civilians.[99] However, the new insurgencies obtain local resources often despite, rather than because of, the local populace.

By ending support to African insurgencies, the Soviet Union, China, and the United States withdrew a guns-for-correct behavior condition. Snow argues that the United States "would have been terribly embarrassed had the forces it supported in Angola committed atrocities with American-provided weapons on the scale that occurred in Somalia; it would have let Jonas Savimbi and his followers know that should they engage in such acts, it would have to dump them."[100] Contemporary insurgencies such as the RUF, which purchase weaponry from ideologically disinterested sources, have more autonomy of action.

Attacks on relief groups are now common, a practice that first gained attention in Somalia where widespread armed thuggery helped to prompt U.S. and UN military intervention. Describing "the new face of war," Médecins sans Frontières notes that "the end of the Cold War has changed the nature of war. . . . Superpowers are no longer sponsoring warring factions. Now military groups must supply themselves. Cynically, they often look at humanitarian organizations as great resources—trucks to be hijacked, hostages to be held, supplies to be stolen."[101]

Clapham contends that "NGOs [nongovernment organizations] provide the most important vehicle for complex processes of 'asset transfer' that turn warfare into a profitable long-term operation."[102] For example, Liberian factions seized over $20 million worth of transportation, communication, medical, and food supplies in April 1996. Laurent Kabila's rebel forces stole fuel from the UN high commissioner for refugees and trucks and food from other sources. Various groups, and especially Kabila's ADFL, seized NGO assets for their military purposes.[103]

Attacking relief agencies hurts African development in both the short and the long term. Innocent civilians are deprived of food, or may assist the insurgency out of necessity, and the factions turn vehicles, radios, medical supplies, and foreign exchange into instruments of war that prolong the country's suffering. The agencies' increasingly assertive role of entering hotly contested areas lessens the appearance of impartiality and encourages combatants to attack these usually undefended supply sources.

Factors Intensifying Regional Conflicts

Growing interstate conflict compounds the difficulty of discerning how African states can defend themselves. Classic geopolitics developed in Africa during the 1990s as states increasingly deployed their militaries regionally to either attack or defend their neighbors.[104] Just as many of Africa's domestic conflicts have a multiplicity of actors, so also do the continent's regional wars. The interlinking of conflicts will complicate the resolution of any one struggle—Congo being the leading example—given the large number of actors.

An incomplete listing of cross-border operations includes Nigeria fielding the equivalent of a combat division in Liberia and Sierra Leone; Uganda fighting in Rwanda, Sudan and Congo; Angola intervening twice in Congo and once in Congo-Brazzaville; Rwanda sending its forces into Congo twice, Ethiopia and Eritrea moving their forces across each other's borders; and South Africa (with Botswana) intervening in Lesotho. The Congo fighting, which has involved some 25,000 troops from seven countries, epitomizes how Africa's tendency toward interstate conflicts has pulled in a wide range of players.[105] The *New York Times* writes that

> troops from as far south as Namibia and as far north as Chad are fighting inside the vast equatorial basin of the Congo river. Would-be presidents, waiting to step forward if Laurent Kabila is overthrown, are preening in hotel rooms from Cape Town to Brussels. Mining companies from South Africa to Canada are holding their breaths—and checkbooks—waiting to see how things turn out. . . . Every force in the Congo fights for a different reason. Sadly, greed and hatred are the two strongest.[106]

The reasons behind greater regional conflict include a partial redefining of sovereignty, economic aggrandizement, greater availability of long-range weapons systems, and personalities of various leaders—most of which are represented in Congo's war.[107] Consequences sometimes include greater privatization of militaries for personal gain, shifting of economic resources toward intervening regimes, or loss of foreign exchange for sophisticated weapons systems.

A Partial Redefining of Sovereignty

Until 1990, the international community had regarded self-determination for third world states as coterminous with freedom from colonial rule and with maintaining existing national boundaries. The UN advanced the concept of *uti possidetis,* which perpetuates the territorial continuity of a political unit regardless of the sovereignty transfer or of the boundary's original legal merit. The UN General Assembly's Resolution 1541 in the early 1960s stated that self-determination could be sought only by the existing political units, and not by subgroups within those units.[108] Recent changes in interstate relations suggest a growing disregard for *uti possidetis,* with its automatic entitlement of sovereignty, and a possible return to the more traditional concept of a state's exercise of effective political and military control. The concept of sovereignty as responsibility holds that claims of sovereignty depend on a state's being able to furnish basic human and economic rights to its citizens.[109]

The OAU, in its 1963 charter, championed a strongly conservative approach to sovereignty. Its first five principles called for "the sovereign equality of all member states . . . noninterference in the internal affairs of states, respect for the sovereignty and territorial integrity of each state . . . peaceful settlement of disputes . . . [and] unreserved condemnation . . . of political assassinations as well as of subversive activities on the part of neighboring states."[110] African states generally complied, forsaking military invasions or incursions, and the superpowers discouraged endeavors in military expansionism by refusing to supply offensive weaponry.

As noted, the end of the Cold War has stimulated a growth in cross-border military operations, either to subvert or support a neighboring government. Rarely has fighting tried to change national boundaries (the Ethiopian-Eritrean conflict providing the major exception).[111] Some of the reasons and results, such as economic gain, availability of weaponry, and leaders' personalities, are examined later. Other reasons include preemptive self-defense, containment of conflict, and the absence of countervailing restraints.[112]

Preemptive self-defense is a major motivation. Following the end of the Cold War, African states appear more willing to invade or subvert other states that harbor insurgent forces. Angola stands as the primary example of preemptive self-defense, intervening three times in 1997 and 1998 against UNITA's support areas in nearby countries. Angola fought against Mobutu's pro-UNITA Zaire (1997) and then for Kabila's

Congo (1998). Angola swung the tide of battle when it intervened to help former President Denis Sassou-Nguesso and his Cobra faction to overthrow Pascal Lissouba in Congo-Brazzaville in 1997.

The little-noticed Angolan invasion of Congo-Brazzaville marked a watershed in Africa's new interventionism. Angolan soldiers, planes, and tanks entered to help overthrow Lissouba's democratically elected government, which had been tacitly supporting UNITA. This marked the first time that an outside military helped to topple a popularly elected president, and the lack of strong criticism, both African and non-African, was especially striking. This silence, as suggested below, may implicitly encourage future invasion.[113]

Rwanda and Uganda also cited self-defense for their Congo aggressions.[114] Rwanda invaded to close down Hutu camps in eastern Congo from which Interahamwe groups were infiltrating into Rwanda. Uganda intervened, in part, to attack Ugandan rebels (the Allied Democratic Forces) transit areas, whereas Angola entered Congo to close down UNITA's supply links.

Sometimes states mount self-defense operations to prevent instability from spreading regionally rather than to attack a specific foe. As the drop in superpower patronage undermined already weak states, the resulting fragility sometimes prompted neighboring militaries to intervene. For example, ECOMOG peacekeepers went into Liberia partly because the ECOMOG countries feared increased refugee flows and the spread of armed groups into neighboring countries.

An absence of effective sanctions also contributes to preemptive military operations. While the outside world will often disapprove of forcible violations of sovereignty, it will likely continue to play a relatively marginal role. The upsurge in interstate conflict has rarely prompted other states to invoke effective sanctions, and this apathy implicitly supports future regional strife. The rare cross-border operations before 1990 received broad condemnation: even Tanzania's toppling of Uganda's Amin garnered scant public support. Yet the invasions of the late 1990s have not triggered significant criticism, even when overthrowing democratically elected governments, as with Angola's action in Congo-Brazzaville. Even France, which had militarily supported other Francophone presidents when they were threatened, declined to intervene in Congo-Brazzaville just as it had demurred on trying to rescue President Mobutu. The lack of non-African, and particularly French, objections probably suggests to African leaders international non-intervention in comparable future actions. The post-1990 weakening of many African states' effective sovereignty offered a green light to aggressor states. "Respect for borders means little," writes Marina Ottaway, "when the state no longer exists."[115]

Motivation is often difficult to discern because of the sometimes complex reasons and justifications, especially as states increasingly invoke the sovereignty-as-responsibility motivation. South Africa's President Nelson Mandela summarized this change from tradition when he stated that "we must all accept that we cannot abuse the concept of national sovereignty to deny the rest of the continent the right and duty to intervene when, behind those sovereign boundaries, people are being slaughtered to protect tyranny."[116]

Economic interests have helped to alter the traditional respect for sovereignty. "Warlord rulers and their allies [also] disrupt authority in other states," notes William Reno. "They ignore the significance of frontiers if they obstruct efforts to control markets, clandestine or visible."[117] A Western intelligence officer, referring to Charles Taylor's continuing assistance to Sierra Leone's RUF, states that "the name of the game for Taylor is control of the diamond producing areas in Sierra Leone. The Taylor enterprise is about the creation of wealth."[118] Taylor has supplied several thousand former National Patriotic Front of Liberia (NPFL) troops, provided camps for several South African and Ukranian mercenaries to train RUF soldiers in small-unit combat, and allowed his country to be the transit area for new RUF military equipment. Diamond desire also encouraged President Campaore to send Burkinabe soldiers to fight alongside the RUF against UN peacekeepers.

Economic Aggrandizement

Predator states existed during the Cold War, but their rulers restricted their appetites to domestic resources. Examples of growing military mercantilism include Charles Taylor acquiring diamonds in Sierra Leone through his support of the RUF and Zimbabwe's Robert Mugabe and other party officials benefiting from Zimbabwe's military defense of Kabila's Congo. Such mercantilism is another form of Africa's security privatization.

This eclipse of ideology by economics as a motive for war parallels what has occurred in numerous insurgencies. The *Economist* implicitly notes that "the main players in Congo are seen by many as greedy warlords, with ready-made armies at their disposal and a clear interest in enriching themselves. Continued war could be their best way of doing this."[119]

High-ranking officials and officers have economic interests in neighboring countries and sometimes deploy their national militaries to protect these interests. Zimbabwe's well-documented military mercantilism could be the major reason for its intervention and reflects a still nascent but potentially important concept of "the state as mercenary."[120] After all, Angolan and Libyan payments persuaded Chad to provide 2,000 troops to Kabila's Congo.

The increased regional fighting and its military mercantilism appear to be creating a new regionalism, for better or for worse. Zimbabwe's growing political, military, and economic ties with Congo, should the ties last and prosper, may provide Zimbabwe (or numerous Zimbabwean elites) with remarkable regional influence. Two economic announcements in late 1999 underscored Zimbabwean-Congolese economic ties. Zimbabwe's Agricultural and Rural Development Authority received more than a half-million hectares of farming land in Congo for maize, soy beans, and livestock. The authority's director, Dr. Joseph Made, trumpeted the agreement as promising "enormous business opportunities for Zimbabwean companies."[121] Zimbabwe's transport minister announced plans to build a railway line from Zimbabwe that would pass through Zambia and then link into Congo.[122]

The Zimbabwean government in 1997 may have deliberately begun its Congo intervention to boost Zimbabwe's business as well as its regional political influence. An initial grant of about $25 million to Kabila's rebel ADFL facilitated mining, timber, and retail agreements between leading Zimbabwean politicians and Kabila's government. The government-owned Zimbabwe Defence Industries provided $250 million in arms to Kabila's rebel group and has continued to assist the Kabila government.[123] The 1998 rebellion against Kabila by domestic dissidents who were aided greatly by Rwanda and Uganda endangered these arrangements, and Zimbabwe quickly responded with up to 12,000 troops backed by tanks, planes, and helicopters. Zimbabwe supplied more than $90 million in arms shortly after the current round of fighting, which began in August 1998. Philip Chiyangwa notes his country's assistance to Kabila in 1997 and argues that "for what we went to do in Congo [in 1997], we should be paid. And the only fair way to be paid is in business."[124]

A Zimbabwean became executive chairman of Gecamines, Congo's major mining company, which holds rights to some of the world's richest cobalt, copper, and zinc deposits.[125] Zimbabwean officials, rather than the Congolese state, reportedly will receive a majority of the company's profits.[126] Several Zimbabwean generals have gained lucrative contracts, passing some of them onto contracts on to friends and family.[127] The U.S. State Department writes that Zimbabwe's commander in Congo won a government contract for his private transport company to ferry military goods to that country.[128] As elaborated in Chapter 4, Zimbabwean and Congolese officers on active duty have formed the Osleg Company, a militarily run firm that plans to market Congolese minerals.

The war benefits Zimbabwe's regime but weakens the state: the "Congo effect" is an often-cited term to describe the economic ramifications of the Congolese war.[129] John Makumbe, a professor at the University of Zimbabwe and local director of Transparency International, argues that "it won't be Zimbabwe as a nation that benefits. Instead, a number of individuals in the political elite will enrich themselves."[130]

Investec Securities wrote in late 1998 that Zimbabwe's Congo intervention was stripping Zimbabwe's economy: "We are drawing closer to an end game in Zimbabwe. The coffers are finally bare, plundered by the [ruling ZANU-PF] party and squandered on the ruinous intervention in the [Congo], meaning that the economic day of reckoning is at hand."[131]

Zimbabwe's economy was near collapse by 2000, according to the *Economist* Intelligence Unit.[132] The publication forecast real GDP growth at a negative 6 percent while predicting that inflation could reach 78 percent by year's end.[133] Worsening export commodity prices and reduced foreign investment assisted this decline, but the war undoubtedly played a major role. The Zimbabwean government acknowledged that for the year 2000 it would raise defense spending by 62 percent over the 1999 outlay. In late 1998, the Zimbabwean government also raised military pay by 100 percent for all personnel, amid published allegations of several foiled coup attempts and anger at Zimbabwe's Congo involvement. The war has also hurt Zimbabwe's ties with Uganda and possibly Zambia.[134]

To what extent is economic gain a motive for, rather than a result of, cross-border operations? Angola's primary motive appears to have been the elimination of UNITA support networks, but Angola also apparently exploited Congo to help pay operating costs. Richard Cornwell, a South African security expert, contends that Angolan troops agreed to fight only if they received the right to pillage.[135] Nigeria's and Guinea's economic gains in Liberia were probably more after the fact. They exploited local economic assets either to pay for the war's cost, to enrich individual officers, or to compensate otherwise unpaid soldiers.

On the other hand, while economic gain will usually not be the primary motive for entering a conflict, it certainly can sustain a force's continuing commitment. Greed may prolong a conflict, as has been noted in Liberia and Uganda, if such a continuation benefits the fighters. Zimbabwe's financial holdings in the Osleg mining venture suggest that its military has an incentive to remain in the DRC, which, if true, could hamper troop withdrawal and peace negotiations.

Several leading Ugandan military and civilian leaders reportedly have transport and mineral holdings in Congo but, once again, the security desire to eliminate foreign-based subversive groups appears as the primary cause for invasion. Ugandan newspapers report that "the illegal trade between Entebbe and Kisangani, Congo's third largest city, is monopolised by senior army officers who mostly deal in salt . . . beer . . . electronics . . . [and] timber," and suggest that two air charter companies owned by Gen. Salim Saleh may be smuggling goods between Entebbe and Kisangani.[136]

Low-cost purchasing or pillaging of resources from war zones has assisted the economies of some of the intervening states. "Uganda's intervention in the Congo's civil war is having immense economic implications. Raw material from the Congo are flooding the Uganda market and driving down prices," writes The *New African*.[137] Numerous observers in the Congo, including Rwandan army officers, contend that Ugandan units have engaged in military mercantilism, sometimes with the systematic looting of valuable assets. A U.S. intelligence official confirms African allegations that the UPDF has brought back significant amounts of gold, coffee, diamonds, and timber for Ugandan export.[138] Several Ugandan military officers, as well as Salim Saleh, have acquired mining rights in Congo: the *Washington Post* contends that the Ugandan forces "also happen to be occupying a Congolese gold mine."[139]

Such exploitation may become more institutionalized. Namibia's minister of home affairs told his National Assembly that "the government would accept an invitation to explore any mineral enterprise, if invited by the Congolese people."[140] *Africa Confidential* in November 1999 reported that "Rwanda plans to set up export processing zones along its frontier with Congo and to establish a twin-town relationship between Bukavu and Rwanda."[141]

Rebels also exploit economic areas to sustain and prolong their military activities; Congolese rebels created a minerals-marketing firm in South Africa, the Little Rock Mining Company, to parcel out concessions in their military-controlled areas.

Availability of Long-Range Weaponry

African states are increasingly obtaining aviation and artillery systems that greatly enhance their force projection capabilities (while small arms still create the majority of casualties). The private market, using pilots and planes decommissioned following the end of the Cold War, now provides critical airlift capability to the extent that the U.S. Defense Intelligence Agency argues that "without contract air transport, many of the victories we have seen on African battlefields in the past several years would not have been possible."[142] Some of the planes are largely new to Africa, notably the Su-27 and MiG-29 fighters used in fighting between Eritrea and Ethiopia, whereas older aircraft, such as MiG-21 and MiG-23 fighter-bombers, are receiving markedly improved avionics, engines, and armament. The Soviet MI-24 Hind attack helicopter is highly sought after and is used by some twelve African militaries.

Artillery advances are especially noticeable in the Ethiopian-Eritrean conflict where Ethiopia has fielded the 2S19 152mm self-propelled howitzer, which defense experts regard as "a quantum leap in sophistication over the post-WWII designed artillery commonly found in Africa."[143] MANPAD surface-to-air missiles and multiple rocket-launching systems are appearing more frequently. The Soviet T-55 tank "is fast becoming the 'battle queen' of Africa, and is now a prime player in wars from the Horn to Angola, and from Rwanda to Guinea," according to the U.S. Defense Department.[144]

The traditional assumption that high costs would prevent such poorer nations as Ethiopia, Eritrea, and Rwanda from purchasing such sophisticated force projection equipment is proving false. One nation's acquisition of a new weapons system often will encourage neighboring states to follow suit. Governments barter not only diamonds but timber, gum arabic, cotton, sesame, and animal skins and trophies for weaponry. Citizens of these three countries living abroad send foreign exchange back home, and foreign countries will support fighting, as well (Reportedly, Israel has helped to finance Eritrea's struggle against Ethiopia, while Sudan has helped Ethiopia.) Protracted conflict is driving the richer African countries deeper into debt: Angola and other countries use future exports as collateral for weapons purchases or to repay past loans.[145] Finally, banks in Asia, Europe, and the Middle East, as well as lenders in the British Virgin Islands, Hong Kong, the Seychelles, and Singapore, have arranged financing of weapons purchases.[146]

Personality

Africa's continuing penchant for personal rule can encourage interventionism, given the absence within these systems of domestic and regional institutionalized checks and balances. Paul Kagame of Rwanda, Yoweri Museveni of Uganda, Meles Zenawi of Ethiopia, Isaias Afewerki of Eritrea, Robert Mugabe of Zimbabwe, José dos Santos of Angola, and Sam Nujoma of Namibia used military force to gain power, a fact that may explain why all of them are now using their forces against nearby states. Friendship forged among Nujoma, Mugabe, and dos Santos during the apartheid years helped persuade Nujoma to commit some 1,000 of Namibia's soldiers to assist Zimbabwe's and Angola's forces in the Congo. Numerous observers believe that Mugabe's desire "to project himself out of the shadows of then-South African President Nelson Mandela"[147] was a significant reason for Zimbabwe's crossing into Congo. Museveni's pan-Africanist philosophy probably also helps to explain Uganda's involvement in neighboring conflicts.

By mid-2000, international actions by international organizations, governments, and businesses were starting to address the above trends. The UN, ECOWAS, and Western states have acknowledged the need for greater peace enforcement, in large part because of events in Sierra Leone. Britain's dispatch of 1,600 combat troops halted the RUF offensive, which the UN peacekeepers had been helpless at stopping. In August 2000, a UN-convened panel recommended that future UN peacekeepers be given the capability "to confront the lingering forces of war and violence [and] to defeat them."[148]

ECOWAS, which had received mixed reviews for its prolonged Liberian and Sierra Leonean campaigns, announced plans in July 2000 to create a standby, combat-capable force. ECOWAS's executive secretary, Lansana Kouyate, stated that "I will like to see us go beyond a strong peacekeeping mandate to a peace enforcement mandate."[149]

The United States, in what a senior administration official characterized as "an agonizing reappraisal,"[150] announced that it would provide combat training to West African battalions engaged in Sierra Leone. Congressional Republicans generally welcomed the shift toward more aggressive training.[151]

Rising worldwide anger at diamond-financed insurgencies tried to restrict the financing of rebel operations. Heightened publicity and condemnation has seen the UN publicly accuse two currently serving African presidents (Blaise Campaore of Burkina Faso and Gnassingbe Eyeadema of Togo) of breaking 1998 sanctions against UNITA by accepting diamonds for military considerations.[152] The United States asked the Security Council to create a special court to try Foday Sankoh and other human rights violators in Sierra Leone.[153] The British Foreign office has publicly accused several businessmen of contravening the UNITA sanctions, and the United States has informed West African countries and the media about Taylor's and Campaore's support of the RUF in exchange for diamonds.

Specific measures have followed. The UN agreed in July 2000 to an embargo of diamonds from RUF areas. Britain persuaded the European Union to withhold $47 million of aid from Taylor's Liberia, which has laundered much of RUF's diamond output. The United States began sending several hundred Special Forces ("Green Berets") soldiers to provide combat training to up to seven West African battalions (about 3,500 men) against the RUF. The United States also called for sanctions against Liberia and Burkina Faso. And, the International Diamond Manufacturers' Association, worried about a possible public campaign against "conflict" or "blood" diamonds, has initiated greater self-regulation.

These measures, while laudable, carry some inherent weaknesses. The UN may lack both the political will and the financial means (the United States owes about $1 billion to the UN) to sustain peace enforcement operations. ECOWAS, whose ECOMOG has traditionally relied upon Nigerian funding, faces similar problems. ECOWAS hopes, perhaps vainly, that its members will impose a levy of 0.5 percent on all imports into West Africa to finance the proposed standby force. And, human rights abuses by U.S.-trained troops or fears that combat training could later make the United States escalate its proposed military involvement could undercut public support.

Diamond boycotts face difficulties. Diamonds are easy to smuggle, certificates of origin have been sold by corrupt officials, and existing technology cannot always determine a diamond's origin. Finally, the Sierra Leone conflict may not provide a lasting precedent. The horrific imprecations of the RUF triggered much of the above concern: future insurgencies, if less brutal, will attract less concern.

The following section examines how international attitudes toward intervention changed during the 1990s and why Africa now has a growing responsibility for its own defense.

The Rise and Fall of
Humanitarian Western Interventionism

The Interventionist Impulse

The suffering in collapsing states in the early 1990s suggested a moral imperative to intervene militarily.[154] An aggressive liberal internationalism briefly supplanted the more realist globalism of the Cold War. Some world leaders envisioned a new world order and a more activist role for a UN no longer hamstrung by Cold War rivalries. The concept of sovereignty as responsibility and a growing international human rights concern began to triumph over traditional deference to claims of sovereignty.

Between 1989 and 1994, the UN initiated more peacekeeping missions than it had in the previous forty-three years of its existence. Its peacekeeping budget rose from $700 million in 1991 to $3.6 billion in 1994. UN peacekeeping operations had 10,000 troops in 1989; that figure had jumped to 70,000 by 1995. The UN authorization of a military rescue of the Kurds in northern Iraq broke new ground in the sovereignty-as-responsibility school. The French government spoke about "the duty to interfere."[155] President Mitterrand noted that the authorization reflected a "new right . . . that is quite extraordinary in the history of the world . . . a sort of right to interfere inside a country when a portion of its population suffers persecution."[156]

The "new interventionists," as Stephen Stedman terms them, sought "a new humanitarian order in which governments are held—by force, if necessary—to higher standards of respect for human life."[157] This new order sought to elevate the importance of international values over national interest or to link distant suffering to an international interest. The realist school of international relations traditionally argued that a nation should use its military only to protect its narrowly defined national economic, political, or strategic interests. Yet the world, and the West in particular, had been widening its arena for humanitarian intervention. Many of the West's interventions during the early 1990s occurred in states where national interest appeared minimal: the UN shield for Kurds and Shiites in Iraq, the UN military effort in Cambodia, and the U.S. and UN intervention in Somalia.

The Gulf War's success encouraged such optimism. Operation Desert Storm presented a unified collection of states, no longer fearing retaliation by a rival superpower, and exercising military might for humanitarian right (as well as defense of crucial oil supplies). The intervention seemed to underline two points. Multinational intervention could be effective; after all, a hastily assembled coalition of largely democratic states had routed the world's fourth largest army and humiliated a tyrannical ruler. And advanced Western military technology, such as "smart bombs," could help to minimize civilian casualties.

The proliferation of NGOs contributed to the redefining of sovereignty. NGOs increasingly attract publicity by attempting what governments traditionally could not, or would not, do. The title of *Médecins sans Frontières* reflects the goal of numerous NGOs: to transcend traditional concepts of sovereignty and political niceties in order to aid the innocent victims of natural or manmade disasters.

Humanitarian NGOs, often helped by a close relationship with the media, shape political attitudes that can create pressure for state intervention. Relief groups enjoy wide public acceptance, based in part on what Mary Anderson terms their perceived "purity of motivation."[158] Anderson writes that the organizations "may serve to dehumanize the perpetrators of these atrocities in the minds of the wider public."[159] Barry Blechman writes that "their reports and activities reinforce (and sometimes help to form) popular pressure in foreign capitals for some kind of official action."[160] Finally, as Richard Betts and others note, the NGOs' presence in a conflict situation alters the existing power balance and may turn them into a target, which in turn could increase pressure on Western governments to intervene.[161] This occurred in Somalia in late 1992 when President Bush announced Operation Restore Hope, an attempt to protect the delivery of relief supplies.

Reaction Against "The New Interventionism"

Values-based interventions encountered unforeseen difficulties and, by the mid-1990s, two emerging obstacles had forced governments to reevaluate the moral arguments for intervention. First, various discrepancies between the interveners' goals and their capabilities arose, particularly during the interventions in Somalia and Bosnia. At the same time, a growing Western reluctance to use military means to resolve conflicts curtailed the chances of Western military intervention. UN peacekeeping operations had used 70,000 soldiers in 1995; the figure had declined to 19,000 by 1998. France had been the major non-African intervener but had started to cut back the size of its national army and its commitments to Africa. As one government official stated, France "refuses to be brought into the internal conflicts or to intervene in the interior affairs of its African partners."[162]

The tensions between the interveners' goals and capabilities include the following:

National interest versus national values. A potential intervener may have to reconcile conflicting motivations about foreign military intervention. National values, such as democratization and human rights, are highly emotive and can quickly unite a diverse domestic constituency. Yet such appeals often fade rapidly, especially when challenged by casualties or heightened involvement, unless assisted by appeals to the nation's economic, strategic, and political interests. The aphorism "CNN got us into Somalia and CNN got us out of Somalia" reflects this dichotomy.

Desire versus knowledge. It can prove difficult to assist innocent victims rapidly when lacking essential knowledge of the conflict and the country.[163] Humanitarian disasters often result when the West knows little about a conflict, yet quickly needs a strong information base for successful intervention.

Normative hopes versus real situations. Interveners in a "humanitarian crisis" enter chiefly to assist individual victims, yet face great problems when trying to remain both humanitarian and neutral in a highly partisan and often violent environment. Intervention, regardless of motive, can quickly make the intervener a player and thus a target in a contentious situation.[164]

Interveners may be tempted to rely on local individuals and groups for valuable manpower and intelligence. Yet the employment of these people or groups can endanger the intervention by jeopardizing the foreigners' desired neutrality and by compromising important intelligence about the mission.

Time versus need. It can be difficult to reconcile the intervener's time constraints with the immensity of the problem and the longer time horizon of the combatants. A values-based intervention usually faces significant time limitations because it lacks the staying appeal of national interest.

Mandate versus capabilities. It is necessary to match the operation's political mandate with both the interveners' military capabilities and their own domestic political support.

Interveners in Somalia and elsewhere have confronted a menu of mandates. For example, peacekeeping, sanctioned by Chapter VI of the

UN Charter, is the positioning of a neutral (and lightly armed) force between combatants that have agreed to a ceasefire. Self-defense is the only justification for combat by peacekeepers. Peace enforcement, which falls under Chapter VII of the UN Charter, calls for significant aggressive combat, if necessary, to maintain a peace agreement.[165]

The United States and the UN in Somalia struggled, often unsuccessfully, to match their mandate with the changing Somalian events—were they peacekeepers or peace enforcers?[166] Traditional limitations of ad hoc multinational forces, such as lack of knowledge, differentiated military strategies and capabilities, and changing political commitments, also helped doom this well-intentioned intervention. Individual contributing states can always reinterpret or disregard the multinational mandate.

Actions taken in pursuit of immediate ends may endanger long-term goals. Interveners have sometimes accomplished short-term goals only to realize that a successful withdrawal required a greater commitment of time—and financial resources—than originally planned. The forces of intervention may need to rebuild a political or economic infrastructure, disarm local factions, or train a new police force. These long-run goals can quickly sap domestic political support for the operation. Some interventions that began as peacekeeping became more costly peace-enforcing operations when interveners entered combat operations. Finally, the interveners may lack the suitable military capabilities to enforce their mandate.

William Durch summarizes what he terms "the dilemma of humanitarian intervention":

> Either the outsiders feed, vaccinate, and stand aside, letting the local parties settle feuds in their own uniquely bloody way while providing some minimal protection to non-combatants: or the outsiders quash local power centers and look for more acceptable local alternatives. The "local alternatives," by definition, have not been strong enough to win on their own. . . . This approach obligates the international "surgeon" to complete the course of treatment but he rarely has the time or attention span; in fact, he really has only the foggiest idea how to do the surgery and he fears the sight of blood, especially his own. Given these choices, the long-term prognosis for humanitarian intervention is not good.[167]

"Humanitarian military intervention now must be *multilateral* to be legitimate," writes Martha Finnemore, but the trend toward multinational intervention generally compounds the above difficulties.[168]

Multinational intervention offers several possible advantages, but few of them are military. A multinational coalition does speak with a more resonant political voice than does a unilateral intervention, and at least in theory, it distributes among its members the political, financial, and military costs of the operation, a joint effort possibly achieving what one nation would hesitate to do by itself.

Yet Somalia, and Bosnia, demonstrated that multilateralism is by nature a politically and militarily unwieldy undertaking: its limitations often endanger an intervention's success and can prolong a conflict. Multilateral military forces face several major organizational challenges of composition, capabilities, and integration as well as the absence of incentives (initial and continuing) and mandates.

A force must quickly gain the participation of competent national militaries and then integrate these units into an interoperative force. Ad hoc rather than permanent forces have been the rule. Although this tendency appears financially cheaper and politically less threatening to standing governments, it has contributed to past failures by not allowing for united doctrine, tactics, and weaponry.

Other issues that arise include whether an intervention force should be a standing or a designated force,[169] and whether military ability should be the major (or sole) criterion for determining membership. Furthermore, nations possessing large and/or effective militaries often may carry heavy political baggage.[170]

John Ruggie reflects that "in several major UN peace operations, neither the UN nor its member states have fully known what they have been doing or how to do it. Frustration and failure therefore have been inevitable."[171] He quotes the UN commander in Bosnia: "There is a fantastic gap between the resolutions of the Security Council, the will to execute these resolutions, and the means available to commanders in the field."[172]

A force must keep itself together despite often unforeseen military and political threats that will challenge the original mandate or lessen the contributors' political will. The necessary conditions for multilateral creation—converging interests and a willingness to pool resources for collective action—can be misinterpreted or else lose their attractiveness. The infamous "mission creep" of the UN's Somalian intervention, in which the foreign force enlarged its original mandate from peace-keeping and humanitarian aid to one of nation building and peace enforcement, is an oft-cited example.

A multinational force risks a clash between its supranational needs and the national demands and aspirations of each of its contributing states. Contingent commanders have primary loyalty to their political leaders and to their soldiers, rather than to an ad hoc and temporary coalition. When national loyalty claims precedence, as it often does, it may threaten the multinational unit's mandate as well as its physical safety. Especially prolonged operations may prompt poorer countries to ask why they should lend some of their security forces to a foreign operation (unless, of course, they receive adequate compensation).

Rwanda's horrific genocide of April 1994, some six months after the Olympic Hotel firefight in Somalia, revealed the world's departure from humanitarian intervention. The Hutu-controlled Rwandan government and the Tutsi-dominated Rwandan Patriotic Front (RPF) signed the Arusha Peace Accords in August 1993 to end their four-year civil war. The UN in December supplied a 2,500-man peacekeeping force, the UN Assistance Mission in Rwanda (UNAMIR). The force's mandate, hurriedly approved by the Security Council the day after the Olympic Hotel firefight, was, *inter alia,* to monitor the cease-fire and the general security situation, train in land mine removal, and assist certain humanitarian endeavors.

The peace disintegrated following the mysterious shooting down of the aircraft carrying the presidents of Rwanda and Burundi. Within hours, Hutus killed both the prime minister and ten UNAMIR Belgian troops who were protecting her. As both government and RPF forces began fighting, UNAMIR's foreign contributors, already alarmed by the Belgians' deaths, began to withdraw their forces and the UN Security Council authorized the reduction of UNAMIR to 270 personnel. Prunier reports that Belgium's government and public "had both been paralysed by the torture and death of their ten Blue Helmets" and stated that its army "would never again take part in any peace-keeping operations under a UN command."[173]

The Security Council members, and especially the United States, were haunted by the Somalia precedent and concerned with mission creep and "exit strategies." Meanwhile, about 800,000 Rwandans were dead and some 2 million Rwandans had fled to neighboring countries.

Maj. Gen. Roméo Dallaire, UNAMIR's Canadian commander, has forcefully stated that the UN and UNAMIR's contributors share major responsibility for tacitly allowing the genocide. Referring to UNAMIR's effective departure from Rwanda, Dallaire said that "I came to the United Nations from commanding a mechanized brigade group of 5,000 soldiers. If I had had that brigade group in Rwanda, there would be hundreds of thousands of lives spared today."[174] Most experts agree that Dallaire is probably correct.

The Wariness of the West.   Western-supported intervention faces another problem. War and its supporting culture may be becoming suspect in the West's consciousness, with serious implications for international security.[175] Some observers speculate that this disenchantment may become permanent. John Keegan writes that war "may well be ceasing to commend itself to human beings as a desirable or productive, let alone rational, means of reconciling [their] discontents."[176] "The age of mass conscription is over for good," predicts Michael Ignatieff, "and with it ends the imprinting of military rituals and codes of masculinity throughout our schools, public institutions, and family life . . . [now] war has become, within the last fifty years, a vestigial memory for most of us . . . throwbacks to forms of insanity that we have left behind."[177] Keegan, Ignatieff, and others may be overstating their case, but what is undeniable is a prevailing disinclination in the United States, Britain, France, and Germany to deploy combat forces overseas.

Western Europe's longest period of peace since medieval times has affected its—and the United States'—views about warfare and intervention. The end of the Cold War removed an apparent threat and then encouraged Western democracies to significantly reduce their militaries. The budget and manpower of the U.S. military have shrunk by 40 percent since 1989, and France, Britain, and Germany have likewise trimmed their services. Many strategists have worried that operations other than war, such as peacekeeping, jeopardize overall readiness by depleting smaller units even further and by diminishing their military training.

Recent interventions, especially peace-enforcing missions, have soured attitudes toward foreign deployment. The above-mentioned difficulties of conventional Western military intervention has served to caution some policymakers against future interventions: "doing something" to alleviate serious suffering may prove worse than doing nothing. Marina Ottaway explains international reluctance to intervene by noting that "intervention always creates resentment: the experience of the United States in Somalia shows that it is easy for the intervener to be hailed as a savior one day and denounced as an enemy the next." Noting the failure of the two United Nations Angolan Verification Missions, she suggests that "the failure of earlier intervention is also a deterrent."[178] Boutros Boutros-Ghali's *Addendum to the Agenda for Peace* of 1995 no longer suggested the creation of a UN standing army, as had the 1992 original *Agenda,* but proposed instead greater regional and nonstate participation in conflict resolution.[179] The U.S. government, which in early 1993 had called for "assertive multilateralism," featured President Clinton in September of that year declaring that "the UN must know when to say no" and issuing Presidential Decision Directive 25, which stipulated a long list of conditions for U.S. intervention.[180] Fighting and suffering in Somalia was still occurring by late 1999, but the West no longer expressed any willingness to assist in ending the conflict.

A gnawing worry about Western inaction is that, as Ignatieff writes, "we are losing our capacity to do good in the world because we are no longer willing to risk the moral danger of doing evil."[181]

The Rwanda genocide illustrated just how far the international pendulum had swung against military intervention for humanitarian purposes. The world quickly learned of the widespread savagery inflicted by the Hutus against the minority Tutsis, but the United States and other countries declined to label it as genocide because they then might have felt public pressure and legal obligations, as signatories to the Genocide Convention of 1947, to send combat troops into the Rwandan maelstrom. Two months after the killings had begun, the U.S. State Department still maintained that genocide was not occurring.[182] The United States refused to jam electronically Rwanda's hate radio stations that were championing the genocide, and the Clinton administration dragged its feet when supplying armored personnel carriers to the UN.[183] Only belatedly, in late June 1994, did France and several allied African countries send troops to establish the safe havens. Even this move, Operation Turquoise, was widely criticized as a French attempt to prevent the Tutsi-dominated RPF from winning a clear-cut victory in Rwanda.

The Shift of Security Responsibility

The growing security threat to many African states, and the West's disinclination to intervene militarily to resolve conflicts, has forced African states to assume a greater responsibility for their own security. In some cases Western nations have tried to promote African military self-reliance; in other instances the affected regions/states have taken the initiative. Impatient at foreign inaction, they have peremptorily assumed greater security responsibility, either by forming multilateral military organizations or by employing private security companies to assist their national militaries.

Such initiatives have occurred at the regional and national, rather than the continental, level. Since 1990, the OAU has not fielded any combat forces and has usually failed to negotiate peaceful settlements to the various conflicts.

This shift of responsibility may achieve a dual objective: to increase the defensive capabilities of weaker states and to lessen the political pressure on Western states or the UN for intervention. A successful shift would facilitate the security and thus, probably, the economic, social, and political development of fragile states: a technically proficient military can stop a conflict faster, and usually with fewer casualties and less destruction, than an incompetent force. Greater trade and investment opportunities, as well as less need for Western economic assistance, would result.

Yet such a shift faces numerous problems, and an unsuccessful attempt could further endanger fragile states. Inherent in the shift is an unpredictable relationship among sovereignty, responsibility, and power. Sovereignty connotes responsibility, but state power—the ability to influence or control citizens' actions—is required to implement that responsibility. The West and the UN have the economic and military capacity to assist the world's more fragile states but, following the end of the Cold War, they feel less responsibility to do so unless a conflict clearly threatens their own national or international interests. In these circumstances, African states need to find adequate military measures to protect themselves.

Notes

1. In 1978 South Africa, Zimbabwe (former Rhodesia), Mozambique, Angola, and Namibia had interrelated conflicts that many experts felt could continue into the twenty-first century. By the mid-1990s all these countries, except Angola, had domestic peace.

Stephen Stedman correctly cautions that "if Africa is home to the collapsed state (Liberia, Somalia, and Sierra Leone) it is also home to the negotiated settlement (Zimbabwe, Namibia, South Africa, and Mozambique) and the reconstituted state (Uganda and Ghana)." Stephen Stedman, "Conflict and Conciliation In Sub-Saharan Africa" in Michael Brown, ed., *The International Dimensions of Internal Conflict,* p. 235.

2. A listing of the "new leaders" usually includes Yoweri Museveni of Uganda, Paul Kagame of Rwanda, Meles Zenawi of Ethiopia, and Issaias Afewerki of Eritrea.

3. Caroline Thomas, *In Search of Security: The Third World in International Relations* (Boulder, Colo.: Lynne Rienner Publishers, 1987), p. 1. See also Jessica Tuchman Matthews, "Redefining Security," *Foreign Affairs* 68, 2 (Spring 1989).

Writers also differ over whether "security" refers only to defense of the state and its values against external or also against domestic insurgencies. See, for example, Morton Berkowitz and P. G. Bock, "National Security," in David L. Sills, ed., *International Encyclopedia of the Social Sciences.*

Domestic crime is a destabilizing influence, sometimes representing a greater threat than an armed political opposition. African crime, especially in overcrowded urban areas, often is appalling. Steven Ellis states that South Africa may "have the highest incidence of murder of any country in the world not at war" and that the country "has become Africa's capital of organized crime." Steven Ellis, "The New Frontiers of Crime in South Africa," in Bayart, Ellis, and Hibou, *The Criminalization of the State,* pp. 49-50.

4. Peter Lock, "Africa, Military Downsizing and the Security Industry," *Peace, Profit, or Plunder?* p. 21.

5. A good summary of irregular warfare is Jeffrey B. White, "Irregular Warfare: A Different Kind of Threat," *American Intelligence Journal,* 1996, p. 57.

6. Figures for defense expenditures by African states are usually incomplete and often unreliable. The *Military Balance, 1998–1999* notes that Africa's defense spending is approximately $8.8 billion for 1998–1999, but judges this figure as too low "because of lack of transparency" and "the heavy involvement of paramilitary forces in internal security and the off-budget funding of much military activity, including armed opposition groups and mercenaries." International Institute of Strategic Studies, *Military Balance, 1998–1999,* p. 236.

7. *The Military Balance, 1998–1999* lists Ethiopia as having 120,000 soldiers and Angola 114,000. Neither Somalia (which has no government) nor Mauritius have an active state military. *Military Balance,* pp. 241, 250.

8. Examples include the secessionist attempts by Katanga Province in the Congo in the early 1960s and Biafra in Nigeria during the late 1960s. Examples of warfare for control of the government include UNITA against the Angolan government (1975 to the present). Many such intrastate wars have seen foreign involvement, usually including some regional support for rebel forces. These intrastate conflicts can be seen as interstate conflict by other means.

9. More of the pre-1989 operations constituted defense rather than attack against a threatened regime. The OAU dispatched the Inter-African Force of three peacekeeping countries into Chad (1982–1983) and Zimbabwe sent some 5,000 of its troops into Mozambique to stage offensive operations against the RENAMO insurgents. Somalia's irredentist invasion of Ethiopia's Ogaden (1977) and Tanzania's overthrow of Uganda's Idi Amin (1979) were major exceptions to Africa's general acceptance of the OAU's strictures. The present Congo fighting has witnessed some nine national militaries enter the country to assist either the government or the Congolese rebels. For a typology of African conflicts, see Dana Francis, "Peacekeeping or Peace Enforcement? Conflict Intervention In Africa," World Peace Foundation, 1998, pp. 15–16, and for a useful distinction between insurgencies, see Christopher Clapham, "Introduction: Analyzing African Insurgencies" in Christopher Clapham, ed., *African Guerrillas* (Oxford: James Curry, 1998), pp. 5–9.

10. For example, all of the five foreign forces in the Congo during the early 1960s were non-African, but all of the five foreign forces in the Congo in 1997 were African.

11. Donald Snow, *Uncivil Wars,* p. 109.

12. Shelpidi, quoted in "We Are Pushing Out Rebels," *West Africa,* March 1- 14, 1999, p. 1.

13. See, for example, Crawford Young, *The African Colonial State in Comparative Perspective.* Among those scholars examining the general deleterious effects of European rule are Walter Rodney, *How Europe Underdeveloped Africa,* and Martin Kilson and Wilfred Cartey, eds., *The Africa Reader.* Peter Duignan and Lewis Gann offer a minority, procolonial rebuttal in *Burden Of Empire.*

14. "At that time [1960] the cleavages of cultural pluralism—ethnic, linguistic, regional, religious, or racial—were widely believed to be transitional tensions, to be effaced by the progressive tides of national integration." Crawford Young, "Self-Defense and the African State System," in Deng and Zartman, eds., *Conflict Resolution in Africa,* p. 333.

15. Robert Jackson and Carl Rosberg, "The Marginality of African States," in Carter and O'Meara, eds., *African Independence,* p. 51.

16. David Welsh, "Ethnicity In Sub-Saharan Africa," *International Affairs* (July 1996), p. 489.

17. Jean-François Bayart, Stephen Ellis, and Beatrice Hibou, "From Kleptocracy to the Felonious State," p. 19.

18. Marina Ottaway, "Keep Out Of Africa," *Financial Times,* February 25, 1999.

19. One may, of course, argue that underlying moral considerations often motivated Cold War strategists.

20. Richard Grimmett, "Trends in Conventional Arms Transfers in The Third World by Major Supplier, 1981–1988," Congressional Research Service, Report 89-434F, p. 36. Referred to in Raymond Copson, *Africa's Wars and Prospects for Peace,* p. 94.

21. The International Campaign to Ban Landmines estimates that 100 million mines worldwide still threaten innocent civilians and kill 12,000 yearly. The International Committee of the Red Cross believes that 20 million mines are in Angola alone, with 3 million in Mozambique and between 500,000 and 1 million in Somalia, Sudan, Ethiopia, and Eritrea. Mines reduce the amount of arable land, can divert large amounts of money to individual victims, and prevent these victims from contributing to national development. Some common mines cost $2 to produce but $1,000 to remove from the ground. Angola has perhaps 20 million buried land mines, and the highest percentage per capita of quadriplegics in the world. As noted later, weapons supplied by the Cold War's contestants have recirculated between various African wars.

22. Writing about the worldwide effect, Joseph Nye suggests that "the end of the Cold War dramatically transformed some nations, changed the external environments of others, and barely affected others." "Epilogue: The Liberal Tradition," in Diamond and Plattner, eds., *Civil-Military Relations and Democracy,* p. 151.

23. The ending abetted private South African crime. "For as long as the

country existed in its Cold War deep-freeze, it was relatively insulated against major international trends such as the narcotics trade. . . . the South African Police did not even have a unit to combat organized crime until 1993." Stephen Ellis, "The New Frontiers of Crime in South Africa," in Bayart, Ellis, and Hibou, *The Criminalization of the State,* p. 51. The dropping of trade and travel sanctions allowed the entry of a distressingly large number of sophisticated criminals, especially in the drug trade.

24. For example, the United States refused to supply Somalia's Siad Barre with the offensive equipment he sought to invade Ethiopia following his failed attempt in 1977. The Soviets and the Cubans reportedly dampened Ethiopia's desire to counterattack in retribution.

25. Morocco also supplied troops to the two operations. For the second operation, Senegal, Togo, Gabon, the Central African Republic, and Egypt contributed smaller units.

26. The disappearance of Soviet military assistance, which often was free or concessionary, meant that countries had to purchase replacements and spare parts on the more expensive open market. A Zambian officer estimates that many previously inexpensive items became two or three times more expensive. Interview, September 1999.

27. William Reno, "Mines, Money, and the Problem Of State-Building in Congo," *Issue* 26, 1 (1998).

28. Stedman, "Conflict and Conciliation in Sub-Saharan Africa," *International Dimensions,* p. 243.

29. Ibid., p. 244.

30. Edward Mansfield and Jack Snyder agree with the belief that democratic states rarely fight each other, but that during democratization, that is, the process leading to democracy, "countries become more aggressive and war-prone, not less . . . [and] formerly authoritarian states where democratic participation is on the rise, are more likely to fight wars than are stable democracies or autocracies." Mansfield and Snyder suggest that democratization creates new and unstable domestic groupings and that ambitious elites will invoke nationalism to secure political control. The upshot could be interstate conflict. This scapegoating encouraging invasion has rarely occurred in Africa. "Democratization and War," *Foreign Affairs* (May–June 1996), pp. 79–80.

31. Jeffrey Herbst, "Securing Peace in Africa," p. 14.

32. As defined by deaths per week, rather than the total accumulation.

33. Eboe Hutchful writes that "the winding down of the Cold War has [also] empowered internal constituencies within individual African states to challenge former client regimes in ways unimaginable in the past." "Understanding the African Security Crisis," in Musah and Fayemi, *Mercenaries,* p. 210.

34. "Arms sales to the region [Africa] are hard to measure as the majority of transactions involve unreported light weapons and ammunition shipments." *Military Balance,* p. 239.

35. Bureau of Intelligence and Research, "Arms and Conflict in Africa," U.S. Department of State, 1999, p. 3.

36. "Monitoring state-to-state weapons transfers is relatively easy because there normally is only a seller and a buyer. The gray and black arms trafficking

businesses are significantly more complex operations involving African and non-African, corporate, and individual suppliers and an array of transshipment points, brokers and financiers." Bureau of Intelligence and Research, "Arms and Conflict in Africa." p. 8.

Weaponry started becoming exceptionally widespread by the mid-1980s. A Ugandan educator in the mid-1980s recalls that "submachine guns could be traded for a carton of cigarettes, and a few packets of cigarettes could buy a hand gun. Ammunition was a more common commodity than many consumer goods." W. Senteza-Kajubi, "Background to War and Violence In Uganda," in Cole P. Dodge and Magne Ruandalen, eds., *War, Violence and Children in Uganda* (Oslo: Norwegian University Press, 1987), p. 39.

37. Small arms generally include single-man, portable weaponry: guns of 50 caliber or less, rocket-propelled launchers, mortars, and land mines.

38. Christopher Smith, "Light Weapons and the International Arms Trade," *Small Arms Management and Peacekeeping in Southern Africa,* Disarmament and Conflict Resolution Project, UNIDIR, 1996, p. 1.

39. See, for example, "Russian Arms Hot Sellers. Weapons Industry Not Too Particular About Its Customers," *Rocky Mountain News,* October 13, 1997. Human Rights Watch's Arms Project notes that Sudan's arms trade "appears to be a largely profit-driven trade, rather than politically-motivated intervention. The largest of these arms merchants, China, also deals freely with Sudan's hostile neighbors, Eritrea and Ethiopia." Both Iran and Iraq supply weaponry to the Sudanese government. Human Rights Watch, "Global Trade, Local Impact. Arms Transfers to All Sides in the Civil War in Sudan," August 1998, p. 2.

40. Human Rights Watch, "Bulgaria. Money Talks: Arms Dealing With Human Rights Abusers," April 1999, p. 12.

41. Ibid., p. 3.

42. Nonattributable source, "Conference on Nigeria," Meridian International Center, Washington, D.C., May 5, 1999.

43. "Revealed: Ex-Soviet Officer Turns Sanctions Buster," *Financial Times,* July 10, 2000.

44. Gérard Prunier, *The Rwanda Crisis: History of a Genocide* (New York: Columbia University Press, 1995). p. 119.

45. The *Military Balance* reports that South Africa exported weaponry to Congo-Brazzaville, Togo, Eritrea, Democratic Republic of Congo, Uganda, and Rwanda. *Military Balance,* p. 239. In April 1998 the South African government stated that it had sold weaponry worth some $656 million to ninety-one countries since 1994. "Asia trip Promises S. African arms trade windfall," Reuters. Http://www.infoseek.com/Content?arn

Governments increasingly use private weapons merchants, and Kathi Austin notes a geopolitical advantage: "Traffickers give foreign governments plausible deniability. Today, Africa is being 'weaponized' by private arms networks, which . . . is sometimes seen as an instrument of foreign policy, a way to keep the playing field level." Kathi Austin, "The Illicit Gun Trade, Fanning Flames of Conflict," the *Washington Post,* January 24, 1999.

46. The U.S. Defense Department estimates that at least half a dozen sub-Saharan states "are capable of producing light arms and their production capa-

bility far exceeds their own needs." "Africa: Military and Security Issues
Through 2010. Prepared by the Defense Intelligence Officer and His Team."
January 2000, p. 5.

See also, "Arms Flows to Central Africa/Great Lakes," Fact Sheet
Released by the Bureau of Intelligence and Research, U.S. Department of State,
November 1999. Http://www.state.gov/www/global/arms/bureau_pm/
fs_9911_armsflows.html

Nigeria's once promising weapons production reportedly has fallen into
significant disrepair by the late 1990s but reportedly produces the NR-1, the
Nigerian army's assault rifle, as well as all the 7.62mm ammunition that ECO-
MOG needed in Sierra Leone.

47. Uganda's invasion of Congo has seen five new air companies charter-
ing their services to the Ugandan military.

48. Public radio broadcasts have benefited governments more. The obvious example is Radio Television "Libre des Mille Collines," which incited
Hutu mobs against Tutsis and some Hutus during Rwanda's genocide.

49. Http://members.tripod.com/~lordsmovement/index.html

50. Adolescent Dinka males traditionally had the responsibility of guarding cattle with spears against the Muraheleen. When the Muraheleen began
appearing with firearms, the Dinka obtained rifles for the child guards. See
Famine in Sudan, p. 122.

51. Austin, "The Illicit Gun Trade."

52. Paul Richards believes that recent increasing social dislocation in
Africa—often fed by conflict and by a deliberate rebel strategy "to detach
youth from local civil society"—have increased the supply of often rootless
youth to opportunistic insurgencies. Paul Richards, "Rebellion in Liberia and
Sierra Leone: A Crisis of Youth," in Furley, *Conflict in Africa,* p. 135.

Richards believes that "the political culture of youth" is "a key to understanding the spread of endemic low-intensity warfare in both countries [Liberia
and Sierra Leone]." Richards, Ibid.

53. The U.K. Coalition to Stop the Use of Child Soldiers, referred to in
"Report Cites Plethora of Child Soldiers," the *Washington Post,* April 20, 1999.

54. Human Rights Watch, *Easy Prey: Child Soldiers In Liberia* (New
York, 1994), pp. 2–3.

55. Interviews, London and Washington, 1999. About 5,000 are in the
RUF, while 2,500 are with the government-assisted irregulars, the Civil
Defence Forces. A recent case is that of Namibian civilians, including women
and children, being forcibly recruited by the Angolan military to fight against
Jonas Savimbi's UNITA. "Exposed: Namibia's Child Soldiers," *Sunday Times,*
January 23, 2000.

56. Child soldiers may have some advantages. As a former child soldier
recalled, "Kids have more stamina, are better at surviving in the bush, do not
complain and follow directions." Quoted in Ilene Cohn and Guy S. Goodwin-
Gill, *Child Soldiers: the Role of Children in Armed Conflict* (Oxford:
Clarendon Press, 1994), p. 26. Some writers believe that child soldiers are more
difficult to control.

57. Paul Richards, in Furley, *Conflict in Africa,* pp. 136, 137.

58. Comfort Ero, "Vigilantes, Civil Defence Forces, and Militia Groups: The Other Side of the Privatisation of Security in Africa," *Conflict Trends,* June 2000. Http://www.accord.org.za/publications

59. Juan Linz, "The Process of Breakdown," in Juan Linz and Alfred Stepan, eds., *The Breakdown of Democratic Regimes* (Baltimore: Johns Hopkins Press, 1978), p. 58.

60. Prunier, *The Rwanda Crisis,* p. 231.

61. Kaldor writes that paramilitaries and self-defense units "lack the hierarchy, order and vertical command systems that have been typical of guerrilla forces." Kaldor, *New and Old Ways,* p. 95.

62. See, for example, "IRIN Special Report: The Caprivi Secessionist Crisis," UN Integrated Regional Network, August 9, 1999. Http://www. africanews.org/south/namibia/stories/19990809_feat7.html and "Complex Motives in the Caprevi," *Business Day,* August 4, 1999.

63. Created in the late 1970s, as the two Zimbabwean guerrilla groups were increasingly succeeding against the Rhodesian government, Pfumo reVhanu consisted mostly of individuals who would not have had the qualifications to enter the regular military. The resource-stretched government provided them with inadequate training and support and placed them into the inhospitable Gokwe region of Matabeleland. Defeats at the hands of the guerrillas weakened whatever unit integrity existed and many of the irregulars began pillaging or aiding the guerrillas. An overt mutiny by them was put down by gunfire from Rhodesian helicopters. Interview with ex-Rhodesian Selous Scout, July 1999.

64. *Famine in Sudan,* p. 13.

65. "War Not Over for the Mai-Mai." *Business Day,* September 16, 1999. Http://www.africanews.org/...go-kinshasa/stories/19990916_feat4.html. The Kabila government in the Congo has provided weaponry to the Mayi-Mayi, a collection of various militias that have no deep loyalty to the Kabila government and could later turn against the Kinshasa government.

66. Human Rights Watch, "Angola Unravels," p. 40.

67. This certainly has not only been an Africa-only view. "Ethnic antagonisms helped fuel the conflict," Steven David writes about the former Yugoslavia, "but they would not have led to war without the collapse of authority." Steven David, "Internal War: Causes and Cures," *World Politics* (July 1997), p. 558. Michael Ignatieff overstates the issue when contending that "now [following the Cold War] these states have been left to their own devices and bereft of outside support they have broken up along ethnic and tribal lines. In these regions, low-intensity conflict has become a way of life. War, like a virus, has worked its way into the very tissue of the Great Lakes regions, part of West Africa, the southern Caucasus and the Afghan region. It is the major employer, the chief economic activity. All power comes from the barrel of an AK-47." Michael Ignatieff, "The Gods of War," *New York Review of Books,* October 9, 1997, p. 12.

But whether an actual increase in ethnic hostilities and conflicts has occurred remains unclear. Patrick Glynn and Francis Fukayama debated the issue in *Commentary.* Patrick Glynn, "The Age Of Balkanization," *Commentary,* July 1993, and Francis Fukayama, "Against the New Pessimism,"

Commentary, February 1994. David Tucker sides with Fukayama in "Fighting Barbarians," *Parameters,* Summer 1998.

68. Frances Deng, Sadikiel Kimaro, Terrence Lyons, Donald Rothchild, and I. William Zartman, *Sovereignty as Responsibility,* p. 21.

69. Jack Snyder, "Nationalism and the Crisis of the Post-Soviet State," *Survival* (35, I), Spring 1993, p. 5. Quoted in Mohammed Ayoob, *The Third World Security Predicament,* p. 171.

70. Referring to the "rise and flowering of ethnic militia and politically-inspired killer mobs," Nigeria's *Post Express* states that "the political elite of each ethnic faction has been emboldened by the virtual collapse of most institutions of national cohesion." "Ethnic Militias and National Security," *Post Express,* July 28, 2000.

71. This is not limited to Africa. Ignatieff writes that "in Afghanistan and Chechnya wars that began as genuine national uprisings against foreign occupation have degenerated into vicious fights for territory, resources, drugs, and arms among militias who are often no different from criminal gangs." Ignatieff, *Warrior's Honor,* p. 125. Admittedly, the distinction between political protest and economic crime is sometimes blurry.

Political or economic grievances may motivate people to join rebel groups but they or the groups rarely use these complaints as a raison d'être. Nor do they actively campaign for public acceptance or create local political organizations. This markedly contrasts with the liberation movements of the 1960s and 1970s.

72. RENAMO, or the Mozambique National Resistence Movement, was clearly more of a military than a political cause during the 1980s. Neither the United States nor the Soviet Union supported this group, which initially relied upon support from Rhodesia and later from apartheid South Africa.

73. Copson, *Africa's War,* p. 84.

74. Kaldor, *The Old and the New,* p. 82.

75. Donald Snow, *Uncivil Wars,* p. ix, and Hutchful in Musah and Fayemi, *Mercenaries,* p. 219.

76. Bayart, Ellis, and Hibou, *The Criminalization of the State,* p. 18.

77. "Taylor's skill at controlling and cultivating sources of foreign exchange . . . has allowed him to arm his soldiers and conquer areas with easily exploitable resources." William Reno, "The Business of War in Liberia, *Current History* (May 1996), p. 212. RUF obtained perhaps $5 million worth of diamonds that it then moved through Liberia and Guinea for foreign sale. "Loot, not better government, has motivated the psychotically brutal guerrillas of Sierra Leone." "The Business of War in Africa," *New York Times,* August 8, 1999.

78. The RUF earns between $30 million and $125 million from illegal diamond sales yearly, according to Richard Holbrooke, U.S. ambassador to the UN. "U.S. Accuses Liberia and Burkina Faso of Fueling Sierra Leone War," Associated Press, August 1, 2000.

79 "Angola II: Deadly Diamonds," *Africa Confidential,* April 16, 1999, p. 7.

80. Human Rights Watch, "Angola Unravels," pp. 132–133.

81. Interviews, U.S. State Department, October 1999.

82. Bayart, Ellis, and Hibou, *The Criminalization of the State,* p. 26.

83. Snow, *Uncivil Wars,* pp. 106, 178.

84. "UN Sees Violation of a Diamond Ban by Angolan Rebels." *New York Times,* March 11, 2000.

85. Clapham, "Introduction: Analysing African Insurgencies," *African Guerrillas,* p. 5.

86. Ibid.

87. Lock, "Africa, Military Downsizing," p. 30.

88. William Reno, "The Business of War in Liberia."

89. Ibrahim Abdullah, "Bush Path to Destruction: The Origin and Character of the Revolutionary United Front," *Journal of Modern African Studies,* pp. 208, 222.

90. Ibid., p. 235. Dislike of the often barbaric methods of RENAMO or the RUF should not overlook the previous regimes' developmental shortcomings. Rebel groups such as the RUF or Mozambique's RENAMO have lacked a defining ideology, strong leadership, or national organization but as political "lightning rods" still have attracted some following in reaction against the status quo rather than as a force for specific change.

91. "Profits Fuel Angola's War," *Guardian Weekly,* July 8–14, 1999. The article mentions the commission claim by *Angolense,* "a newspaper sympathetic to the MPLA [government]." Human Rights Watch writes that "in 1998 senior Angolan government officials [also] assisted UNITA in its procurement of fuel." "Angola Unravels," p. 130.

92. Clapham, "African Security Systems: Privatisation and the Scope for Mercenary Activity," in Mills and Stremlau, *The Privatization of Security,* p 35. Jonas Savimbi, leader of Angola's UNITA's rebel movement for some thirty years, has discarded his Cold War ideological trappings in favor of overt personal and economic goals. UNITA's struggle for military and political control is probably unwinnable, yet its economic gains are considerable. UNITA reportedly earned $3.7 billion between 1992 and 1999 by controlling most of Angola's diamond-producing areas. Some Western intelligence officials speculate that some high-ranking Angolan officers who have benefited financially from the continued struggle harbor ambivalence toward a peaceful settlement.

93. Heike Behrend, "War in Northern Uganda," in Clapham, *African Guerrillas,* p. 116.

94. Beltekheksport, a private Belarussian company, sold some twenty-eight BMP-1 armored personnel carriers to the Angolan government and "chartered a Ukranian Air Force transport plane to fly the cargo." Human Rights Watch, "Angola Unravels," pp. 103–104.

95. Defense Intelligence Agency, "Africa: Military and Security Issues," p. 5.

96. Sergio Vieira de Mello, the UN under secretary-general in charge of emergency relief, worries that "in internal conflicts, often—if not always—helping civilian populations that live in territory controlled by the adversary is almost automatically seen as assisting the enemy. This is a fundamental change in contemporary conflict." "The World Expected Peace, It Found a New Brutality," *New York Times,* January 24, 1999.

97. Snow, *Uncivil Wars,* pp. 145–147.

98. "Olive Branch from the Rebels," *New African,* June 1999, p. 20. Relief experts believe that many amputation victims died from hemorrhagic shock before reaching medical facilities. An apparent prisoner of the RUF recollects that "life was ruthless and very rough and women were frequently raped. Half a dozen RUF members would fall on a woman and subject her to repeated rapes. No one enforced any form of law whatsoever. RUF fighters were most of the time under the influence of drugs. They did what pleased them." "Life with the RUF . . . a Woman Abducted by the RUF," *West Africa,* March 1–14, 1999, pp. 125–127. Reports indicate equally serious human rights atrocities in Uganda's Lord's Resistance Army.

99. China was the primary military provider to FRELIMO during its guerrilla campaign against the Portuguese. The Warsaw Pact supplied the Zimbabwean Peoples' Revolutionary Army, the armed wing of (ZAPU), and the Peoples' Republic of China aided ZANLA, the military wing of the ZANU. The Warsaw Pact assisted Umkhonto we Sizwe, the South African ANC's military wing.

100. Snow, *Uncivil Wars,* p. 147.

Ayoob reaches the same general conclusion: "By removing the restraints that had been imposed upon local protagonists by . . . the superpowers, the end of superpower rivalry may have simultaneously signaled the beginning of an era of less restrained and more bloody conflicts in the Third World." Ayoob, *The Third World Security Predicament,* p. 141.

101. Médecins sans Frontières, "Humanitarianism Under Fire," 1998 (undated).

102. Clapham, "Introduction: Analysing African Insurgencies," in *African Guerrillas,* p. 16.

103. See Mark Malan, "The Crisis in External Response," in Cilliers and Mason, *Peace, Profit or Plunder?* p. 40.

In March 1997 Kabila seized 15,000 gallons of fuel from the UN high commissioner for refugees to fly his troops for fighting at Lubumbashi. His forces also stole trucks and food. Mobutu's FAZ hijacked UN-charted planes to carry weaponry to Rwandan Hutus who were living in UN-administered refugee camps. Aid organizations increasingly have placed themselves in harm's way.

104. "This is European balance-of-power [maneuvering] come to the heart of Africa," notes a U.S. expert commenting upon conflicts in central and southern Africa. "Up in Arms in Southern Africa," *Washington Post,* October 5, 1998. See also Col. Terrence Taylor, editor of *IISS Military Balance,* in "Changing Face of Conflict in Africa," Panafrican News Agency, October 22, 1998.

105. At the peak of its involvement in 1998, Zimbabwe fielded between 6,000 and 10,000 troops, Angola about 5,000, Sudan and Chad about 1,500 each, and Namibia perhaps 1,000 fighting for Kabila in Congo. Fighting against Kabila were Rwandans, Ugandans, and several Congolese rebel groups. Private soldiers, perhaps several hundred mostly from South Africa or Eastern Europe, split in their affiliations.

106. "A War Turned Free-for-All Tears at Africa's Center," *New York Times,* December 6, 1998.

107. "The unmaking of Congo points to several trends reshaping Africa and its component states: the privatization of diplomacy alongside the growth of informal business networks; the irrelevance of the Organisation of African Unity's strictures on interfering in the affairs of sovereign states and the inviolability of colonial borders; [and] the primacy of personal (often criminal) enrichment over nation state strategy." "Emerging Maps: Africa Scrambles for Africa," *Africa Confidential* 40, 1 (January 8, 1999), p. 1.

108. Onyeonoro S. Kamanu, "Security and the Right to Self-Determination: An OAU Dilemma," *Journal of Modern African Studies,* 1974.

109. An excellent study is Deng et al., *Sovereignty as Responsibility.*

110. The OAU Charter quoted in Jon Woronoff, *Organizing African Unity,* p. 643.

111. The only significant boundary change has been the splitting-off of Eritrea from Ethiopia in 1993. The subsequent Ethiopian-Eritrean war is one of Africa's few interstate conflicts fought primarily over boundary issues.

112. "Without an external or effective regional brake on their activities, emergent local powers can and will take the military option when they believe their vital interests are at stake," Defense Intelligence Agency, "African Military and Security Issues," p. 3.

113. The United States did suspend military-to-military relations for two years. The OAU suggested a peacekeeping force but few, if any, African states were willing to provide funds or materiel, and France declined to support such a force. France's policy of probable support of Sassou-Nguesso's (and Angola's) toppling of Lissouba is interesting but perhaps exceptional, given France's worry over Lissouba's cooperation with the U.S.-based Occidental Petroleum. See John F. Clark, "Foreign Intervention in the Civil War of the Congo Republic," *Issue* (1998).

114. Peace talks over Congo revealed regional animosities. Congo's foreign minister opined that "Rwanda has a problem of space. The danger which is lurking is the ambition of our Rwanda brothers. It is very dangerous. They have expansionist ambitions." It was further alleged that Uganda, Rwanda, and Burundi had a "hidden agenda" to massacre Hutus. "Delegates From DRC, Rwanda, Uganda Hurl Abuse," Panafrican News Agency, October 27, 1998. Http:www.africanews.org/PANA/news/19981027

115. Marina Ottaway, "Post-Imperial Africa at War," *Current History,* May 1999, p. 205.

116. *Cape Times,* June 10, 1998, quoted in Hutchful, "Understanding the African Security Crisis," in Fayemi and Musah, *Mercenaries,* p. 218. Kofi Annan echoes the thought: "State sovereignty . . . is being redefined. . . . States are now widely understood to be instruments at the service of their people, and not vice versa." Kofi Annan, "Two Concepts of Sovereignty," *The Economist,* September 18, 1999.

117. William Reno, *Warlord Politics and African States* (Boulder, Colo.: Lynne Rienner Publishers, 1998), p. 2.

Some observers speculate that Taylor is interested in subverting other West African states, including Guinea, for a combination of political and economic reasons. Brig. Gen. Max Khobe, a Nigerian officer serving as Sierra Leone's

chief of defense staff, maintains that "what [Taylor's supporters] have promised
. . . was that after the capture, and therefore change of government in Freetown,
the next place was to be Guinea. After Guinea, the rebels will come to Ghana
since they have their troops in Sierra Leone. Then, after Ghana it will be
Nigeria." "Military Probes Liability for Freetown," *Guardian* (Nigeria, undated) http://www.ngrguardiannews.com

Other countries reportedly also lend some support. Well-placed Guinean
officials (possibly including the government's "Red Berets" special operations
unit) helps protect the RUF's Sierra Leone-Guinea diamond route. Burkina
Faso, possibly with Libyan encouragement, has supplied several hundred fighters to the RUF. Muammar Qaddafi may have shifted his revolutionary desire
away from the Middle East by 1998 and toward Africa. Western intelligence
sources believe that Libya had supplied several dozen advisors and some equipment to the RUF.

118. "Fatal Transactions: Liberia Stokes African Gem War," *Financial
Times,* July 10, 2000.

119. "Congo: War Turns Commercial," *The Economist,* October 24, 1998,
p. 43.

120. Some analysts believe that Mugabe deployed troops into Congo to
uphold the OAU's Charter and its principle of supporting sovereign governments. Yet Mugabe had materially assisted Laurent Kabila's guerrilla forces
against President Mobutu.

121. "World: Africa—Zimbabwe Accused of Economic Colonialism,"
BBC Online Network, October 1, 1999. Http...//news.bbc.co.uk./hi/english/
world/africa/newsid

122. "Zimbabwe to Build Railway to DRC," Panafrican News Agency,
October 24, 1999. Http://www.africanews.org/...go-kinshasa/stories/
19991024_feat1.html

123. U.S. State Department Bureau of Intelligence and Research, "Arms
Flows to Central Africa/Great Lakes."

124. Ibid. The *Wall Street Journal* describes Chiyangwa as "a leading
businessman and the head of a Zimbabwean government economic committee."
"General Partners: Zimbabwe's Elite Turns Strife in Nearby Congo into a Quest
for Riches," *Wall Street Journal,* October 9, 1998. This clearly collides with
Kabila's insistence that "we pay the bills, we buy all the materiel for the planes,
pay the troops' salaries in hard currency. . . . So these people [foreign allies] do
not have to take anything from their budget." "Kabila Says Congo Picking up
War Bills of Allies," Reuters, March 17, 1999.

125. "Congo Names Zimbabwean Head of Mining Concern." The *Daily
Telegraph* remarked, "That's handing over your most valuable resources to a
foreigner. You would not agree to that unless you owed someone a huge
favor."

126. Billy Rautenbach, who heads up the Zimbabwean-based Ridgepointe
Company, is Gecamines chief executive. According to *Africa Confidential,*
"Profits from the sale of Gecamine's copper and cobalt are divided 62.5 per
cent to the Congo government and 37.5 per cent to Ridgepointe. From the government's share, 20–30 per cent of profits are meant to go the Zimbabwe government in part payment for its military support. Business people party to these

transactions say that some highly placed Congolese and Zimbabweans have received *ex gratia* payments from both Ridgepointe and Congo." "Zimbabwe/Congo-K. Rhodies to the Rescue," *Africa Confidential,* November 5, 1999, p. 5.

127. Some government agencies did benefit. The state-owned Zimbabwean Defense Industries in late 1998 had a $53 million contract to supply Congo's army.

128. See U.S. State Department Bureau of Intelligence and Research, "Arms Flows to Central Africa/Great Lakes." Other sources believe that General Zvimavashe's brother heads the family's transport company (Zvimavashe Transport). The distinction may be largely irrelevant, given that the contract strongly suggests the use of public office for personal (or family) gain.

129. See, for example, "As SADC Split Deepens, Kabila's Allies Renew Commitment to War," *Zimbabwe Independent,* April 16, 1999. Http://www.africanews.org/south/zimbabwe/stories/19990416_feat8.html

130. Quoted in "Zimbabwe Accused of 'Economic Colonialism,'" BBC Online Network, October 1, 1999. Http://news.bbc.co.uk/hi/english/world/africa/newsid

131. "General Partners: Zimbabwe's Elite Turns Strife in Nearby Congo into a Quest for Riches," *Wall Street Journal,* October 9, 1998.

132. "Country Report Zimbabwe," *Economist* Intelligence Unit, August 11, 2000. Http://db/eiu.com/report

133. Ibid.

134. Uganda Airlines canceling plans for a joint venture with Air Zimbabwe in late 1998 is one such example. See "Air Zimbabwe Deal Soured by Politics," http://www/bday.co.za/98/1116/world/w24.htm

135. Cornwell states that intervention forces "are living off the local population, stealing food and extorting money." "A War Turned Free-for-All," *New York Times.*

136. "Smuggling Booms at Entebbe," *New Vision* (Kampala), reprinted by Africa News Service, March 28, 1999.

137. "Uganda's Congolese Treasure Trove," *New African,* May 29, 1999, p. 20. See Chapter Three for Liberia. *The Economist* mentions Uganda in "A Dirty War That Can't Be Won," *The Economist,* October 4, 1997, p. 52, and Sierra Leone in "War Without End," p. 48 ("Intervention has brought Nigeria international approval, and gained its troops access to Sierra Leone's diamond fields"). See also remarks by Prof. John Makumbe in "Combatants Feel Congo Effect," *Washington Post,* January 29, 1999.

138. Interview with U.S. State Department official, November 1999.

139. "Uganda's Glow Fades," *Washington Post,* February 7, 1999.

140. "Congo-Kinshasa. Precious Little Peace," *Africa Confidential,* November 5, 1999, p. 4.

141. Ibid.

142. Defense Intelligence Agency, "Africa: Military and Security Issues," p. 6.

143. Ibid., p. 5.

144. Ibid.

145. "Oil output of 780,000 barrels per day produces little revenue. Almost every oil cargo this year . . . went directly into repayments on earlier loans, leaving almost nothing for the pot . . . roughly three years' worth of future oil production was earmarked for loan repayments." "Angola: Oil-Fired Warfare," *Africa Confidential,* May 14, 1999.

146. U.S. State Department Bureau of Intelligence and Research, "Arms Flows to Central Africa/Great Lakes," November 1999. Http://www.state.gov/ www/global/arms/bureau_pm/fs_9911_armsflows.html

147. "Up in Arms in Southern Africa," *Washington Post,* October 5, 1998. "Relations between Zimbabwe and South Africa are strained over the war in Congo and a contest of wills between Mr. Mandela and Mr. Mugabe for moral leadership in Africa." "Fugitive Zimbabwe ex-President Has Odd Meeting with Mandela," *New York Times,* December 4, 1998. Numerous analysts believe that Mugabe, who had enjoyed his reputation as a leader of southern Africa's front-line states during the anti-apartheid struggle, felt upstaged by Nelson Mandela's release and subsequent worldwide adulation. Some of the rivalry has occurred within SADC's institutions. During 1998–1999 Mandela served as chairman of SADC, whereas Mugabe had been chairman of SADC's Organ for Defence, Politics, and Security. Mugabe has worked to provide the organ with greater autonomy to make SADC security decisions, whereas Mandela and others believe that SADC, and not the organ, should have responsibility for security policy.

148. "Overhaul of UN Peacekeeping Is Urged, *Washington Post,* August 24, 2000. Among the recommendations were authorization of UN missions only with firm troop commitments, deployment within 30 days for most peace-keeping forces, and designated units within individual militaries for rapid deployment.

149. "West African Defence, Security Chiefs End Meeting," Panafrican News Agency, July 21, 2000. Http://www.africnews.org/PANA/news/2000

150. "G.I.s to Be Sent to Train Africans for Sierra Leone," *New York Times,* August 9, 2000.

151. Ibid.

152. Robert R. Fowler, "United Nations Security Council Report," Http:/www.un.org/news/dh/latest/angolareport_eng.html.2000

153. "U.S. Urges War Crimes Court for Sierra Leone," *Washington Post,* July 28, 2000.

154. Major works reflecting this school include Boutros Boutros-Ghali's *Agenda for Peace,* and the Commission on Global Governance's *Our Global Neighborhood* (New York: Oxford University Press, 1995). *Agenda for Peace* suggested that the UN acquire a standing military and that the UN become involved in Charter 7 activities, that is, peace enforcement. Brian Urquhart, the UN's former under secretary-general, hoped that "the new role of the Security Council, functioning for the first time as a collegial body as anticipated in the Charter rather than as a battleground for the great powers, opens up a number of possibilities for regional conflict management." Quoted in Terrence Lyons, *Somalia: State Collapse, Multilateral Intervention, and Strategies for Political Reconstruction* (Washington, D.C.: Brookings Institution Press, 1995), p. 4.

155. Bernard Kouchner, minister of humanitarian affairs, quoted in Minear and Guillot, p. 19.

156. Frances Deng and Larry Minear, *The Challenges of Famine Relief: Emerging Opportunities in the Sudan* (Washington, D.C.: Brookings Institution Press, 1992), p. 8.

Boutros-Ghali wrote that "the authority of the United Nations system to act in this field [human rights] would rest on the consensus that social peace is as important as strategic or political peace. There is an obvious connection between democratic practices—such as the rule of law and transparency in decision-making—and the achievement of true peace and security in any new and stable political order." *Agenda for Peace,* p. 34.

157. Stephen Stedman, "The New Interventionists," *Foreign Affairs,* September 1992, p. 3.

158. Mary Anderson, "Humanitarian NGOs in Conflict Intervention," in Chester Crocker and Fen Osler Hampson, *Managing Global Chaos: Sources of and Responsibilities to International Conflict* (Washington, D.C.: U.S. Institute of Peace, 1996), p. 346.

159. Ibid. p. 348.

160. Blechman, "Emerging from the Intervention Dilemma," in Crocker and Hampson, *Managing Global Chaos,* p. 289.

161. Betts, "The Delusion of Impartial Intervention," in Crocker and Hampson, *Managing Global Chaos,* pp. 333–342.

162. Malan, "The Crisis in External Response," p. 47.

163. A former U.S. defense analyst on Africa comments about "the inability/unwillingness of Western intelligence agencies to devote sufficient analytical resources . . . [When confronted with a crisis] what the agencies do is to 'surge,' which involves assigning everyone from secretaries to administrators to analytical positions. 'Surged' personnel have no knowledge of the area in question yet they provide assessments to policy makers as soon as they get on the job." Private correspondence, February 1999.

164. Richard Betts writes of an "Olympian presumption," his term for the belief that a foreign force can "be both limited and impartial, because weighing in on one side of a local struggle undermines the legitimacy and effectiveness of outside involvement." Betts, "The Delusion of Impartial Intervention," p. 333.

Forced impartiality affected Gen. Roméo Dallaire, Canada's commander of UNAMIR, the UN force in Rwanda. He turned to alcohol as a result of his frustrations from not being able to save doomed Tutsis during the Rwandan genocide. He characterized his feeling of military impotence as a "new generation of peacekeeping injury." Canada's *National Post* described it as "the chilling result of being trained to do a job, being sent to do it and then being held back at the last minute by convoluted and frequently changing rules of engagement, which most often prevent soldiers from engaging in combat." "Price of Waging Peace," *National Post,* July 15, 2000." Http://www.nationalpost.co

165. John Ruggie compares the two: "Peacekeepers are not intended to create the peace they are asked to safeguard. They accept the balance of forces on the ground and work with it. In short, peacekeeping is a device to guarantee transparency, to reassure each side that the other is carrying out its promises. It

is a noncombatant mission carried out by military personnel." John Gerald Ruggie, *Winning the Peace: America and World Order in the New Era,* p. 94.

166. Some contingents in Somalia (Italian most notably) concluded secret agreements with various Somali factions. As a result, UN contingents sometimes found themselves opposing each other's goals.

The financial price to the UN of Somalia's and Cambodia's peacekeeping missions—about $2 billion for each—dampened UN enthusiasm for future interventions.

167. William J. Durch, "Introduction to Anarchy: Humanitarian Intervention and State-Building in Somalia," *UN Peacekeeping, American Politics and the Uncivil Wars of the 1990s,* p. 329.

168. I am using John Ruggie's definition of multilateralism, which is "coordinating relations among three or more states in accordance with certain principles." John Gerald Ruggie, *Multilateralism Matters,* p. 8. Finnemore, "Constructing Norms," p. 176.

169. The intervention force comprises units from other countries whose major allegiance is to the multinational force and who are permanently assembled together. A designated force can call upon specific multinational units that sometimes train together and have established common doctrine and materiel stockpiles, but that permanently reside in their own countries and whose duties usually are for their own governments. One major advantage of a permanent force would be its higher level of competence, given its greater time to train together. A major disadvantage could be the loss to a national government of a portion of its force. Relatively high financial costs pose another problem.

170. An intervention force needs units that are well supplied and well trained and that possess specialist skills in engineering, maintenance, signals, and logistics. Yet inclusion in the force also sends a political message, an implicit acceptance of a particular regime, and may cause problems within the multinational force. Additionally, transfers of technology/knowledge to a regime's military to gain or assist in its multinational cooperation will enhance repressive capabilities in that country. Military assistance to a nation having a competent military but a woeful human rights record may cause domestic political concerns for the donor. Should the West aid the militaries of nondemocratic states? Selection into the force confers an implicit political acceptance of a particular regime: Should a multinational force use only military criteria to determine leadership? This rarely succeeds, given the forces' varied military capabilities, the lack of incentives, the lack of joint training/exercises, or the scarcity of common strategy, tactics, and equipment. In other words, too many differently trained cooks suddenly converge in a relatively unfamiliar kitchen.

171. John Gerald Ruggie, *Winning The Peace,* pp. 93–94.

172. Lt. Gen. Francis Briquemont, quoted in Ruggie, *Winning the Peace,* p. 92.

173. Prunier, *The Rwanda Crisis,* p. 274.

174. Dallaire quoted in Col. Scott Feil, "Could 5,000 Peacekeepers Have Saved 500,000 Rwandans?: Early Intervention Reconsidered." *ISD Reports,* Georgetown University, April 1997, p. 1.

175. The NATO air attacks against the former Yugoslavia would appear to argue against this point. It should be noted, however, the special historical con-

cern about Balkan insecurity for the world community, and that NATO was strongly hesitant to employ ground troops for fear of public opinion turning against NATO's involvement, Even assuming a non-African willingness to employ air power in Africa, it likely would have minimal success against decentralized, rurally based, and nonmechanized irregular forces.

176. John Keegan, *A History of Warfare* (New York: Vintage, 1994), p. 59. John Mueller believes that warfare may suffer the same fate as dueling: once acceptable physical aggression that now faces social opprobrium. John Mueller, *Retreat from Doomsday: The Obsolescence of Major War.*

177. Ignatieff, " The Gods of War." Patrick Morgan, "Multinationalism and Security: Prospects In Europe," in Ruggie, *Multilateralism Matters,* notes various other reasons for Western views about war's inutility. See also Edward Luttwak, "Toward Post-Heroic Warfare," *Foreign Affairs,* May–June, 1995. Stephen J. Cimbala, "Military Persuasion and the American Way of Life," *Strategic Review,* Fall 1997, pp. 33–43. Edward Luttwak believes that the decline of certain American social indices, notably "high birthrates, large families and a hypernationalist population that sanctioned with equanimity" will work against the United States militarily intervening in relatively unimportant states." Luttwak, "Toward Post-Heroic Warfare," p. 115.

178. Ottaway, "Post-Imperial Africa at War," p. 207.

179. The UN's former secretary-general, Boutros Boutros-Ghali, modified his 1992 *Agenda for Peace* and increasingly urged more cooperation by African states with the UN.

180. Some of this directive's underscored criteria for intervention were a clear threat to U.S. national interests, clear objectives and available means for intervention, and a method for successfully departing the situation. For an analysis of the directive and its international context, see Adam Roberts, "The Crisis in UN Peacekeeping," Crocker and Hampson, *Managing Global Chaos.*

181. Ignatieff, "The Gods of War," p. 13.

182. Two months into the genocide, a U.S. State Department spokesperson stated that "although there have been acts of genocide in Rwanda, all the murders cannot be put into that category." Quoted in Prunier, *The Rwanda Crisis,* p. 274, emphasis in the original.

183. Department of Defense personnel disagree as to whether the U.S. Air Force could have jammed the small and portable radio stations. Interviews, October 1999 and August 2000.

4

ECOMOG AND REGIONAL PEACEKEEPING

The corrosive effects of personal rule on national militaries, as well as changes in Africa's post–Cold War security, helped to spark and then prolong the Liberian and Sierra Leonean conflicts. West Africa's institutional reaction, in the form of ECOMOG (Economic Community of West African States Ceasefire Monitoring Group), dramatized the pitfalls of using often unprofessional forces for ad hoc multinational intervention. Established in 1990, ECOMOG became Africa's first permanent multinational peacekeeping force. This chapter focuses on the Liberian conflict, which caused ECOMOG's founding and also presaged many of contemporary Africa's security problems.[1] The chapter then follows ECOMOG to Sierra Leone and concludes with a glance at the future of regional peacekeeping in Africa.[2]

The absence of any significant armed threat until the early 1990s allowed rulers in both Liberia and Sierra Leone to disdain their militaries' functional autonomy. Instead, they encouraged their armies' political loyalty, often through "ethnicization," at the expense of technical capabilities. Personal rule in Liberia led to the woefully incompetent and repressive Armed Forces of Liberia (AFL). President Samuel Doe's ethnicization of the AFL during the 1980s encouraged its repression of civilians and then its battlefield ineptness. Both of these factors greatly assisted Charles Taylor's National Patriotic Front of Liberia (NPFL) to gain quick control of much of the country in early 1990. The damaging of the civil-military divide by several Sierra Leonean presidents, most notably Siaka Stevens and Joseph Momoh, eliminated whatever degree of professionalism the British had instilled. The Republic of Sierra Leonean Military Force proved abysmally incapable of repelling the RUF insurgency. Similarly, the mediocre Nigerian military, which formed the bulk of ECOMOG, had suffered from personal rule's cross-ing of the civil-military divide. ECOMOG failed to render military solutions in Liberia and Sierra Leone and probably helped to prolong, at least, the Liberian war and its suffering.

The end of the Cold War helped to facilitate the Liberian conflict. During the 1980s, the Reagan administration had assisted the Doe gov-ernment with about $500 million of aid to a country of 2.5 million peo-ple. Yet in early 1990, with the Cold War finished, the United States declined to intervene to save the Doe regime from an initially weak NPFL of 100 fighters. Emboldened by U.S. inaction, the NPFL spread quickly throughout Liberia and soon began aiding the RUF in neighbor-ing Sierra Leone.

The NPFL and subsequent factions vividly illustrated the changing nature of African conflict by their access to weaponry, large number of armed groups, economic rather than ideological goals, and the targeting of noncombatant populations (including the recruitment of child-sol-diers). The NPFL soon challenged the sovereignty of neighboring Sierra Leone, which was part of ECOMOG, by assisting Foday Sankoh's RUF, an insurgency that shared many of the characteristics of the NPFL.

The inability of the Liberian military to contain the insurgency, the U.S. refusal to aid its historically close ally, and the war's suffering per-suaded some West African states to form ECOMOG in August 1990.[3] ECOMOG soon intervened in Liberia (1990–1998) and then in the related conflict in Sierra Leone (1998 to present).

A regional force, such as ECOMOG, may enjoy several major advantages over nonregional interveners. These benefits can lessen the traditional gaps between an intervener's hopes and abilities. Each of these advantages strongly relates to military professionalism.

1. A regional force's greater knowledge of the nearby situation increases its ability to reach its hoped-for goals.
2. Its greater political acceptance lessens the gap between its nor-mative hopes and actual situations.
3. The regional force's more relevant military capabilities, along with its political knowledge, allows the regional intervener to match its military capabilities with the intervention's political mandate. Similar topography, terrain, and climate should encourage equivalent equipment and training. These capabilities could offer significant financial savings over Western military intervention.
4. The regional's greater commitment to its own region means less

of a gap between both its interests and values and also between its time constraints and the longer time horizons of the local combatants.

Supporters of regional forces also argue that these multinational militaries could "convince small states like Sierra Leone and Gambia that the protection of their territorial integrity does not necessarily depend on a standing army . . . [and] reduce the relevance of mercenary outfits in Africa."[4]

This chapter maintains that ECOMOG failed to live up to these claims, but ECOMOG's lessons, while generally negative in themselves, are important because multilateralism remains the preferred method for military interventions and because ECOMOG (or some variant) will likely continue in West Africa.

ECOMOG's intervention established several important precedents. ECOMOG became the first regional military force in the third world since the end of the Cold War *and* the first regional military force with which the United Nations agreed to work as a secondary partner. Liberia was one of the first conflicts in which both the UN and the major regional organization, the OAU, redefined traditional ideas of sovereignty to permit external intervention.

Background to the Liberian Struggle

When ECOMOG arrived in Liberia in August 1990 it entered a country with a challenging geography, exploitable natural resources, and strong ethnic/historical divisions. Liberia is about the size of Tennessee and has a low coastal plain that soon merges into forested hills and mountains. Much of the interior is impassable by automobile, especially during the rainy season. The country has seventeen ethnic groups, none of which comprises more than 20 percent of the population. Among these groups, besides the "Americo-Liberians," who ruled Liberia until 1980, are the Mano and Gio in the north, the Mandingo in the west, and the Krahn in the northeast. Liberia's prewar population was slightly over 2 million. Considerable amounts of iron ore, timber, some gold and diamonds, and rubber constitute Liberia's major resources.

Scholars such as Gus Liebenow and Christopher Clapham have documented the historical roots of Liberia's present conflict.[5] The American Colonization Society, assisted by the U.S. Navy, resettled freed slaves on "Liberia's" shores in the 1820s. These "Americo-

Liberians" never made up more than 5 percent of Liberia's population, but gained national political control. Liberia became independent in 1847, and the Americo-Liberians' True Whig Party soon began a continuous rule that lasted until 1980. Political domination, economic exploitation, and the lack of widespread education prevented a common Liberian nationalism. Many observers believe that the Americo-Liberians soon displayed some of the worst traits of the antebellum U.S. South. Victims of American slavery became the victimizers of "the natives."[6] Economic exploitation of natural resources and labor without adequate compensation were common. Future governments did begin political reform, but two trends in the 1970s sealed the True Whig's fate: a major drop in trade (higher oil prices and lower commodity export prices) and the AFL's perception of government underfunding.

The AFL had represented the interests of the minority True Whig party: most of the AFL officers were still Americo-Liberians, even into the 1970s. Yet political responsibility was suspect, as evidenced by the arrest of officers in 1969, 1970, 1973, and 1977 for alleged coup plotting. The "native" enlistees had ample cause for frustration. Frederick Ehrenreich observed that "with their low pay, no housing allowance and only a limited number of overcrowded crumbling barracks available, many enlisted men lived in conditions of near squalor."[7] Military capabilities were lacking, in part because of the illiteracy of the majority of enlistees. English was not a prerequisite for acceptance (despite Liberia's close ties to the United States), and the troops had a limited ability "to communicate with one another as well as . . . to operate and maintain modern weapons and equipment."[8]

On April 12, 1980, indigenous, noncommissioned officers successfully toppled Americo-Liberian rule in a coup that initially enjoyed widespread support. But Samuel Doe (a Krahn who humbly promoted himself from master sergeant to five-star general) drove the country into deeper ethnic hostility and economic ruin and paved the way for Liberia's civil war. The new Doe government began its rule violently by publicly executing leading officials of the ancien régime.

The United States strongly supported the True Whig and then the Doe government. Many observers characterized Liberia as a U.S. quasi-colony, and Liberia certainly had enjoyed especially close relations with the United States since its independence in 1847. The United States had viewed Liberia ever since World War II as having some strategic importance and could count on Liberia for support of its international policies. Liberia housed various U.S. strategic installations and strongly supported the United States in most foreign policy debates.

The United States ensured that Doe's Liberia remained pro-Western, despite overtures from Libya's Muammar Qaddafi. Washington did press Doe to hold national elections in 1985 but, despite gross election irregularities, it continued to publicly align itself with the Doe regime.[9] Widespread corruption and the flight of Americo-Liberians continued to inflict economic chaos.

Doe's regime destroyed whatever professionalism still existed in the notoriously unprofessional AFL.[10] Throughout the early 1980s, discipline was often nonexistent (one of the first instructions by the coup makers to the enlistees was for them not to obey their immediate officers).[11] Doe forced out many of the most experienced officers and heavily politicized—ethnicized—the AFL, making it essentially a Krahn instrument. Political responsibility also was lacking. Doe accused several groups of officers of plotting against him, and the AFL had killed as many as 3,000 Mano and Gio civilians following a coup attempt in 1985. Civilian anger would later greatly assist Charles Taylor's NPFL drive against Doe.

The United States provided funding for Doe's military and his Executive Mansion Guard (a presidential guard of 1,000 soldiers, out of the AFL's total of 6,700), but the foreign support failed. "We wanted to professionalize the military," recalls a senior State Department official. "It was a failure. It was an unmitigated failure."[12]

Existing regional competition intruded into the worsening Liberian situation. Oil-rich Nigeria, by far the most powerful West African state, was seeking expanded political influence. It competed vigorously against continuing French influence in the region (as well as becoming black Africa's leading opponent against South Africa's apartheid regime). Nigeria had used economic assistance to strengthen its ties with neighboring Anglophone states; Doe's Liberia was one of the leading examples. Nigeria's President Ibrahim Babangida provided Liberia with debt relief and some road and educational financing.

Several French-speaking nations, notably Côte d'Ivoire and Burkina Faso, intensely disliked the Liberian government, especially because of Nigeria's support of Doe, its dominance in ECOMOG, and its perceived anti-Francophonism. Several personal factors also played a role.[13]

Having survived numerous coup attempts, Doe initially paid little attention to the small NPFL, comprised of one hundred or fewer men, which entered Nimba County from Côte d'Ivoire on Christmas Eve, 1989. Charles Taylor, a former Doe official and alleged embezzler of $900,000 from the government, led the largely Mano-Gio force.[14] Libya had trained a core of his fighters, Burkina Faso had supplied them with Libyan weaponry, and Côte d'Ivoire had allowed them free transit across the border into Liberia. Taylor's force espoused no ideology beyond "democracy" and opposition to Doe, but drew significant support from Liberians united in their opposition to the Krahn (and Mandingo) rule of Samuel Doe.

The threat from Charles Taylor's NPFL was real. Doe belatedly rushed a battalion of the AFL to Nimba County. The troops ravaged the local population in a replay of the 1985 violence and generated more hostility against the already unpopular Doe. Taylor took advantage of this anti-Doe backlash, and his NPFL quickly spread through much of Liberia. By July 1990, Taylor's forces numbered perhaps 10,000 and had reached Monrovia's outskirts. On July 2 Taylor began his onslaught against Monrovia. NPFL forces singled out Krahn and Mandingo civilians for slaughter, while the AFL, ostensibly a more disciplined unit, committed its own atrocities. AFL personnel killed about 250 civilians seeking sanctuary in St. Peter's Lutheran Church on July 29 and wounded several hundred others. The bodies were left to rot on church pews for three months. Immediately following this massacre, the AFL pursued survivors to a vacant U.S. Agency for International Development compound, where it killed several hundred more. By August, Doe's government had clearly lost control of Liberia, his shrunken regime hunkering down in government buildings.

Mediation efforts by religious and other organizations (Liberian and non-Liberian) failed: Doe refused widespread demands, including one by Charles Taylor, that he resign.[15] Monrovia's refugee-swollen population feared mass starvation and an incipient cholera epidemic. After July 2, relief ships dared not enter Monrovia because Lloyds of London refused to insure them.

The proliferation of factions became a hallmark of Liberia's war. The Independent National Patriotic Front of Liberia (INPFL) split off from Taylor's NPFL in January, shortly before ECOMOG's arrival.[16] The INPFL, led by Prince Yourmie Johnson, fought both the AFL and the NPFL. Other factions would later emerge.

The factions lacked significant military training and respect for established rule or individual human rights. The result was twofold: Taylor's onslaught, and its counterreaction, created significant savagery, and the NPFL's poor command-and-control system failed to keep its soldiers' attention on fighting and away from the more attractive looting. The fighting killed far more civilians than soldiers, and undisciplined "soldiers" began destroying Liberia's economic infrastructure. About 30 percent of the factions' fighters were under the age of 17.

Would anyone intervene? The members of the Economic Community of West African States (ECOWAS) had been watching the nearby devastation with growing trepidation. Some in ECOWAS feared that the war would increase refugee flows and political instability in their already impoverished states and further persuade already hesitant foreign investors not to invest in West Africa. Several in ECOWAS worried about significant numbers of their citizens trapped in Liberia, and many West Africans felt dismay over the war's brutality.[17] The Doe government could not contain the conflict, and no outside force wanted to intervene. ECOWAS, founded in 1975, was the only West African organization that included all sixteen of the region's states (nine Francophone states, five Anglophone, and two Lusophone).[18] Its mission was economic, to increase trade and self-reliance through trade liberalization and currency convertibility, not military. It also called for the free movement by West Africans through the region. ECOWAS had never fielded a military force, although it had two defense protocols for mutual self-defense.

No major power had expressed a desire to intervene militarily. Although the United States had many more ties to Liberia than did any other country, it limited its involvement. Washington assisted initial mediation efforts but never seriously considered military intervention to end the conflict. Several officials questioned any lasting benefits of a military intervention, given the depth of Liberia's problems. The Soviet Union—a major reason for U.S. involvement in Africa after 1960—had ceased to exist. Iraq's invasion of Kuwait (and the possibility of future U.S. intervention) was holding U.S. attention by August 1990. The United States had no desire to save its former client Doe, and Washington disliked both Taylor and Johnson.[19] Additionally, the American media—especially television—had not significantly covered Liberia's conflict and the civilian suffering.

The OAU and the UN paid scant official attention to Liberia's suffering. The OAU, Africa's major continent-wide organization, had always opposed military interference without invitation in the internal affairs of a fellow African state. Several nations in 1990 opposed UN involvement. African supporters of Taylor, notably Côte d'Ivoire, argued against UN involvement, as did the two African members of the UN Security Council, Ethiopia and Zaire, which, according to David Wippman, "evidently wished to avoid creating a precedent [of intervention] that might someday apply to them."[20] In July 1990, Liberia's UN ambassador tried but failed to have the Security Council consider the crisis. But not until January 1991, thirteen months after the war's start and five months after the formation of ECOMOG, did the Security Council publicly comment upon the war, and then without specifically mentioning ECOMOG.

The Birth of ECOMOG

Anglophone Nigeria was the leading supporter of a West African force for Liberia. In May 1990, at the urging of Nigeria's President Babangida, a group of five ECOWAS members established a Standing Mediation Committee (SMC) to resolve Liberia's conflict peacefully.[21] For three weeks in July an all-inclusive grouping of Liberian movements attempted and failed to obtain a peace settlement leading to elections: by August, no peace settlement existed among the combatants. Seeing no alternative, and believing that any further delay could witness a final bloodbath in Monrovia, the SMC on August 7 created ECOMOG. The SMC, still hoping for a political resolution, also called for a broadly based interim government of Liberians to rule until elections could be held under international supervision.

ECOMOG received a broad mandate that encompassed both peacekeeping and peace enforcement. ECOMOG was "to conduct military operations for the purpose of monitoring the cease-fire, restoring law and order to create the necessary conditions for free and fair elections to be held in Liberia" and "to aid the release of all political prisoners and prisoners of war."[22]

Other, more implicit and less Liberian oriented, goals helped prompt ECOMOG's creation. Chike Akabogu of Nigeria's Concord Newspapers wrote that a successful ECOMOG intervention would strengthen a largely moribund ECOWAS and create a precedent of regional cooperation that the rest of Africa could follow. Additionally, "it would signal to the rest of the world that African nations were also ready and capable of responding to the critical economic, political and security challenges of the new world order, without prompting from erstwhile colonial powers."[23]

Sustenance of Nigeria's personal-rule regime may have played a significant role. Abdel-Fatua Musah cites economic factors: the drop in world oil prices and the availability of cheap diamonds "presented another appealing proposition to diversify sources of income to the

Nigerian military."[24] The chance for President Babangida to deploy possibly coup-inclined officers overseas may have also played a role.[25]

ECOMOG faced immediate problems of political unity, military capabilities, and uncertain funding. ECOWAS itself was badly divided, mostly between English- and French-speaking states, over ECOMOG's existence. France had continued close political and economic links with its former colonies, most of which, Côte d'Ivoire in particular, feared Nigerian dominance of the region: Nigeria's gross national product and population approximated that of all the other ECOWAS members combined. During the Nigerian civil war of 1967–1970, Côte d'Ivoire had actively assisted Biafra's attempted secession from Nigeria. The different colonial legacies, continuing disparities, and the domestic interests of the individual members continued to impede regional cooperation in the early 1990s.

Demonstrating ECOWAS's disunity was the fact that most of the ECOMOG contributors were Anglophone states—Nigeria, Ghana, Sierra Leone, and Gambia (Guinea initially was the only Francophone state). Nigeria would supply about 70 percent of ECOMOG's men and materiel over the next five years. Although its name (ECOWAS Cease-fire Monitoring Group) suggested ECOWAS approval and sponsorship, only the SMC members had decided to create the force. By ECOMOG's August inception, ECOWAS's supreme body had not officially sanctioned ECOMOG and its "Operation Liberty."[26]

Some Francophone states in ECOWAS, notably Burkina Faso and Côte d'Ivoire, supported Taylor. Blaise Compaore, president of Burkina Faso, along with Charles Taylor warned prophetically of ECOMOG's hostile reception. In August, Compaore expressed "total disagreement" and warned prophetically of "an eventual expansion of the internal conflict, which could break out among member countries if an intervention force is sent to Liberia."[27]

ECOMOG also faced internal political divisions. Contributing members to ECOMOG disagreed about ECOMOG's goals and methods: Should, for instance, ECOMOG act only as a peacekeeper or, if necessary, also as a peace enforcer against Taylor's NPFL? Nigeria's dominance in ECOMOG was a continual concern, although this was rarely expressed publicly.

The ECOMOG states had varying military capabilities. Most observers regarded the small Ghanaian military as the most professional, whereas the much larger Nigerian force had serious internal command and administrative problems, notably corruption, and a dearth of relevant counterinsurgency materiel and training. Partly to lessen tensions among contributors, ECOMOG diversified its command structure: despite Nigeria's status as the major supplier of men, materiel, and money, Ghana was to provide the force commander, Guinea the deputy commander, and Nigeria the chief of staff. All five countries received some command positions. Nigeria provided economic incentives (e.g., concessionary oil) for nations to join and remain in ECOMOG.[28]

ECOMOG could not call on a strong history of regional military cooperation. It was an ad hoc creation because West Africa lacked a standing regional force. Joint military activities had been intermittent, at low level, and not notably successful.[29]

Funding was a problem. The SMC established the Special Emergency Fund, whose initial goal was to collect $50 million from African states and any other donors. But the international passivity toward the conflict and the parlous financial state of most ECOMOG members resulted in incomplete funding for the new force.

Troops Are Deployed

Notwithstanding these problems, the ECOMOG force of about 2,700 men arrived in Sierra Leone in mid-August. Sierra Leone, Liberia's western neighbor, agreed to serve as ECOMOG's forward staging base. It would become a fateful decision.

Gen. Arnold Quainoo of Ghana, ECOMOG's force commander,[30] believed that the NPFL would lay down its arms once ECOMOG made clear both its determination and armed capability. General Quainoo was wrong. On August 25 ECOMOG landed on Monrovia's beaches into hostile fire.

The three Liberian factions differed in their reactions. Prince Johnson's INPFL eagerly offered cooperation, as did the AFL. Yet Charles Taylor's NPFL artillery quickly zeroed in on ECOMOG's forces. The INPFL and the AFL cooperated with ECOMOG for two self-serving reasons: each was too weak to challenge ECOMOG directly, but each could benefit from ECOMOG's protection and from any destruction ECOMOG inflicted on Taylor. The INPFL's initial aid to ECOMOG won it special privileges, which included unhindered armed access to ECOMOG headquarters. Many Liberians therefore perceived ECOMOG as taking sides shortly after its landing.

ECOWAS/ECOMOG's overall strategy was for its conventional military force to intimidate the three factions while an interim government would help resolve political differences and prepare Liberia for peaceful elections. On August 27 the SMC convened the "All Liberia Conference" of seventeen Liberian political groupings and parties. The conference endorsed the SMC's peace plan and selected an interim president, Prof. Amos Sawyer, and a legislature. ECOWAS hoped to limit its political responsibilities and thus avoid being perceived as an army of occupation. The interim government of Liberians, rather than ECOWAS/ECOMOG, was to exercise sovereignty over Liberia.

Military problems, some of them caused by ECOMOG's inexperience, added to the force's political liabilities. ECOMOG established a beachhead, but at first moved slowly against the NPFL. ECOMOG's force commander, General Quainoo, considered his role as that of a peacekeeper rather than peace enforcer. A surprise NPFL attack caught ECOMOG unaware and almost overran its headquarters.

On September 9 INPFL forces killed seventy Doe bodyguards—at ECOMOG's headquarters—and then captured President Doe himself, whom they murdered the next day. The AFL thereupon suspected ECOMOG connivance, and AFL soldiers torched sections of Monrovia. Their chants of "No Doe, no Monrovia" summed up the "national" military's priorities. Soon afterward, the INPFL detained a platoon of Nigerians until ECOMOG traded two 105mm howitzers for them. A close observer of these events recalls that "Quainoo was rattled, he simply wasn't capable."[31] Yet Quainoo was subject to conflicting pressures from officials in ECOWAS, ECOMOG, the Nigerian government, the Nigerian military, and his own Ghanaian government.[32]

Nigerian officials worried that ECOMOG, which Nigeria largely had created, might not survive. Quainoo reportedly had convened a meeting at which he called for ECOMOG's withdrawal from Liberia. Nigerian Brig. C. K. Iweze, Quainoo's second in command, acknowledged that "most of the soldiers welcomed the thought of the said withdrawal."[33] Nigeria asserted its dominance of ECOMOG by having ECOWAS's Dawda Jawara, who was chairman of ECOWAS's Authority of Heads of State and Government, replace Quainoo with the more aggressive Maj. Gen. Joshua Dogonyaro of Nigeria.[34]

Nigeria also persuaded ECOMOG to shift temporarily from peacekeeping to peace enforcing. Nigeria (and Ghana) supplied 3,000 additional men, more offensive weaponry, and limited offensive air capability. ECOMOG now took the offensive. By October, Dogonyaro was using Nigeria's 77th Airborne Battalion and the two Ghanaian battalions to outflank a retreating Taylor and push him beyond Monrovia. The military pressure forced Taylor to sign a cease-fire at Bamako, Mali, on November 28. Between August and the end of November 1990, ECO-

MOG had moved from peacekeeper to peace enforcer and then, with the Bamako cease-fire, back to peacekeeper.

The Cease-Fire, 1990–1992

ECOMOG member states had had little previous knowledge of Taylor and assumed (or hoped) that he had signed the cease-fire in good faith. ECOMOG controlled Monrovia, while Taylor in late 1990 controlled what he termed "Greater Liberia," practically all of the rest of Liberia.

ECOMOG's offensive certainly saved thousands of lives by preventing an AFL-NPFL-INPFL battle for Monrovia and by restoring peace that allowed food and medical supplies to enter Monrovia. The offensive also provided breathing space for subsequent negotiations. The cease-fire, although increasingly shaky, lasted for two years. Joshua Iroha of Nigeria served as ECOWAS's special representative in trying to reach a lasting peace settlement.

As the relative peace allowed all sides in the conflict to rebuild themselves, Burkina Faso resupplied Taylor's limited insurgency needs. Taylor built his own resource base by extorting resources from several large businesses and by selling gold, diamonds, and hardwoods to commercial middlemen. A stalemate emerged, with each side possessing enough resources to continue fighting but none acquiring enough strength for a total victory.

Taylor spread the war beyond Liberia by harboring, arming, and supplying manpower to the Sierra Leonean Revolutionary United Front (RUF), composed mostly of dissidents from that nation. Taylor wanted to stop Sierra Leone from serving as ECOMOG's forward staging base. Additionally, he believed correctly that ECOMOG troops would be diverted from Liberia to fight the RUF in Sierra Leone.[35] The RUF invaded Sierra Leone, a major ECOMOG supporter, in March 1991.[36] Taylor would remain instrumental in the RUF's fortunes for the rest of the decade.

The cease-fire also allowed new factions to form. Johnson's INPFL already had spun off from Taylor's NPFL and fought until late 1992. Many anti-Taylor refugees, mostly Krahn and Mandingo, had fled to Sierra Leone. These refugees, among whom were many former AFL soldiers, reacted to the RUF by forming ULIMO (United Liberation Movement of Liberians for Democracy) around May 1991. Soon ULIMO was skirmishing with the RUF and by February 1992 had crossed into Liberia. ULIMO later split into two forces (the mostly

Mandingo ULIMO-K of Alhaji Kromah and later the mostly Krahn ULIMO-J of Roosevelt Johnson). The AFL remained, but many of its soldiers joined ULIMO-J or another Krahn faction, George Boley's Liberian Peace Council (LPC) that operated in southeast Liberia. The Krahns' armed power far exceeded their numerical strength: they constituted only 4 percent of Liberia's population and therefore feared for their survival, given their close identification with the repressive Doe regime. Not surprisingly, the Krahn had equipped themselves heavily from AFL armories or from covert ECOMOG deliveries.

Military unprofessionalism, including economic motives, ethnic defensiveness, and personal loyalty to a faction leader, became hallmarks of the Liberian conflict. Few, if any, of these groups voiced ideological positions. Self-enrichment was often a major goal; all the factions helped support themselves by looting various resources that they then sold to international middlemen.

Child soldiers greatly benefited the factions. Some 10 percent of the possibly 60,000 fighters were under the age of 15 (and another 20 percent were between 15 and 17). Some had their own unit (e.g., the NPFL's "Small Boys Unit"). These children often proved willing fighters. As a Liberian who worked with ex-combatants remarks, "Adults need a good reason to take up arms. It is easier to convince kids to fight for almost nothing, with small promises of money and loot. . . . They are easy prey for the factions."[37]

These youths performed as ammunition porters, front line soldiers, spies, executioners, checkpoint staffers, and, according to Human Rights Watch, "as cannon fodder to draw the fire of adversaries."[38] Command and control of faction fighters in general, many of them financially rather than politically driven, and armed but poorly trained, was often nonexistent. Human Rights Watch rated the factions' human rights record as "suspect to abysmal."[39] The U.S. State Department wrote that

> the factions committed summary executions, torture, individual and gang rapes, mutilation and cannibalism. They burned people alive; looted and burned cities and villages; used excessive force; engaged in arbitrary detentions and impressment, particularly of children under the age of 18; severely restricted freedom of assembly, association and movement; and employed forced labor.[40]

ECOMOG at times provided the ULIMO-K, ULIMO-J, and LPC with arms, ammunition, intelligence, transport, and free passage to press the war against Taylor. ECOMOG, for example, provided ammunition in 1990 to the INPFL and AFL. Although documentation is sparse, ECOMOG at the military unit level apparently provided transport and protection for the factions' loot shipments that raised capital for these groups. (Nigeria first supported the ULIMO-K, but later switched its support to the breakaway ULIMO-J; Guinea supported the mostly Mandingo ULIMO-K before and after ULIMO-J's startup and permitted Kromah to reside in Conakry.)

During its first several weeks in Monrovia, ECOMOG realized the usefulness of factions when it employed Prince Johnson's INPFL for combat and intelligence against the NPFL. The INPFL provided special assistance by guiding ECOMOG troops through the baffling swamps of Monrovia. ECOMOG air-lifted ULIMO units into Monrovia during Taylor's unsuccessful Operation Octopus against Monrovia in 1992, and the ULIMO, as INPFL before it, then guided ECOMOG troops through the swamps.

Largely Nigerian ECOMOG contacts with the factions occurred for two reasons. Some ECOMOG officers had become frustrated with ECOMOG's political and military limitations in adhering to a peace-keeping mandate, fear of high body counts and escalating financial costs, and scant counterinsurgency capability—and they saw the factions as an effective proxy force to realize their goal of defeating Taylor. The Liberians knew the countryside better and cost less to employ since they largely lived off the land, and if they got killed did not cause possible political problems back in ECOMOG countries. Individual greed was a second reason for ECOMOG-faction contact. For personal gain, some ECOMOG officers assisted the factions in their looting by providing armed protection and transport.[41] Support of the factions added to the conflict's uncontrollability, most notably by dissipating ECOMOG's command effectiveness, and prolonged the war.

Peace talks, notably those at Yamoussoukro, Côte d'Ivoire, between July and October 1991, vainly attempted to bring a more lasting peace. The Yamoussoukro accord provided for a cease-fire, disarmament, restriction to camps, an interim government, and various steps toward elections. To increase the non-Nigerian presence in ECOMOG, Senegal, with U.S. financing, sent two battalions to ECOMOG in late 1991.

The Liberian conflict soon claimed its first regional state victim. By early 1992, Sierra Leonean soldiers, mostly ECOMOG veterans, were fighting the RUF. The war was destroying Sierra Leone's economy, and the soldiers suffered from missing paychecks, irregular supplies, and minimal logistics support. In April 1992 these soldiers overthrew their president, Joseph Momoh.

The cease-fire between the NPFL and ECOMOG continued

throughout much of 1992, despite the growing fighting between the ULIMO and NPFL. (Between ECOMOG's August 1990 landing and October 1992's Operation Octopus, the worst single day of casualties occurred when twenty-seven ECOMOG officers died from drinking wood alcohol marketed as Scotch whisky or as gin). ECOMOG soldiers began dispersing throughout much of Liberia, as called for by the Yamoussoukro accord, in late April 1992.

Yet events on the battlefield were undermining conference agreements. Citing the spread of ULIMO forces—by August 1992, they had captured much of northwestern and some of central Liberia—Taylor refused to disarm and continued to fight the ULIMO and to mistreat some ECOMOG peacekeepers.[42] In one case, the NPFL surrounded a Nigerian contingent that ECOMOG had ordered to withdraw to Monrovia. Following intervention by former President Jimmy Carter, the NPFL released the Nigerians but only after stripping them of their uniforms, weapons, and personal effects. This and other actions by Taylor's forces (e.g., the killing of three Nigerian journalists) further embittered ECOMOG, especially Nigerian officers, against the NPFL. All this time, Jimmy Carter and the International Negotiations Network of the Carter Center were working for a Liberian cease-fire: Carter visited Liberia and met with Taylor in late 1991. However, many Liberians felt that Carter was too accepting of Taylor, especially when the former proposed that ECOMOG remove all its offensive weaponry from Liberia during the cease-fire.

Operation Octopus and Continued Fighting

On October 15, 1992, the NPFL irrevocably broke the cease-fire by mounting Operation Octopus, a two-month siege of ECOMOG-held Monrovia. Burkina Faso soldiers may have led the NPFL's offensive.[43] ECOMOG's departing field commander, Gen. Ishaya Bakyut, reflected ECOMOG's, particularly Nigeria's, disenchantment with Taylor: "I now realize that I was wrong about Taylor's intention. It is quite clear that Taylor is not sincere about disarmament nor is he willing to let anything stand between him and the Executive Mansion."[44]

Taylor's aggression again had pushed ECOMOG into peace enforcement: ECOMOG began some five months of fighting—its first peace enforcement actions in almost two years. By late December, ECOMOG Gen. Adetunji Olurin of Nigeria had pushed the NPFL beyond Monrovia's suburbs. By April ECOMOG had taken the major towns of Harbel and Kakata and then the port of Buchanan, 90 miles from Monrovia.

By mid–1993, Taylor was in retreat throughout much of Liberia and losing his economic base. *Africa Confidential* observed that Taylor was "in the difficult position of leading a guerrilla force which has to hold vast swatches of territory on a sharply declining revenue base."[45] ECOMOG had captured Taylor's major revenue sources, the Firestone rubber plantation and the port of Buchanan, and the French and Lebanese trading interests that had been aiding the NPFL fled.

ECOMOG's aggressive peace enforcement once again forced Taylor to negotiate. A July 1993 meeting in Cotonou, Benin, saw the combatants agree to another cease-fire, a coalition interim government, and free elections within seven months of the cease-fire. The Cotonou agreement attempted to assuage continuing worries about a biased, Nigerian-dominated ECOMOG by incorporating UN involvement and by sanctioning the inclusion of East African troops in ECOMOG.

Cotonou marked the first time that the UN had agreed to cooperate with a non-UN peacekeeping force. The UN dispatched the UN Observer Mission in Liberia (UNOMIL).[46] In early 1994, 368 UN observers arrived in Monrovia. About the same time, a battalion each of Tanzanian and Ugandan troops, under ECOMOG command and partially financed by the United States, also arrived.[47]

The Liberian factions began working against ECOMOG's wishes. Just as a new group, the ULIMO, had help scuttle the Yamoussoukro talks, so in late 1993 another ECOMOG-supported faction, the LPC, threatened the Cotonou accord and quickly began fighting the NPFL. Supporters of Alhaji Kromah's ULIMO-K also began disregarding ECOMOG; in mid-December at Kakata they blocked food aid intended for NPFL areas. ECOMOG, particularly Nigeria, grew increasingly angry at Kromah's independence and aided, if not incited, a split-off of the ULIMO-J. In March 1994 ULIMO officially split into the ULIMO-K and ULIMO-J. (Other armed groups included the Lofa Defense Force and the Bong Defense Force.) Continued fighting forced the UN to drastically reduce its observer mission, from a peak of 368 down to about sixty in mid-1995.

Fighting continued in mid-1994, despite a Cotonou-decreed new government (the Council of State) and ECOMOG attempts at demobilization. In July a coalition of forces, comprising the Krahn AFL, the LPC, and the ULIMO-J, captured Prince Taylor's headquarters at Gbarnga with ECOMOG's blessing. Yet Taylor recaptured Gbarnga in September. Clearly the stalemate of three and a half years was to continue.

The Liberian conflict then claimed another political casualty. Gambian soldiers in ECOMOG (about thirty at any given time) had claimed, inter alia, that they had not received their extra pay for serving in ECOMOG. On July 23, 1994, the Gambian military overthrew the president, Sir Dawda Jawara.

The Peace Settlement

Mid-year meetings in 1995 between Taylor and Sani Abacha, Nigeria's head of state, in Abuja, Nigeria, paved the way for a peace settlement on August 19. By early April 1996 an eminently fragile peace floated above Liberia. The country faced two possibilities: if ECOMOG controlled its former allies, the elections scheduled by the Abuja accord for August 1996 would occur, but, ironically, Charles Taylor might win the national elections and thus come to power peacefully under the eyes of ECOMOG soldiers.

The other possibility—ECOMOG's not controlling the factions—unfortunately came about, as former allies turned on ECOMOG. In early January 1996, ULIMO-J fought ECOMOG at Tubmanberg over access to a diamond mine. The fighting resulted in at least fifty dead ECOMOG soldiers and ECOMOG's loss of significant weaponry to ULIMO-J. Then in April 1996 the NPFL, temporarily aligned with ULIMO-K, attacked the three Krahn groups, the LPC, ULIMO-J, and AFL in Monrovia. The fighting killed several thousand Monrovians and destroyed sections of the capital. Factions targeted the relief organizations and, within a few days, stole some $20 million in foreign exchange and equipment, including 480 vehicles. ECOMOG took significant losses but, assisted by political negotiations, eventually regained control. The "Abuja Two" agreement of August 1996 established the cease-fire that led to the July 16, 1997, elections, which provided Charles Taylor with the presidency of Liberia. All ECOMOG troops left Liberia in October 1999. The Obasanjo government in late 1999 announced that Nigeria alone had lost 500 soldiers in the conflict at a cost of $8 billion.[48]

Significance of the Liberian Conflict

Liberia offered a preview to many of the security trends of the post–Cold War era. Its unprofessional military helped to trigger the fighting and then proved unable to end it. Two of the major trends—

superpower nonsupport of fragile regimes and the relative growth of insurgent capabilities—helped prolong the conflict's suffering and duration. Secondary trends, most notably economic motivation by all armed groups, child-soldiers, and weapon availability, prevented centralized control over the combatants. Regional intervention, when conducted by a largely unprofessional military force, further extended the conflict.

The U.S. disinclination to provide economic assistance to the corrupt Doe government in the latter 1980s and then its refusal to provide military support against Taylor certainly allowed Taylor's ragtag forces to enter and then spread rapidly throughout Liberia. Belated responses by the OAU and the UN, however temporarily, provided more favorable conditions for Taylor's NPFL.

The nature of Liberia's conflict thoroughly ravaged that country—not just during the war but, given the subsequent lack of outside investment, for years to come. The factions' economic strategy, as illustrated by their seizure of foreign businesses and NGO assets, provided the factions invaluable financial, communication, and transportation capabilities and lessened their desire for political resolution of the conflict (and this undoubtedly appealed to many combatants in a country with a 90-percent unemployment rate). This economic strategy helped the NPFL to compensate for its organizational limitations (i.e., no indigenous taxing ability) and its lack of state recognition (i.e., more difficulty in obtaining military materiel). Looting by the factions, and by some ECOMOG units, has mortgaged part of Liberia's economic future. Child-soldiers contributed to the carnage, prolonged the conflict with their willingness to fight, and now represent a serious threat to Liberia's peacetime stability.

The availability of weapons assisted the factions' growth. These groups compensated for the lack of superpower support by obtaining small arms from several African states and from ECOMOG soldiers by using money from their sale of minerals and hardwoods to European arms dealers and private African middlemen. The factions may or may not have totally disappeared, but the weapons remain to threaten Liberia's—and West Africa's—development in the face of banditry or political subversion.

Why ECOMOG Failed in Liberia

The world in 1990 had welcomed ECOMOG, hoping that it might become a model for future regional forces that, as opposed to Western military units, might exhibit political and military advantages. Such a force could display more knowledge about a contested country's political issues and physical geography, enjoy greater political acceptance, employ more suitable military capabilities, and maintain a greater commitment to ending a nearby struggle whose suffering could slop over into neighboring states. Such assumptions did not consider ECOMOG's basic limitations, as described below. ECOMOG clearly demonstrated the dangers of a security dilemma: external assistance, regardless of motives, can prolong a conflict.[49]

Greater Knowledge?

The West's limited knowledge of the developing world can endanger military interventions, as the United States and UN realized in the case of Somalia. Greater knowledge of the conflict could assist potential interveners in deciding whether to intervene and, if so, what form of mandate—peacekeeping or peace enforcing—would match their military capabilities and domestic support. Will countries from the same region necessarily have adequate (or superior) knowledge? Not necessarily, according to ECOMOG's experience.

Despite geographical proximity, neighboring states in Africa often have surprisingly limited knowledge about each other. Ignorance about Liberia hurt ECOMOG's military operations and the framing of a precise mandate. West Africa has a wide range of ethnic-linguistic-cultural groupings, as well as a lack of regional transport and communication and political-economic cooperation.

West African states knew Liberia better than did any others (with the exception of the United States), but ECOMOG's initial understanding of Charles Taylor and his motives proved negligible. ECOMOG certainly misjudged his willingness and ability to resist the multinational force. ECOMOG officers note that ECOMOG lacked substantial understanding about Taylor's organization and the strength of his domestic support. These officers acknowledge that ECOMOG initially assumed that the superior firepower of their conventional, professional force would a priori intimidate the ragtag NPFL.[50] This fatal assumption encouraged the broadness of ECOMOG's mandate—that it could quickly achieve the cease-fire it was to monitor. Furthermore, both ECOWAS and the United States underestimated the willingness of Burkina Faso, Côte d'Ivoire, and private businesses to assist the NPFL and thus prolong the conflict. Lack of intelligence hurt ECOMOG's tactical capabilities: C. K. Iweze writes that ECOMOG based its initial planning on a "tourist map of Monrovia,"[51] and ECOMOG lacked adequate topographic maps until the United States provided them.[52]

ECOMOG/ECOWAS compounded their initial ignorance of the conflict by not adequately supporting its political special representative. Ambassador Joshua Iroha, who later became Nigeria's ambassador to Liberia, did serve as the ECOWAS special representative, but a lack of funding, disagreements over areas of responsibility, and personality differences led to his withdrawal after two years.

Knowledge, along with military capabilities, is crucial for specifying whether the interveners should pursue peacekeeping or peace enforcing. ECOMOG's ignorance encouraged the new force to seek numerous—and contradictory—goals. ECOMOG first assumed that it would be a peacekeeper, a Cyprus-like interpositional force between armed but peaceful forces. It believed that the NPFL would cease fighting when confronted by ECOMOG, and that ECOMOG's conventional strength would quickly defeat Taylor's forces if the NPFL did choose armed resistance. Until 1992's Operation Octopus, much of ECOWAS believed that Taylor would settle for a power-sharing agreement. Only after Octopus did ECOWAS/ECOMOG fully realize Taylor's unqualified political ambition.

The uncertain mandate, which was interpreted differently by contributing nations, weakened ECOMOG's initial military capabilities. Iweze writes that "because the structure of the Force was not clear from the onset, many troops arrived without personal weapons. . . . Some contingents comprised . . . para-military forces [having] essentially those [weapons] of customs and immigration duties."[53]

ECOMOG's mandate "to keep the peace, restore law and order and ensure respect for the cease-fire"[54] was, as one leading Western diplomat in Liberia concluded, "way too mushy."[55] It simultaneously attempted impartial peacekeeping (without a peace to keep) and biased peace enforcement against Taylor's NPFL. The title "Cease-fire Monitoring Group" suggests the former interpretation, but the active NPFL antagonism sometimes forced the latter.

ECOMOG planners had not realized how easily the rebel NPFL could sustain itself economically and militarily. The French government aided commercial ties in NPFL territory, including the promotion of a major iron-ore mining operation. Such action worked against Nigerian commercial influence and supported the anti-ECOMOG stance of Burkina Faso and Côte d'Ivoire. In 1991 Taylor's "Greater Liberia" was "France's third largest supplier of tropical timber," according to William Reno.[56]

Prolongation of a conflict allows such networks to grow. Taylor developed a parallel economy in his "Greater Liberia." Reno writes as late as 1995 that "Taylor's 'Greater Liberia' boasts a vigorous trade in timber, agricultural products and minerals, and hosts numerous foreign firms and regional trade networks."[57] Taylor sold timber concessions to foreign companies—and sometimes sold the same concessions several times over.

Greater Political Acceptance?

Will Africans accept other African peacekeeping forces more willingly than those from outside the continent? Peacekeepers face great problems when trying to remain "humanitarian" and "neutral" in a highly partisan and often cruel situation. Nonregional interveners can quickly face accusations of insensitivity, neocolonialism, and racism. Perhaps regional interveners can appeal to such commonalities as race, ethnicity, and region, which could lessen mistrust. Such acceptance could lessen the combat hostilities, allow entry of relief supplies, and encourage peace negotiations.

The Liberian experience underscores that such acceptance is not automatic; indeed, it may be more difficult for a regional force to obtain.[58] Two factors, the existing political realities and the military's ongoing behavior, determine acceptance of the intervener. Existing regional (and bilateral) differences could pose serious problems since a new regional force will carry existing baggage. Regional cleavages, such as Francophone versus Anglophone, and such resentments as that of Nigeria's status as West Africa's largest economic and military power created difficulties for ECOMOG (including initially not having a mandate from ECOWAS). Robert Mortimer notes that "the multilateral, but Nigerian-dominated, force is more a classic study of competing national interests in the West African subregion than . . . a case study in regional peacekeeping."[59] Burkina Faso and Côte d'Ivoire supported Taylor, while Guinea and Senegal supported ECOMOG. Most other Francophone states favored ECOMOG as a peacekeeper rather than peace enforcer and, at least by 1992, were seeking a stronger UN presence to lessen Nigeria's influence. Serious Anglophone-Francophone divisions occurred also within ECOMOG. According to Iweze, to the Guineans, "being asked to fight was a deliberate attempt by the Anglophones to eliminate the Franco Phones [sic]."[60] During Operation Octopus, Nigeria and Sierra Leone pursued a major offensive against Taylor's NPFL. Most of the Francophone states resisted, believing that a peaceful UN involvement would lessen antagonism between ECOMOG and the NPFL.[61]

A regional hegemon may underwrite the costs of a regional force, but that country's commitment may heighten regional fears and noncooperation. "The same incentives that make a regional power more likely to act," writes Mortimer, "render that actor more threatening than a more distant patron."[62] Nigeria's effective control over ECOMOG's operations irritated numerous non-Nigerian officers: "Big Brother" was a term heard frequently by this author to refer to the Nigerian contingent. Nigeria wisely declined to insist on an enforcement mechanism to ensure effective agreement, even after November 1990 when all ECOWAS members—even Burkina Faso and Côte d'Ivoire—belatedly endorsed the SMC's peace plan. ECOWAS took no disciplinary action against these two states, which despite their endorsement continued to aid the NPFL against ECOMOG.

The national aims of contributing states may collide with those of the regional force. The immediate result—increased tension within the multinational force and a corresponding drop in efficiency—may prompt a contingent to abandon the alliance.

Instances of national desires aggravating ECOMOG tensions soon appeared. Nigeria had agreed that a Ghanaian should always command ECOMOG but, following General Quainoo's apparent incompetence, Nigeria pushed to have him removed. After late 1990 only Nigerians commanded ECOMOG, a fact resented by non-Nigerian officers. ECOMOG had ordered, in August 1990, that fighting vehicles should be the first to land on Monrovia's beaches but, as Iweze recalls, "some countries decided [otherwise] and started bringing in their five and ten ton trucks loaded with fish and rice. . . . We were lucky that the opposing forces did not meet us with a higher degree of opposition . . . we would have been sitting ducks." ECOMOG suffered from many other examples of independent decisionmaking.[63]

The political background of a regional force's participating governments will affect the force's political legitimacy and probably also its acceptance. The personal rule of most of the contributing countries did not provide an imprimatur of legitimacy. ECOMOG's mandate included "creat[ing] the necessary conditions for free and fair elections," a novel function for most of ECOMOG's forces.[64] Few of the governments contributing to ECOMOG had been democratically elected; most, indeed, had gained power through military force, as Taylor himself was attempting, and few of them tolerated much domestic dissent (Max Ahmadu Sesay compares the presidents of the five initial contributors to "the unholy alliance of reactionary regimes in nineteenth century Europe").[65] Stedman bluntly concludes that ECOMOG, "whose member states were mostly dictatorships, had no credibility in pushing an election as a solution to the conflict. Nigeria, led by a regime that came to power through a military coup and in existence as a state because it triumphed in a civil war, had no credibility when it came to urging parties to resolve their conflict peacefully."[66]

Existing political baggage may limit Western support. U.S. "decertification" of Nigeria for involvement in the international drug trade exacerbated ECOMOG's serious financial plight. As a result, the United States provided bilateral assistance to all nations except Nigeria until late 1995. ECOMOG officials correctly claim that bilateral funding contributed to disparate military capabilities and jealousy among its members. Some Nigerian officers argue that the U.S. embargo on military equipment hurt their acquisition of spare parts, most notably for their previously obtained C-130 transport planes.

A regional force's conduct will, ipso facto, affect the force's acceptance. A major worry for an intervention force is that a prolonged presence may change public perception of the force from an army of liberation to an army of occupation. ECOMOG partly avoided this by wisely not assuming sovereignty for Liberia. ECOMOG, arguably, did not unduly interfere with Liberia's government: it did not indulge in military praetorianism by staging a coup or physically disrupting political meetings among factions.[67] The ECOWAS SMC had encouraged a Liberian interim government, and ECOMOG publicly cooperated with local authorities. But ECOMOG never signed a status of forces agreement, which delineates the respective roles of the host government and the intervention force, although several peace agreements mandated ECOMOG to do so.[68] ECOMOG's monopoly of military coercion in Monrovia probably restrained any Liberian tendencies to deviate from ECOMOG policy or to criticize ECOMOG conduct. Many Monrovians were of two minds about ECOMOG: a heartfelt, sometimes tearful, appreciation for its saving Monrovia in 1990 and 1992 was often balanced by anger about alleged widespread corruption and highhandedness.

ECOMOG contingents successfully handled a classic problem of political responsibility that confronts multilateral operations: whether to obey their national governments or the regional authority when disagreements arise. ECOWAS's weak financial and organizational capabilities helped ensure that Nigeria (the major funder) rather than the regional organization would create ECOMOG's policies.[69] Individual

contingents sometimes did disagree strongly with some ECOMOG policies but apparently never countermanded them. For example, there is no
known example of a contingent refusing ECOMOG combat orders.
Nigeria's underwriting of the costs of some of the contingents probably
encouraged this responsible behavior.

The national contingents rarely stepped over the divide between
political rule and military deference. The coups in Gambia and Sierra
Leone were the two exceptions. This lack of pretorianism is somewhat
surprising, given both the anger of many officers toward the decision by
their governments not to conduct offensive operations and frustration
felt by the soldiers about substandard living conditions. Funmi
Olonisakin writes that "many ECOMOG officers . . . believed that the
enforcement strategy should have been pursued further . . . to settle
Liberia's armed conflict once and for all."[70] She continues that "it was
normal for the same troops to be in the area of operation for up to twen-
ty-four months without being rotated . . . [and this was] compounded by
infrequent payment of operational allowance, which was delayed by up
to four months in the case of the Nigerian contingent."[71] Nigerian
troops also lacked adequate uniforms, including boots, and had to purchase them from other contingents.

ECOMOG soldiers too often mistreated Liberian citizens, although
their behavior shone when compared to that of the various factions.
"They [ECOMOG soldiers] may beat or steal from us," commented
several Liberians, "but the factions will kill you."[72] ECOMOG's crimi-
nality and general unprofessionalism will continue to hurt Liberia's
development. An unnamed "Western diplomat" in the *New York Times*
stated that "by the time the Nigerians really got serious about bringing
the war to an end . . . they had taken just about everything that there
was to take from Liberia."[73] The UN's chief of security stated that
ECOMOG units had pilfered raw rubber, timber, housing material, UN
rice, scrap metal (including cars and railroad tracks), ammunition, guns,
and drugs. ECOMOG should also be held partly responsible for the
often reprehensible abuse of human rights by the anti-Taylor factions.

Alliances with local factions, while offering an outside force some
military advantages, may lessen the interveners' political standing. A
regional force's acceptance of, and by, some factions will lessen its
acceptance by others. Torture, rape, pillage, and isolated examples of
cannibalism by ECOMOG-supported factions lowered ECOMOG's
general political acceptance, and demonstrated that a regional force has
less control over factions, and their misdeeds, than over its own troops.

ECOMOG's African composition by itself did nothing to gain its acceptance by Charles Taylor. He had distrusted ECOMOG before it landed, and ECOMOG's quick military cooperation with the AFL and INPFL cemented his anger. He could then call for Liberian unity against supposed Nigerian hegemony. And the AFL and INPFL had welcomed ECOMOG not so much as fellow African peacekeepers but as possible allies against the NPFL. Surprisingly, ECOWAS may not have anticipated this challenge to its neutrality. Iweze writes that at the creation of ECOMOG, "we asked the ECOWAS Secretariat for our anticipated reaction to the leaders of the warring factions should we meet them. Unfortunately, the leadership could not provide an answer."[74]

In this circumstance, UNOMIL could have acted as a watchdog, or ombudsman, over ECOMOG, but UNOMIL had little independent authority. ECOMOG cooperated grudgingly, at best, with UNOMIL, some of whose officials complained that ECOMOG did not want its presumed partner, UNOMIL, observing activities relating to arms flows, human rights abuses, and food shipments.[75] (Gen. John Inienger, ECOMOG's field commander in 1995, vigorously disputed allegations about corruption, human rights abuses, and aid to the factions).[76] The overall result was that ECOMOG lost a chance to restore some of its desired neutrality and public acceptance.

Greater Military Capabilities?

Does a third world regional grouping enjoy some military advantages over a Western force? Military capabilities include equipment, maintenance, manpower, administration, and intelligence. Such a third world force conceivably could field equipment and personnel well suited for the terrain, an adequate intelligence capability, and a strong strategic sense—all at a reasonable cost—and possible cultural similarities, notably language and religion, could also assist the force. This strong military capability could allow the interveners to bridge the traditional gap between mandate and capabilities.

Despite being an African force, ECOMOG lacked much of the suitable equipment, maintenance, manpower, administration, and intelligence required for counterinsurgency effort in Liberia. The years of personal rule had taken their toll on national military capabilities. So ECOMOG increasingly resorted to sponsoring the factions, whose low-tech capabilities were more cost-effective than ECOMOG's.

ECOMOG's order of battle (OB) was not suited for counterinsurgency operations, even though it was impressive at first glance. Nigeria alone had 257 tanks, ninety-five combat aircraft, an 80,000-man army, artillery, and a navy with several frigates, corvettes, and missile craft. But, an OB can often be deceiving about military capability. Modern counterinsurgency warfare almost invariably requires heavy use of helicopters and spotter aircraft, but Nigeria's decentralized procurement policy that encouraged kickbacks plagued ECOMOG's military capabilities. In mid-1995, ECOMOG's only helicopter was for the field commander's personal travel (previously, one Nigerian helicopter had been in Monrovia and two were in Sierra Leone). Other equipment, such as main battle tanks, was costly and ill suited for Liberia's heavily forested interior.

Communications posed a basic problem. National contingents arrived in 1990 with various mixtures of Western and Eastern Bloc equipment. During the 1990–1992 cease-fire, Nigeria provided compatible radio equipment at the battalion level, but even then companies in different national contingents could not communicate with each other, often because of different frequencies. ECOMOG's forward checkpoints in October 1992 lacked radios to inform ECOMOG headquarters of the start of Taylor's Operation Octopus. For too long, ECOMOG lacked full radio communications capability both within and between national contingents. ECOMOG's communications capability improved, but even by mid-1995 ECOMOG officers, including General Inienger, and Western observers emphasized ECOMOG's lack of radios. Communications with the ECOWAS Secretariat in Lagos, Nigeria, were, at least initially, problematic: fairly soon after ECOMOG's arrival, one important ECOWAS decision did not reach ECOMOG headquarters for a month.[77]

Inadequate maintenance, often a serious problem in third world militaries, plagued ECOMOG. Several countries did have helicopters, yet much of the equipment was not battle ready (or else the countries preferred to shepherd it for their own domestic defense). Defense analysts in late 1995 noted that most of Ghana's eight helicopters and Nigeria's fifteen armed helicopters had not flown for several years, owing to the expensive maintenance—generally, four hours of maintenance for every flying hour—that helicopters require.[78]

A possible selling point of ECOMOG was its cheapness, relative to the more sophisticated first world forces. Pay scales and logistical support certainly were less expensive. Yet ECOMOG's overall lack of military capabilities prolonged the war, and therefore its costs. Plundering by some ECOMOG contingents, sometimes because of insufficient pay, also raised the indirect price of the conflict. Extortion may have been necessary to finance its continuing presence.

ECOMOG's manpower, which varied from a maximum of about 14,000 to an occasional low of 2,700, was too small for peace enforcement or even for effective peacekeeping. Several West African officials speculated that ECOMOG would need 20,000 men for peace enforcement, rather than the 6,000–10,000 it usually had. After all, some of ECOMOG's checkpoints were as far apart as 22 kilometers. ECOMOG's size and amount of equipment was large enough to prevent a final battle for Monrovia, but the force was not large enough to push the factions into successful peace talks. Prolongation of the war was the result.

A generally inept force under fire understandably may order its most competent contingent to shoulder disproportionate responsibilities. The Senegalese contingent was ECOMOG's best force, and ECOMOG used it as a quick-reaction/strategic reserve unit. A close observer of the fighting recalls that the Senegalese "conducted platoon through battalion level missions in support of (and in the zones of) virtually every national contingent, as needed."[79] Senegal's dislike of this role— and the accompanying casualties—contributed to its pulling out of ECOMOG in January 1993.[80]

Inclusion of nonregional forces can provide mixed results. The addition of Tanzanian and Ugandan soldiers in February 1994 provided more men and "de-Nigerianized" ECOMOG, which was a longstanding Taylor and Francophone demand.[81] Limited information about the Tanzanian and Ugandan ECOMOG experience, however, suggests that these two non-West African forces displayed even less commitment to the mission than did the West African contingents. The Tanzanians and Ugandans rarely saw combat and, when they did, they sometimes performed inadequately. In a 1994 situation the NPFL confronted a few Tanzanian companies—a total of about 300 men—which decided not to fight but to surrender all their equipment, including U.S. radios and their personal weapons and kits. The Tanzanians may have been stretched too thin, but this episode lowered morale by angering other ECOMOG officers.[82]

ECOMOG lacked adequate administration and control, and its poor integration began at the top. A weak regional organization can create only a weak military force. West African states of ECOWAS traditionally had not supported the organization sufficiently because of pressing domestic concerns and generally moribund economies. Limited institutional allegiance does result in unkept promises, financial shortfalls, and lack of effective enforcement for the military force. ECOMOG thus had difficulty in maintaining its "logistical tail," which involved shipping relevant supplies quickly, usually from Lagos, to Freetown, and then to Liberia.

ECOMOG never supplied its officers and troops with rules of engagement (ROE). These rules, which are given in all UN and many other military operations, specify what constitutes justifiable force and what exceeds the force's mandate. Without ROE, junior ECOMOG officers made quick decisions in the heat of battle, and these actions caused unnecessary casualties.[83]

A multilateral force reflects the existing ethos of each of its members; the record of the ECOMOG forces was mixed. Most observers gave high marks to the Ghanaians and Senegalese but criticized others, especially the Nigerians. The high level of corruption in some units drained significant resources from ECOMOG's military capabilities or, when pilfered from in Liberia, angered Liberians who previously had been grateful for the presence of ECOMOG. Some Western and African diplomats in Freetown felt that Nigeria's corruption was contagious and encouraged theft by members of other contingents.

A regional force requires, beyond sheer numbers, an effective joint command (a major challenge to multinational forces), strong administrative and intelligence capabilities, and suitable training. ECOMOG generally lacked these capabilities. ECOMOG suffered especially from a structural problem, "ad hocism," which plagues most multilateral intervention forces. Lack of administrative skills and effective oversight of possible corruption are especially likely in a hastily assembled multilateral force. This was especially true of ECOMOG: most of its members had had few, if any, joint training exercises, and their forces were often inept. For example, Iweze reveals that ECOMOG's logistical planning did not contain any logistics officers.[84]

However, initial problems may have been unavoidable, given the speed of ECOMOG's creation. ECOMOG's rapid formation probably accounted for its "stovepiping" of responsibilities, that is, each contingent was responsible for most of its military capabilities, including logistics, area of operations, and indirect fire support.[85] A 1997 high-level conference that included ECOMOG's former commanders noted that "joint training did not occur; common doctrine did not exist. Each country continued to bear the expenses of its own forces; each country's troops were under the command of their own officers. It is obvious that command and control questions, central to any military operation, were often unresolved."[86]

A Western defense attaché recalls that "throughout the conflict, each contingent trained separately at the national level prior to sending troops to Liberia. Each country had its own training standards . . . so the quality of training for the contingents varied widely."[87] The lack of horizontal training remained a serious problem for several years. Stovepiping maintained the often very wide discrepancies between the various contingents' military capabilities and lessened the chances for combined combat operations.

An external force will often lack basic tactical intelligence—which, despite their geographic closeness to Liberia, ECOMOG contributors lacked.[88] Adjunct to this, language incompatibility (English versus French) was a relatively minor problem. Few ECOMOG officers knew Liberian languages, but this would have been a serious problem only if ECOMOG had conducted intensive peace enforcement.

A regional force may not have experience even with nearby physical geography. No other African forces had fought in terrain similar to Liberia's; their recent peacekeeping experiences having been in Chad and Lebanon. ECOMOG members had little counterinsurgency experience, and in 1990 only Ghana and Senegal had any functional jungle warfare training centers.[89]

Few ECOMOG pilots had flown in combat. They did succeed in harassing supply lines and lowering troop morale in the NPFL when counterattacking Operation Octopus. Yet, too often, ECOMOG planes accidentally hit relief convoys and medical facilities, and the ensuing protests (along with inadequate maintenance) helped curb ECOMOG's air power.

ECOMOG faced difficult problems inside Liberia beyond those of equipment or personnel. The traditional advantages of an indigenous irregular force against a conventionally trained foreign force often reasserted themselves. Liberia's vegetation, often mountainous terrain, and its long rainy season from July to December posed natural impediments to any major mechanized operations. "It's good ambush country, almost anywhere outside of Monrovia," notes a Western military analyst.[90] The lack of interior roads, coupled with the complete lack of transport helicopters, offered obvious logistical difficulties.

Distinguishing between combatant and noncombatant proved difficult, especially since the NPFL had no uniforms and often employed children (e.g., Taylor's "Small Boys Unit") as soldiers.[91] ECOMOG's morale plummeted when its soldiers had to fire in self-defense upon child-soldiers.

By the time of Operation Octopus, two years after ECOMOG's arrival, Western observers could still note glaring military limitations in ECOMOG. U.S. State Department cables stated that "ECOMOG [since

October 15] has not acquitted itself with distinction; with the notable exception of the Senegalese and Guineans, some elements have been worse than useless." The cables described Nigerians as "unmotivated and poorly-led" (until the arrival of ECOMOG's new field commander, Adetunji Olourin).[92]

Theft hurt ECOMOG's effectiveness as well, even though it was sometimes committed to help finance ECOMOG's continuing in Liberia.[93] More often, however, thievery was personal. Officers selling soldiers' food or keeping their pay occurred too often. Hutchful mentions that Nigerian troops, though "technically better funded, complained frequently of a lack of food at a time when the Ghanaians were being well fed."[94] He describes a major "who banked the salary of his troops in a foreign bank for several months and collected the interest" and that "this kind of practice by peacekeeping commanders could not have been unusual: earlier, seven Lieutenant-Colonels and their paymasters who [previously] had served in the Middle East were dismissed by General Quainoo . . . for similar corruption."[95]

Crime by ECOMOG soldiers (who certainly were not the only or worst plunderers in Liberia) drained or diverted material and manpower resources and served as a bad example. General ECOMOG morale declined as non-Nigerian forces sometimes privately complained that Nigerian dominance of ECOMOG resulted in the lack of prosecution of Nigerian officers for alleged criminal improprieties. Desire for continued access to Liberia's resources probably lessened some units' desire to engage Taylor militarily and end the war quickly. Rapaciousness led to at least one firefight that threatened to shatter Liberia's cease-fire when, in January 1996, ECOMOG fought ULIMO-J for control over profits of a Tubmanberg diamond mine: ECOMOG alone suffered some sixty casualties.

ECOMOG's cooperation with the Liberian factions weakened its purported neutrality. Furthermore, these factions constantly tried to use ECOMOG for their own purposes. For example, the INPFL ransomed Nigerian ECOMOG soldiers for weapons and the LPC wanted ECOMOG to garrison areas around Buchanan captured by the LPC so that it could use as many of its troops as possible for forward operations. Factions sometimes attempted, through the use of false intelligence, to provoke ECOMOG attacks against other factions. "Every faction comes here to use us—we can't trust any of them," complained a highly placed Nigerian intelligence officer.[96]

By supporting the factions, ECOMOG risked creating

Frankensteins that could threaten any peace settlement. A diplomat in Liberia commented that "the factions at various [times] have been uncontrollable."[97] Looting and smuggling provided the factions with some independent financing. All the factions eventually skirmished with ECOMOG forces and several times engaged them in significant firefights. Also, prolongation of the war risked devolution of faction power away from central command and to smaller units.[98] Factions continued their struggle by linking up with private businessmen: this external support not only aided the groups' military capabilities, but made them reluctant to settle for political negotiations that would end their profitable pillaging.

Factions lacked a clear command-and-control system: individual fighters did not receive standardized military training or the political indoctrination that helps mold an esprit de corps. Individual (or perhaps small-unit) gain was the guiding raison d'être, rather than any sacrifice for an ideology. With no central ethos or control of communications, faction leaders ran the risk of losing control to local commanders; the lack of clear command and control allowed faction "soldiers" to switch sides.

Such a diffusion of power poses a policing problem to the regional force. Lack of control may allow local human rights abuses that discredit the political reputation of a faction and its sponsors. Lack of control may lead to the kind of localized actions that trigger international reaction. Another possible result of the decentralized, somewhat apolitical forces is a concerted resistance to a political settlement that tries to close down pillaging operations—which is what occurred in early 1996 at Tubmanberg.

Greater Commitment?

Regional forces, simply by their existence, evince a strong commitment to their own region. This commitment should lessen the gap between (a) their interests and their values in the conflict and (b) their time constraints and the time horizons of the local combatants. National/regional values, such as ending starvation, are congruent with interest because a conflict's civilian suffering can threaten neighboring states with spillover fighting ("hot pursuit"), increased refugees, and the deliberate destabilization of neighboring states. The geographical proximity increases the chance of common ethnic, family, and business ties. This overlapping of values and interest undoubtedly prolonged ECOMOG's commitment in Liberia.

African states did have real national interests involved in Liberia's war. Nigeria hoped to use ECOMOG to assert itself in West Africa, especially against France and her former colonies, and to use its sponsorship of ECOMOG to gain political credits from Western nations otherwise critical of Nigeria's authoritarianism. Other ECOMOG states received important financial assistance from Nigeria in return for their ECOMOG participation. Ghana, for example, received subsidized fuel shipments shortly before its 1992 elections. Several ECOMOG nations had significant numbers of their citizens threatened by the fighting within Liberia.

The overlapping of values with interest also shortened the gap between the interveners' and combatants' commitments. Unlike in Somalia, where national interests of member states were largely absent, the insurgents in Liberia could not assume that unexpectedly high casualties or financial costs would prompt an early withdrawal by the foreign force.

ECOMOG did "stay the course"; the prolonged war failed to destroy the will of the outside interveners. The ECOMOG states at first clearly did not expect the war to last very long: a top Ghanaian Foreign Ministry official thought of six months as the absolute maximum period.[99] Yet all of the original five contributors remained, despite the financial and human costs. The reasons ranged from humanitarianism to regional stability to fear of losing political face. Nigeria suffered about five hundred killed in action, and it claims to have spent $8 billion on a conflict that did not directly affect its own security. (And this was from a country whose 1995 foreign debt stood at $35 billion; no Western nation, especially following the Somalian intervention, could match such commitment.)

Yet ECOMOG's undeniable commitment needs more explanation; its remaining in Liberia depended on its acting as a peacekeeper, rather than a peace enforcer, and on its using dangerous surrogates for much of the fighting. As noted, prolonging the conflict and its suffering became the result. Furthermore, the undemocratic nature of most of the contributing states helped facilitate ECOMOG's protracted commitment. These states proscribed political parties, unfettered media, and restricted information about the war's financial and political costs; this authoritarianism at home restricted possible debate and aided the continuance of ECOMOG.

Although the original five ECOMOG contingents remained in Liberia, they did not actively attempt to end the war militarily. Rather than acknowledge failed commitment by withdrawing from a prolonged conflict, a regional force may alter its strategy; this more conservative strategy—the use of surrogates and the adoption of peacekeeping rather than peace enforcement—paradoxically may further prolong the struggle. By not carrying the war outside Monrovia, except when attacked in late 1992, ECOMOG allowed Taylor to recover from his two defeats (1990 and 1992) and to loot much of the Liberian countryside.

Deciding upon and then maintaining a mandate is often difficult: regional, domestic, and local politics affect the process. Nigeria and Ghana strongly disagreed about Charles Taylor. For much, although not all, of ECOMOG's first three years, Nigerian officers considered Taylor the main impediment to peace and hoped to pursue him vigorously, sometimes with airstrikes and assassination attempts. Ghana, however, felt that the powerful Taylor was essential to Liberia's peace, and that demonizing and actively pursuing him would only make the war last longer.[100]

Local political realities also affect a mandate. Taylor's initial popularity (and Doe's unpopularity) weakened ECOMOG's solidarity. The AFL had committed most of the atrocities by August 1990, and, at least until Doe's death, Taylor did not appear clearly as the enemy to some ECOMOG members. Taylor had started and led the crusade against the despotic Doe, and he had a substantial following of Liberians.

ECOMOG increasingly supported the surrogates, who demonstrated more commitment to fighting Taylor than did ECOMOG itself. Because these factions operated out of ECOMOG's sight and because their goal of containing Taylor aided ECOMOG, they generally had carte blanche in their everyday operations. So abuse of human rights became the norm. Taylor increasingly could not engage ECOMOG because of multifront pressure from ULIMO-K, ULIMO-J, and LPC. But this led to the growth of quasi-independent factions, a further loss of ECOMOG's neutrality, and greater devastation of rural Liberia. ULIMO's fighting against the NPFL helped undermine the Yamoussoukro accord, while the LPC's attacks against the NPFL hurt implementation of the Cotonou agreement. When ECOWAS/ECOMOG finally gained a peace settlement with Taylor in 1995, the factions had come to oppose ECOMOG.

That most ECOMOG states were not democratic hurt ECOMOG's military and political capabilities but assisted ECOMOG's commitment.[101] Nigeria's personalist governments had stripped the military's effectiveness by allowing, inter alia, corruption (especially in procurement), by reshuffling the officer corps, and by creating parallel militaries. The military's above-the-law tradition in Nigeria carried over to Liberia. Stedman writes that "because the Nigerian military was not accountable at home, it was not accountable for how it behaved in Liberia."[102]

Repressive home states that refused to divulge ECOMOG's human and financial costs and denied their publics the opportunity to voice objections faced little questioning of ECOMOG's commitment. Official information about the national militaries' commitment, size, and financial cost; their rate of casualties; or their overall performance (including human rights conduct) was not forthcoming. The opposition press in these states faced various official and unofficial constraints in reporting about ECOMOG.

The five original ECOMOG states, all basically undemocratic, remained in Liberia for the war's duration. The three countries, Senegal, Tanzania, and Uganda, that entered later had more open political systems, and each of these three countries withdrew after a specified period. Only Senegal, probably the most democratic of the contributing states, witnessed any serious domestic debate. Following the NPFL's killing of six Senegalese soldiers in May 1992, "public opinion in Senegal was deeply shocked by this loss of life . . . [and] turned even more sharply against this policy," according to Mortimer.[103] Soon thereafter, the Senegalese contingent withdrew to the relatively safe confines of Monrovia and then left Liberia in January 1993. Security considerations also influenced Senegal's departure: it resented serving as the "fire brigade" for endangered ECOMOG forces and worried about its soldiers acquiring corrupt practices from other contingents.

The undemocratic states did fear the possibility of domestic debate, and these fears lessened commitment to a quicker military resolution of the conflict. Nigeria's concerns about the political and economic costs of a possible Vietnam-like quagmire increasingly weakened that nation's peace enforcement strategy. Herman Cohen mentions that "Nigeria worried about its participation in ECOMOG becoming a domestic issue . . . and worked to keep it from becoming one."[104] Field commander appointments fluctuated between aggressive leaders such as Dogonyaro and Olurin, who pressed the war but caused more casualties, and the more passive generals, such as Kupolati and Bakyut, who only maintained the stalemate but incurred less cost and fewer casualties.

The Lessons of Failure

The failures of ECOMOG, many of which the organization was power-less to affect, are just as significant as ECOMOG's successes as lessons for future regional forces. ECOMOG's general deficit of suitable military capabilities and, to a lesser extent, a lack of political responsibility prevented it from realizing the hypothetical advantages of a regional intervention force. Reliance on unprofessional national forces courts disaster.

Potential interveners should maintain constant expertise in regional affairs and should be able to judge whether their own political and military capabilities are equal to a proposed task. ECOMOG's experience demonstrates an obvious but important peacekeeping lesson: it is infinitely easier to enter than to leave a conflict. Cooperating with local factions offers some short-run tactical advantages to a peacekeeping force but threatens its necessary neutrality and poses long-term political problems.

Intelligence helps determine mandate. The hastily assembled ECOMOG lacked the acceptance, knowledge, and military capability to act as an effective peacekeeper or as a peace enforcer. The difficulties of ECOMOG's attempts at peace enforcement suggest strongly that states should not enter an ongoing conflict, or else should intervene only with an adequate force. Temporary coalitions, especially of relatively poor states, should limit their mandate to that of peacekeeping rather than peace enforcement. A future regional force should hesitate about emotionally intervening for strictly humanitarian reasons before assessing the possible military, political, and economic pitfalls.

Perhaps future regional peacekeeping forces could be a "first reactor" that could enter quickly upon agreement by the warring parties, and then step aside for (or operate alongside) a better equipped UN peacekeeping force.[105] A major advantage that ECOMOG had over typical UN peacekeeping forces was its ability to form and begin operations quickly. Two major disadvantages, though, which a stronger UN force could have addressed, were ECOMOG's lack of suitable military capabilities and its loss of its initial neutrality. Admittedly, the UN's present difficulty in fielding new forces makes this suggestion less likely for now.

Interveners should avoid "ad hocism," even though various political and economic considerations rule out permanent forces throughout the third world. An alternative is designated forces, which keep their own national military structures but that share common doctrine and equipment and conduct joint operations with each other for future joint operations. ECOMOG never had uniform training standards and it "stovepiped" many essential functions (it is noteworthy that since late 1994 the chiefs of staff of the ECOMOG forces began meeting with some regularity to discuss greater coordination of national units).

Such forces should emphasize relatively low-cost and available counterinsurgency items (e.g., spotter planes and interoperable radios rather than jet fighters and main battle tanks). Several ECOMOG countries had aircraft, but all too often a lack of maintenance or spare parts grounded their planes and helicopters. A future regional force, especially one involved in peace enforcement, will need an adequate support system, or logistical tail. Ad hocism delays establishing this very necessary function.

A regional military force should have a centralized structure whose authority lessens the influence of a major contributor.[106] It could also lessen the troops' pay frauds that plagued some of ECOMOG's national contingents. Rationalized administration in most individual ECOMOG militaries could have lessened their mediocrity, even as hasty amalgamation of these systems multiplied the problems. Finally, external aid on a regional, not bilateral, basis can increase the compatibility and the equality of equipment.

An intervention force is as much a political as a military instrument and must act accordingly. By obtaining prompt blessing of the force by nonregional forces, the OAU and the UN will aid a regional force's credibility. A future force should consider an overt political presence: an in-country political representative could assist negotiations between the warring parties, as well as the ad hoc negotiations that arise among the forces or with the relief agencies. "We had to do these talks, but that's not what we were trained in," mentions a high-ranking Nigerian officer in Liberia. "We would have welcomed a professional negotiator."[107] A special representative should also oversee the regional force's adherence to human rights, which would strengthen the force's neutrality and acceptance. The involvement of a neutral, outside monitoring group may provide the same function of monitoring human rights. A future force should also consider a civic action program: well-publicized initiatives in basic health and education offer a more beneficent image of the foreign intervention and encourage necessary intelligence flows to the outside force.

In the end, ECOMOG proved unable to end the Liberian conflict, but instead prolonged it. This encouraged a spillover of the conflict into Sierra Leone,[108] the toppling of the Gambian government, and an increase of refugees in several countries. Regional stability was a goal of ECOMOG; greater regional instability was the result.

All in all, however, the nations of ECOMOG richly deserve credit for trying to end Liberia's carnage and for creating ECOMOG so quickly while the rest of the world stood by. These underfunded African states allowed serious humanitarian concerns to erase their traditional hesitation to interfere in another state's internal affairs.

Continued Failure in Sierra Leone

That ECOMOG entered Sierra Leone in 1997 following seven years of possible lessons in Liberia raises a basic question: How much did ECOMOG improve as a result of its Liberian experience? Answering that question helps to determine whether ECOMOG should continue as a multinational force.

Sierra Leone has a similar recent history to that of Liberia: discredited previous personal-rule governments that had engaged in wide-scale corruption, manipulated ethnic divisions, undermined the national military, and produced unusually violent insurgencies. The collapse of the state's legitimacy encouraged the appearance of an insurgent movement, the RUF, in 1991 which brutalized many civilians in its areas of control. (Liberia's Charles Taylor would strongly support the RUF throughout the 1990s.) The dense bush and lack of roads in both Liberia and Sierra Leone gave operational advantages to rebel movements, and Sierra Leone's alluvial and kimberlite diamond areas attracted rebel and outside military interests. Government officials also used the conflict to avail themselves of diamonds.[109]

The weakness of the Republic of Sierra Leone Military Force (RSLMF) persuaded Sierra Leone in 1995 to hire a foreign force, Executive Outcomes (EO), which helped to gain a temporary but deceptive peace. EO and a decentralized militia force quickly pushed the RUF away from the capital, Freetown, and the diamond areas, and secured sufficient stability for a relatively free February 1996 election and a subsequent peace agreement in November of the same year. A combination of the RUF and "sobels" overthrew the largely unprotected Kabbah regime in late May 1997, several months after EO had left Sierra Leone. The toppling of the democratically elected government by the newly formed Armed Forces Revolutionary Council and the subsequent plundering and brutalization brought instant and continuing international protest. No country recognized the new regime.

ECOMOG began hostilities shortly after the May coup. (ECOMOG in Liberia was about 70 percent Nigerian; ECOMOG in Sierra Leone was about 90 percent Nigerian.) It was initially counterproductive; a naval shelling of Freetown in June failed to dislodge the RUF but did hit several civilian areas. ECOMOG did not venture much out of Lungi Airport for the next six months. Then, in February 1998, Nigerian forces attacked and quickly liberated Freetown. Subsequent operations proved more difficult, especially in the Kono-Kailahun diamond areas, despite predictions from ECOMOG commander Gen. Timothy Shelpedi of imminent military victory. Difficult terrain slowed and then halted ECOMOG's progress, and the RUF's "shoot and scoot," small-scale actions had killed several hundred Nigerians by November 1998.

The war's Tet-like turning point occurred in late 1998 and January 1999 when RUF irregulars infiltrated Freetown and then battled ECO-MOG for several weeks before withdrawing into the bush. ECOMOG killed substantial numbers of RUF fighters, but the Freetown episode demonstrated that the war had become a military stalemate. Gen. Abdulsalami Abubakar, Abacha's successor as president of Nigeria, voiced a desire in January 1999 that Nigerian troops leave Sierra Leone by the end of May of that year. Although Abubakar and his elected successor, Gen. Olesegun Obasanjo, subsequently agreed that Nigerian troops would remain to safeguard an election process, it was clear that Nigeria had become disenchanted with its ECOMOG involvement in Sierra Leone. In July 1999, the Kabbah government and the RUF reached a peace settlement in Lomé, Togo. Like the NPFL, the RUF had won political legitimacy not through force of ideas or popular support, but because national militaries had proven capable of stopping a quasi-terrorist rebellion.

Numerous reasons explain ECOMOG's failure, but its inability to learn from Liberia looms as decisive. ECOMOG gained little counterinsurgency capability during its largely "peacekeeping" (i.e., nonaggressive combat) mission in Liberia. A former high-ranking U.S. special operations officer who worked with ECOMOG forces in Sierra Leone in early 1999 recalls that "they had no counterinsurgency doctrine, preferred conventional assault, and flew aerial reconnaissance at 5,000 feet."[110]

Nigeria and other ECOMOG countries by 1999 still had not emphasized counterinsurgency capabilities, possibly reflecting fears by insecure rulers of a too-effective military. ECOMOG lacked sufficient appropriate counterinsurgency equipment and manpower. ECOMOG in Sierra Leone grievously suffered from logistic shortages. It rarely risked its planes or helicopters in combined ground-air operations against the RUF—a single MI-17 helicopter piloted by two white South Africans played a pivotal role in defending ECOMOG, as noted below. British government sources maintain that no ECOMOG member has ground attack helicopters, suggesting that the governments' fear of military coups was a major factor. ECOMOG in Sierra Leone once again relied on two U.S. companies, International Charter, Inc., and Pacific Architects and Engineering, for its helicopter and truck transportation needs.[111]

ECOMOG after nine years still lacked basic capabilities in communications and intelligence collection and/or analysis. The force reportedly needed encryption and frequency-hopping radio capabilities: "RUF could listen to ECOMOG radio traffic: they heard all of ECOMOG's commos [communications]," observes a U.S. government analyst.[112]

ECOMOG continued to lack both aggregate manpower or the skills that would allow it to rely on fewer personnel. ECOMOG generals felt that they needed a force level of 20,000 soldiers to mount offensive operations in Liberia and Sierra Leone, but only rarely did they have more than 12,000. A few West African nations offered troops for Sierra Leone but only as peacekeepers—especially as these nations came to realize the RUF's combat capabilities. ECOMOG needed local allies, as it had in Liberia, but it worried that strengthening the Civil Defence Forces (that outnumbered ECOMOG by at least two to one) might encourage a Liberian-like Frankenstein against ECOMOG or the Kabbah government.

A higher skill level would have allowed ECOMOG to rely on fewer troops for its combat operations; after all, EO's 200-man force had succeeded against the RUF. Predeployment training remained insufficient: ECOMOG militaries apparently had not engaged in joint, let alone similar, training by mid-1999—some nine years after ECOMOG's formation. Lack of maintenance for high-technology items is as an especially glaring weakness to this day. Nigerians acknowledge a problem and blame the lack of money for spare parts, as well as the U.S. decertification.

ECOMOG's political responsibility did generally improve, beginning with General Malu's cracking down on illegal activities in Liberia. ECOMOG apparently did not interfere with the political operations of the democratically elected Kabbah government, except to insist in early

1999 that Kabbah begin negotiations with the RUF. ECOMOG's internal discipline has remained commendably intact. Nigerian soldiers have not received the credit they deserve for refraining from mutinies or from disobeying or "fragging" their officers during the frustrating and dangerous campaign against the RUF.

Yet some problems of responsibility continued, especially before and following the Freetown fiasco. Nigeria's unilateral changing of ECOMOG's mandate from peacekeeping to peace enforcement angered most of the ECOWAS countries, although few expressed such open criticism as Burkina Faso's Blaise Compaore.[113]

Nigerian troops began illegal diamond mining and exporting in Sierra Leone by mid-1998 and had engaged in limited harassment of civilians. Economic goals sometimes claimed priority over any military resolution of the conflict: ECOMOG soldiers "soon found that digging diamonds was more profitable than imposing peace," writes *The Economist*. "They made local deals with the RUF, in one place mining on opposite sides of a river bank."[114] Payroll theft continued to plague the Nigerian military; British, U.S., and Nigerian sources believe that some Nigerian officers may have skimmed up to 50 percent of their soldiers' pay, which forced some soldiers to steal from the already hard-pressed Sierra Leoneans.[115]

RUF's grinding guerrilla campaign and then its surprising invasion of Freetown prompted additional instances of ECOMOG mistreatment of Sierra Leonean citizens. A UN report in February 1999 criticized the force for "numerous incidents of ill treatment . . . whipping, beating, [and] varying types of public humiliation."[116] Human Rights Watch suggests that ECOMOG forces may have been largely responsible for "over 180 summary executions of rebel prisoners and their suspected collaborators."[117] ECOMOG's overall conduct still remained reasonably good when compared with RUF's terrorism, just as it had in Liberia when contrasted to the factions' brutality.[118]

It should be noted that UNAMSIL (United Nations Military In Sierra Leone), which entered in late 1999, fared worse than did ECOMOG, repeating many of ECOMOG's initial mistakes of 1990 and inadvertently aiding the RUF. The *Washington Post* reported in early June 2000 that "more than half of the [UN] troops [which then totaled about 8,000] did not bring the arms, communications equipment and logistics support they were required to by a UN checklist." One diplomat said, "We are sending ill-equipped troops out into the field with the same vulnerabilities as before. It is mind-boggling."[119] Only after ECOMOG's departure from Sierra Leone did the RUF take some 500

UNAMSIL peacekeepers hostage. RUF appeared ready to re-enter Freetown in mid-2000 until the British combat troop deployment.

The Future of ECOMOG

ECOMOG's nearly ten-year record, as well as uncertain underwriting and a widespread desire for less Nigerian control, suggest an uncertain future. ECOMOG has not achieved the possible advantages of a regional peacekeeping force largely because it has lacked sufficient military capability, which is partly a result of unaccountable political systems. ECOMOG's record is at best uneven, but both its successes and failures offer valuable lessons for future regional military forces.

ECOMOG garnered significant worldwide praise following Liberia's peaceful elections in 1997. Official U.S. judgment of ECOMOG since Liberia's elections was typical. The U.S. State Department spokesman, James Rubin, commented that

> the patient determination and commitment of ECOWAS to bring peace and security to Liberia is a tribute to the ability of the West African subregion collectively to solve its problems. The U.S. is proud to have played a supporting role in this effort. . . . We also look forward to working with ECOWAS to help resolve peacefully other regional issues of mutual concern such as the crisis in Sierra Leone.[120]

Some observers believe that the Nigerian military, in particular, has learned invaluable lessons since 1990.[121] Human Rights Watch noted a growth in ECOMOG's political responsibility, with "significant improvements in its conduct since its intervention in Liberia," stemming from "improved supervision, more regular payment of salaries, and a sensitivity to past criticisms."[122]

Yet wishful thinking for an idealized ECOMOG, rather than the force's actual performance, had generated such praise. And ECOMOG was the only horse on the track during the decade throughout the 1990s; no multinational alternative ever appeared. Policymakers, at least in the United States, prefer to work with the imperfect institution rather than hope for a new one.

Political as well as the military problems may suggest a dicey future for ECOMOG. Regional reaction to a future ECOMOG was guardedly favorable by mid-2000. Many states would support a future ECOMOG but only if they received greater control over it vis-à-vis Nigeria, the regional hegemon. Many of ECOWAS's sixteen states favor a permanent regional military capability, but not a standing force, and one which has a broader based leadership.[123]

Several 1998 ECOWAS meetings provided insight into regional attitudes toward ECOMOG. The foreign ministers' communiqué in March of that year acknowledged ECOMOG's "dedication, courage, and professionalism" and expressed hope for a "peacekeeping mechanism . . . that will have ECOMOG as its backbone."[124] The ministers then revealed their objections to the current ECOMOG by seeking a "redefinition" that would include "the judicial statute, the constitution of the troops, the decision-making process—that is the relations of the troops with the political authorities—the conditions of their mission, their deployment, the political and diplomatic management of the crisis, the methods of command, the training, the financing, and so on."[125]

Quite a redefinition! The ministers of defence meeting in July 1998 made a series of wide-ranging recommendations, some of which strove to address problems resulting during ECOMOG's Liberian and Sierra Leonean campaigns. The ministers concurred that ECOMOG should continue, but that any interventions should feature a strong political component, a wider regional membership, and an authorization of any mission prior to its departure.[126] The ministers recommended an early-warning system, that various committees (e.g., a council of elders) should hold informal meetings and negotiations to head off possible conflict, and that ECOMOG should assist with humanitarian support. The communiqué of the meeting notes that such aid "is one of the most important tools of conflict prevention and . . . [that ECOWAS had] not adequately supported its peacekeeping activities with humanitarian action."[127]

A proposed Mediation and Security Council would provide the necessary mandate for ECOMOG's future interventions. Its rotating membership would have nine member states, and interventions would need a two-thirds majority of those nine. Intervention would occur only in conflicts that have significant outside involvement or in conflicts between states if peaceful methods fail. ECOMOG could undertake a range of other duties, including preventive deployment, policing, and anticrime activities.

These goals are admirable but they raise the long-standing problems of mandate, financing, and regional unity. Many of the above situations, though listed in the communiqué as "peacekeeping," could easily involve ECOMOG in combat: interposing itself between states when negotiations have failed, attempting to disarm factions, or cracking down on crime. ECOMOG's 1990 entry into Liberia as a peacekeeper soon saw the well-intentioned force under fire from recalcitrant factions. West African states have shown great reluctance to commit their ill-trained and poorly equipped forces to any probable combat situation. They fear the financial and political costs of a military stalemate or defeat, as well as the anger of especially junior officers who may cause political unrest—though common training and equipping of these national militaries could increase the chance of their entry into future conflicts.

Uncertain financial backing also confronts ECOMOG's future. ECOWAS hopes to greatly expand its conflict resolution capability, but as the communiqué candidly acknowledges, member states have not been financially forthcoming ("the difficulty with which Member States pay their contributions to the Community Institutions and the enormous amounts of arrears of contribution").[128] The communiqué states that all of ECOWAS's members should pay for troop upkeep "irrespective of whether or not their contingents are involved in the operation, In view of limited resources, troop-contributing states may have to bear the cost of military operations for the initial three months, after which ECOWAS will take full responsibility."[129]

Troop-contributing nations might hesitate to pay initially for putting their troops into harm's way with only a promise of "full responsibility" after three months from a presently impoverished organization.

ECOWAS has never been fully united, and regional schisms have not lessened since ECOMOG's creation. Previous conflicts in West Africa usually saw ECOWAS members divided in their sympathies and, therefore, in their financial or military support. The hope in 1990 that a successful ECOMOG could encourage greater regional cooperation has proven illusory. Nigeria's predominance (and that of other Anglophone countries) in ECOMOG indicates a continuing Anglophone-Francophone divide.[130] Many ECOWAS states disapproved of ECOMOG's (basically Nigeria's) January 1998 Freetown offensive and some of the French-speaking countries have turned to particularly French attempts to create a regional peacekeeping capability, a move that irritated the Abacha government.[131]

An internally changing Nigeria may curtail its support for ECOMOG. Should Nigeria continue on its democratization path, public demand for domestic spending may preclude any significant finding for ECOMOG. Nigeria's pressing domestic problems, including an economy that has seen per capita income drop fourfold since 1990 but that has undergone a dramatic climb in inflation and foreign debt, may convince Abuja to cut funding to ECOMOG. ECOMOG's Sierra

Leone commander, Abu Ahmadu, reflected in late 1998 that "it's not an easy thing to keep us here. We wonder what will happen if a civilian comes to power [in Nigeria]. . . . When a democratic government takes over after the elections, it may well be more sensitive to Nigerian soldiers' death."[132] Nigerian criticism directed at ECOMOG's record rose following President Abacha's death in mid-1998. Gen. Olusegun Obasanjo, now Nigeria's president, remarked in August 1998 that

> Nigeria can go to Liberia, and make a mess up there, and spend and waste our money, because what we got after five years of ECOMOG in Liberia, we would have got without sending one single troop to Liberia, because it's the same thing we got at the end. Taylor would have been there if we hadn't sent one single soldier. Taylor was there after five years—we have the same difference.[133]

Writing in the spring of 1999, Mortimer suggested that "Obasanjo would terminate Nigeria's almost nine-year expedition into regional peacekeeping."[134]

Yet ECOMOG could offer some continuing political advantages to Nigeria. Many Nigerians feel that it symbolizes Nigerian leadership in the region and that ECOMOG can help stabilize the region. A future ECOMOG that distributes responsibilities and funding more evenly would appeal to many Nigerians seeking greater domestic spending. Finally, President Obasanjo has appeared determined to reprofessionalize Nigeria's military, and a competent force could attract significant Western financial backing.

The RUF's entry into Freetown in early 1999 and the deaths of about 1,000 Nigerian soldiers, coupled with Nigeria's belief that Kabbah was relying on ECOMOG for a military solution rather than entering into peaceful negotiations with the RUF, helped to prompt the Nigerian government in late January 1999 to announce a pullout from Sierra Leone over the following several months. Some Nigerian officials realize that regional fears of Nigerian hegemony could restrict desirable peaceful cooperation. The Babangida, Shonekan, and Abacha governments had used ECOMOG's peacekeeping to defuse Western criticism of Nigeria's domestic authoritarianism: a democratizing Nigeria would not require such military means of attracting foreign approval.

ECOMOG's future may hinge on whether Nigeria will continue to pay most of ECOMOG's expenses—especially during a prolonged operation—while surrendering its predominance to neighboring states, some of whom are Francophone and opposed to many of Nigeria's policies. More states forming ECOMOG policies but having less funding could jeopardize ECOMOG's effectiveness. In July 2000, ECOWAS announced plans to impose a 0.5 percent surcharge on all imports into West Africa to pay for a future combat-ready force.

Western cooperation will be less than many African states desire, largely because of ECOMOG's general incompetence, the political advantages of bilateral assistance, and a continuing rivalry among Western states. ECOMOG's record has discouraged financial assistance, even though the United States and Britain increased their financing to ECOMOG beginning in the mid-1990s.[135] The West's general belief that ECOMOG lacks responsible procurement and payroll practices helps to circumscribe its aid: Britain insisted that it—not ECOMOG—purchase needed equipment with the $16 million grant. France, in particular, is funneling significant funding into its bilateral assistance programs, and provided no support to ECOMOG in either Liberia or Sierra Leone.

Other Regional Cooperation

Despite ECOMOG's spotty accomplishments, Western and African states gradually are increasing and coordinating their regional peacekeeping resources. Most observers agree that African regions, or blocs within them, are increasingly assuming primary security responsibility. The West has helped to underwrite, but not to supervise, multinational military exercises in southern and eastern Africa. ACRI has provided peacekeeping training to battalions from seven African countries, beginning in 1997. The British African Peacekeeping Initiative, begun in 1995, has aided peacekeeping training through various means including British military advisory and training teams (BMATTs) at staff colleges in Zimbabwe and Ghana. France began its Renforcement des Capacités Africaines de Maintien de la Paix, or RECAMP, in 1997. RECAMP trains mostly Francophone African soldiers in peacekeeping skills, and it has pre-positioned vehicles and medical supplies in Senegal for possible future multilateral regional operations. These three initiatives have remained separate, although much of their doctrine and equipment are similar (the French supply larger items, such as armored personnel carriers and trucks). In addition, France has created a peacekeeping school in Côte d'Ivoire and provided about $6 million to "Guidimakha '98," a West African training exercise. Much of the

French supplies for Guidikmakha later supported the Mission Internationale de Surveillance du Accords de Bangui (MISAB), which halted a 1997 army mutiny against President Ange-Félix Pataseé.

Regions other than West Africa have increased military cooperation, usually with substantial Western assistance, but have not yet developed regional military groupings. The OAU has expressed growing interest in having a peacekeeping capability. These region-wide attempts will continue the growing trend toward interoperable intervention capability.[136]

Southern Africa, which has several of Africa's most competent and experienced militaries, has explored the possibility of a future force and has staged several joint exercises. Zimbabwe and Britain co-hosted "Blue Hungwe" in April 1997, the largest field exercise to date, including nine nations and 1,500 troops. Its goals followed those of the African Crisis Response Initiative (ACRI): "to enhance regional liaison, co-operation, military skills and interoperability by means of a multinational joint field training exercise in the tactics and techniques of international peacekeeping."[137] Blue Crane, a subsequent exercise in April 1999, saw the participation of 4,000 military and police personnel from ten Southern African Development Community countries. It involved a wide range of participants, including human rights and relief groups. It worked on developing standardized doctrine and tactics for future peacekeeping. The U.S. Central Command, along with the reconstituted East African Community of Kenya, Tanzania, and Uganda, conducted Exercise Natural Fire in 1998.[138]

Yet interstate warfare could further divide some regions into several different political blocs, thus undermining a common regional identity and cooperation. The Liberian and Sierra Leonean wars aggravated Anglophone-Francophone differences, while Charles Taylor's possible regional aspirations add a new complication.[139] By late 1998, Angola and Zimbabwe (and perhaps Namibia) had formed a de facto grouping that had championed cross-border military operations in the Congo, whereas South Africa, Botswana, Mozambique, Malawi, and Zambia generally preferred political negotiations.

The OAU has become more concerned about African security during this decade, but it lacks the resources and political consensus to mount its own peacekeeping operations. In 1993, the OAU formally adopted a conflict mechanism that created two security organizations, but one of the mechanism's major goals was peaceful settlements without any armed capability. The lack of an international response to the Rwandan genocide and subsequent events deeply bothered Salim Salim, the OAU's secretary-general, and other African officials. A chiefs of staff 1997 meeting agreed that "the OAU could undertake peace support operations excluding peace enforcement."[140]

But long-standing problems, including the tension between supranational and national priorities, will prevent creation of an OAU force. African states desire to retain their scarce resources for national goals and to control their use, rather than turn them over to a poorly funded continental grouping. For that reason the Military Experts' Report of October 1997 suggestion that "member states should be encouraged to send officers to work *at their country's expense* at the OAU for a period not exceeding three years [emphasis added]" is probably a nonstarter.[141] Perhaps twenty African governments are behind on their OAU dues, again preferring to keep resources for domestic purposes. The OAU depends fully on suggested contributions and lacks any formal enforcement capability to collect its assessed dues. The chiefs of staff suggestions for funding indicate the unlikelihood of significant contributions: "soliciting for individual donations in cash and in kind and involving business corporations . . . [and] the issuance of Commemorative Stamps by OAU member states and other options such as the organization of soccer matches."[142] A major final concern is that the fear that a short-term peacekeeping operation could unexpectedly descend into a long-term and much more costly peace enforcement operation.

Total dismissal of the OAU is unwarranted. It will continue to serve a useful, though limited, political function by encouraging peaceful resolution, sending military observers into politically troublesome areas, and presenting a continent-wide voice against arms flows into Africa. But, as with its backseat status during the Liberian war, it will continue to defer to regional organizations.

Notes

1. An article that examines the Liberian war's prototype status is "Liberian Slayings Began a Brutal Trend In Africa," *New York Times,* February 4, 1998.

2. This chapter only fleetingly examines ECOMOG's entry into Guinea-Bissau in 1998 as peacekeepers in a dispute between the recently dismissed chief of general staff of the armed forces and President João Bernardo Vieira. Togo, Niger, Gambia, and Benin were the troop-donating countries (Senegal and Guinea, which had entered earlier in 1998, were not part of this force). For an analysis of the conflict, see "Guinea-Bissau. Human Rights in War and

Peace." Amnesty International Report AFR July 30, 1999, http://www.amnesty. org/ailib/aipub/1999

3. This analysis of ECOMOG presents a largely critical view of its Liberian and Sierra Leonean interventions. Yet the nations and soldiers that constituted ECOMOG deserve praise for their rapid response and continuing commitment to lessen Liberia's suffering, especially given the West's inaction. ECOMOG's relative professionalism is especially evident in that it certainly treated civilians far better than did the factions. And, while many observers (including this writer) criticized the Nigerian contingent for improper conduct, there would have been no ECOMOG without Nigeria.

4. Abdel-Fatua Musah, "A Country Under Siege: State Decay and Corporate Military Intervention in Sierra Leone," Musah and Fayemi, *Mercenaries,* p. 33

5. J. Gus Liebenow, *Liberia: The Evolution of Privilege,* and *Liberia: The Quest For Democracy;* Christopher Clapham, *Liberia and Sierra Leone.*

6. "In what came to be called the Americo-Liberian community, an early distinction was made by the settlers and others between themselves and the 'natives,' as they called the indigenous population." Robert Rinehart, "Historical Setting," in Harold Nelson, ed., *Liberia: A Country Study,* p. 22. In 1931, the League of Nations reported that Liberia "represents the paradox of being a Republic of 12,000 citizens with 1,000,000 subjects." Nelson, *Liberia: A Country Study,* p. 45.

7. Frederick Ehrenreich, "National Security," in Harold Nelson, ed., *Liberia: A Country Study,* p. 276.

8. Ibid., p. 268.

9. An interesting article on this time period is Reid Kramer, "Liberia: A Casualty of the Cold War's End?" *CSIS Africa Notes* (July 1995). Kramer argues that the United States supported Doe as part of its strategy to destabilize Libya's Muammar Qaddafi. See also Mark Huband, *The Liberian Civil War,* pp. 27–33, for a discussion of U.S. policy during the Reagan administration.

10. Doe did provide better funding for pay and housing—with U.S. urging—and started some military civic action programs.

11. "Over four years later, according to observers, the reluctance of most officers to impose discipline had combined with the unwillingness of more than a few enlisted men to accept it." Kramer, "Liberia," p. 273.

12. Unidentified official, quoted by Huband, *Liberian Civil War,* p. 28. Ehrenreich records that "observers noted, however, that after the [U.S.] advisers were removed, all but the few well-led units rapidly lost the skills they had acquired in training." Ehrenreich, *Liberia,* p. 275.

13. President Houphouët-Boigny, the late octogenarian ruler of Côte d'Ivoire, disliked the youthful and semiliterate Samuel Doe, who violently seized power and executed former Liberian officials. Doe condemned to death A. B. Tolbert, the brother of President William Tolbert. Daise Tolbert, the widow of A. B. Tolbert, was Houphouët-Boigny's goddaughter. She went on to marry Blaise Compaore, the president of Burkina Faso. Not coincidentally, Houphouët-Boigny and Compaore helped Charles Taylor, Doe's major opponent.

14. The NPFL did not champion an ethnic agenda, despite its early membership. Doe's Krahn rule had singled out the Mano and Gio, and Taylor chose

to enter their territory in late 1989, realizing that they would likely support any anti-Doe force.

15. Herman Cohen, the U.S. assistant secretary of state for Africa, offered Doe passage from Liberia and asylum in Togo. Huband, *Liberian Civil War,* p. 139.

16. The split did not become public until May when Taylor acknowledged it.

17. Significant numbers of Guineans, Nigerians, and Ghanaians were living in Liberia. Of these there were perhaps as many as 30,000 Guineans. At one point Taylor held 3,000 Nigerians hostage on the Nigerian embassy's grounds. Huband mentions that Muslim leaders in Nigeria feared attacks on Liberia's Muslims, especially the Mandingo ethnic group. Huband, *Liberian Civil War,* p. xxi. Private Nigerians held some significant investments in Liberia, though specific figures are lacking.

18. The major Anglophone countries involved in the Liberian war were Nigeria, Ghana, and Sierra Leone. The major Francophone states were Côte d'Ivoire and Burkina Faso, both of which supported the NPFL, and Guinea and Senegal, which contributed troops to ECOMOG.

Most authorities agree about ECOWAS's failure to reach its goals. The causes include states placing their own needs (and finite resources) above those of the region. National and regional instability have also lessened ECOWAS's effectiveness. In 1990 Ruby Ofori wrote that ECOWAS's "15-year history has been rocked by border disputes, mass deportations, and mini wars, not to mention the personal animosities between rival heads of state and deep seated rifts in anglo-francophone relations . . . [which] offer further analysis of ECOWAS' level of accomplishments," Ruby Ofori, "Dream of Unity," *West Africa,* May 28–June 3, 1990, p. 882.

19. The United States staged three limited military interventions, in 1990, 1992, and 1996, to extricate U.S. and other foreign nationals from the fighting. The United States supplied $.5 billion of relief to Liberians and gave about $75 million in military assistance, mostly to individual ECOMOG countries. Washington also supported, both financially and politically, several major peace conferences. Critics accuse the United States, especially after the 1993 Cotonou and 1995 Abuja agreements, of delaying delivery to Liberia of needed logistical equipment.

20. David Wippman, "Enforcing the Peace: ECOWAS and the Liberian Civil War," in Lori Fisler Damrosch, ed., *Enforcing Restraint,* p. 165.

21. Three Anglophone (Nigeria, Gambia, and Ghana) and two Francophone states (Mali and Togo) made up the SMC. The three Anglophone states would become heavily involved in ECOMOG, whereas the two Francophone states did not.

22. "ECOWAS Standing Mediation Committee." Decision A/DEC. August 1, 1990 on the Cease-fire and Establishment of an ECOWAS Cease-fire Monitoring Group for Liberia, Banjul, Republic of the Gambia, August 7, 1990. Cited in Mark Weller, ed., *Regional Peace-Keeping and International Enforcement: The Liberian Crisis,* p. 68.

23. Chike Akabogu, "ECOMOG Takes the Initiative," in Margaret Vogt, ed., *The Liberian Crisis,* p. 86.

24. Abdel-Fatau Musah, "A Country Under Siege: State Decay and

Corporate Military Intervention in Sierra Leone," in Musah and Fayemi, *Mercenaries,* p. 104.

25. Musah makes this claim: "In 1989, a study commissioned by Babangida into ways of turning the tide against the spate of junior officer coups in West Africa recommended keeping junior officers busy in peacekeeping operations outside Nigeria." Ibid., p. 103.

26. ECOWAS did provide formal approval in November 1990.

27. Compaore, quoted in BBC Monitoring Report, "Taylor to Visit Banjul; Burkinabe Leader Rejects ECOWAS Intervention, 13 August 1990," Weller, *Regional Peace-Keeping,* p. 85. Charles Taylor threatened a "very, very high price" that ECOMOG would pay for any Liberians killed and that "we'll fight to the last man . . . I've given orders to open fire on any strangers setting foot on our territory." Taylor, quoted in BBC Monitoring Report, "Banjul Talks Begin; ECOMOG Again Delayed; Taylor Warns He Will Fight, 21 August 1990," Weller, *Regional Peace-Keeping,* p. 86.

28. Nigeria supplied concessionary, or possibly free, oil to President Jerry Rawlings of Ghana before Ghana's 1992 presidential elections.

29. Between November 1981 and June 1982, the OAU sponsored a three-nation West African intervention force in Chad. But, as Herman Cohen notes, the force lacked a clear mandate and, among other things, "suffered from severe financial and logistical handicaps." Herman Cohen, "African Capabilities," in Smock and Crocker, eds., *African Conflict Resolution,* p. 80. These deficiencies would reappear after ECOMOG became operational.

30. Quainoo, a three-star general, was ECOMOG's only force commander. Subsequent commanders, all of them two-star generals, have been ECOMOG field commanders.

31. Telephone interview with a former U.S. government official who was stationed in Monrovia in 1990 and 1991, October 15, 1995.

32. Comments at the Regional Collective Security in West Africa conference, Akosombo, Ghana, July 1999.

33. C. K. Iweze, "Nigeria in Liberia: The Military Operations of ECOMOG," in Vogt, *The Liberian Crisis,* p. 233.

34. Sir Dawda Jawara was also president of Gambia from 1966 until a 1994 military coup.

35. Taylor had more personal reasons: Joseph Momoh, president of Sierra Leone, had jailed him in the late 1980s when Taylor was seeking support for his NPFL.

36. The Nigerian, Guinean, and Sierra Leonean troops did not fall under ECOMOG's command because they were stationed outside Liberia.

37. Quoted in Janet Fleischman and Lois Whitman, *Easy Prey,* p. 3.

38. Ibid.

39. Fleischman and Whitman, *Easy Prey,* p. 9.

40 . "Country Reports on Human Rights Practices for 1996." Report submitted to the U.S. House Committee on Foreign Relations by the Department of State, February 1997, p. 149.

41. A 1995 example offered by diplomats in Liberia was that of a Nigerian colonel who traded timber rights in his command sector for a monthly payment of $500.

42. See BBC Report, "AFP Report on Jimmy Carter's Proposals at Yamoussoukro Summit, 1 November 1991"; Weller, *Regional Peace-Keeping*, p. 21.

43. Interview with Margaret Vogt, International Peace Academy, February 18, 1996.

44. "Bakyut Says He Has 'No Confidence' in Taylor," Agence France Presse, October 10, 1992. Quoted in Kevin George, *The Civil War In Liberia: A Study of the Legal and Policy Aspects of Humanitarian Intervention* (Unpublished ms., Washington, D.C., 1993), p. 63.

45. "Liberia: The Battle for Gbarnga," *Africa Confidential*, May 23, 1993, p. 2.

46. UNOMIL was "to monitor the cease-fire, to monitor the UN and ECOWAS arms embargo, to assist in the disarmament and demobilization of combatants, to observe and verify the election process, to help with coordination of the humanitarian aid effort [and] to report on human rights violations." "UN Observer Mission In Liberia," full-page UNOMIL advertisement in *The Eye* (Monrovia), June 23, 1995, p. 6.

47. The United States provided $32 million, which paid for transport to and from Liberia, eleven 5-ton trucks and fourteen Humvee vehicles, tents, and battalion-level radio equipment for the two battalions. The United States had also discussed with Zimbabwean and Egyptian officials the possibility of financing troops from those two nations. Financing was one problem, at least with Zimbabwe. Some U.S. officials claim that Zimbabwe initially wanted $100 million in cash and equipment from the United States before Zimbabwe would provide two battalions to ECOMOG.

48. "Nigeria Says It Spent 8 Billion Dollars in Peacekeeping," Panafrican News Agency, October 26, 1999. Http://www.africanews.org/PANA/news/19991026/featl2.html

49. Stephen Stedman writes that ECOMOG "demonstrates the limitations of sub-regional organizations with respect to such [peace enforcement] operations. . . . Almost every aspect of ECOWAS reasoning about the intervention was suspect. . . . Indeed, the ECOWAS intervention created the very situation it hoped to prevent." Stephen Stedman, "Conflict and Conciliation in Sub-Saharan Africa," in Michael Brown, ed., *The International Dimensions of Internal Conflict*, pp. 250–252.

50. Interview with Ghanaian diplomat, June 16, 1995; also various discussions with ECOMOG/ECOWAS personnel.

51. Iweze, "Nigeria," in Vogt, *The Liberian Crisis*, p. 220.

52. The United States withheld some intelligence from ECOMOG but did furnish maps. No country, including the United States, had 1:50,000 scale maps of all of Liberia (which ECOMOG officers wanted) even though, as one U.S. military analyst noted, "This was the part of Africa we knew best." Interview, October 15, 1995.

53. Iweze, "Nigeria," in Vogt, *The Liberian Crisis*, p. 221.

54. ECOWAS Authority of Heads of State and Government, "DEC.A/DEC 2/ November 1990, Relating to the Adoption of an ECOWAS Peace Plan for Liberia and the Entire West Africa Sub-Region, Bamako, Republic of Mali," November 28, 1990, in Weller, *Regional Peace-Keeping*, p. 112.

55. Interview with U.S. diplomat, June 23, 1996. Ibrahim Gambari, Nigeria's ambassador to the UN, concurs that the mandate "at least at first, was ambiguous. Neither the diplomats nor the soldiers charged with implementing it knew what to make of it. They did not know whether they were a peacekeeping or a peace-enforcing body. . . . Consequently, 'complications, dissensions and dissonance' were rife in their interpretation of the ECOMOG mandate." Ibrahim Gambari, "The Role of Foreign Intervention in African Reconstruction," in Zartman, ed., *Collapsed States,* p. 231.

56. William Reno, "Global Commerce, 'Warlords,' and the Reinvention of African States." Paper presented at the African Studies Association annual meeting, Orlando, Florida, November 1995, p. 14.

57. Reno, "Global Commerce," p. 12.

58. Comfort Ero, a Nigerian security analyst, writes that "because the forces were black and from the region, intervention was no less objectionable." Comfort Ero, "The Future of ECOMOG in West Africa," *Peacekeeping to Complex Emergency: Peace Support Missions in Africa* (Johannesburg and Pretoria: South African Institute of International Affairs and the Institute of Strategic Studies, 1999), p. 60.

59. Robert Mortimer, "Senegal's Role in ECOMOG: The Francophone Dimension in the Liberian Crisis," in Karl Magyar and Earl Conteh-Morgan, eds., *Peacekeeping in Africa,* p. 162.

60. Iweze, "Nigeria," in Vogt, *The Liberian Crisis,* p. 226.

61. Wippman, "Enforcing the Peace," in Damrosch, *Enforcing Restraint,* p. 173.

62. Robert Mortimer, "From ECOMOG to ECOMOG II," in Harbeson and Rothchild, eds., *Africa in World Politics,* p. 203.

63. Iweze, "Nigeria," in Vogt, *The Liberian Crisis,* p. 222. Soon after landing, the Guinean battalion was to capture territory around Spriggs-Payne Airfield and wait for a linkup with the Ghanaian battalion. But, perhaps on orders from Conakry, the Guineans, without notifying ECOMOG headquarters, decided to leave the captured territory in order to liberate their embassy. The NPFL surrounded them, and the Ghanaian battalion finally rescued them with loss of men and materiel. The Ghanaian battalion landed with a well-stocked mobile hospital but disregarded a common pooling policy. Therefore, writes Iweze, "only Ghanaian soldiers were being given attention in terms of surgery." Iweze, "Nigeria," in Vogt, *The Liberian Crisis,* p. 237.

64. Weller, *Regional Peace-Keeping,* p. 68.

65. Max Ahmadu Sesay, "Collective Security or Collective Disaster? Regional Peacekeeping in West Africa," *Security Dialogue,* 1995. Hutchful comments that "from the point of view of political legitimacy, there was often little to choose between the official heads of state in the region and the warlords whom they were fighting." Eboe Hutchful, "The ECOMOG Experience with Peacekeeping in West Africa," in Mark Malan, ed., *Whither Peace-Keeping In Africa?* p. 75.

66. Stedman, "Conflict and Conciliation," p. 253.

67. ECOMOG did become a political actor, as does any intervention force in an active conflict. ECOMOG also took sides among the factions as part of its strategy to defend the capital city and the existing Liberian government.

68. For example, section C, article 4, clause 6, of the Akosomba agreement of October 14, 1994, states that "the Liberian National Transition Government shall enter into a Status Of Forces Agreement with ECOWAS within 30 days from signing this agreement."

69. An interesting discussion of this is in 'Funmi Olonisakin's "When the Military Is the Political Moderator of Peacekeepers: The Case of ECOMOG" (Unpublished paper, Centre for Defence Studies, University of London, Spring 1999).

70. Ibid., p. 20.

71. Ibid., p. 19.

72. Conversations with Liberians, January 1996.

73. *New York Times,* June 26,1997.

74. Iweze, "Nigeria," in Vogt, *The Liberian Crisis,* p. 219.

75. ECOMOG resented the UN's late involvement in the war and UNOMIL soldiers' enjoying a higher standard of living.

76. General Inienger also argued that the UN should "come to Liberia's aid by providing resources [to ECOMOG]. We can perform the job." Interview with Gen. John Inienger, June 29,1995.

77. Iweze, "Nigeria," in Vogt, *The Liberian Crisis,* p. 238.

78. Apparently for the same reason, Nigeria used only two of its twenty-one Alpha ground attack fighters in Liberia (reportedly none flew in Liberia during 1995). Nigeria rarely committed any of its approximately twenty-two MiG-21 fighters, and only two of its fifteen Jaguar reconnaissance fighters have seen even limited use.

79. Interview with Anthony Marley, August 13, 1998.

80. Other reasons included the NPFL's kidnapping and murder of Senegalese soldiers and security problems in Senegal's Casamance area.

81. The two contingents, a battalion from each country, had most of their expenses paid by the United States (which also allowed them to retain U.S.-supplied equipment).

82. One high-ranking Nigerian intelligence officer bitterly complained that "the Tanzanians were here just to satisfy their country, not because of any commitment. The Ugandans were worse: they didn't want to work with anyone." Interview with a Nigerian intelligence officer, July 1995. A pay differential may account for some of the anger toward the East Africans. The UN funded the Tanzanians and Ugandans at a higher rate than the ECOMOG-paid troops.

83. Several aerial bombings of civilian targets, for example. Information from a Western military analyst, 1997.

84. Iweze, "Nigeria," in Vogt, *The Liberian Crisis,* p. 236.

85. A Western military analyst in Liberia at the war's outset writes that "when ECOMOG first arrived, EVERYTHING except fuel was stove-piped within the national contingents." Personal correspondence, August 13, 1998.

86. Jean Herskovits, "Africans Solving African Problems: Militaries, Democracies, and Security in West and Southern Africa," p. 9.

87. Western military analyst, personal correspondence.

88. Iweze characterizes the ECOMOG operation as "a classical case of

launching troops into a theatre of operation without any form of intelligence."
Iweze, "Nigeria," in Vogt, *The Liberian Crisis,* p. 240.

Maj. Gen. Rufus Kupolati acknowledged that "definitely we had problems at the start of the operation. You need good intelligence of where you are going to operate. That was definitely lacking. And to get good intelligence you need very good maps and [we] found these were just not available." The U.S. government provided ECOMOG's best maps. Kupolati, quoted in Jimmi Adia, "ECOMOG Force Commanders," in Vogt, *The Liberian Crisis,* pp. 256–257.

89. Some ECOMOG countries, notably Nigeria, subsequently gave their Liberia-bound troops jungle warfare training.

90. Western military analyst. Interview, September 3, 1995.

91. Fleischman and Whitman, *Easy Prey,* for information on child-soldiers. Human Rights Watch/Africa estimated that 10 percent of the some 60,000 fighters were under the age of 15.

92. "Liberia: Listening in to Washington," *Africa Confidential,* November 20, 1992, p. 7. U.S. officials verify the accuracy of these leaked cables.

93. "Using fire to fight fire, ECOMOG increasingly adopted a sort of warlord/counter-warlord strategy in order to keep its own costs down." Mortimer, "From ECOMOG to ECOMOG II," in Harbeson and Rothchild, *Africa in World Politics,* p. 190.

94. Hutchful, "The ECOMOG Experience," in Malan, *Whither Peacekeeping?* p. 72.

95. Ibid., p. 83.

96. Interview with Nigerian intelligence official, July 1995.

97. Interview with diplomat, July 5, 1995.

98. A UNOMIL representative worried that "regional commanders are becoming local heroes . . . they make independent statements, [and] chang[e] sides . . . everyone wants to be president." Interview with UNOMIL official June 15, 1995.

99. Interview with Ghanaian diplomat, June 16, 1996.

100. A top-ranking Ghanaian diplomat felt that "Guinea, Sierra Leone, and Nigeria saw the NPFL as the enemy. This preoccupation was not helpful— it drove the NPFL into a corner." Ibid.

101. Gen. Sani Abacha disagreed, arguing in late 1997 that "Nigeria has not allowed its form of government to affect its duty towards the security of our sub-region. Indeed, it is doubtful that a democratically-elected government could have acted otherwise." Jean Herskovits, "Africans Solving African Problems," p. 14.

102. Stedman, in Brown, *International Dimensions,* p. 253.

103. Mortimer, "Senegal's Role," in Magyar and Conteh-Morgan, *Peacekeeping in Africa,* p. 130. The attack occurred in May 1992.

104. Herman Cohen. Interview, October 1995.

105. For a general elaboration of a layered response, see Timothy Sisk, "Institutional Capacity-Building for African Conflict Management," in Smock and Crocker, eds., *African Conflict Resolution.*

106. By mid-1996 Nigerians were divided about the wisdom of future regional forces. A permanent force under the ECOWAS Secretariat would, according to Iweze, "eliminate the possibility of mis-conceptualizing the situa-

tion from a military angle." Iweze, "Nigeria," in Vogt, *The Liberian Crisis,* p. 239.

When asked if Nigeria should participate in a future regional force, Ambassador Iroha replied, "I doubt it, if we have to pay for our own troops." Interview with Ambassador Iroha, July 2, 1995. The Nigerian government claims that ECOMOG has cost it over $8 billion.

107. Nigerian intelligence officer. Interview, July 1995.

108. "The collapse of Liberia into warlord zones engulfed Sierra Leone, thus making it ripe for what would eventually become ECOMOG II." Mortimer, "From ECOMOG to ECOMOG II," in Harbeson and Rothchild, *Africa in World Politics,* p. 191.

109. "Under cover of rebel-caused insecurity, Strasser and his military colleagues enriched themselves in the illegal diamond trade." Ibid., 194.

110. Telephone interview, July 28, 1999. Washington, D.C.

In mid-1998 several thousand, mostly Nigerian, ECOMOG troops remained in Liberia, while some 10,000 Nigerian troops were in Sierra Leone and along the Nigerian-Cameroonian border, where troops from the two countries were fighting a sporadic, low-level conflict over the disputed Bakassi Peninsula. All three contingents needed ground and air assets, and one U.S. defense analyst noted that Nigerian troops along the Cameroonian border had no air support or much logistical support. Nigeria had already dispatched much of its operable equipment to ECOMOG in Liberia and Sierra Leone. Interviews with U.S. intelligence officers, Washington, D.C., June 1998.

111. Pacific Architects and Engineering ran the truck operation, and International Charter, Inc., its subcontractor, was responsible for the three helicopters. These companies first worked for ECOMOG in the latter stages of ECOMOG's Liberian stay.

112. Interview with State Department official, January 1999.

113. Compaore asserted that Nigerian soldiers "conduct themselves quite simply like an army of occupation. . . . ECOMOG is going well beyond the mandate that was entrusted to it." He also rhetorically asked, "Just what might be the intentions of those who have employed force for the restoration of President Kabbah?" Interview with Blaise Compaore, "Je ne suis pas un fauteur de troubles!" *Jeune Afrique,* February 16–22, 1999, p. 18. Cited in Mortimer, "From ECOMOG to ECOMOG II," in Harbeson and Rothchild, *Africa in World Politics,* p. 201. Quoted in *Sud Quotidien,* February 18, 1998, and cited by Mortimer, p. 200.

114. "Sierra Leone: Diamond King," *The Economist,* January 29, 2000, p 52.

115. Various interviews, 1999.

116. "UN Accuses Peace Force in Sierra Leone Atrocities," *International Herald Tribune,* February 13, 1999.

117. "Getting Away with Murder, Mutilation, and Rape," Human Rights Watch, June 1999, p. 42. The report notes a Nigerian justification: "We have a proper code of conduct. We know about the Geneva Conventions and have taken prisoners in the past, but this time was different. The things these people [RUF/AFRC] do. This time my unit took very few prisoners." "Getting Away With Murder," p. 32.

118. Another "ECOMOG" force, composed of troops from Togo, Niger,

Gambia, and Benin, entered Guinea-Bissau in late 1988 to stop fighting between rebel military units and the government of President João Viera (it followed a joint Senegalese-Guinean deployment). Comfort Ero reflects the views of many when she writes that "[T]he failure of ECOMOG to prevent the coup was an indication that the force level provided was an inadequate response to the conflict in Guinea-Bissau." Ero, *Peacekeeping to Complex Emergency,* pp. 68–69.

119. "Old Problems Hamper U.N. in Sierra Leone," *Washington Post,* June 11, 2000.

120. "U.S. Congratulates ECOWAS on Liberia Election," August 8, 1997. U.S. Information Service Archives, gopher://198.80.36.82:70/OR44935754-44937917-range/archives/I997/pdq.97

121. Liz Blunt, the BBC's West African correspondent during much of ECOMOG's history, writes that "invaluable lessons have been learned [and] senior soldiers in ECOWAS are now keen that the region should build on the experience with some permanent form of co-operation," Focus on Africa, BBC World Service, http://www.docklands.bbs.co.uk/worldservice

122. Human Rights Watch, "Sierra Leone. Sowing Terror: Atrocities Against Civilians in Sierra Leone," July 1998, p. 37.

123. These states envision designated ECOMOG units that would usually remain under national chain of command. Only an ECOWAS-sanctioned operation would bring them together into a supranational brigade force under ECOMOG command.

124. "Côte d'Ivoire: ECOWAS Meeting Ends: Communiqué Issued," *Fraternité Matin,* March 15, 1998. FBIS-AFR-98-074.

125. Ibid. ECOWAS's secretary-general, Lansana Kouyaté, summarized the feeling of many leaders when stating that ECOWAS should exercise initial, not ex post, authorization: "[T]he states should never be placed [sic] a fait accompli." "Côte d'Ivoire: ECOWAS Secretary Comments on Conflict Resolution Mechanism Document," Radio France International, March 15, 1998. FBISAFR-98-075.

126. ECOMOG's 1998 offensive, according to *The Economist,* "had not been officially sanctioned by either ECOWAS, the Organization of African Unity (OAU) or the UN, and several member states, including Liberia, Ghana, and Côte d'Ivoire, have questioned its legitimacy, alleging that the offensive was unilaterally initiated at the behest of the Nigerian government." "Sierra Leone," *Economist Intelligence Unit Country Report,* 2d Quarter, 1998, p. 27.

127. "ECOWAS Mechanism for Conflict Resolution for Conflict Prevention, Management Resolution, Peace-Keeping and Security." Meeting of Ministers of Defence, Internal Affairs and Security, Draft Mechanism. July 1998.

128. Communiqué, Meeting of Ministers of Defence, p. 18.

129. Ibid.

130. "Of the francophone states, only Guinea aligned itself squarely with Nigerian policy." Mortimer, "From ECOMOG to ECOMOG II," in Harbeson and Rothchild, *Africa in World Politics,* p. 202.

131. Units from Senegal, Mali, and Mauritania, as well as several other

countries, participated in Guidimakha '98, a French-organized training exercise that was part of the larger RECAMP (Reinforcement of African Capabilities for Peacekeeping) program. Nigerian Foreign Minister Tom Ikimi criticized "foreign countries working to weaken our inter-African organizations by dividing us along anglophone-francophone lines." Senegal's foreign minister riposted that Guidimakha's participants did not want "anyone prevent[ing] states from training their police, gendarmerie, and army or freely choosing their partners." Mortimer, "From ECOMOG to ECOMOG II," in Harbeson and Rothchild, *Africa in World Politics,* p. 200.

132. "War Without End," *The Economist,* November 21, 1998, p. 48.

133. Transcript of President Obasanjo's speech in Washington, D.C., sponsored by the Center for Strategic and International Studies, August 4, 1998. Taylor won the election after seven, not five, years of ECOMOG's presence.

134. Mortimer, "From ECOMOG to ECOMOG II," in Harbeson and Rothchild, *Africa in World Politics,* p. 201.

135. In 1996 the United States granted $30 million to ECOMOG (which represented most of the U.S. total contribution up to that point); Britain gave $500,000 for spare parts to ECOMOG. Britain announced in early 1999 that it would provide about $16 million of equipment to ECOMOG in Sierra Leone.

136. Col. Dan Henk writes that "the exercises are indications of a maturing collective African approach to conflict management. . . . [T]hat is likely to continue." Dan Henk, *Uncharted Paths,* p. 26.

137. Michael Nyarnbuya, "Zimbabwe's Role as Lead Nation for Peacekeeping Training in the SADC Region," in Mark Malan, ed., *Resolute Partners: Building Peacekeeping Capacity In Southern Africa,* p. 92.

138. The United States gave funding and logistics support, as well as 460 participants.

139. Some observers fear that Taylor has financially benefited from Sierra Leone's instability and that he seeks to destabilize several of the ECOMOG countries that fought against him, most notably Guinea and Ghana.

140. "Report of the Meeting of the Working Group of OAU Military Experts," OAU/MRT/Exp./Rpt (11) Rev.1 October 1997, p. 8. Most observers assume that Taylor has financially benefited from Sierra Leone's instability and some believe that he seeks to destabilize several of the ECOMOG countries that fought against him, most notably Guinea and Ghana.

141. Ibid., p. 23.

142. "Draft Report of the Second Meeting of the Chiefs of Defence Staff of the Central Organ of the OAU Mechanism," OAU/CHST/CO/DRAFT/rpt (11), n.d., p. 20.

5

EXECUTIVE OUTCOMES
AND PRIVATE SECURITY

As noted in the previous chapters, the personalist nature of the African state, the longstanding unprofessionalism of many African militaries, the post–Cold War refusal of the West to intervene militarily, the shifting coercive balance, and the decidedly mixed record of African multinational military groupings (as exemplified by ECOMOG) have contributed to a security crisis in a number of countries. This instability has encouraged some governments and businesses to hire private security firms. This still nascent trend represents the extreme of power devolution: from the West or the UN, to the African state, and then to state-sanctioned private companies.

This chapter begins with an overview of the concept of private security and then uses the former Executive Outcomes (EO) to illustrate several valuable lessons about African security in particular.

Private Security: An Overview

The term "mercenary,"[1] usually defined as a foreigner who receives payment for military services, encompasses an extraordinarily wide range of individuals, motivations, and functions.[2] Some soldiers fight overseas primarily for financial gain, whereas others espouse personal, ideological, or religious reasons. Possible tasks include combat but also numerous noncombat functions: guarding, support (including administration and logistics), training, demining, equipment procurement, and intelligence collection and advising.[3] Although mercenaries are often equated with instability, they have sometimes helped to prop up existing authority.[4] The imprecision of this term has policy considerations, as noted below, in terms of possible regulation or prohibition.

Security theoreticians and futurists suggest that state coercive power is waning and that private security could regain some of its historical importance. Alvin and Heidi Toffler ask: "Why not, when nations have already lost the monopoly of violence, consider creating volunteer mercenary forces organized by private corporations to fight wars on a contract-fee basis for the United Nations, the *condottieri* of yesterday armed with some of the weapons . . . of tomorrow?"[5]

The private security industry is enjoying tremendous growth: worldwide revenues were $55.6 billion in 1990 and are projected to climb to $202 billion by 2010.[6] *Jane's Intelligence Review* estimates that 9,800 firms exist in Russia alone, and Alex Vines believes that South Africa by itself has almost 6,000 companies regulated by the Security Officers Board (the vast majority in both countries are for domestic purposes).[7] Defence Systems Ltd. (DSL) had 130 contracts worldwide, with 115 clients (private and government) in twenty-two countries by early 1999.[8]

Private security in Africa is assuming an increasingly central role: Jakkie Cilliers notes that "private security companies are increasingly supplanting the primary responsibility of the state to provide both security for its peoples and for lucrative multinational and domestic business activities."[9]

Recent History

Private soldiers have existed throughout history[10] and they have fought in Africa for some 150 years. They furthered British business interests, notably the United African Company, and French interests, especially the Compagnie Française Ouest Afrique Occidentale and the Société Commerciale Ouest Africaine. Mercenaries often reflect a problem even more than they may contribute to it; they largely were absent from Africa between 1900 and 1960, given colonialism's enforced stability.

Combat units began appearing shortly after the independence of various African nations. The departing colonizers had not created strong national institutions—including professional militaries—in their former colonies, and both opportunistic politicians and foreign businesses sought to exploit this power vacuum. Mercenaries usually sided with insurgencies (especially secessionist attempts), thereby identifying themselves as opposing Africa's new, black-led states.[11] Most Africans and Africanists regarded mercenaries, in the words of Wilfred Burchett and Derek Roebuck, as "neo-colonialism's last card . . . a faceless . . . reserve of cannon fodder, not identifiable with governments and their policies, immune to public criticism and debate. The perfect substitute for the expeditionary forces."[12]

Among their first actions were fighting for Moïse Tshombe, secessionist leader of the breakaway Katanga region, against the central Congolese government and UN soldiers during the early 1960s. Union Minière, a Belgium mining house with extensive Katangan holdings, probably financed the private force. Mercenaries in the Congo acquired the sobriquet of "les affreux"—the frightful ones—for their often rapacious behavior. Many mercenaries acted unprofessionally and sported criminal or drug backgrounds or dishonorable discharges. A surprising number of mercenaries in the Congo had no previous military background.

Subsequent operations occurred, inter alia, against the governments of Nigeria, Guinea, the Comoros, and Benin (former Dahomey). Non-African countries sometimes condoned, or encouraged, mercenary operations: France, for example, arranged for mercenaries for Biafra. About a thousand South Africans, Englishmen, and Americans fought for Rhodesia in the 1970s. Mercenaries appeared increasingly irrelevant by the mid-1970s, given the growth of competent Soviet and Cuban military assistance, the general discrediting of secessionism, and several incompetent mercenary operations.[13] Foreign-supplied "passive" security continued quietly from 1960 to 1990. For example, Britain's Watchtower International (an offshoot of the British Special Air Service) provided personal security for Zambian President Kenneth Kaunda and for the Lonrho congolomerate in Zambia's copper belt.

Many contemporary observers claim that the private security business has changed recently and that several of these shifts may aid African stability. First, the business is burgeoning: post–Cold War demobilizations have dumped significant numbers of well-trained ex-soldiers on the free market. Highly specialized soldiers from the United States' Delta Force, ex-Soviet Union's Spetnaz, Britain's Gurkhas, and South Africa's Reconnaissance Commando have joined private security groups, as have pilots, communications specialists, trainers, and logisticians. Private service overseas offers combat opportunities and lucrative salaries, two attractions often absent from many Western militaries.

Several new companies combine former adversaries from Western and former communist elite forces. International Charter Incorporated (ICI) is an American company created in 1992 that works closely with two Russian ex-state aviation firms. In ICI's Liberian and Sierra

Leonean operations, Eastern European pilots ferried former U.S. special operations soldiers who were advising on logistics and security.[14] DSL, whose leadership is made up of former Special Air Service (SAS) personnel, employs among others, a former White House security advisor and an officer in the former KGB's Alpha commando unit. The dramatic increase in the supply of private soldiers has resulted in an upgrading of professionalism: no longer need an employer rely on the unprofessional soldiers so evident in the Congo during the 1960s.

The business's increasingly permanent and corporate nature also may increase military professionalism. "Rather than being ragtag bands of adventurers, paramilitary forces, or individuals recruited clandestinely . . . the modern mercenary firm is increasingly corporate . . . [and they] now operate out of office suites, have public affairs staffs and web sites," writes David Isenberg.[15] Mercenary groups during the Cold War invariably were hastily created, ad hoc collections of soldiers who displayed a wide range of professionalism and often cared little about how others perceived their capabilities. Juan Carlos Zarate believes that the established private security companies (PSCs) need a good record of military professionalism, not only strong military capabilities but also political accountability and correct human rights behavior.[16] Unprofessional activity would undermine business prospects by prompting unfavorable media reporting and angering both the companies' host states and future possible contracting governments.

This heightened respectability manifests itself in client selection and military behavior, which works against a central assumption that private soldiers will hire out to the wealthiest bidder. EO officials maintained that their force fought only for sovereign governments and had refused any contracts from criminal or insurrectionist groups or from pariah states.[17]

Zarate, Isenberg, and others believe that the better known companies exert strong control over their employees. Three recent developments may aid this control: the large pool of retired but highly professional soldiers, the time for established companies to check the backgrounds of applicants and the ability of these companies to offer future employment, which may improve the soldiers' behavior. (In addition, many employers have known these soldiers from past service together.) Tim Spicer, O.B.E., a former colonel of the Scots Guards and UN peacekeeper, and now director of the Sandline military advisory group, argues that "we would like to conduct ourselves in the way most people would expect a First World army to conduct itself."[18]

Western nations increasingly permit, and sometimes encourage, companies to send proxy training and advising teams to favored states. These firms can perform services governments approve of but hesitate to attempt themselves because of various costs of foreign military intervention. Brian Boquist, executive vice president of ICI, maintains that

> the collapse of the Cold War status quo continues to manifest itself globally through an explosion of civil conflicts. . . . In West Africa and elsewhere, we have worked closely with international peacekeeping forces on behalf of the U.S. government. This *"proxy peacekeeping"* strategy has saved the United States millions of dollars while effectively pursuing peaceful resolutions that save lives and promote democracy.[19]

Western governments increasingly are assisting PSCs based in their countries, and David Isenberg states that "no PMC [private military company] thus far has worked against the interest of its home state."[20] Military Professional Resources, Inc. (MPRI), an Alexandria, Virginia-based company, claims to house "the greatest corporate assemblage of military expertise in the world."[21] It employs seventeen retired U.S. generals full-time; by late 1999, its African focus was primarily Nigeria.[22] Britain and France allow private security companies to contract with foreign clients, including national governments ("Great Britain remains the center of mercenary recruitment in the world," notes Zarate).[23] The British government has exceptionally close ties with DSL, which has worked for the UN, various foreign embassies and governments, and major firms (e.g., British Petroleum, Shell, Mobil, De Beers). Even the ANC-dominated South African government permitted EO to dispatch troops to Angola and Sierra Leone during most of the 1990s.

A nascent relationship is developing between some relief agencies and PSCs. Agencies may require increased protection in Africa's post–Cold War environment. Armed theft from relief groups has grown tremendously throughout the 1990s, and humanitarian supplies (food, medicine, transport, communications, and money) commandeered by factions have prolonged various conflicts—a 1999 University of Toronto study concluded that "huge sums are routinely lost to theft, looting and outright extortion."[24]

Somalia in the early 1990s was the first major example of such behavior and helped persuade the United States and the UN to intervene militarily. Armed rebels stole about $20 million and 470 vehicles from relief groups in Liberia during April 1996. While Western states often provide valuable relief supplies, they will not provide protection for food and medicine. The UN's undersecretary general for humanitarian affairs notes that Western states are not "averse to letting humanitarian staff go where they dare not send their invariably better equipped, better trained and better protected [troops]."[25]

A heated debate has divided the relief community over the wisdom of hiring security personnel, either as advisors or armed guards. The University of Toronto study proposes that relief groups "should consider the privatization of security for humanitarian purposes. . . . Since the core dilemma humanitarians face is the ability of predators to prey on civilians at will, and since nations and the UN are increasingly hesitant to furnish the necessary means to provide that security, it is worth exploring whether . . . the privatization of security is [also] appropriate."[26]

The support by many companies of relatively legitimate governments, rather than despots or destructive insurgencies, is another change. Burchett and Roebuck wrote some twenty years ago that mercenaries' "primary function has been to supply tyranny with a fighting force without the risks involved in arming the people, who might turn their arms and training on the tyrant."[27] Established security groups since the late 1980s have often aided African governments against insurgencies, and several have contracted with relief agencies operating in conflict areas. Supporting governments or relief agencies instead of insurgent groups generally provide the PSCs with greater legitimacy and perhaps a more assured payment source.

Possible Advantages

Industry growth has occurred since established private security groups offer possible advantages over state-centric militaries. The former can attempt tasks that many governments approve of but hesitate to attempt themselves because of financial or political costs. Although the UN and some governments may deploy peacekeeping forces, they rarely will agree to sending peace-enforcing, or combat, units. *Harper's* magazine notes that EO "offers to do what the United Nations blue helmets cannot and will not do: take sides, deploy overwhelming force, and fire 'preemptively' on its contractually designated enemy."[28]

Private forces can handpick from a pool of highly trained combat veterans, an especially large pool since post-Cold War demobilizations. A significant number come from very professional Western units in which political responsibility and military capabilities are cardinal principles.

These forces often will cost less than government forces because the companies work only when under contract, and they lease, rather than own, their equipment. Training costs are minimal because the PSC soldiers already possess the required skills. The Logistics Management Institute believes that PSCs cost about one-third the price of a national military.[29]

Established private forces can be deployed faster than multinational (and even some national) forces, and may carry less political baggage, especially concerning casualties, than government militaries.[30] Additionally, PSC forces have a clearer chain of command, more readily compatible military equipment and training, and sometimes greater experience of working together than do ad hoc multinational forces. Some writers even contend that private security firms offer exceptionally loyal forces to the hiring government. Zarate notes that "rulers still find it convenient to hire foreigners to act as guards so as to avoid arming their respective nationals and to prevent a challenge to their power."[31]

Possible Disadvantages

Until recently, several objections precluded serious discussion about the use of private security to stabilize states. Max Weber noted that the modern state arose because it "successfully upheld a claim to the monopoly of the legitimate use of physical force in the enforcement of its order."[32] Critics believe that private military groups cannot aid national development by protecting a weak state against armed insurrection. Instead, they maintain that the growth of such nonstate forces necessarily threatens the state's security and its legitimacy.[33]

Machiavelli counseled his prince that mercenaries were unprofessional: militarily ineffective and disloyal—"disunited, ambitious without discipline, unfaithful . . . you cannot trust them because they will always aspire to their own greatness, either by oppressing you who are their boss or by oppressing others outside of your intention."[34] Mercenaries in Africa during the Cold War generally proved Machiavelli correct. In Biafra, they stirred resentment among the Biafran soldiers and, as John de St. Jorre notes, "Biafra got very little in return for the vast sums of precious foreign exchange that were doled out to the mercenary leaders."[35] Most recently, a 400-man force of mostly Eastern Europeans, covertly and hastily organized by the French government, failed to stem Laurent Kabila's offensive in the former Zaire.

The assumption that mercenaries, who are foreign, fight primarily for money leads many to question foreign soldiers' acceptance by a local population, their knowledge of the situation, and their commitment to their employers' cause.[36] Alex Vines offers a warning that economic pressures can persuade ostensibly noncombat security companies to adopt violence.[37] Private soldiers can switch sides and take valuable intelligence with them, especially if prompted mostly by financial considerations.

Doubts about commitment touch on a foreign force's accountability and the belief that a largely autonomous mercenary group is more inclined than local soldiers to commit atrocities or pillage the local economy. The UN special rapporteur on mercenaries asks, "Who will be responsible for any repressive excesses that the security companies may commit against the civilian population. . . . Who will take responsibility for any violations of international humanitarian law and of human rights that they may commit?"[38]

Numerous critics contend that otherwise democratic states can circumvent public or legislative oversight by hiring private security firms. Ken Silverstein argues that "corporate entities are used to perform tasks that the government, for budgetary reasons or political sensitivities, cannot carry out."[39] Some local private security groups, especially in Latin America, have violently upset their hiring countries' security situation. Andres Oppenheimer notes that "private armies have long been active in countries like Colombia, where they have often ended up working for drug lords and paramilitary organizations with gruesome human rights records. . . . In Mexico City alone, there are 2,700 private security firms, which regularly employ tens of thousands of armed guards, many of which have criminal records."[40] Critics assert that Western companies, even if well intentioned, provide training and equipment that can then be used for human rights abuses.[41]

Other issues about accountability have arisen. Do PSCs assist personal rulers to bypass national institutions, especially the military, and thereby lessen the regime's accountability? Does private military expertise encourage governments to forgo more peaceful means of conflict resolution?

Charges of "neocolonialism" have tarred private soldiers and their African employers. Mercenaries, some of whom fought for minority or racist causes, often have drawn their pay from Western sources— either governments or private businesses (usually mining companies). Mercenaries thus often give a kiss of political death, or guilt by association, to their employers. To whom are such mercenary groups ultimately accountable, ask the critics: the African state or the Western government or corporation? Finally, how lasting a settlement can result from a foreign-imposed military victory?

Executive Outcomes

These concerns have immediate importance since the use of private groups worldwide, but especially in Africa, appears to be growing rapidly. The Angolan and Sierra Leonean governments, in 1993 and 1995, respectively, turned to Executive Outcomes (EO) for military protection against hitherto successful insurgencies. EO, which received financial help from a multinational mining company, helped to achieve rapid military victories, at a seemingly low financial cost, with several hundred combat soldiers and a small aircraft wing. It stopped operating in early 1999, but many of its personnel joined, or started, other security firms.

Background

The world's largest and best known "mercenary" group during the 1990s, EO marketed itself as a defender of African state security. It was a military anomaly: a feared force that had neither a standing army nor major weapons stockpile,[42] picking its employees as needed from a list of 2,000 proven and trusted South African combat specialists (it hired very few foreigners).

Most of EO's soldiers came from South Africa's former 32 Battalion, the Reconnaissance Commandos, the Parachute Brigade, and the paramilitary Koevoet ("Crowbar"). These four groups were South Africa's spearhead of military destabilization throughout southern Africa. They gained a thorough knowledge in Angola of UNITA's guerrilla capabilities and of the Angolan terrain, and several times plucked UNITA's leader, Jonas Savimbi, from the jaws of defeat. The South African Defense Force (SADF) Special Forces and the 32 Battalion saw especially heavy service in Angola during the 1980s. The 32 Battalion, composed largely of Portuguese-speaking Angolans, became South Africa's most highly decorated unit since World War II. Blacks made up about 70 percent of EO, but most of them served as combat soldiers.

Three of EO's officials reflected this elite unit background. Eeben Barlow, EO's founder and chairman until mid-1997, had been second in command of the 32 Battalion's reconnaissance unit (and later a top official of the Civil Cooperation Bureau). Laffras Luitingh, head of recruitment, had been a major in 5 Reconnaissance Commando.[43] Nic van den

Bergh, chief executive officer, had been a lieutenant colonel in the Parabats. In July 1997 Barlow and Luitingh resigned from EO; van den Bergh took over the chairmanship.

EO promised attractive financial benefits to its soldiers (although various press accounts exaggerated the amounts).[44] The average salary for a soldier was about $3,500 per month, with top helicopter pilots and country commanders earning about $7,500.

In some important ways, EO was different from past mercenary groups; differences suggesting that EO assisted political stability, but only in the short run. EO was an established firm that carefully picked its soldiers from a generally professional (though politically unsavory) military, the former SADF. EO claimed to support only sovereign states and, in the case of Sierra Leone, that its military operations helped create the stability necessary for democratic elections. EO's human rights record in Angola and Sierra Leone compared favorably with other armed groups in those two countries.

Yet the rapid success and commercial acumen of this organization pose a crucial question about entrusting national security to private groups: do they weaken or stabilize already fragile states? How professional are these groups; have any demonstrated both technical capabilities and political loyalty?

EO's commercial ties raised concerns about its effects on the de facto sovereignty of some African states. Critics worried that EO, or some of its subsequent offshoots, could become far more than an effective intervention force. Abdel-Fatau Musah cautions about a new scramble for Africa, observing that "the role of mercenaries in Sierra Leone (and also in Angola) has pushed the debate about the political recolonization of Africa from the realm of fantasy to that of real possibility."[45] The Branch Group, a British multinational holding company, benefited financially from its close ties with EO, as noted below. Some observers speculated that EO and other groups could form the military tip for a multinational economic wedge that, in this era of worldwide privatization, may be obtaining significant influence in fragile states. Britain's *Guardian Weekly* described EO as "arguably the world's first fully equipped corporate army . . . the advance guard for major business interests engaged in a latter-day scramble for the mineral wealth of Africa."[46]

Other worries arose. EO and other groups evoke a security dilemma: Does a private military force increase the instability of the nation it has contracted to protect?

How did EO succeed militarily on a continent where counterinsurgency victories are so infrequent? Most importantly, EO's soldiers came from a system that, unlike most African governments, generally encouraged military professionalism. Pre-liberation South Africa had two characteristics not found in personal-rule systems: an institutionalized political system and a sense of urgency, both of which encouraged the military's functional autonomy. South Africa's apartheid governments fit Weber's definition of a rational-legal (rather than personal) authority, and they institutionally separated civilian from military powers. The civilian rulers rarely intruded into purely military matters, and the militarily powerful SADF did not engage in pretorian activity.[47]

Fear of the regimes' opponents and the government's implicit faith in its military allowed the SADF to exercise functional autonomy and expertise. The often evoked *laager* metaphor emphasized the strength of a united and skilled minority against a larger but less competent opposition.[48] And meritocratic rather than subnational criteria (other than race) generally determined selection and promotion, procurement, and training.[49]

The division between civil and military responsibilities allowed the security forces to develop unusually effective skills. The white governments saw no security dilemma between military capabilities and political responsibility, and the SADF became one of the very few African militaries to emphasize counterinsurgency capabilities. The Reconnaissance Commando, South Africa's primary special operations unit, grew rapidly during the 1970s and 1980s at the behest of the apartheid government. The SADF's mechanized and armored units effectively supported operations of over 1,000 miles into Angola in the same decades. The South African Air Force became highly proficient in transportation, surveillance, bombing, and the close air support of ground units. The SADF, unlike most African forces, had traditionally trained its smaller units (i.e., squads, platoons, and companies) to be innovative when under pressure, rather than act purely defensively while awaiting orders from their superiors.

There were other contributing factors to the SADF's capabilities that would later empower EO. The SADF preached—although it certainly did not always practice—correct treatment of innocent civilians: specifically to obtain "the goodwill, support and cooperation of the local population by alleviating friction points, grievances and dissatisfaction, [and by] improving their standard of living."[50] The military schools taught the writings of Roger Trinquier (a French légionnaire involved in Algeria), André Beaufre (a French general), and John McCuen (a U.S. lieutenant colonel), all of whom emphasized the political aspects of counterinsurgency and the need—especially for a military that represented an unpopular government—to win the hearts and minds of civilians.[51] South Africa learned how to build effective networks for weapons procurement, intelligence, and "dirty tricks" operations in foreign countries.[52]

Finally, EO came from a tradition of the military not interfering in civilian politics. South Africa by 1999 had never faced a coup or even a coup attempt in the almost ninety years of its national military.[53] The SADF arguably never crossed the military-civil divide to restyle apartheid policies, simply because it agreed with white domination. Yet President F. W. de Klerk's reforms, which began around 1990 and helped to facilitate majority rule, angered many SADF combat veterans. However, even though disagreement with the reforms ran high in the SADF, its officers accepted the dramatic changes.[54] EO would maintain this abstinence from pretorianism in Angola and Sierra Leone.

The above political and military factors contributed to EO's being an already experienced single structure when it entered the Angolan and Sierra Leonean conflicts. EO's order of battle was generally much smaller than that of ECOMOG's members, but it was of higher quality. EO had a single and well-practiced set of tactics, as well as exceptionally experienced troops and functioning equipment. As a result, this small but highly competent force could check an advancing insurgent force.

Angola

EO arose out of southern Africa's radically changed political landscape. The 1988 Brazzaville accords signaled an end to Soviet, Cuban, and South African military involvement in Angola and Namibia. As South Africa retired its regional destabilization policy, many of its combat soldiers left the SADF. By 1992 the Reconnaissance Commandos and the Parachute Brigade stood at approximately half their 1989 strength, and South Africa officially disbanded the largely Angolan 32 Battalion and the largely Namibian Koevoet.

Observers worried that these unemployed upholders of the old order could derail political reforms and subsequent majority rule. Instead, EO was an apparently stabilizing force. Angola's MPLA government contracted with EO (members of which in the 1980s had fought against the MPLA) to defeat Jonas Savimbi's UNITA—an insurgency for which most EO personnel had once fought.

Escalating fighting within Angola had prompted EO's entry in early 1993. After the 1991 peace agreement between UNITA and the MPLA that resulted in September 1992 elections, UNITA's Savimbi disagreed with the incomplete returns that showed the MPLA winning. Returning to fighting, Savimbi soon controlled 80 percent of Angola's countryside, and the MPLA desperately sought help. But the MPLA and foreign oil companies could no longer draw upon support from Cuba and the Soviet Union.

UNITA continued on the offensive throughout much of Angola. Heritage Oil and Gas, which is part of the Branch Group, hired EO to capture two important oil towns, Kefekwena and Soyo, in early 1993: Soyo being an important economic site with an $80 million pumping station. An increasingly desperate MPLA recognized EO's capabilities and signed a one-year contract for $40 million in September 1993 ($20 million for military supplies requested by EO and $20 million directly to EO). The Angolan government would renew this contract until mid-1996.[55] For the MPLA, it was money well spent because EO helped to halt UNITA's military drive.

Executive Outcomes served primarily as a "force multiplier"—a small group whose specialized skills enhance the effectiveness of a much larger force. EO fielded a maximum of about 550 soldiers and trained about 5,000 government troops and thirty pilots.[56] At Longa special operations training base, near Luanda, EO personnel instructed the Angolan Armed Forces (FAA) in such fields as motorized infantry, artillery, engineering, signals, and medical support, as well as sabotage and reconnaissance. EO's major triumph occurred in June 1994 when the EO-trained Angolan 16th Brigade triumphed over a strong UNITA force at N'taladonda, a strategic town outside Luanda. N'taladonda was the newly constituted brigade's first battle; with joint EO-FAA planning it suffered only four casualties. "That battle changed the whole attitude of the Angolans," recalls Barlow. "Everything else fell into place for us in Angola and word spread throughout Africa."[57]

Executive Outcomes personnel sometimes fought, rather than just trained and advised. EO-trained soldiers proved instrumental in seizing N'taladonda, and EO personnel helped recapture the diamond areas of Cafunfo in mid-July 1994 and the oil installations at Soyo by November, as well as Uige. Pilots belonging to Ibis Air, which possibly was a Branch Group company, flew combat sorties in Mi-8 (Hip), MI-17 (Hip-H) helicopters, and MiG-23 fighters. Defense strategists generally credit EO with greatly assisting the MPLA to turn back the resurgent UNITA.[58] About twenty EO personnel died in Angola from combat, training, and health problems.

A chastened Savimbi signed the Lusaka Protocol in November

1994. The protocol ended the fighting and prepared the ground for another round of elections. It also called for the repatriation of all mercenaries in Angola, but EO remained for another thirteen months at the MPLA's request. On December 12, 1995, the Angolan government announced the imminent withdrawal of EO from Angola, the first group leaving for South Africa on January 11, 1996. EO and the Angolan government followed the letter, but probably not the spirit, of the withdrawal: up to half of EO personnel remained in Angola legally, often taking jobs in government-encouraged PSCs.[59]

Sierra Leone

EO's rapid military successes against one of Africa's most capable guerrilla armies attracted attention elsewhere on the continent.[60] In May 1995, Sierra Leone contracted with EO to help its faltering four-year campaign against the RUF. The Branch Group apparently entered into an agreement with the government during this same time. Tony Buckingham, the CEO of Heritage Oil and Gas, helped introduce EO to the Freetown government, and Michael Grunberg, Branch Group's owner, negotiated EO's contract.[61] The RUF, aided by a general breakdown in order and disloyal government soldiers, had advanced by May 1995 to within 20 miles of the capital of Freetown. The RUF's strength was several thousand at the most. A high-ranking U.S. official believes that the RUF's "hard-core" fighters may not have numbered more than 350; any others were situational opportunists.[62]

The war had devastated the country. One-and-a-half million of Sierra Leone's 4 million people had become refugees, and at least 15,000 had been killed since 1992. The economy was in shambles: the RUF had largely closed road traffic as well as diamond and bauxite mining. The war's disruption of Sierra Leone's extensive diamond and titanium dioxide (rutile) deposits saw the gross national product decline by at least 10 percent in 1995 (and inflation soar by 35 percent). Clandestine diamond and agricultural production cost the government about $200 million: government domestic revenues came to only $60 million.[63]

The Republic of Sierra Leone Military Force (RSLMF) evinced many of the military limitations that have encouraged the growth of private militaries. The RSLMF hardly qualified as an army, despite its size of perhaps 14,000 soldiers (two-thirds of whom had been hastily recruited). The RSLMF lacked the basic attributes of military organization. The governments of Siaka Stevens and Joseph Momoh had "ethnicized" the military and cut its budget. The World Bank and the International Monetary Fund (IMF) increasingly pressed the government to lower military funding, following the army's hasty buildup from about 3,000 to about 11,000. The military displayed no lack of corruption. The term "sobels" ("soldiers by day, rebels by night") described soldiers who also engaged in banditry or rebel activities, and was a common reference to RSLMF members. RSLMF units sometimes even fought each other.

EO submitted a proposal to the financially strapped government of Valentine Strasser. "They said they couldn't pay," recalls EO's Lafras Luitingh. "We said they could pay us when they could afford it."[64] Barlow and Luitingh maintain that EO insisted that the Strasser government begin a democratization process. According to Barlow, "When Strasser started reneging, we threatened to withdraw. We insisted on a timetable for democracy—within one to one and a half years. We kept on pushing, pushing . . . ten months later the (election) occurred." Other observers strongly downplay EO's requests for democratization.[65]

EO's military progress was rapid. Once again, as a force multiplier it provided technical services, combat forces, and limited training. Thirty EO soldiers arrived around May 1995 and within weeks had trained 150 government soldiers. EO claims that the Sierra Leonean military feared the capabilities of an EO-trained force and therefore did not offer any trainees after the first 150. EO thus turned to the Kamajors, a locally based paramilitary.

EO's first tasks were to push the RUF away from Freetown, protect the Kono diamond district, and open the roads to Freetown for food and fuel transport. By late January 1996, EO-backed forces had retaken the southern coastal rutile and bauxite mines, notably those belonging to Sierra Rutile and Sieromco. Brig. Bert Sachse, EO's commander in Sierra Leone, states that EO suffered two killed during EO's year-and-a-half of combat.[66]

EO's activities helped to facilitate a cease-fire, as they had in Angola. In February 1996 the Julius Maada Bio government, which had seized power from Strasser, scheduled elections that took place without serious complications. The new government headed by Ahmed T. Kabbah took power on March 29 and continued the war against RUF and the sobels. On November 29, the Kabbah government and the RUF signed a peace settlement that continued into early 1997. EO departed Sierra Leone upon completion of its contract in January 1997.[67]

EO's military assistance aided Sierra Leone's economic and political situation. William Reno, generally a critic of EO, notes that the force created the stability that attracted more foreign investors, whose revenue helped lower the foreign debt 20 percent in 1995 and 1996 and that allowed nationwide elections in March 1996.[68]

Retired Canadian Gen. Ian Douglas, a UN negotiator, acknowledges that "E.O. gave us this stability [in Sierra Leone]. In a perfect world, of course, we wouldn't need an organization like E.O., but I'd be loath to say they have to go just because they are mercenaries."[69]

EO's military successes prompted dramatic speculation about its future influence in Africa. A Western European intelligence source stated in 1996 that EO had "unlimited potential for expansion and self-enrichment certainly within Africa and there is little evidence of the bandwagon slowing down.[70] A British intelligence report predicted that "Executive Outcomes will become ever richer and more potent, capable of exercising real power, even to the extent of keeping military regimes in being. If it continues to expand at the present rate, its influence in sub-Saharan Africa could become crucial."[71]

Military Effectiveness

Executive Outcomes largely disproved Machiavelli's contention that mercenaries are usually ineffective; it demonstrated the ability of a small, highly trained group to change the military tide. John Leigh, Sierra Leone's ambassador to the United States, implicitly recognized how the RSLMF contributed to his nation's security dilemma when he acknowledged that "the government of Sierra Leone believes EO can do a better job than the Sierra Leone army."[72] EO's expertise in combat operations and, especially, as a force multiplier garnered widespread respect. EO's troops proved instrumental in several battles, for instance, at Cafunfo in Angola and Kono in Sierra Leone. Its pilots, often flying MiG fighters and MI helicopters, greatly assisted ground and intelligence operations.

EO's upgrading of local military capability in Angola proved more important than its combat capability. Training and intelligence are two major aspects of force multiplication. EO's officers proved excellent trainers of African recruits: many of EO's officers had trained and officered black units of the former SADF.

EO provided the Angolan FAA, for example, with specialized services that Angola's Cuban and Soviet patrons had never furnished. EO gave the MPLA and the FAA its close knowledge of Savimbi's capabilities. EO planes and helicopters conducted aerial, including infrared, reconnaissance flights. Long-range reconnaissance and aerial surveillance provided visual identification of enemy camps. Its radio operators could listen to, and reportedly jam, UNITA and RUF communications. Defense experts also believe that EO was highly skilled in signals and communication and photo interpretation.[73]

Sources inside EO have revealed that the organization in Sierra Leone also conducted counterintelligence operations, intelligence operators at times identifying possible informants, isolating and training them, and then supplying them with communications equipment.[74] EO also quietly drew on threatened businesses for local intelligence.

Rapid acquisition of intelligence was especially essential for EO: as a private foreign force it presumably lacked official South African (or Western) intelligence and yet faced pressures to achieve quick victories. Inadequate intelligence had hamstrung other recent African interventions, most notably that of ECOMOG in Liberia. EO achieved strong intelligence capabilities in short order—which may seem surprising, given its foreign, white officership and its history in apartheid South Africa.

EO's actions to increase its political acceptance also aided its intelligence gathering. During the 1980s the SADF had stressed (though often did not practice) that counterinsurgency was 80 percent political and 20 percent military. EO countered any criticism from outside and gained valuable internal support and information with its generally good behavior toward African civilians and minimal civic action programs.[75] "We train our soldiers to behave with the locals," says Eeben Barlow "and not [to] become their enemy . . . we build trust and acquire more intelligence."[76] EO's signals intercepts, its reconnaissance (ground and air), its very limited medical aid for civilians, and its host governments' contributions added to its intelligence base.

EO did not mount any major civic action programs; its military ability to defeat rebel groups and its correct behavior toward the general population created some popularity with civilians. (Although, as a World Bank critic of EO rejoins, "It doesn't take much [in Angola or Sierra Leone] to look pretty good.")[77] The company's apparently stabilizing actions contrasted with those of its opponents: UNITA and the RUF enjoyed only limited domestic and international support. Savimbi's refusal to accept the 1992 election results and his subsequent return to warfare greatly reduced his already limited credibility. The popular perception of the RUF was that it was a nonideological, often brutal spinoff of the forces of the Liberian warlord, Charles Taylor.

EO could not count on Sierra Leone's corruption-ridden military but, as noted above, did use a locally based network of hunters, the

Kamajors, which grew to over 10,000 fighters during EO's stay and, along with EO, turned the war around militarily. The Kamajors knew the terrain, enjoyed excellent relations with the paramount chiefs, and resented the RUF's intrusions. EO strengthened the military capability of the Kamajors with food supplies, intelligence, training, and some strategic planning. (However, such support of local, parallel militaries backfired later in Sierra Leone).

EO's military successes, combined with its generally correct behavior toward civilians, muted any criticism of these profit-seeking soldiers out of the old apartheid system. A leading human rights activist in Sierra Leone notes that "our country had so much destruction and devastation [that had] never been seen here before. Most of us didn't understand apartheid. . . . our country is far from South Africa and is 80% illiterate. . . . Call them [EO] whatever, they were coming to save us. My survival over somebody else's apartheid?—Never an issue."[78]

Political Responsibility

The concept of a foreign soldier fighting for money strongly suggests a purchasable and changeable loyalty. Could a government trust EO, given the company's profit-driven ethos and its opposition to UNITA, which EO personnel had previously supported when fighting for the SADF? EO apparently remained loyal to current regimes, but the favorable economic contracts it obtained could have deprived the contracting states of future revenue. In return for significant payments, EO remained loyal to its employers. It did not switch sides, threaten any government, or shirk combat—the three traits of mercenaries noted by Machiavelli and others.

EO provided valuable military assistance to the Angolan government and then left when requested in late 1995. Equally, EO stood by the Sierra Leonean government (although it threatened to leave in late 1995, apparently because of nonpayment) and did not become involved in the several coup plots of 1996. EO reportedly forestalled a planned coup against the 1996 elections.[79] Business pragmatism largely determined EO's loyalty, and in Barlow's words, EO hoped "to live a long time as a company."[80] So an undisputed record of loyalty, as well as military success and a good human rights record, appeared essential to generate future business.[81]

It has to be noted that EO maintained remarkable discipline over its soldiers as long as the contracts were in force. But militaries for hire provide only short-term employment and, as Carl Albert told this author in 1997, loyalty lasts only as long as the contract does.[82] Some ex-EO soldiers in Angola and Sierra Leone now assist UNITA and the RUF. Albert points out a major worry about mercenaries: transferable loyalty. He flew initially for EO and the Sierra Leonean government against the RUF, but reportedly later took his services and the specialized knowledge about Sierra Leone gained during his EO employment to the RUF and Charles Taylor. Some intelligence analysts believe that more ex-EO soldiers were fighting for Savimbi than for the MPLA by late 1999.[83]

Finally, EO's budget ($40 million yearly in Angola and far less in Sierra Leone) *seemingly* paled when compared to the national military budgets of Angola and Sierra Leone. The International Institute for Strategic Studies *Military Balance* notes that Angola's defense spending in 1995 average was at least $515 million, whereas Sierra Leone's military budget for 1995 was $41 million.[84]

Yet, as with much else about EO, the story was more complicated and eluded full understanding. EO did not succeed all by itself: it worked with several units of the Angolan FAA, notably the 16th Brigade, as with the Kamajors in Sierra Leone. The announced $40 million yearly in Angola and about $12 million yearly in Sierra Leone constituted only a part of payments to EO-Branch Group. Angola also secretly provided the Branch Group with an unknown number of valuable mineral concessions. The Yetwene mine in northeastern Angola, which produces about $24 million worth of diamonds yearly, is but one example.[85] The Branch Group's ownership of the mine, which was a partial payment for EO's services, remained secret until UNITA attacked the mine in late 1998, almost three years after EO had left the country. Sierra Leone reportedly awarded significant mining concessions to the Branch Group when the government could not pay EO's monthly fee.

Role in National Development

Did EO assist state development in Angola and Sierra Leone? The organization did demonstrate both military efficiency and political loyalty to its clients. Yet, its record—including linkages with Western commercial interests, support of usually unaccountable personal rulers, and often less-than-permanent victories—raises several issues that are difficult to resolve.

EO apparently helped the Branch Group to obtain highly advantageous concessions. Some Western and African diplomats speculate that in return for a temporary security fix, EO/Branch Group was "gaining a host of dirt-cheap long-term concessions which mortgage a country's future to this foreign company that can call upon both economic and military force . . . and get a foothold."[86] Khareem Pech cites other sources when she writes that "EO's operations facilitated the granting of some of the richest diamond concessions in the world, valued at over US $3 billion."[87] CBS's "Sixty Minutes" claimed that "as soon as EO cleared the rebels out of the diamond fields, the government of Sierra Leone awarded Branch Energy a huge diamond concession. There have been similar coincidences in other countries where EO has ventured."[88] The Branch Group rejects these accusations of extraordinary leverage and claims only that it introduced EO to the Angolan and Sierra Leonean governments, served as a "consultant" to EO, and disbursed the government's pay to EO.

Other observers believe that the connections went beyond "consultancy" and that Branch perhaps financed some of EO's initial, and then ongoing, costs when the Sierra Leonean government fell into arrears. Sources close to the Branch Group reveal that the Sierra Leonean government paid nothing—despite an agreement to pay almost $2 million monthly—during EO's first eight months, and that for EO's duration (May 1995 to January 1997) the government paid only $15.7 million of a $35.2 bill.[89]

EO may have retained some profits from its Angolan campaign, but it is most unlikely that it could have paid its approximately 200 men in Sierra Leone and provided them with equipment from Angolan profits. Branch (and other mining companies) depended on EO for security and had the resources to assist EO. Tony Buckingham of Heritage Oil and Gas aided, and seemed to speak for, EO when he flew to Freetown in December 1995 and told the Kabbah government that EO would leave within two weeks if the government did not provide adequate funding.

The importance of the Branch Group's possible financial connections to EO is that the former could have used its EO connections to obtain more favorable terms on its concessions. Possibilities include a stretched tax holiday or customs exemptions from the Bio and Kabbah governments in Sierra Leone, which desperately needed both EO's physical protection and Branch Group revenues. Highly favorable concessions could constrict national development by lessening future government revenue. In other words, was this a short-term reprieve in exchange for a long-term curse?

EO and the Branch Group denied that their activities threatened present or future state development—in fact just the opposite. Grunberg and Spicer argued that a professional military (i.e., EO) could quickly restore stability—sometimes in countries that have witnessed obscene human rights violations. Further, the Branch Group/SRC companies offered technology and finance that most African states desperately need. These companies, therefore, claimed to be no different from other private enterprises that help develop a country in return for a profit. Furthermore, any possible Branch Group underwriting of EO's expenses provided a necessary service by aiding state stability. Neither the Sierra Leonean government alone nor the West would have paid EO's bill.

The Branch Group and SRC claimed that they could act as economic subcontractors following the peace that EO had achieved and introduce into a struggling state, such as Lierra Leone, other corporations that EO can continue to protect.[90] Even if the Branch Group did barter EO's muscle for favorable concessions, Michael Grunberg asks, "What's wrong with bartering: a country uses whatever assets it can during bargaining?"[91]

The short and less-than-transparent history of EO/Branch Group cannot firmly answer whether either exerted undue security and economic influence. The Sierra Leone experience certainly exhibited Branch Group influence, but apparently no control over major policy decisions. Other powerful international actors added a counterbalancing influence. The Sierra Leonean government depended on EO for its security throughout 1995 and 1996 but, as a result of IMF pressure, rejected Branch Group attempts to obtain the country's national petroleum company and its maritime surveillance contract through noncompetitive bidding. Such international actors as the World Bank and the IMF insisted that the government conduct a transparent and competitive bidding process. As a result the Branch Group gained neither concession. The IMF also successfully insisted in mid-1996 that the Sierra Leonean government cut its overall spending, which resulted in fewer payments to EO (the government owes $19.5 million to EO). Reportedly, Executive Outcomes bid for a contract to train a downsized RSLMF, but outside funding sources, notably Britain, told Sierra Leone's government that they would not finance any EO training operation. The proprietary nature of Branch Group's mineral contracts prevents knowledge of the terms.

Several critics believe that EO/Branch Group benefited African personal-rule "compradors" by pursuing an "enclave development," which, unlike previous foreign-imposed control, would be "imperialism by invitation."[92] William Reno casts this thesis into the post-Cold War era:

rulers of weak states can use a foreign partnership to compensate for the lack of great-power patronage.[93] The availability of private security services helps personal rulers in not trying to develop professional militaries.

The Branch Group and SRC have brought leading Africans—especially military figures—into their economic tent. U.S. State Department officials state that Gen. João de Matos, Angola's chief of staff, has an economic interest in a Branch/Diamondworks concession as well as in the Alpha-5 security force, reportedly an EO spinoff.[94] In 1997, the Branch Group and the Sierra Leonean government were partners in a major diamond concession (the firm having majority ownership).

African employers of EO apparently preferred foreign agents to local actors: an EO-Branch Group combination would loyally and efficiently serve the regime, whereas African military officers or businessmen might pose a greater threat. Angola's legal requirement that foreign companies hire their own (almost always foreign-officered) security force lends credence to this view and demonstrates the extent to which rulers see threats not only from rebel groups but also from disloyal state agents. Even though such a policy serves the interests of the regime, it may work against the concept of "nation building" by retarding growth of a civic culture and an indigenous business community. Reno notes that Ahmed Kabbah's "reliance on Executive Outcomes and related private firms such as Branch Mining gave him a measure of autonomy vis-à-vis local rivals and the global economy."[95]

A high-ranking U.S. diplomat contends that the Sierra Leonean government pressed Sierra Rutile Company to hire EO (or Lifeguard, its guard subsidiary) as a permanent guard force.[96] This strategy would grant special treatment to the foreign companies in particular economic areas. The Sierra Leonean government officially invited EO, an outsider, whose initial deployment was to secure the capital and the nation's mineral areas—areas where Branch Group had gained concessions. Paul Kamara, the editor of Sierra Leone's *For De People,* wonders whether his government paid EO to protect Branch Energy with official funding.[97] In effect, he asks, did Branch get something for nothing?

How lasting are the settlements forcibly obtained by foreign soldiers? A military solution to longstanding social-economic divisions may prove financially costly and of only temporary value. Sierra Leonean soldiers sympathetic to the rebel RUF overthrew the democratically elected Kabbah government some four months after EO left. The growth of the Kamajors as a parallel force was a major cause of this coup (the RSLMF despising this parallel military force), and the first act of the new government was to demobilize the Kamajors. The coup's aftermath plagued Freetown with its only serious destruction during the six years of war. (Meanwhile, the Branch Group had obtained at least one very valuable long-term concession, and EO had collected about $16 million from a foreign-exchange-strapped country.) EO officials countered that the 1997 instability showed EO's capability; an extended EO presence would have provided breathing space for the Kabbah government.[98]

EO officials also contended that its personnel are not nation builders; they only obtain a military settlement, which will, with any luck, assist political reconciliation. They argue that a deployment of UN observers, or a UN peacekeeping contingent, could have provided stability after EO's departure. Neither the regional superpowers, South Africa and Nigeria, nor the OAU campaigned strongly against EO: the right of a sovereign state to a secure self-defense, regional geopolitics, and widespread dislike of both insurgencies were the major reasons.[99] Indeed, the OAU reportedly held some security discussions with EO. Britain's *Independent* newspaper in 1996 reported that "a recent South African intelligence assessment concluded that the Organization for African Unity (OAU) may be forced to offer [EO] a contract for peacekeeping continent-wide."[100]

Critics contend that private security groups such as EO can undermine a state's security by causing dissension in the existing national militaries and by raising countries' general levels of militarization and destabilization. Existing national militaries have not always appreciated EO's assistance, and their anger can destabilize national governments and EO's achievements. EO was better paid and enjoyed better weaponry, as its mere introduction suggested government dissatisfaction with an existing military.[101]

EO had to face "turf battles" with the established national militaries in Angola and Sierra Leone.[102] In Angola, EO faced a special problem: cooperating with a former enemy. "The FAA had a lot of hostility towards us," recalls Barlow. "They couldn't forget very quickly a lot of past engagements."[103] Luitingh remembers that the MPLA was "hesitant to divulge force levels and deployment which we needed for our operational planning."[104] EO's quick successes, notably at N'taladonda, lessened FAA hostility.

Mutual suspicions sometimes remained, however, because EO

operated outside of the normal chain of command in Sierra Leone. There it reported directly to the president, who was also the minister of defense, and to the deputy minister of defense. EO continued to keep much of the operational intelligence to itself because the Sierra Leonean soldiers' allegiance was often questionable. EO's operations room at Defence Headquarters was off limits to almost all of Sierra Leone's officers.

EO's victories produced different reactions from the militaries of Angola and Sierra Leone. EO's successes in Angola, where the military supported the government, apparently lessened the antagonism between EO and the FAA. But battlefield victories in Sierra Leone, notably at Kono, convinced some RSLMF personnel that EO was both showing them up and lessening their opportunity for diamond theft. EO soldiers and Ibis pilots maintain that government officials, presumably involved in smuggling, restricted EO's activities following the retaking of Kono. Also, EO reported RSLMF soldiers who had looted civilian or government property to their military commanders.[105]

Obviously, the extent of a military's loyalty to its governments helps explain the difference. The RSLMF was more factionalized than the FAA; the former, which contained numerous sobels, had a history of military coups, whereas the FAA remained loyal to the Angolan government. EO did not spark any reported violence from the RSLMF during EO's stay, but EO's high salaries and assistance to the Kamajors later encouraged the May 25, 1997, coup against President Kabbah. "What they do not do is address the root causes of the conflicts they've been involved in," contends 'Kayode Fayemi. "They scratch the surface. The minute [Executive Outcomes] left Sierra Leone—what they drove underground rose up when they left."[106]

Another worry was that EO's training and combat skills would only increase the militarization and the destabilization of a desperately poor continent. Endangered governments could turn to EO rather than to peaceful negotiations to answer insurgents' demands. Britain's Parliamentary Human Rights Group speculated that EO's Sierra Leonean success "may lead to a situation where any government in a difficult position can hire mercenaries to stay in power."[107] Skeptics also believe that a company that depends on strife for its profit might initiate or prolong conflict.[108] Others worry that training and equipping irregular forces (e.g., the Kamajors) could threaten future stability because such forces are often less controllable than are trained regular militaries. Finally, EO inspired, or assisted, a number of corporate security companies in Sierra Leone, Angola, and elsewhere within Africa. Critics charge that such groups—often encouraged by both foreign companies and national governments—may become forces unto themselves.[109]

A high-ranking former U.S. diplomat believes that EO's presence may have exacerbated Sierra Leone's security dilemma by (1) compelling the RUF to adopt butchery of civilians as its only, albeit counterproductive, means of retaliation; (2) hurting potential negotiations stemming from EO's pressure on the RUF; and (3) lessening the legitimacy of a government that had found it necessary to call on "mercenary" support.[110] Yet the RUF had already started such butchery before EO' engagement (although EO's actions may have increased the RUF's penchant for amputations), and EO's generally correct treatment of civilians garnered more approval than did actions of the poorly trained RSLMF and the sobels.

What is certain is that any foreign intervention, no matter how well intentioned, can destabilize an already fragile situation. West Africa offers an interesting comparison of how regional versus private forces may affect militarization. ECOMOG, a multinational African peacekeeping force, tried for six years to end a devastating civil war in Liberia. The results were dramatically different from those sought. The wars that had EO as a player did have important differences, including differences in mandates. ECOMOG entered Liberia in 1990 as a peacekeeping force, whereas EO clearly entered Angola and Sierra Leone as a peace enforcer, that is, a combat (and training) unit.[111] Even after serious attacks against it in 1990 and 1992, ECOMOG did not maintain military offensives to crush Charles Taylor's NPFL.[112] EO helped put down Sierra Leone's insurgency (and facilitated a relatively democratic election) during its stay of a year and a half, whereas ECOMOG did not achieve peace in Liberia during its first six years there. In fact, several national contingents in ECOMOG prolonged the Liberian conflict by arming and abetting several of the factions, which subsequently turned against their regional benefactor and thereby prolonged the war.[113]

EO's combat success has not spawned any similarly competent competitors, thus limiting fears of greater militarization of conflict. EO's composition of proven veterans with shared training and experience and its already established structure proved unique in the African context. Ad hoc multinational mercenary collections may draw inspiration from EO, but such groups usually will achieve only mediocre results.

Termination

EO closed its operations on January 1, 1999. The reasons were varied, and included legislation in South Africa, EO's murky connections with the Branch Group and its secretive business dealings, its less-than-permanent solutions (and difficult relations with national militaries), Branch Group's own qualms about closely identifying with the high-profile EO, EO's own military limitations, and a lessening manpower pool. EO itself adopted a lower profile following its failed 1997 involvement with the Sandline operation in Papua New Guinea, sending only small groups of specialists (e.g., combat helicopter pilots) to African governments and performing usually uncontroversial domestic advising and guarding operations, such as antirustling activities in South Africa.

South Africa's Regulation of Foreign Military Assistance Act in 1998 may have persuaded EO to close up shop. Although EO publicly claimed that it welcomed the legislation—which levied stiff fines against unauthorized private security operations—it may have concluded that the legislation's demands for disclosure and permission were too restrictive. Many of EO's employees joined other, less prominent, private security firms following the company's 1999 closing.

EO never gained full political acceptance from the international community, despite having been hired by sovereign governments to fight against discredited insurgencies. Traditional suspicions about mercenaries, including their unaccountability and behavior toward civilians, as well as the apartheid-connected past of EO's present soldiers and EO's links to Western capital continued to create suspicion.[114]

Basic fears about unaccountability restricted the appeal of EO and any other private combat groups. Heavily armed ex-SADF soldiers of battalion strength operating with few constraints in a fragile state—despite generally correct behavior—hurt EO's appeal, while suggesting that the state system may have been surrendering by default one of its basic prerogatives. Jakkie Cilliers and Christian Dietrich note that "responsibility for global peace and security, for law and order, cannot be diverted to a private body, a mercenary outfit, which is beyond the control of either government or international bodies, but is purely commercial in its undertaking."[115]

Sandline, which had close links to EO, contracted to fight for the Papua New Guinea government in 1997 against an insurgency force. It raised accountability concerns with its Papua New Guinea contract that read in part that "all Sandline personnel will be furnished with the necessary multiple entry visas without passport stamps and authorization to enter and leave the country free from hindrance at any time."[116] Such a provision should hinder investigation and prosecution of suspected abusers of human rights.

EO's actions presented a racially based insult to many critics: EO's soldiers were former gangsters of an apartheid regime, who now claimed the status of saviors of an "independent" continent that could not save itself. That is to say, thirty-five years after Africa's independence, a white-led group of ex-SADF soldiers was killing black Africans for profit—both for itself and for multinational business interests. Chief R. O. A. Akinjide of the International Law Commission writes that "the crime of mercenarism is particularly obnoxious within the African context. In Africa, the mercenary is seen as the representative of colonialism and racial oppression—an assassin hired to kill freedom fighters in wars of national liberation and wars against racial oppression."[117]

EO's highly publicized combat operations, rather than its training and advising ones, exacerbated worries about muscular neocolonial/ racist domination. Zarate argues that international protests about EO/Sandline's contract in Papua New Guinea "focused on the direct offensive role to be played by EO soldiers, especially the alleged plan to decapitate the BRA [Bougainvillle Revolutionary Army] by assassinating its leaders. The international community . . . may be averse to the direct, aggressive involvement of foreigners in an ongoing civil strife."[118]

Even though EO justifiably claimed to have stabilized several African states, however temporarily, Barlow's rhetoric sometimes moved beyond simple paternalism. For example, he stated: "We understand the cultures, we understand the people of Africa. We have to be around for a long time. . . . Who else will solve Africa's problems?"[119] The United States publicly disagreed with this sentiment, and President Clinton successfully pressed President José dos Santos of Angola to expel EO.[120] A State Department official noted in 1996: "We tell [African governments] that we're opposed to EO."[121]

The Branch Group, EO's main contractor, reportedly disliked being linked to the high-profile EO with its battalion-sized combat units and Eeben Barlow's colorful personality, both of which spurred critical articles about "Diamond Dogs of War."[122] *Africa Confidential* observed in late 1998 that "EO now seems to limit its operations to South Africa (partly because Branch-Heritage/DiamondWorks want to distance themselves from the South African mercenary image). Sandline has become EO's real successor."[123]

Paradoxically, EO's military successes and its lack of military capabilities most likely slowed its growth. Continued successes by the highly visible EO probably proved to be self-checking. Princeton Lyman, the U.S. ambassador to South Africa during EO's Angolan campaign, predicted that EO would become a victim of its own success: "A serious political backlash [could occur] if the growth became extensive."[124]

In helping to reverse the Angolan conflict, EO was blessed by very unusual circumstances. It had extraordinary knowledge of UNITA's various capabilities, longstanding experience with southern Angola's topography and terrain, and major financing by this oil-rich state. In Sierra Leone, EO initially had little knowledge about the enemy, but, by all accounts, the RUF was more a bandit force than a serious enemy. It lacked grassroots support, did not hold and politicize any territory, and allowed EO total air superiority because it had few, if any, operable antiaircraft guns. "Suppose RUF had UNITA's military capabilities," posits a Western military analyst. "EO would've had the devil of a time defeating it."[125]

The "white knight" status conferred on EO by several writers is misleading.[126] Indigenous groups, notably the FAA in Angola and the Kamajors in Sierra Leone, provided indispensable backing by supplying intelligence and large numbers of men for combat and garrison duty. Military analysts agree that EO hastened these wars' endings, but they disagree as to whether EO turned the tide or simply hastened an inevitable conclusion.

Executive Outcomes itself limited its operations, trying not to overextend its resources or enter politically harmful conflicts. Sources close to EO acknowledge that the Sudanese government approached it to provide security to oil companies but that EO declined. Aligning itself with a fundamentalist and repressive government would damage EO's reputation with most other states: supporting sovereignty per se is not necessarily supporting legitimacy. Also, some states could possibly draw EO into conflict with other sovereign states. Supporting Sudan could antagonize Uganda, where Branch Energy had a major investment. Equally, aiding the discredited Mobutu government (and its Kabila successor) in eastern Zaire/Congo could have pushed EO soldiers into conflict with Rwandan and Ugandan forces.[127]

Executive Outcomes limited its involvements by assisting governments, not insurgencies. EO faced an aging and finite manpower pool of South African-trained and tested combat personnel. Part of EO's unique ability stemmed from a force with similar training, outlook, and combat experience. Yet the former SADF had deemphasized combat capability and stopped its regional destabilization operations by 1990. Eeben Barlow acknowledged in 1997 that this problem of aging would trouble EO more and more.[128] EO could have drawn soldiers from other countries, but this would probably have lowered EO's combat capabilities. Its refusal to employ its soldiers permanently meant that if EO did not land frequent contracts, its soldiers would have to seek more permanent employment and decline subsequent EO possibilities.

A British intelligence assessment that EO would enjoy "unlimited potential for expansion within Africa" proved wrong.[129] EO's mixed record and its closing in 1999 prove that the Tofflers' suggestion of modern-day condottieri and "free companies" will not soon appear. Yet EO did modify attitudes toward private security and it provided several important military lessons for African security and foreign intervention.[130] Among those lessons are the following:

1. An established private company can field a professional force that may help win counterinsurgency wars in Africa and not threaten its employer. Even a small unit may tilt the power balance in domestic wars by acting as a force multiplier of existing assets. This is especially true in many third world conflicts where the insurgents lack significant military strength and a defining ideology. The provision of a limited amount of reliable air support (transport, reconnaissance, or combat) can prove surprisingly cost-effective, given most insurgencies' lack of counterfire. Foreign advisers—or elements of professional African militaries—can obtain information quickly, especially through good military-civilian relations and a relatively small investment in technology (e.g., spotter planes, radios, signal-interception equipment). A single force, with already established unit integrity, including agreed strategy, tactics, and equipment, has distinct advantages over an ad hoc multilateral force. Established firms, whose members are often rooted in Western military professionalism, are likely to prove loyal to their employer and not significantly abuse the human rights of the civilian population.

2. A private security company can, however, add to a nation's security dilemma. A foreign-imposed military victory may prove temporary unless it significantly upgrades the professionalism of the national military. Such a victory, especially when quickly followed by the security firm's departure, needs a replacement military force as well as a concerted nation-building program of political reconciliation and

economic development. A foreign-imposed victory underlines the inadequacy of a government's local security capability and may encourage insurgents to simply await the company's departure before renewing hostilities or a military resentful of competition to turn against its government. Furthermore, a powerful private force could persuade its employer to depend on military power, rather than work to address the underlying causes of the conflict.

3. A private force should support, rather than supplant, existing forces and actively cooperate with them whenever possible. Acceptance of the foreign officers by the national military will greatly assist their success. Conversely, a politically divided military may use the private company's presence as a pretext to challenge officials who hire it. A supporting force will be smaller in size than EO's combat battalion and will concentrate on training, advising, and combat support. By not directly engaging in combat operations, a private force will lessen potential international disapproval of its employer and its own presence.

4. Financing will remain a problem. Private security combat groups tied to multinational businesses will suffer from suspicions of neocolonialist military and economic domination. Small stand-alone advising or support companies that pose little threat to the host government (or the local military's ego) should attract governmental contracts and public support. Yet this separation could make the financing of a private force more problematic. Fragile states and international organizations may lack the funding to hire a private force, whereas a private company (e.g., the Branch Group) could bankroll a security operation that would protect and expand the company's economic capabilities. Western governments will not support mercenary combat forces. Problems of financing will encourage small training and support groups rather than larger combat units.

Private Security Companies in the Post-EO Era

Supply and demand variables—sophisticated equipment and foreign specialists coupled with the lack of adequately professional African armed forces, the unwillingness of non-African states to intervene militarily, and the use of PSCs by both non-African and African governments to further their policy goals—will ensure private security as a growth industry. The growth of African-controlled companies will help to entrench regime interests, often at the expense of those of the state.

Private security has taken a cue from EO's demise and is modifying its size, function, and autonomy to accommodate new political realities.

Continuing Supply and Demand

Private soldiers were fighting in all of Africa's major conflicts in mid-1999. Angola, the two Congos, and Sierra Leone had over 1,000 mercenaries (this excludes several thousand Liberian and Burkina Faso soldiers in Sierra Leone).[131] Some mercenaries come as part of an integrated supply package that includes pilots, planes, spare parts, and maintenance. In a fairly new development, mercenaries from the same country have faced each other in several conflicts: Russian pilots flying for both Eritrea and Ethiopia, South African infantry specialists assisting the Angolan government and UNITA, and South African pilots serving both the RUF and ECOMOG in Sierra Leone.[132]

Nongovernment groups will continue to hire private security. Rebel groups, especially in those countries with abundant mineral resources, employ mostly South African and Eastern European combat and logistics specialists (the diamond-extracting RUF employed a smattering of South Africans and perhaps two hundred Ukrainians). The growth in the number of insurgent groups often increases demand for foreign personnel.

Businesses hire private security in advisory and guarding roles. Such security enhances a company's ability to obtain contracts in some cases, and then to extract raw materials under difficult circumstances. A Canadian expert on the Branch Energy–related DiamondWorks was asked by the Canadian Broadcasting Corporation how investors would react to news about the mercenaries (i.e., EO's involvement with DiamondWorks). The answer was: "Probably quite well . . . this is not a stock market negative, this is a stock market positive."[133]

As they have increasingly come under attack, relief agencies have begun hiring private security advisors and guards, a trend that occasions debate in the relief community.[134] UNICEF, the International Committee of the Red Cross (ICRC), and the World Food Program (WFP) have hired security advisors. Defense Systems, Ltd., and Lifeguard Security help protect UN and private relief operations. Relief agencies have always hired private pilots, some of whom have at different times flown arms supplies or mercenary soldiers into the same conflict-torn country.

Non-African governments use PSCs as extensions of their foreign policies, and embattled African regimes increasingly rely on private security for state and individual enrichment.

Movement Away from the EO Model

EO's size, function, and autonomy helped to spell its demise. Established companies now offer small, specialized, and usually non-combat services that attract less attention and criticism than did EO. Paradoxically, such apparent diminution of power may augment the companies' effectiveness.

Size. Battalion-sized private combat units will not likely resurface. The reappearance of large units will be prevented by the political factors of domestic and international disapproval; the economic demands of foreign exchange or mineral concessions for salaries, insurance, and equipment; and the concerns about most large mercenary groups' performing inadequately in combat and angering the existing national military.[135] EO proved the rare exception to Machiavelli's dictum that units of combat mercenaries are generally incapable. (The incompetent "white legion" of some 300 European mercenaries in the former Zaire during 1997 was far more typical of hired warriors' combat abilities.)[136]

Yet less may be more. Smallness of size lessens public visibility and interest and therefore stands less chance of provoking international regulation. Specialists' relatively small numbers sometimes belie the impact of their special military skills. Mercenaries, especially those from South Africa, have demonstrated high levels of technical competence, and these small groups of foreign personnel will influence conflicts unless African armies become professional.

Post-EO Sierra Leone of early 1999 provides a graphic comparison between a minuscule but professional group and a much larger nonprofessional force. A motley group of four mercenaries—two South African pilots, a former British SAS officer from Fiji in his late 50s, and an Ethiopian helicopter mechanic—played a pivotal role during ECOMOG's defense of Freetown. The *London Times* reported that

> ECOMOG officers admit that they would have lost Freetown last month without Mr. Marafuno [the ex-SAS officer] and his comrades, "Juba" Joubert and Neil Ellis, both South Africans, and their Ethiopian engineer, Sindaba. "Without these guys, we would have run out of food and ammo and fled the front. They are amazingly brave. I know they do it for money, but I wouldn't do it for anything," said a Nigerian lieutenant colonel.[137]

The smallness of this force disinclined media attention.

Function. Nonlethal, rather than combat, capability will be the norm for established PSCs.[138] Weapons deliveries, communications, tactical training, weapons handling, and aerial support and reconnaissance will be the major offerings. Such support functions can prove just as lethal (albeit indirectly) as combat soldiers, but will appear much less visible or threatening.

"Private" security is increasingly a misnomer. Western and African governments influence the functions of the companies both negatively (through restraining legislation) or positively (through government contracting or introducing company representatives to foreign officials). Fayemi observes that DSL is "sometimes regarded in the business as Britain's officially-backed 'mercenaries.'"[139] Governments are becoming more involved in these companies because the PSCs offer some possible advantages over official involvement, notably the fulfillment of national goals with financial and manpower savings and less public scrutiny.[140]

Western governments prefer to assist nonlethal companies. Aiding white-officered mercenary companies to help kill Africans can easily stir opposition in Western democracies, especially if the support appears *sub rosa* and the arrangement features lethal capability.

Sandline's "Arms to Africa" controversy illustrates this point. Some officials in the British government in late-1997 apparently offered tacit support to Sandline to ship some 38 tons of Bulgarian military supplies (including assault rifles) and a small number of advisors to the exiled Sierra Leonean Kabbah regime. Many observers had by then formed a critical opinion of Sandline, which, with numerous ex-EO soldiers as well as close ties to Branch Minerals, had recently been thrown out of mineral-rich Papua New Guinea where it had planned crippling helicopter attacks against insurgent strongholds.

Britain's apparent approval of the plan sparked enough controversy in that country for additional reasons: a disreputable banker with diamond interests in Sierra Leone had provided the funding, the action threatened a sovereign (though unrecognized) African state, and it seemingly violated a UN arms embargo.[141] That the government had kept secret its cooperation until press revelations further angered many observers.

Several factors helped the Blair government to eventually weather the storm: the weaponry and advisors were to help a deposed democratically elected government against a vicious, universally unrecognized junta, and the UN belatedly reinterpreted its embargo to restrict weaponry only to the junta, not to pro-Kabbah forces. But it was a Pyrrhic victory, and the Sandline affair demonstrated to Britain and France the domestic political risks of supporting combat-directed PSCs. Some governments will continue quietly to facilitate mercenary operations: France and Yugoslavia reportedly assisted the "white legion," which served Mobutu in his waning days.

Sandline's recent operations illustrate these shifts in size and function. Its planned Papua New Guinea force had some seventy soldiers, pilots, and advisors who probably would have engaged in some ground and air combat (about forty of these fighters having previously served with the much larger EO) in operations independent of the chain of command in Papua New Guinea. In Sierra Leone, in January 1998, only about twelve Sandline personnel appeared and they focused on weapons procurement, helicopter transport and maintenance, and some advising while closely coordinating their actions with the Kabbah government and ECOMOG commanders. These personnel did not engage in any offensive missions. Most of Sandline's foreign personnel in Sierra Leone are former EO soldiers in Sandline's Lifeguard Security, a guard force. But they attracted far less attention than did EO because they formed a smaller contingent and did not engage in offensive operations.[142]

MPRI exemplifies the growing government-company relationship. The U.S. Agency for International Development in 1999 contracted for seven MPRI employees to present a proposal to the Obasanjo government on how to professionalize the Nigerian military. Specific areas included the role of a military in a democracy and such manpower issues as accurate payroll distribution.

Although established PSCs will emphasize nonlethal support, some private foreign companies and individuals will continue to supply weaponry or combat assistance in return for lucrative concessions or payments. Following the Branch-EO model, foreign natural-resource extraction firms are developing linkages with security firms or developing their own military wings.

The personal-rule regimes in Sierra Leone, Liberia, and Angola provide three examples of a growing mineral-military symbiosis. Foreign private security personnel are becoming diamond business procurers, and diamond executives are becoming weapons merchants. The purpose, as it was with the Branch Group and EO, is using military skills to gain lucrative contracts from besieged governments that benefit the regime—but which, in the longer run, may hurt the state.

Sierra Leone is illustrative in this regard. Rex Diamond Mining, based in Antwerp, created an arms-procuring company to sell Bulgarian-supplied arms to the Kabbah government, which then awarded diamond mining leases to Rex. Fred Rindle, a retired SADF officer, reportedly has supplied training, and perhaps weaponry, to the RUF and Charles Taylor in exchange for diamonds. The RUF's late 1998 offensive against Freetown exhibited "textbook South African army" tactics, according to a South African military source, a view seconded by U.S. officials.[143]

Individual regime officials have benefited from the PSC-mineral linkage. Charles Taylor, rather than Sierra Leone or Liberia, has been the primary African beneficiary of Sierra Leone's smuggled diamonds. Liberia can produce only 60,000 carats yearly of rough gemstones, but the country exported some 8.3 million carats during 1997 and 1998.[144] Analysts contend that Taylor personally retains much of the $601 million gemstone revenue and suggest that he is now a billionaire.[145] Burkina Faso, which serves as the major transit point for Ukranian arms flights, also profits from the Sierra Leonean-Liberian diamond smuggling.

The damage to Sierra Leone is massive because most of its diamonds and their income are bypassing state coffers. Sierra Leone's Government Gold and Diamond Office contends that the country exports "a very, very marginal part" of its total production through official agencies.[146] Leonid Minin of Ukraine runs the Exotic Tropical Timber Enterprise in Liberia, but a senior ECOMOG officer contends that its "real business is diamonds and arms supply."[147] The trucking of timber apparently disguises the smuggling of weapons to the RUF. In Liberia, helicopter pilot Carl Albert and two associates reportedly formed a mining company that has received lucrative mining rights in return for Albert's highly valued helicopter skills and the company's weapons importation.

The Santos government of Angola awarded sales of oil equity stakes in 1999 to Naptha, Pro-Dev, and Falcon, which, according to *Africa Confidential,* "have links to defence and security specialists but little apparent expertise in upstream oil production."[148] Naptha, for example, is closely linked to Israel's Levdan security company and to two companies that have diamond and oil interests in Angola. In 1997, after Levdan successfully completed a security assignment for the Congo-Brazzaville government, Naptha conducted successful business negotiations with the Brazzaville government and paid Levdan about $300,000 "when [Levdan] brought us the project in Congo," according to Yossie Levy, Naptha's chief executive.[149]

Autonomy. Non-African and African governments use the "private" firms as a tool of foreign policy. Other than former SADF personnel, Africans are increasingly entering the security business by forming PSCs and militarily operated mineral firms for both contractor-state and personal gain.[150]

Governments can employ private security firms, and manipulate their contract negotiations, to further foreign policy objectives. The U.S. government used MPRI as a bargaining tool with the Angolan government, restricting MPRI's attempts to gain training contracts in 1997 until there were Angolan reforms. MPRI had submitted a proposal in August 1997, but the U.S. government refused permission for MPRI to operate unless the MPLA government would integrate seven UNITA generals into the new Angolan army's command structure. MPRI subsequently received authorization following the integration, but the U.S. government then suspended the authorization to express disapproval of the Angolan military's deployment of troops to Congo-Brazzaville to assist Sassou-Nguesso to overthrow the sovereign Lissouba government. The British government has warned several PSCs, including Sandline, not to accept some foreign offers.[151] France has proven more circumspect, although probably more active, in its ties to private security forces. Its Direction de la Surveillance du Territoire has reportedly coordinated with GeoLink, a Paris-based communications firm, to hire the mostly non-French mercenaries of the "white legion."[152]

The growth of African-owned PSCs has gone largely unnoticed. Local ownership or control creates some appreciable political symbolism, but it benefits financially only a handful of regime officials, rather than the country as a whole. Two locally controlled firms, Teleservices and Alpha 5, dominate the large Angolan market; Teleservices has responsibility for coastal, mostly oil, security, while Alpha 5 protects the diamond areas. Gen. João de Matos, Angola's chief of staff, helped found Teleservices, and Vines reports that "Teleservices' main shareholders are [de Matos], the commander of ground forces, the head of intelligence and the current Angolan ambassador to Washington."[153] De Matos's brother runs Alpha 5, which had close ties to EO. To further demonstrate the blurring of public and private spheres, Endiama, Angola's state-owned diamond mining company, is Alpha 5's principal shareholder. In Uganda, Gen. Salim Saleh (President Museveni's brother) owns about 30 percent of Saracen-Kampala, an offshoot of EO. Despite partial or total African ownership, foreign soldiers (often South African) are responsible for most of the PSCs' operational aspects.

These local private security companies, backed by government legislation, aggressively protect their own interests. Angolan legislation requires foreign diamond companies to contract for their own security, and Angola now has over ninety PSCs.[154] But Teleservices and Alpha 5 dominate the market, and several Western diplomats contend that the Angolan government presses foreign companies to hire their security from either Teleservices or Alpha 5. Attempts by foreign security companies to retain full autonomy over their operations may threaten future contracts. Alex Vines writes that "the expulsion of DSL from Angola was partly due to its poor efforts to 'Angolanise' its staff."[155]

Local officials can blur the line between state and private security when diverting active duty state personnel into their private companies. Once again, the regime benefits at the state's expense. Elements of Angola's security forces, especially the "Ninja" rapid reaction force, reportedly assisted Alpha 5 in the mid-1990s. In Uganda, General Saleh had about 400 government soldiers assigned to Saracen-Kampala by the military. Saracen in 1997 was the only private company allowed to import and operate automatic weapons into Uganda. And other government officials use their offices to obtain a variety of commercial benefits. Private companies may sometimes also protect the mineral holdings of government officials, compounding the privatization of state resources.

Several regimes, including those of Congo and Zimbabwe, have formed private companies, in part to mislead Western lending agencies and governments about the levels of national military spending. The World Bank and several governments in 1999 threatened to reduce foreign assistance because regional military operations were consuming dwindling foreign exchange assets and siphoning money from domestic investment and social spending.

Senior Congolese and Zimbabwean officers created Osleg Private Ltd., apparently in late 1998, to market gold and diamonds to fund military costs in an extra-budgetary procedure. Osleg is a merger of a Congolese military company (Comiex) and the Zimbabwean military's Osleg. Movan Mahachi, Zimbabwe's defense minister, explained that "we saw this as a noble option. Instead of our army in the DRC [Congo] burdening the treasury for more resources, which are not available, it embarks on viable projects for the sake of generating the necessary revenue."[156] As Chapter 6 notes, Uganda employs a different means of hiding its defense spending from international donors—it takes monies ostensibly appropriated, but never intended, for civilian ministries.

Osleg's beginning came about during increased international concern about Zimbabwe's soaring defense budgets and subsequent skepticism about Zimbabwe's explanations. The IMF had approved a staggered $193 million financial package in August 1999, after Zimbabwe asserted to the fund that it was spending only $3 million monthly on its military operation in the Congo. Subsequent revelations indicated that $27 million was a more accurate figure. The Dutch government then terminated its $15 million annual aid package to Zimbabwe, and the World Bank postponed considering a major credit until the IMF was confident that the initial Zimbabwean claim could be substantiated.

Unaccountable officials do not see foreign or local PSCs as a Trojan horse, as long as these firms support the regime's interests.[157] Indeed, they may well prefer foreign security over national militaries because the latter could use force to advance their local national interests. Foreign personnel, conversely, may neither know nor care about local politics and their seemingly arcane ethnic, regional, or religious appeals. Personal contracts between a president's office and a foreign firm may help to ensure loyalty; after all, the overthrow of the ruler may terminate the contract. "Guard" companies can sometimes fulfill a military role: many of the foreign guards of Angolan mineral companies are well-trained former South African military (and sometimes EO veterans as well). These guards reportedly had engaged in offensive operations against UNITA in 1998.[158]

Indigenous PSCs, such as Alpha 5 or Saracen-Kampala, offer their own advantages to personal rulers. Company officials can handpick personnel who will be directly beholden to them, rather than having to rely on long-serving army officers whose loyalties are unknown or questionable. The payroll and insurance expenses of local hires will be considerably less than those of foreign soldiers.

The growth of private companies aids regimes but often hurts countries. For instance, sometimes governments are willing to cede geographically limited sovereignty to foreign security companies. The Kabbah government of Sierra Leone in early 1997 was considering granting Lifeguard, through Sierra Rutile, security responsibility for a radius of about 15 miles that encompassed the lucrative Sierra Rutile concession (in January 1996, RSLMF looters had caused about $20 million of damage to the site). The plans required the country's military to request permission to enter the Lifeguard-controlled area and that Lifeguard could monitor the national army during its entry. The May 1997 coup stopped the plan's progress.[159]

Local PSCs assist the personal, noninstitutional nature of African regimes: the PSCs' leadership, funding, composition, and mission are unaccountable to the citizenry, and their usually narrow, but well-armed, specific ethnic composition can aggravate longstanding social tensions. PSCs, unless they are primarily trainers, reduce a regime's need for a competent national military. The siphoning of military resources into the private companies further lowers morale and military capabilities. Local companies are usually ethnically based and therefore less likely to function as a national body that integrates differing groups and creates a common nationalism. Parallel and competing forces undermine local security force morale, as shown by the EO-Kamajor example in Sierra Leone.[160]

For-profit state military companies can destabilize African security by increasing the temptation for some states to militarily destabilize neighboring countries for profit. Whether more frequent deployment for financial profits can increase a force's capabilities is questionable; the military mercantilism that stretches from Sierra Leone to Uganda often diverted soldiers from military duties. Nine years of ECOMOG saw some officers and their units more occupied with mineral extraction than peacekeeping, and even by late 1999, according to the *Washington Post*, "Nigerian soldiers complained [in Sierra Leone] that officers were neglecting the troops, spending their time and ECOMOG money to run mining operations."[161] Michael Quintana, editor of the Zimbabwe-based *Africa Defence Journal,* states that Osleg "would be dreadful for military discipline . . . everyone is going to be an entrepreneur first and do his job second."[162] Other concerns about profit-motivated militaries include the possible use of force against local inhabitants, probable lack of public accountability, and reluctance to leave other countries. The Zimbabwean force in Congo will prove an interesting case study.

By raising these objections, are non-Africans posing possibly unreachable norms for governments that sometimes are barely functional and that desperately require immediate security? Developing quickly a local professional military for immediate needs is often impossible, given the prerequisites that Huntington and others suggest. Perhaps alliances of these firms with local officials may provide some stability and economic development, which may be all that can be expected, given Africa's present lack of political institutionalization. But this view would consign Africa to a continuance of rentier regimes that in frequent alignment with foreign companies will restrict a state's economic growth and political accountability.

PSCs can perform a valuable service to African countries if they help to stabilize relatively accountable governments, especially against such extreme violators of human rights as Sierra Leone's RUF. Their provision of technical training can strengthen local military professionalism and their guarding of valuable economic assets can protect economic development. Foreign PSC personnel may encourage democratization among local military officers more effectively than could civilian groups. Their use of former military officers to promote both a greater political responsibility to the state, as well as a more transparent and accountable military, could significantly assist African military professionalism. Yet PSCs, at best, should be a short-term and well-regulated supplement, given their numerous and already mentioned limitations.

Regulation and the Future of Private Security Companies

Attempted prohibition of private companies will prove impossible and probably counterproductive. Yet unrestricted PSC actions can rapidly expand a war's suffering. International regulation of the goals and methods of these companies appears desirable, even though any action will prove incomplete given definitional problems, the number of countries with their often competing national interests, and the lack of effective enforcement.

Since the companies' role is clearly growing, governments and international organizations should seek ways to regulate, rather than ignore or eliminate, PSCs. Legislation cannot void the supply of, and a demand for, hireable security. (Prohibition of "mercenaries" would be akin to outlawing alcohol or prostitution: a durable supply and demand for any product will mock such legislation.) It must be kept in mind that even though irresponsible PSCs can easily harm Western and African interests by acting as force multipliers for clearly repressive or criminal causes, the current minimal regulation and accreditation still allow a dangerously wide range of companies and individual soldiers to sell their services.

Legislation can impose some degree of transparency and accountability. Pech writes that "mercenary contracts are kept secret—unlike training contracts. EO and other private military companies have confidentiality clauses written into their contracts with both client companies and their hired forces."[163] Most security companies operate from Western nations where government and the private market provide limited control over their activities. American companies, for example, need government approval, the terms of which are stipulated by the International Trafficking in Arms Regulation, the Arms Export Control Act, and the Export Administration Act. PSCs must submit their African proposals to the U.S. State Department, which sends them to its Africa Bureau and Human Rights office, to the Defense Department, and sometimes to Treasury or Energy departments. A rejection by any of the above usually suffices to stop the licensing process, thus preventing the company from accepting the foreign proposal. Regulation may provide the PSCs' country of origin with some leverage over the contracting combatant forces and the war's conduct.

Established companies support regulation because it places an implicit official imprimatur upon well-behaved companies, and thus may increase contracts. "[T]he international community's fear of mercenaries," suggests Zarate, "lies in that they are wholly independent from any constraints built into the nation-state system."[164] Regulation lessens such worries. Retired Gen. Ed Soyster of MPRI contends that "we as a company want the regulations," in part because they increase the company's credibility to prospective clients.[165]

Some observers of PSCs claim that the commercial need for security companies to display a good human rights record helps check abridgments of human rights. Observers also note that the personnel of these companies usually come from first-world, professional militaries that teach respect for human rights. And inquisitive media might also restrict PSC abuses.

But international regulation is necessary. Governments and the media may learn of objectionable behavior, and often after the fact. (The media face numerous difficulties when trying to enter operational areas.) The need to establish a good business record means little to those PSCs that seek only a one-shot but very lucrative contract, and companies can quickly relocate offshore and then restart under a different name. As Sandline itself notes, such companies can become very nomadic to evade nationally applied legislation that they regard as inappropriate or excessive.[166]

International regulation should benefit trustworthy companies by providing them with greater legitimacy while separating them from those truly mercenary groups willing to fight for any organization capable of paying them.

Regulation should be a multistep process and involve registration, which would determine the applicant's initial qualification; specific project approval; and then operational oversight, which should include observer units from recognized human rights organizations. Finally, an enforcement capability would be essential, both during the military operation to lessen abuses and then following the operation. Several companies, including Sandline and MPRI, agree to these suggestions in principle.

Many details in regulation would need resolution, such as the

appropriate international regulatory body and the extent of its enforcement capabilities. Specific problems include client confidentiality and
the client's need for quick action versus the regulators' requiring time
and contractual information before granting project approval. The companies' links to mineral companies, such as those of EO and Sandline to
the Branch Group, need close scrutiny: stand-alone security companies
might be preferable.

Regulation is necessary, but definitional and legal problems will
pose serious obstacles. Trying to define "mercenaries" has stymied
international organizations, the UN and the OAU most notably. If one
cannot adequately define a term, how can one adequately prohibit its
activity? For example, what constitutes military service? Would MPRI's
advising the Nigerian government on democratization and military
administration, which both the Nigerian and U.S. government support,
be a prohibited activity? And, wouldn't proscribing combat soldiers but
permitting noncombat personnel be condoning people whose duties
may prove just as lethal, however indirectly, as those of the warriors?

Do sovereign states have the right to self-defense? Are only those
foreigners who oppose established authority to be considered mercenary? The OAU's Convention for the Elimination of Mercenarism in
Africa of 1977 (adopted in 1985) suggests so. It hopes to ban only those
soldiers who fight "against any African state member of the
Organization of African Unity." Private soldiers fighting for a government receive implicit approval.[167] The UN disagrees, arguing that "the
mere fact that it is government that recruits mercenaries or contracts
companies that recruit mercenaries for its own defences or to provide
reinforcements in armed conflict does not make such actions any less
illegal or illegitimate."[168]

How enforceable are international restrictions on PSCs? National
interests will render regulation and enforcement necessarily incomplete:
states benefiting from private security may well ignore or undermine
the regulations. African states whose officials own local PSCs would
probably avoid regulating these companies effectively.

Several countries have signed antimercenary accords—only to hire
mercenaries at a later date. The UN General Assembly drafted the
International Convention Against the Recruitment, Use, Financing, and
Training of Mercenaries (Convention) in December 1989. It required
ratification of twenty-two countries, but by 1998 only twelve nations
had signed—and at least two of those signatories (Angola and Zaire)
subsequently hired mercenaries. "African countries . . . were obviously
reluctant to propose any sort of international regulation which would

limit their own ability to maneuver," writes Jeffrey Herbst.[169] Governments and international organizations may hesitate to agree to international regulation for another reason: such action would confer some legitimacy on nonstate military actors.

Therefore, the supply of skilled foreign soldiers, the pressing demand for effective security, and the world's inability to monitor and to regulate PSCs effectively make the need for African military professionalism—which could blunt the need for mercenaries—even more compelling.

Notes

1. As noted, "mercenary" is a highly imprecise and value-laden term. Foreign soldiers fighting for financial gain may not include idealistic volunteers or personnel seconded by another country. PSCs dislike the label since it suggests a total lack of principle (other than profit) and does not convey the wide range of noncombat services available, for example, communications, advising and training, maintenance and construction.

2. Additional protocol 1 to article 47 of the Geneva Convention (1949) lists six classifications, which include a foreigner who is prompted to fight "essentially by the desire for private gain," "not a member of the armed forces of a party to the conflict," or seconded as a serving soldier of another state. See Alex Vines, "Mercenaries, Human Rights and Legality," in Musah and Fayemi, eds., *Mercenaries,* p. 170.

3. Many, and perhaps most, private security employees are unarmed. Defense Systems Limited has 5,000 employees worldwide but allows only one hundred to carry weaponry.

4. A. E. Housman's poem "Mercenaries" presents the mercenary as defender of a desirable status quo: "Their shoulders held the sky suspended/They stood and earth's foundations stayed/What God abandoned, they defended/And saved the sum of things for pay." Ironically, Housman was referring to the British army, which Kaiser Wilhelm had labeled as mercenary. "Epitaph on an Army of Mercenaries," *The Poems of A. E. Housman,* p. 104.

5. Alvin and Heidi Toffler, *War and Anti-War: Survival at the Dawn of the 21st Century,* p. 273.

6. Securities Corporation, *Equitable Securities Research,* August 27, 1997, quoted in Alex Vines, "Mercenaries, Human Rights and Legality," in Musah and Fayemi, eds., *Mercenaries,* p. 169,

7. Mark Galeotti, "Boom Time for the Russian 'Protectors,'" *Jane's Intelligence Review,* August 1997, p. 339. Quoted in Isenberg, "Soldiers of Fortune, Ltd.," p. 2; Vines, "Mercenaries," in Musah and Feyemi, eds., *Mercenaries,* p. 169.

8. Vines, "Mercenaries," in Musah and Fayemi, eds., *Mercenaries,* p. 184.

9. Jakkie Cilliers, "Private Security in War-Torn African States," in Cilliers and Mason, eds., *Peace, Profit or Plunder?* p. 1.

10. Xenophon recorded his mercenary record in *Anabasis,* an account of Cyrus's, a pretender to the Persian throne, employing 10,000 mercenaries in 401 B.C. Xenophon. Mercenaries became a common, if not prevailing, military means by the fifteenth century, with condottieri commanders hiring "free companies." The growth of nation-states following The Thirty Years' War (1618–1648) and then the post-1789 French Revolution's spread of nationalism witnessed national armies eclipsing mercenary forces. States started to write neutrality laws that often forbade enlistment by their citizens in foreign armies. Chartered British companies provided a major exception to the overall decline of mercenary soldiering, with the British East Africa Company and the British South African Company using private soldiers to gain land and mineral concessions from African rulers. The first half of the twentieth century saw some idealistic "mercenaries": Americans forming the Lafayette Escadrille air unit in 1916 prior to U.S. entry into World War I, Americans and British in the International Brigade to fight Spanish fascism in the mid-1930s, and the American Volunteer Group/"Flying Tigers" air unit in China against Japan. By 1960 mercenaries had seemingly faded in importance, with a few anomalies: the Vatican's Swiss Guards, the British army's Nepalese Gurkhas, and France's Foreign Legion.

11. Whites fought for the minority racist regimes, especially in Rhodesia and South Africa. Several governments saw fit to hire foreigners, as with Nigeria against breakaway Biafra (which also employed mercenaries).

12. Wilfred Burchett and Derek Roebuck, *Whores of War,* p. 17. The specific reference is to foreigners fighting for the white Rhodesian government.

13. An especially flawed mercenary operation occurred in Angola in 1976. "Commander Callan," a homicidal commander of a mercenary unit, deliberately shot his own men. The government staged a public trial of several captured mercenaries, which further weakened the image and the romanticism of the mercenary trade. Peter McAlese's account of his mercenary involvement in Angola is contained in his *No Mean Soldier* (London: Orion, 1993), pp. 76–114.

14. Another example of the Cold War's demise supplying private personnel is that of Nepalese Gurkhas formerly of the British army now in several security companies operating from Britain. See Alex Vines, "Gurkhas and the Private Security Business in Africa," in Cilliers and Mason, eds., *Peace, Profit or Plunder?*

15. David Isenberg, "Soldiers of Fortune, Ltd.," p. 2.

16. Juan Carlos Zarate, "The Emergence of a New Dog of War: Private International Security Companies, International Law, and the New World Disorder," *Stanford Journal of International Law,* Winter 1998.

17. A company's ideological preference may restrict its clientele. Military Professional Resources, Inc. (MPRI) refuses to consider any possible contracts with Vietnam, a certain result of its members having fought against the North Vietnamese. Conversation with Ed Soyster of MPRI, October 15, 1999.

18. "I'm No Dog of War Says Former British Officer Held in Papua," the *Daily Telegraph,* April 1, 1997.

19. International Charter Inc. of Oregon, undated promotional material.

20. David Isenberg, "The New Mercenaries. Corporate Warriors Market Combat Expertise," the *Christian Science Monitor,* October 13, 1998.

21. "MPRI," an advertising document of MPRI.

22. One of MPRI's biggest contracts has been in Bosnia-Hercegovina, where MPRI placed a 150–200-man force to train and equip the federation's military force. The U.S. government has officially approved of MPRI's operations and has contributed over $100 million in surplus equipment to ensure MPRI's success in Bosnia.

The Vinnell Corporation, a subsidiary of the McLean, Virginia-based BDM International, has trained Saudi Arabia's 60,000-man National Guard since 1975 and may have been involved in some military actions. In 1979, the monarchy reportedly depended upon Vinnel to retake the Grand Mosque at Mecca from opposition forces. See William D. Hartung, "Mercenaries Inc.," *Progressive,* April 1996, p. 26.

23. Zarate, "The Emergence of a New Dog of War."

24. Michael Bryans, Bruce D. Jones, and Janice Gross Stein, "Mean Times," p. 36.

25. Sergio Vieria de Mello, quoted in Bryans, Jones, and Stein, "Mean Times," p. 35.

26. Bryans, Jones, and Stein, "Mean Times," p. 31.

27. Burchett and Roebuck, *Whores of War,* p. 1.

28. Elizabeth Rubin, "An Army of Their Own," *Harper's,* February 1997, p. 45.

29. "War and Piecework," *The Economist,* July 10–16, 1999, p. 67.

30. "The deaths of the soldiers of a private military company, to be blunt, would not cause the same political problems that the deaths of a country's nationals do." Jonah Schulhofer-Wohl, "Should We Privatize the Peacekeeping?" *Washington Post,* May 12, 2000.

31. Zarate, "New Dog of War," p. 90. See also Reno, *Warlord Politics.* Advantages to the supplying nation(s) include the possible supply of tactical intelligence and the providing of employment to specially trained personnel who otherwise might add to domestic political unrest: this certainly applied to EO personnel and the political transition to majority rule in South Africa.

32. Max Weber, *The Theory of Social and Economic Organization,* p. 154.

33. Other critics worry about the opposite; that mercenaries can bolster repressive regimes. See Ken Silverstein, "Privatizing War," *The Nation,* July 2, 1997.

34. Machiavelli, *The Prince,* pp. 44, 46.

35. John de St. Jorre, *The Brothers' War,* p. 329.

36. A critical African view is the Eddie Iroh's novel, *48 Guns for the General,* about mercenaries fighting for Biafra.

37. Writing about Gurkha Security Guards (GSG), Vines suggests that "a clear lesson from GSG is that small private security firms, with little capacity to see them through difficult financial circumstances, may be more inclined to engage in mercenary-type activity in order to remain viable," Alex Vines, "Gurkhas and the Private Security Business in Africa," in Cilliers and Mason, eds., *Peace, Profit or Plunder?* p. 136.

38. "Report on the Question of the Use of Mercenaries as a Means of Violating Human Rights and Impeding the Exercise of the Right of Peoples to Self-Determination," submitted by Mr. Enrique Ballesteros, special rapporteur, U.N. Doc. E/CN.4/1997/24 (1997), p. 93.

39. Silverstein, "Privatizing War." Deborah Avant states, "It's a tool for foreign policy in a less public way—and that is not a good thing in the long term." Quoted in "The Rise of the Private-Sector Military," *Christian Science Monitor,* July 5, 2000.

40. "The Oppenheimer Report," *Miami Herald,* January 4, 1999.

41. Human rights activists believe that DSL, employed by British Petroleum in Colombia, provided counterinsurgency techniques to the heavily criticized national police. See "BP's Secret Military Advisers," *Guardian* (UK), June 30, 1997.

42. The absence of a standing force and supply stocks has at least two advantages: the host country (South Africa) did not feel a physical threat and EO could reduce its administrative costs.

43. "Barlow was head of an internal CCB [Civil Cooperation Bureau] cell that is allegedly tied to the murder of ANC activists in Europe. Barlow was also engaged in sanction-busting efforts in Europe." Khareen Pech, "Executive Outcomes—A Corporate Conquest," in Cilliers and Mason, eds., *Peace, Profit or Plunder?* p. 84.

44. This author's own article was one example of claiming the exaggerated salaries, "South Africa's 911 Force," *Armed Forces Journal International,* November 1996.

45. Musah, "A Country Under Siege: State Decay and Corporate Military Intervention in Sierra Leone," in Musah and Fayemi, *Mercenaries,* p. 109.

46. Khareen Pech and David Beresford, "Corporate Dogs of War Grow Fat in Africa," *Guardian Weekly,* January 26, 1997, p. 8.

47. The SADF certainly influenced government policy, but as a welcome ally of the executive rather than as an intrusive force.

48. The *laager* was a tightly arranged circle of ox wagons that protected some 400 Afrikaners against perhaps 10,000 Zulu warriors at the battle of Blood River in 1838. Afrikaner history holds that no whites were killed but that some 4,000 Zulus perished, in part because of the Afrikaners' political unity. A small but united and skilled group can thus hold off a much larger force.

49. An important qualification is that the new Nationalist government of 1948 retired numerous English-speaking South African officers and replaced them with Afrikaners. Most South Africans subsequently saw the SADF as an Afrikaner-dominated force.

50. Maj. Gen. Charles Lloyd, quoted in Frankel, *Pretoria's Praetorians,* p. 92.
The 32 ("Buffalo") Battalion's brutal treatment of Angolan civilians in the early 1980s was one such example of SADF brutality. See Gavin Cawthra's *Brutal Force.*

51. South Africa's highly restricted and whites-only democracy did permit limited civilian oversight by parliamentary committees, the media, and other private groups. Parliamentary questioning of the Ministry of Defence, for example, elicited security information that an even less open government would not have made public.

52. South Africa also had a generally strong economy that offered employment opportunities outside of government and access to Western training, intelligence, and equipment (at least until the mid–1970s).

53. Some observers believed that the SADF did carry out a coup by stealth. Kenneth Grundy wrote in the mid-1980s that "the SADF is no longer simply an instrument for policy implementation. It is an active participant in policymaking." Kenneth W. Grundy, *The Militarization of South African Politics,* p. 1.

54. See Herbert M. Howe, "The South African Defence Force and Political Reform." The SADF accepted the reforms on the condition that it would retain functional autonomy. André du Toit writes that "the securocrats have been willing to go along with the new [political] initiatives launched by de Klerk, but on the implicit understanding that they will remain masters in their own house." André du Toit, "The White Body Politic: What Has de Klerk Wrought?" p. 30.

55. Some observers believe that Angola also granted some concessions to the Branch Group as additional payment for EO's services.

56. A U.S. intelligence source believes the maximum figure for EO in Angola was about 1,000 men. Interview, August 1996. Most observers accept Eeben Barlow's claim that the top figure was 570 soldiers. Interview with Barlow, June 1997.

57. Barlow interview, July 1996.

58. This view is not universally held. Sean Cleary writes that although EO "undoubtedly contributed significantly to the FAA's subsequent military ascendancy . . . nothing . . . supports the proposition that EO played any role in inducing Savimbi to negotiate." Sean Cleary, "Angola—A Case Study of Private Military Involvement," in Cilliers and Mason, eds., *Peace, Profit or Plunder?* pp. 156, 158. EO and the FAA did not fully defeat UNITA; the rebel group remained active in several areas, especially along the Cuango River—a major diamond source.

59. UNITA correctly claimed that EO personnel were still assisting the FAA months after the signing. The MPLA clearly did not trust Savimbi and wanted EO personnel to remain on call. Worried that EO's presence had prompted Savimbi's slowness in following the Lusaka Protocol's timetable, President Clinton pressed President dos Santos during a state visit to Washington in December 1995. Some observers believe that Clinton hoped that the MPRI could take over EO's noncombat functions.

60. "The war is a classic post-Cold War conflict, as it owes little to traditional superpower rivalry and much to the post-Cold War reconfiguration of regional power balances." Musah, "A Country Under Siege," in Musah and Fayemi, *Mercenaries,* p. 76.

61. Tony Buckingham, the founder of the Branch Group (and a former British navy Special Boat Services [SBS] officer), introduced EO to Angola and Sierra Leone. This coupling of economic and security power as a package deal undoubtedly assisted both the Branch Group and EO in securing their contracts.

62. Interview with U.S. official, December 1998.

63. See William Reno, "Privatizing War in Sierra Leone," *Current History,* May 1997, p. 228. A provocative study, although too deferential toward the RUF, is Paul Richards, *Fighting for the Rainforest.*

64. Interview with Laffras Luitingh, June 1996.

65. Interview with Eebon Barlow, July 1996. A U.S. diplomat previously based in Sierra Leone questions the extent of EO's democratizing actions. He states that although EO initially pressed for elections when it entered in May 1995, it dropped its insistence during the military campaign. Interview, December 1996.

66. Interview with Brig. Bert Sachse. Sources close to EO state that force levels stood at 160 through May 1995, topped at 350 in January–February 1996, and then declined to 80 until the contract ended in January 1997.

67. The new Kabbah government had mixed feelings about EO's departure. The company had provided far more reliable and competent security than any Sierra Leonean group, but the democratically elected government was stung by criticism of its need to rely upon apartheid-era mercenaries. At least publicly, international lending agencies expressed displeasure about funding EO. In private, several representatives of the World Bank voiced appreciation of EO's presence. Interviews, 1997, 1998.

68. Reno, "Privatizing War in Sierra Leone," p. 229.

69. General Douglas, quoted in Rubin, "An Army of Their Own," p. 48.

70. Information gathered by author, July 1996.

71. Pech and Beresford, "Corporate Dogs of War."

72. Quoted in Zarate, "New Dog of War," p. 97.

73. Interviews in the United States and Europe, 1996 and 1997.

74. Interviews in Britain, Sierra Leone, and Washington, D.C., 1996 and 1997.

75. This remains a point of contention, partly because EO's military operation did cause some civilian casualties. Its Angolan campaign, which involved twice as many soldiers as in Sierra Leone and perhaps the use of fuel-air explosives, undoubtedly killed some innocent civilians. Yet EO seems to have a respectable human rights record, especially when compared to the other combatants. Amnesty International offers a differing view in "Killing for Gain," *Amnesty Magazine,* July–August 1998. Alex Vines of Human Rights Watch believes that EO committed numerous human rights violations in Angola but that "there are fewer reports of EO abuses in Sierra Leone, possibly because EO learnt from its mistakes in Angola." Vines, "Mercenaries," in Musah and Fayemi, eds., *Mercenaries,* p. 175.

76. Interviews in Britain, Sierra Leone, and Washington, D.C., 1996 and 1997. See Zarate, "New Dog of War," p. 97, for more information on EO's relations with Sierra Leone's civilians.

77. Interview with a World Bank official, January 1997.

78. Interview, January 1997.

79. "Our people who are involved in Sierra Leone picked it up, reported it, and then necessary action was taken in order to neutralize the coup d'etat," "Executive Outcomes Head Eeben Barlow Interviewed," South African Broadcasting Corporation, January 22, 1997, in *SWB,* AL2825, p. A/8, January 24, 1997.

80. Interview with Barlow, June 1997.

81. Despite these attractions, South African soldiers knowledgeable about EO claim that some EO soldiers dislike the reportedly harsh and sometimes arbitrary discipline. South African press reports have also featured complaints

by relatives of dead EO soldiers about EO's pensions. *Executive Outcomes, The Business of War,* a 1997 Journeyman Productions documentary film, features family members of dead EO soldiers complaining about the lack of EO's death benefits.

82. Interview with Albert, January 1997.

83. Interviews with Western intelligence sources.

84. *The Military Balance,* 1966–1967, pp. 242, 263.

85. According to a top MPLA officer, "the mine . . . was a reward for Mr. Buckingham's [of the Branch Group] help in organizing mercenaries from Sandline's South African associate Executive Outcomes to fight UNITA." "Murder of Britons Was Revenge for Sandline," *Daily Telegraph,* November 15, 1998.

86. Interview with U.S. State Department official.

87. Pech, "Executive Outcomes," in Cilliers and Mason, eds., *Peace, Profit or Plunder?* p. 90.

88. Transcript of "Dogs of War," "Sixty Minutes," CBS, June 1, 1997.

89. Interviews, July 1997.

90. Barlow and Branch Group interviews, July 1997.

91. Interview, July 1997.

92. Ronald Robinson, "The Eccentric Idea of Imperialism, with or Without Empire," in Wolfgang Mommsen and Jurgen Osterhammel, *Imperialism and After: Discontinuities,* cited in Reno, *Warlord Politics,* p. 35. The term "imperialism by invitation," includes a government faction hiring a foreign force to combat insurgents or to combat rivals in the government.

93. Reno, *Warlord Politics,* p. 227.

94. These same officials state that Gen. Salim Saleh in Uganda, President Museveni's half-brother, owns some 25 to 40 percent of Saracen Uganda (a Strategic Resources Corporation affiliate) and has interests in a Heritage oil concession.

95. Reno, *Warlord Politics,* p. 136.

96. Interview, January 11, 1999.

97. Interview with Paul Kamara, January 1997. EO soldiers did engage the RUF outside the diamond areas after they had secured the capital and the mines.

98. Zarate agrees: "The chaos which followed EO's departure is a testament to its effectiveness in maintaining order," Zarate, "New Dog of War," p. 97. Several journalists following the RUF's near-takeover of Freetown in January 1999, called for a return of EO. Sam Kiley, "Send in the Mercenaries, Mr. Cook," *London Times,* January 22, 1999.

99. EO was fighting against two forces opposed to peaceful conflict resolution. UNITA had deserted an apparently democratic electoral process to which it had agreed, and Sierra Leone's RUF appeared more as a bandit organization not seriously interested in peaceful discussions leading to eventual democratization. EO served the purposes of South Africa in Angola by helping to defeat Savimbi's UNITA, whereas it aided Nigeria's regional policy in Sierra Leone by helping to defeat the RUF. In Sierra Leone, EO several times cooperated with Nigerian forces in anti-RUF offensives.

100. The *Independent,* March 23, 1997. A Western intelligence source

confirms that although no agreement was reached, "discussions [between the OAU and EO] took place and soundings were made." Interview, October 1996. Some observers contend that Branch Group/EO officials deliberately championed discussions only to achieve public legitimacy, while knowing that the OAU was not about to hire the mercenary force.

101. Like armies anywhere, African armies traditionally disliked parallel armed forces that operate outside of their nations' normal chain of command. In some countries, resentment of a newer force answerable only to the president has sparked coups (e.g., Ghana in 1966). Mercenary groups have generally angered existing militaries (Rolf Steiner's 4 Commando in Biafra was such an example). William Thom notes the Zairian military's bitterness about Mobutu's employment of mercenaries to stem Laurent Kabila's advance. William Thom, "Congo-Zaire's 1996-97 Civil War in the Context of Evolving Patterns of Military Conflict in Africa in the Era of Independence," *Journal of Conflict Resolution* (20,2), Fall 1999.

102. The presence of EO soldiers in Papua New Guinea helped to trigger a military coup in early 1997. Sandline International, the military advisory wing of the Branch Group, had signed a $36 million contract with the government of Sir Julius Chan to end a nine-year conflict on Bougainville Island. Ex-EO soldiers formed much of the Sandline force. Brig. Gen. Jerry Singirok initially supported the contract but then, in mid-March, openly broke with his government. Singirok demanded that Chan quit because of his hiring of EO. Chan then sacked Singirok, an action that helped trigger large anti-EO street demonstrations. Sandline and EO ignominiously left the country, and a beleaguered Chan stepped down.

Singirok justified his actions by claiming that EO planned to use force directly against Bougainvillians, most notably with helicopter-launched rockets. Some observers believe, however, that army resentment over EO's capabilities and its high pay was the motivating factor. The *London Observer* writes that "the Sandline contract undermined his standing with his own troops who, frustrated by low pay and poor equipment, were infuriated by the money paid to the mercenaries." "Mercenaries' Chief Held on Arms Charge," *Observer,* March 23, 1997. Sandline officials believe that General Singirok deliberately okayed EO's mission in order to use the mercenaries' presence against Prime Minister Chan.

103. Interview with Barlow, July 1997.

104. Luitingh interview, July 1997.

105. Interviews, July 1997.

106. Fayemi of the Africa Research and Information Bureau, quoted in "Africa/Mercenaries," Voice of America, July 8, 1997. "A chief complaint of the coup makers is that the government paid large sums to Executive Outcomes and other forces [the EO-assisted Kamajors], rather than improving and paying the army." Sierra Leoneans Resist New Rulers," *Washington Post,* June 11, 1997.

107. Parliamentary Human Rights Group, quoted in the *Independent,* March 23, 1997. South Africa's *Cape Argus* states that "EO's presence may even have . . . encourage(d) its clients in both cases [Angola and Sierra Leone] to avoid addressing those underlying causes of instability, knowing they could

always rely on the kind of quick-fix solution which EO provided," "South Africa: War-Mongers or Peace-Keepers?" *Cape Argus,* December 14, 1998.

108. British freelance pilots during the Nigerian civil war deliberately avoided Biafra's major airstrip, the destruction of which would have greatly hastened the war's end. See John de St. Jorre, *The Brothers' War: Biafra and Nigeria,* pp. 319–320.

109. Saracen once was part of Strategic Resources Corporation. Alpha 5 (which some Angolans refer to as "Filho de EO"—"Son of EO") and Lifeguard have close relations to EO. These companies, often composed of numerous EO veterans, practice corporate security. Some observers speculate that EO, and/or its above offshoots, could easily smuggle guns into or out of various countries. It faced only minimal customs or security restraints in South Africa, Angola, or Sierra Leone. Interviews with U.S. and British intelligence officials, 1996 and 1997. EO denies all allegations.

110. Interview, March 1999.

111. See Herbert M. Howe, "Lessons of Liberia: ECOMOG and Regional Peacekeeping," *International Security,* Winter 1996/1997.

112. Ibid.

113. Ibid.

114. Elizabeth Rubin concludes her *Harper's* article by contending that "like a hawk riding the thermals, Barlow is simply capitalizing on the shifting currents. . . . He is accountable to no nation and no legal body. His law is the marketplace. And if the geoeconomic world order should require Barlow to adapt his services for a new kind of client, there isn't much to prevent the chameleon from once again changing colors," Rubin, "An Army of Their Own," p. 55.

115. Jakkie Cilliers and Christian Dietrich, "Editorial Comment: Privatising Peace Enforcement," *African Security Review,* 1996, p. 2.

116. Quoted in Isenberg, "The New Mercenaries," p. 16.

117. Chief R. O. A. Akinjide, "Mercenarism and International Law." Lecture delivered at the International Law Seminar, Palais des Nations, Geneva, May 27, 1995.

118. Zarate, "New Dog of War," p. 99.

119. Barlow, July 1996.

120. The U.S. belief that UNITA's Savimbi was using EO's continued presence as a reason to not comply fully with the Lusaka Accords was a major reason for Washington's criticism.

121. Interview, U.S. State Department, Office of West African Affairs official, April 1996. This official commented that "African states ask us all the time how we feel about Executive Outcomes."

122. For example, Roger Moody's "Diamond Dogs of War," *New Internationalist,* March 1998.

123. "Sierra Leone/Britain. Militias and Market Forces," *Africa Confidential,* October 23, 1998, p. 2.

124. Interview, April 1996.

125. Interview with U.S. Department of Defense official, November 1996.

126. A reputation of invincibility, whether deserved or not, has its own uses. A "Western diplomat" who supported EO's early 1997 departure had sec-

ond thoughts: "In retrospect, it was a mistake to have them leave . . . there was a myth of invincibility about them that was very useful." Quoted in "U.S. Backs Role for Rebels in W. Africa," *Washington Post,* October 18, 1999.

127. EO's lack of French speakers reportedly lessened its desire to provide a large fighting force to Mobutu.

128. Interview with Barlow, June 1997.

129. Information gathered by author, July 1996.

130. The initial periodical and journal articles that examined EO in depth presented ambivalent or guardedly positive views. These include Elizabeth Rubin's "An Army of Their Own," and David Shearer's "Private Armies and Military Intervention," International Institute for Strategic Studies, Adelphi Paper 316, 1998, and his "Outsourcing War," *Foreign Policy,* Fall 1998, and this author's "Private Security and African Stability," *Journal of Modern African Studies,* 1998. Two recent, and more critical, views are Khareen Pech's "Executive Outcome," in Cilliers and Mason, eds., *Peace, Profit or Plunder?* and Musah's "A Country Under Siege: State Decay and Corporate Military Intervention in Sierra Leone," in Musah and Fayemi, *Mercenaries.*

131. Interviews with military specialists, U.S. Department of State, September 1999.

132. See, for example, "Russians Fly for Both Sides in Horn of Africa," *London Times,* February 19, 1999. The *Times* reports that all Russians fighting in Ethiopia and Eritrea arrive "usually as part of a package including the supply of the aircraft, parts and maintenance."

133. John Woods of *Stockwatch* newsletter, quoted. Transcript, "The Fifth Estate," February 4, 1997, p. 1. Examples of foreign guard firms include Lifeguard in Sierra Leone, where, until 1999, it protected Branch Energy's diamond operations at Koidu and the the Bambuna hydroelectric dam.

134. NGO supporters of guard units argue that unprotected relief supplies can prolong suffering when combatants capture them. A private contingent of experienced ex-soldiers could appear to local combatants as more impartial than local hires or troops of a foreign government. Yet other relief specialists argue that armed personnel contradict an essential humanitarian philosophy, and that arming "mercenaries" could call into question their neutrality and jeopardize their mission. These critics charge that the costs of hiring private security personnel will use finances that otherwise could purchase food and medicine. Furthermore, a security presence could heighten insecurity as attackers resort to greater firepower to seize the relief supplies. Foreign guards with sidearms cannot match the more heavily armed local soldiers who know the local culture and physical geography.

135. Alex Vines offers another reason why foreign forces will remain small. Writing about the Angolan government's ouster of DSL, Vines writes that "the company had made little effort to indigenise its workforce and management." Vines, "Mercenaries," in Musah and Fatemi, *Mercenaries,* p. 136.

136. The "white legion" in the former Zaire also helped to discredit the myth of omnipotent mercenaries. Composed of some 300 Europeans, including many Serbs, the hastily formed "legion" cost Mobutu some $50 million but produced few military victories. See Khareen Pech, "The Hand of War:

Mercenaries in the Former Zaire 1996–97," in Fayemi and Musah, *Mercenaries*. A major problem the "legion" faced was the incompetence of Zairean (Congolese) forces. That Zairean soldiers in 1999 in several engagements accidentally fired upon Chadian soldiers, who were fighting for the Zairean government, prompted Chad to withdraw its troops. The European pilots had difficulty in understanding Zairean headquarters' orders and therefore did not provide necessary air cover for ground operations.

137. "Mercenaries' Rage Kindled by Atrocities," *London Times,* January 24, 1999. The one-day exploits in 1997 by Will Scully, a former British SAS officer fighting by himself in Sierra Leone, dramatically demonstrate what a few trained personnel can accomplish against a ragtag insurgency. Will Scully, *Once a Pilgrim.*

138. The U.S. firm of Halliburton Co. (of which Richard Cheney—former U.S. secretary of defense and Republican candidate for U.S. vice president in 2000—was chief executive officer and chairman of the board) is a dramatic example of noncombat capability. Between 1992 and 2000, Halliburton, especially through its Brown and Root Services subsidiary, won more than $2 billion in contracts supporting U.S. peacekeeping missions abroad. It is "doing everything including washing uniforms and setting up tents and toilets for the American services." Cheney said that "the first person to greet our soldiers as they arrive in the Balkans, and the last one to wave good-bye, is one of our employees." "War and Piecework," *The Economist,* July 10–16, 1999, p. 67; "Peacekeeping Helped Cheney Company," Associated Press, August 28, 2000.

139. Musah and Fayemi, *Mercenaries,* p. 18.

140. International Charter Incorporated (ICI) and other companies have demonstrated some financial, political, and intelligence advantages. ICI claims, and U.S. officials concur, that it completed the task for only 35 percent of what a similar operation would have financially cost the U.S. military. Sometimes other countries foot the bill: several Muslim countries are paying for the MPRI training team of almost 200 men in Bosnia. The employment of the private ICI raised few of the sensitive domestic issues in the U.S. Congress that an official U.S. military presence would have provoked (critics contend that this indicates a serious lack of transparency and accountability). Private specialists in ICI and other such similar firms as Sandline or DSL probably also provide valuable, on-the-ground information to their Western governments.

141. "Sierra Leone: How The 'Good Guys' Won," *New African,* July 1998, summarizes the controversy that threatened Tony Blair's government in mid-1998. Also, *Sierra Leone,* Foreign Affairs Committee, House of Commons, HC 166-I, II, February 3, 1999.

142. Bert Sachse, EO's commander in Sierra Leone, became commander of Lifeguard after EO left that country.

143. "Diamond Hunters Fuel Africa's Brutal Wars," *Washington Post,* October 16, 1999. Interviews, Washington, D.C., 1999.

144. "Diamond Hunters."

145. Interviews, U.S. State and Defense Departments, September 1999.

146. Lawrence Ndola Myers, acting director, quoted in "Diamond Hunters."

147. "Diamond Hunters."

148. "Angola. Oil-Fired Warfare," *Africa Confidential,* May 14, 1999, p. 6.

149. Ibid.

150. A variant of indigenous "private security" forces had already existed in Africa, as Chapter 2 notes, since personal rulers had effectively privatized sections of their "national" militaries—presidential guards, militias, and often the militaries themselves—by making them more answerable to the president or a subnational group than to the state.

151. See Vines, "Gurkhas," in Cilliers and Mason, eds., *Peace, Profit or Plunder?*

152. Pech, "The Hand of War. Mercenaries in the Former Zaire 1996-97," Fayemi and Musah, *Mercenaries,* p. 139.

153. Vines, "Mercenaries," in Musah and Fayemi, *Mercenaries,* pp. 185–186.

The *Washington Post* reports that a 300-man private force controlled by de Matos protects the Catoca mine for $500,000 monthly. "Africa's Gems: Warfare's Best Friend," *Washington Post,* April 6, 2000.

154. Figure from Alex Vines, "Gurkhas," in Cilliers and Mason, eds., *Peace, Profit or Plunder?* p. 134.

155. Ibid., p. 137. Vines, "Mercenaries," in Musah and Fayemi, *Mercenaries,* pp. 185–186.

156. "Soldiers to Market Diamonds, Gold," IRIN, UN Office for the Coordination of Humanitarian Affairs, September 25, 1999. http://www.reliefweb.int/IRIN

157. Some professional officials do object, however. Vines quotes "a senior Angolan police commissioner" as complaining that "these private security firms erode the state further. They are dangerous, we cannot regulate them as they are politically controlled by senior government officials." Vines, "Mercenaries," in Musah and Fayemi, *Mercenaries,* p. 186.

158. Teleservices, which is a partnership between two top Angolan security personnel firms and South Africa's Gray Security Services, reportedly "cleared a mine near Luo of residual forces of Uniao Nacional Para a Independencia Total de Angola" in 1998. "Angola: Protection." *Africa Confidential,* June 1998, p. 8.

159. Interviews January 1997.

160. Numerous South Africans and some Russian air specialists were contributing significantly to the Kabila government's defense in 1998. Few, if any, were reported to be combat soldiers.

161. "Diamond Hunters Fuel Africa's Brutal Wars," *Washington Post,* October 16, 1999.

162. "DRC-Zimbabwe Army Business," IRIN, September 27, 1999, http://www.reliefweb.int/IRIN

163. Pech, "Executive Outcomes," in Cilliers and Mason, eds., *Peace, Profit or Plunder?* p. 98.

164. Zarate, "New Dog of War," p. 122.

165. Remarks at Georgetown University, October 15, 1999.

166. "Private Military Companies—Independent or Regulated," March 28, 1998. Http://www.sandline.com.site/index.html

167. Article 6 (c) of the Convention for the Elimination of Mercenarism in Africa, reprinted in Geno J. Naidi, ed., *Documents of the Organization of African Unity,* p. 58.

168. "The Report by the UN Special Rapporteur on the Use of Mercenaries, 1998," reprinted in Appendix Six, Musah and Fayemi, *Mercenaries,* p. 303

169. Jeffrey Herbst, "The Regulation of Private Military Forces," p. 14.

6

ACRI:
U.S. SUPPORT OF AFRICAN
MILITARY PROFESSIONALISM

E COMOG and Executive Outcomes illustrated some of the serious deficiencies of ad hoc regional interveners and foreign security companies. Many of ECOMOG's major problems were those of military capabilities. It was built on national forces of very differing technical resources, especially since some personal rulers had deliberately weakened their own militaries, and it never blended into one force, in part because of its hasty startup. It rarely defeated sometimes ruthless insurgent groups. At the same time, ECOMOG fared better politically as an African-generated and controlled institution: to reverse Mao Tse Tung's observation, what it didn't win on the battlefield it did win on the political table.

In many ways, EO achieved the opposite. It evinced remarkable military professionalism, in part because of its long-standing unity of institutionalized command, training, and equipment acquired from the old SADF. But the nonstate EO triggered widespread suspicions of unaccountability and was shunned by much of the international community.

Africa needs regional intervention forces that combine the best of ECOMOG and EO—in other words, a professional, established, and unified military capability that enjoys international political support. Western security assistance to Africa increasingly has sought this goal

---

* Space considerations prevent me from examining a wide range of important bilateral and, increasingly, multilateral military aid programs for Africa. I selected ACRI both because of its possible importance and the considerable public attention it has received.

since the Cold War's ending, and the U.S.-run African Crisis Response Initiative (ACRI) is the best-known example.[1] ACRI supplies professional military capabilities, but only to those states that are relatively democratic and that observe human rights. By emphasizing peacekeeping rather than combat skills and by providing nonlethal equipment, ACRI also helps to address leaders' concerns of a heightened domestic military threat.

ACRI and other Western programs address several of Africa's key security needs and should assist African professionalism, but these programs are not a panacea. Serious concerns, especially about ACRI's purpose, composition, and control, as well its possibility of spreading African conflict inadvertently, raise questions about ACRI's usefulness to African security. And the continuing presence of personal, rather than institutional, rule could well weaken the initiative.

The U.S.-financed ACRI began training African battalions in 1997 (Senegal and Uganda were the first) as the start of a five-year program,[2] combining Western training and financing with the legitimacy of state-to-state relations and African manpower, and instructing about 11,000 African soldiers in peacekeeping doctrine and tactics. Specific instruction includes border monitoring, convoy protection, and proper human rights behavior. The initial training period lasts about sixty-five days, with five subsequent follow-on training exercises.[3] Two PSCs help provide the follow-on training.[4] Besides upgrading military capabilities, ACRI emphasizes a military's political responsibility toward civilians. It teaches such skills as refugee protection, cooperation with relief groups, and observance of human rights.

Its overall goal is to develop "rapidly deployable, interoperable battalions and companies from stable, democratic countries that can work together to maintain peace on the continent."[5] It seeks a common capacity, rather than a standing force, among designated national battalions that can come together as peacekeepers for specific situations. ACRI hopes that its ongoing sustainment exercises and its "train the trainer" approach will ensure a lasting effect after the program concludes.

ACRI is important for several reasons. Along with British and French initiatives, it represents the first united attempt by major Western powers to help Africa develop a continent-wide integrated peacekeeping capability. ACRI believes that "interoperability"—common training and equipping of battalions from some twelve African militaries—will allow these designated forces to begin effective operations quickly, without the usual problems that confront ad hoc multinational peacekeepers. Second, ACRI's anticipatory, rather than reactive, motivation could allow for more systematic planning and response than any previous ad hoc intervention. Third, ACRI has created a common peacekeeping doctrine drawn from the experiences of the UN, Nordic countries, and other peacekeepers. This doctrine, if tested successfully, may have worldwide applicability. Fourth, ACRI's success would help redress both the domestic balances of coercion and slow the drift toward the privatization of state security. Finally, a successful ACRI will lessen political pressure on Western governments to intervene militarily in African humanitarian crises by helping African states to defend themselves.

Background to ACRI

U.S. Military Assistance During the Cold War

Western nations have cooperated with African states on military matters since independence, and sometimes even earlier.[6] Political loyalty to a foreign patron rather than a regime's intrinsic domestic worthiness was the usual stimulus for assistance during the Cold War. This often led to critics' singling out the United States, for example, for its military support of ideologically correct "anticommunist" but often clearly despotic rulers. U.S. programs included IMET (International Military and Education Training), JCET (Joint Combined Exercises and Training), and MTT (Mobile Training Teams).

These earlier military programs spawned controversy. Did they assist legitimate national interests or did they mostly bolster regimes that repressed the political and economic development? Supporters maintained that the aid helped to stabilize the recipient country and the regime, as well as furnishing intelligence and access to the Western donors.[7]

Critics have maintained that previous military assistance undercut African development by assisting repressive states, undermining diplomatic goals, and adding to a security dilemma by increasing regional military tensions. Another criticism is that some training programs may have denied Western democratic principles, notably accountability. The *Washington Post* wrote about the JCET program that "American special operations forces have established military ties in at least 110 countries, unencumbered by public debate, effective civilian oversight, or the consistent involvement of senior U.S. foreign affairs officials."[8]

The U.S.-based Demilitarization for Democracy project claims that militaries hold significant political power in three-quarters of African nations and that U.S. equipping and training have not lessened the corruption, human rights abuses, and commercial activities of these militaries. Critics have focused on the JCET program as contravening stated U.S. policy.[9] Some critics see a connection between foreign military training and African coups d'état, noting ostensible examples in Liberia, Central African Republic, and elsewhere.[10] Because African militaries control much of the political and economic power, the project states that "U.S. policy still seems locked in its Cold War policy of strengthening the armed forces of non-democratic African rulers . . . [and] there has been no evidence or study submitted to support administration claims that exposure to U.S. military personnel and training programs change officers' attitudes and leads to a transition to democracy."[11]

Supporters of military aid acknowledge some of its drawbacks. Much of the West's assistance during the Cold War propped up personal rulers who often undermined attempts at professionalism. Both the West's and the Soviet Union's approaches were largely bilateral, creating few regional—and no continent-wide—programs. Such assistance helped maintain the wide disparities in regional military capabilities that were to plague any future multinational force. Furthermore, much of the training was a "one-shot" program that offered little follow-up. Training benefits disappeared as soldiers left the military and as the West did not implement continued training.

Trainees perhaps heard only what they wanted to hear: well-intentioned attempts to promote political responsibility that sometimes fell upon deaf ears. Col. Dan Henk notes that "U.S. military training, even that which stresses professional ethics, does not inherently guarantee that its recipients will subscribe to the U.S. models of professional behavior. For instance, relatively large numbers of military officers from Liberia and Zaire attended U.S. military schools in the 1970s and 1980s. However, it has been difficult to see results in resulting behavior."[12]

U.S. Security Assumptions After the Cold War

The end of the Cold War and three major African conflicts in Liberia, Somalia, and Rwanda modified Western concepts of military assistance to African militaries and helped create ACRI. By the mid-1990s Washington had assumed the following about Africa:

1. African conflicts would continue far beyond the end of the Cold War, and their changing nature could seriously jeopardize African development. Such fighting would undermine already weak state institutions (including the military) and heighten the possibility of state collapse.
2. The "Somalia syndrome," the U.S. fear of prolonged commitments of prestige, time, money, and troops in largely unknown areas for ill-defined (or largely nonexistent) national interests, had chilled U.S. intervention policy worldwide. Suffering in Africa, even that not threatening any Western national interests, might marshal public sympathy and force ill-conceived military interventions. Such instances had to be avoided.
3. Africa had primary responsibility for its own security, but the West could assist Africa. Multilateral interventions could best distribute the operations' political and financial costs.
4. African multinational forces could offer several advantages, including greater knowledge, acceptance, military capabilities, and commitment, over non-African forces, but ECOMOG's Liberian experience demonstrated the danger of inserting an ad hoc and largely unprofessional African force into combat.
5. Improving Africa's military professionalism would serve some important purposes by empowering future African intervention forces and enabling national militaries to meet the changing nature of African conflict, while lessening humanitarian pressure on the West to intervene as the force of last resort. Heightened military professionalism also might decrease the incidence of military coups, lessen the possibility of fragmenting armies assisting state "collapse," and provide breathing space to newly democratizing states. Finally, well-trained African peacekeepers could bolster UN peacekeeping efforts outside Africa.

The African Crisis Response Force

Rwanda's 1994 genocide and subsequent destabilization of central Africa deeply troubled Western governments. The killings demonstrated once again how "local" conflicts, whether in Liberia, Rwanda, or elsewhere, could topple fragile states and spark regional economic destruction. The world's inaction during the genocide—including many governments' refusal even to label it as genocide—embarrassed many U.S. officials.

The Rwandan conflict was itself bad enough. What further troubled policymakers was that it could occur again—most likely in Burundi, a neighbor of Rwanda with the same Hutu-Tutsi imbalance.[13] U.S. concern about that eventuality led to the proposal for the African Crisis Response Force (ACRF), which was formally unveiled by Secretary of State Warren Christopher on October 10, 1996. The timing appeared to be good; the ending of the Cold War had lessened African suspicions of U.S. strategic motives, and the United States had backed away from its more objectionable Cold War clients.

The primary purpose of ACRF would be peacekeeping, not peace enforcement. Burundi was its major, and perhaps only, raison d'être, and the United States hoped that the force could be deployed there quickly if necessary. The West would supply training and equipment for a standing force of about eight battalions (about 5,600 soldiers).[14] The United States would largely decide ACRF's membership, the UN would provide specific sanctions, and the OAU and other regional organizations would play an unspecified role.

The plan announced by Christopher underlined four important ongoing assumptions: African states and regions have primary responsibility for their security; the West should play an important but noncombat support role; efforts should be multilateral and established, instead of unilateral and ad hoc; and greater training and basic equipment would assist African military capabilities more than sophisticated weaponry. Significantly, ACRF's "double multinationalism"—Western and African—underlined Washington's refusal to go it alone.

The ACRF plan grew as the United States realized that Boutros Boutros-Ghali would fail in getting a standby force for Burundi. Washington had distanced itself from sole responsibility by emphasizing UN and regional roles; it also wanted the UN to fund any actual deployment. Lessons from past ad hoc UN interventions were implicit in Christopher's worry that "some event will come, such as genocide in Rwanda, and there simply is not time to put together a force because it takes many months to put together a force if you're doing it from scratch."[15]

Yet the ACRF failed before actually getting started, illustrating the difficulty of gaining consensus for multinational security endeavors. Washington's hasty reactiveness was all too typical of U.S. decision-making about African crises.[16] The hastily proposed ACRF failed to gain agreement about the need for such a force from its European and African partners. ACRF architects had not consulted adequately with these putative partners and had not predicted a host of reasonable concerns about purpose, composition, and control, among others. Having witnessed Rwanda's ghastliness, both European and African states sensed the volatile unpredictability that an intervention force (whether "neutral peacekeepers" or not) would face in a tense Burundi.

The West stood divided over the ACRF, and Christopher's team in Europe prior to the October announcement realized that it had not adequately anticipated European sensitivities. France and Britain, ACRF's potential European partners, questioned the need for such a force.[17] Both had current bilateral defense relations, which included training and equipping, with many of their former colonial powers. These programs paid dividends to the ex-metropole, largely because of the bilateral nature. Moving resources from proven and politically valuable programs into an untested and multilateral, U.S.-designed program had little appeal.

The United States as the "new kid on the block" provoked some of the European reaction. Both Britain and France presumed a special knowledge based on a much longer and deeper involvement in Africa, with some sections of the French government still viewing Francophone Africa as its *chasse gardée*. Jeffrey Herbst comments that "what the French really feared was not American indifference to the [African] continent by American activism. . . . The ACRF appeared to be, in French terms, nothing less than the final consolidation of a new American hegemony in Africa."[18]

The French voiced open skepticism and, sometimes, scorn. They had reportedly rebuffed U.S. attempts to dovetail ACRI with France's 1994 call for an African peacekeeping force.[19] Jacques Godfrain, France's minister for foreign cooperation, characterized Clinton as a new arrival to African matters, stating that "I am delighted to see the president showing interest in Africa and making it a priority three weeks before the presidential elections."[20] (Christopher riposted that no longer could Africa "be carved up into spheres of influence, or . . . outside powers . . . view whole groups of states as their private domain.")[21]

Furthermore, Europe's recent experiences with peacekeeping in Eastern Europe and Africa had lessened enthusiasm for ACRF. Christopher had selected the relatively easy option of peacekeeping, but several states, especially in Europe, had been burned by peacekeeping operations and appeared cautious about the ACRF. Holland's memories of the debacle of Srebrenica, in Bosnia, had cooled its ardor, and both the Dutch and the Belgians wanted strict limits to peacekeeping and humanitarian operations. Belgium had just lost ten soldiers in Rwanda and was understandably hesitant about any future African military involvement.

African support was essential, Several key points of the ACRF found favor but unanswered questions about the force prevented a wholehearted response.[22] Few sub-Saharan African states openly opposed it, but Mali and Ethiopia were the only two states quickly to pledge support (Salim A. Salim, secretary-general of the OAU, also endorsed the proposal). Christopher's seeming fait accompli prompted some Africans to see the ACRF as another paternalistic, even neocolonial, Western creation. Africa has always questioned the West's enlisting of African troops to help Western goals. William Foltz's earlier observation proved apt: "Intervention that combines African troops and great power support . . . evokes Trojan horse metaphors from Africans, who are prone to see this as a particularly insidious form of external intervention using African clients as cover."[23]

The foreign creation and ownership of the force irritated many Africans, some of whom wondered whether the ACRF was selecting surrogates to implement U.S. strategic goals in Africa. Many Africans feared that ACRF could relegate them to being mercenary-like instruments of Western security policies. A U.S. State Department official characterized African skepticism and confusion: "Hey, wait a minute, you [the United States] pick the militaries to be involved, you train them, you tell them when and where to go. . . . How is that different from hiring Gurkha mercenaries?"[24]

The United States had not sought advice from African states, even from those it wanted to staff the force; it had only informed several key Africans about the plan.[25] The perceived abrasiveness of some key advocates in Washington, including Susan Rice of the National Security Council, irritated African leaders. Additionally, many critics charged that the ACRF provided the West an excuse to wash its hands of African conflicts and instability that its policies, stretching back to the days of colonialism, had helped to create. A few leaders worried about the possible threat to national sovereignty posed by a supranational force—the same worry that had helped to sink Nkrumah's All-African High Command proposal in 1960.[26]

Both Nigeria and South Africa, sub-Saharan Africa's two regional military powers, refused to give their endorsement. The Abacha government was curt in its refusal. Col. Godwin Ugbo, Nigerian defense spokesman, suggested that "the force in question is an American creation. It is neither a UN nor an OAU affair. . . . The US may have come up with this idea of African intervention force without the contribution of Nigeria just to slight the country."[27] The United States had not sought Nigeria's participation, in part because of "decertification" of Nigeria over possible state involvement in international drug smuggling. Support by South Africa's Nelson Mandela would have helped sell the ACRF to some hesitant states. But Mandela gave it, at best, a lukewarm salute, stating that the UN should have initiated the proposal.[28]

Analysis of the ACRF's views of its purpose, composition, and control is necessarily incomplete: the proposal was hastily formed and quickly discarded. Unexplained were the criteria for intervention, deployment, and departure; its composition and leadership; the site (if any) of the force's headquarters; the financing of operations; and the specific roles of its U.S., European, UN, OAU, African regional, and troop-contributing participants.

Washington's reaction, which largely divided along party lines, did little to help the ACRF. A Republican congressional staffer said that "you can just say that we hate this" because of worries about "costs and risks involved in U.S. participation in international peacekeeping efforts." Europeans "have no interest, zippo."[29] Additionally, the unpopular U.S. and UN interventions in Somalia had turned many Republicans and Democrats away from any military involvement in third world conflicts.

U.S. officials by late 1996 acknowledged that the ACRF had elicited only a lukewarm reaction and that the way in which the United States organized, and then presented, the concept of the force was responsible for much of that response.[30] The Burundi-inspired haste had forced the State Department to sidestep most of the major issues. The difficulty that the United States had just in defining the ACRF's "peacekeeping" illustrates how difficult a seemingly easy task can be.[31] Washington had sought an agreement in principle, something that potential backers hesitated to offer, considering the proposal's vagueness. Fortunately, the ACRF never deployed an ad hoc force in Burundi: a failure would have crippled future chances for any Western-supported peacekeeping force.[32]

The assumption that Africa's wars would continue was accurate. Fears about Burundi were fading by early 1997, but subsequent conflicts in Zaire/Congo, the Central African Republic, and Sierra Leone "reinforced the Clinton administration's desire to upgrade African military capabilities."[33]

From ACRF to ACRI

Washington's next attempt to enhance peacekeeping ability in Africa occurred when Ambassador Marshall McCallie took over leadership of the ACRF in December 1996.[34] He quickly distanced his approach from that of Christopher. McCallie and his staff consulted with potential European and African partners and stressed that the program was a work in progress: the United States would welcome advice and modifications.[35] McCallie held meetings at the UN to solicit opinions and sought support for an international African Peacekeeping Support Group, which would lend an international imprimatur to the proposal.

Western and African reactions slowly warmed to the slower and more realistic U.S. approach to the issues of purpose, composition, and control.

ACRI'S Purpose

ACRI is to undertake only humanitarian and peacekeeping missions, as its Program of Instruction indicates. The U.S. European Command (EUCOM), which directs ACRI's military training, notes that the training's "major emphasis [is] on leadership, communications, logistics operations, and maintenance of equipment."[36] Specific skills include checkpoint operation, coordination with NGOs and the press, vehicle searches, and basic marksmanship for self-defense. African troops gained training in protection of refugees.[37] The peacekeeping training doctrine would be an amalgam of that already developed by the UN, the Nordic states, the United States, Britain, and France.

The nonlethal equipment reflected ACRI's peacekeeping, rather than peace-enforcing, mission: communications gear, mine detecting equipment, water purification devices, portable electric generators, eyeglasses and night-vision goggles, uniforms, webbing, and boots. Each battalion received the same type of equipment, which assists quick coordination of the units when they are deployed. ACRI planners claim that each trained and supplied battalion will gain "an organic logistics sustainment capability . . . [to] permit sustained operations [of] up to six months."[38] Each selected battalion receives approximately $1.9 million in initial training and another $1.2 million in equipment. The four follow-on training sessions would cost $400,000 each. Troop strength would vary, depending on which session was being conducted.[39]

Trained African units would not be thrown quickly into any potentially genocidal conflict. ACRI would offer training and materiel, and the individual countries could decide whether and when to commit their troops. The peacekeeping training would occur at various levels. It would start with a two-month period for a battalion within its own country, move to brigade-size (two or three battalions) training and exercises within the country, and then regional training and exercises of these same units. Follow-on training exercises would occur every six months after the initial training. The U.S. Army 3rd and 5th Special Forces ("Green Berets") Groups would perform much of the initial training, although other qualified countries were also welcome to assist in the training.[40]

ACRI'S Composition

McCallie, in accordance with appropriations legislation, also changed much of the ACRF's composition and structure. Selection criteria quieted some fears of a U.S. "Trojan horse" in Africa. The United States sought relatively competent forces from "stable, democratic countries,"[41] therefore excluding authoritarian states such as Congo (ex-Zaire), which had served U.S. strategic interests during the Cold War. Instead, ACRI strove to enlist militaries that had refrained from human rights abuses or military pretorianism or invasions and that already had basic skills, including previous peacekeeping experience, if any. ACRI hoped to assuage possible Francophone (and French) worries by selecting Francophone Senegal and Anglophone Uganda as the first two countries for training.

No longer was there to be a "force." Addressing African concerns about a standing, supranational force, McCallie stressed that the program would build capacity within designated national units and that these units would join together only when requested by the UN, the OAU, or relevant regional groupings.[42] Hence the renaming of the "force" to the "initiative."

ACRI has stressed inclusiveness, inviting to its exercises observers from neighboring African states and Western governments. Some of ACRI's exercises have included cooperation with relief agencies, an ACRI exercise in Uganda featuring participation by the World Food Program.

Control of ACRI

African states should determine where, when, and how to deploy peacekeeping forces, although the actual sanctioning mechanism has remained vague (i.e., whether approval is necessary from the UN, OAU, and the relevant regional bodies). Significantly, already trained and equipped states may decline to send their troops on a particular peacekeeping mission. ACRI's intention to "train the trainer" would eventually allow greater African control of the initiative. Follow-on training is to occur every six months with battalions previously trained. Finally, ACRI has not specified its command-and-control structure, arguing that Africans should direct this: "It is for Africans themselves to determine what the appropriate command and control structures will be. They will decide when and how to deploy their peacekeeping troops."[43]

Criticisms of ACRI

Observers have raised serious questions about ACRI's composition, control, and mandate. Its peacekeeping purpose could restrict its effectiveness in curtailing conflict, as well as its potential to militarize conflicts further. Concerns about composition include the regional destabilization and unprofessional behavior of some of ACRI's militaries, as well as the limited size of a future ACRI-trained force. Control issues include both the U.S. insistence on determining membership in ACRI and the initiative's reluctance to specify and delegate the political and military command structure.

ACRI trains only at a peacekeeping level: yet most of Africa's conflicts need a peace enforcer to stop suffering from spiraling out of control. The United States and the UN at present refrain from inserting peacekeepers into volatile areas. Joseph Wilson, a former U.S. National Security Council adviser for Africa, states two criteria for the United States and the UN to use in determining "whether or not a peacekeeping delegation is going to be useful. . . . One, the protagonists basically have to agree that there will be a sustainable cease-fire. . . . Secondly, there has to be a genuine commitment to attempt to mediate their differences in a political forum. Otherwise [a situation] just basically puts a lot of people at unacceptable risk."[44] A U.S. State Department official acknowledges that "90 percent of the scenarios in Africa are those like Brazzaville (Congo) or Freetown (Sierra Leone), where an intervention force would have to *impose* peace [emphasis added]."[45] Various observers believe that the quick entry of well-trained combat forces could have prevented much of Africa's recent suffering. UNAMSIL's failure in Sierra Leone—followed by the success of British combat forces during mid-2000—has greatly encouraged this belief. Robert

Rotberg contends that peace enforcement "was urgently needed in Rwanda, to prevent genocide, and in eastern Congo-Kinshasa, to forestall carnage. . . . Had an African-led peace enforcement mechanism been available at the beginning of the Somali civil war, that ex-country's descent into anarchic warlordism could have been prevented."[46]

As noted earlier, Canadian Maj. Gen. Roméo Dallaire, commander of the UN Assistance Mission in Rwanda, believes that 5,000 capable peacekeepers could have stopped most of Rwanda's genocide. Herman Cohen, assistant secretary of state for Africa under President Bush, concurs: "The big mistake [was] not sending an intervention force into Rwanda."[47]

Yet ACRI architects assume that a peace-enforcing level would prompt heightened criticism. The U.S. Congress, which controls ACRI's budget, might worry that U.S. combat training and equipment would increase Africa's instability. African leaders, concerned about their own militaries' enhanced capabilities, threats to national sovereignty, or probable financial and military losses, might oppose a combat mandate. Peace enforcing could create greater postconflict demands. Evoking Somalia's "mission creep" from peacekeeping to nation building, Rotberg asks: "Is the intervention force's job just to impose a cease-fire? Or is it to rebuild civil authority and civil society?"[48]

ACRI seemingly faces a "damned if you do and damned if you don't" dilemma. Nevertheless, it is quietly developing African peace-enforcing abilities with a backdoor, "turnkey," strategy. Continued ACRI nonlethal assistance could strengthen Africa's interoperability capacity to the point where African militaries possess the ability for sufficient peace enforcement. "Nonlethal" is an imprecise concept, since such training and equipment—for example, communications instruction or shipments of boots and radios—can assist a military's combat capability. EUCOM tacitly acknowledges this by stating that ACRI's "focus is to improve basic soldier skills, strengthen combat support and combat service support units."[49]

Most important, African countries will decide the mandate under which their militaries serve and fight. President Alpha Oumar Konaré of Mali suggests ACRI's assistance-providing combat potential to provide assistance: "The ACRI gives us the tools that we need and the opportunity to develop—and enforce if necessary—African solutions to African problems."[50] At present, ACRI's peacekeeping approach is circumventing U.S. congressional worries about encouraging African combat while raising the combat capabilities of selected African states.

Critics question ACRI's composition: some of Africa's "new

rulers," who were offered ACRI training, have recently engaged in regional conflicts, and their militaries have participated in unprofessional practices. ACRI has given training and equipment to Museveni's Uganda, which has a long history of subverting unfriendly neighbors, and it assisted the Rwandan Patriotic Army invasion of Hutu-controlled Rwanda in the early 1990s. Ugandan and Rwandan troops invaded Zaire to fight against Sese Seko Mobutu in 1997. In 1998, Ugandan and Rwandan troops invaded Zaire (by then, Congo) again, trying to topple Laurent Kabila—the man they had helped install as president a year earlier. This intervention helped to spark a counterintervention by other African states, notably Angola and Zimbabwe, that dramatically raised the level of combat and suffering.

The armed conflict between Ethiopia and Eritrea (Ethiopia was to have received ACRI training), as well as the scattered firefights between Rwanda and Uganda, points up an unpredictability: countries that seemingly are allies can quickly turn against each other. Khareen Pech writes of central and southern Africa that "the alliance system is fairly chaotic, with little trust between players, and often the same backers will provide support to different sides of the conflict."[51] Such unpredictability can cause well-intentioned training and equipment programs to intensify conflict and suffering.

Some of ACRI's African partners allow practices that reduce military professionalism. In Uganda, several officers, including Gen. Salim Saleh, have profited from the UPDF's nonaccountability. Uganda's *Monitor* notes that "in Kampala, anything which touches the army is a preserve of the President, High Command, Army Council and a few cabinet ministers. No one is prepared to go on record on serious military matters in the Congo despite the huge military expenditure and human loss."[52]

Kampala's *New Vision* agrees that domestic reform elsewhere has not reached the military: "There should be accountability in the realm of defence expenditure. Great strides have been made in making government more accountable, but regrettably defense transactions have so far been largely obscured from scrutiny."[53]

Personal rule, with its absence of institutionalized restraints, has encouraged this regional destabilization and military unprofessionalism. (Museveni's desire to become a regional power broker and his friendship with his half-brother Salim Saleh is a major example of this.) None of the seven states fighting in Congo ever obtained, or even sought, parliamentary permission to deploy militarily. As long as personal rule continues in ACRI recipient states, the possibility of African forces using U.S. aid for destabilizing or self-enriching purposes will remain. While ACRI's assistance cannot be blamed for regional conflicts, it is possible that U.S. aid has contributed to the conflicts' overall effects.

The total number of ACRI-trained forces represents another composition problem for the initiative. ACRI will train a maximum of 12,000 troops—not a large number—and countries have the option of not contributing their ACRI battalions to a particular future peacekeeping mission. Also, retirements, deaths, and service rotations will deplete the number of ACRI-trained personnel.

Further, Nigeria's and South Africa's nonparticipation in ACRI reduces the number of possible troops and also illustrates state-specific problems that have plagued the initiative. The ACRI-Nigeria relationship illustrates the dilemma of choosing between strategic-military capabilities and political acceptability. How much should an intervention force, which needs ample amounts of manpower, equipment, and money, allow political considerations to determine the force's membership? The South African situation presents different political problems, including the pull of post-apartheid domestic reconstruction and suspicion of U.S. security motives.

The U.S. government placed political above military considerations in Nigeria's case. That nation, whose military's size equals roughly that of all other West African states combined, had served as the linchpin of ECOMOG—despite significant costs (perhaps $8 billion and 500 deaths in Liberia alone). Service in Liberia and Sierra Leone likely generated valuable combat, leadership, and logistical experience, and Nigeria's economic and military might have ensured that its views are listened to, if not always respected, throughout West Africa.

Yet, the United States declined to invite Nigeria to join ACRI and generally refused to provide it with any military support because of the 1993 decertification that denied the transfer to Nigeria of any U.S. military technology or supplies or the financing of military procurement. This understandably offended the Nigerian government, and it claimed that ACRI was an attempt to split Anglophone and Francophone states.[54] Nigeria may have had more pragmatic worries: an effective ACRI would challenge Nigeria's virtual monopoly over peacekeeping in West Africa. Nevertheless, ACRI officials were cautiously optimistic that by mid-2000 Nigeria under President Obasanjo would join the initiative, given Obasanjo's desire to reprofessionalize the country's military.

Political problems of a different sort prevented South Africa, Africa's strongest regional power, from joining ACRI. The United States had especially hoped for South Africa's participation. The com-

bat-tested South African National Defence Force (SANDF, successor to
the SADF) was one of sub-Saharan Africa's most professional force.[55]
Furthermore, the new South Africa enjoyed a special moral standing,
having moved peacefully to nonracial democracy from racist authoritarianism.

Domestic reconstruction, concern about the pitfalls of peacekeeping, and suspicion of U.S. motives explain much of South Africa's hesitation regarding ACRI. The South African government faces demand-
ing, often self-imposed, deadlines for social spending: revenue spent on
foreign military operations could meet with strong opposition. The
SANDF has had to deploy substantial units internally against political
violence in KwaZulu and crime in the major cities; it also has undergone difficult internal changes, absorbing elements of the ANC's
Umkhonto we Sizwe and other liberation forces while witnessing the
departure of many very experienced soldiers and officers of the
apartheid era. The Ministry of Defence also has experienced significant
personnel and philosophical changes as it moved from military to civilian control. South Africa (as well as Zimbabwe, Mozambique, Angola,
and Namibia) suffered through bitter liberation struggles during which
the various opposition groups justifiably felt that the United States was
ambivalent at best toward their movements.[56] Lingering resentment
about past policies, an irritation at the imperiousness of U.S. State
Department officials in 1996, and a suspicion that the ACRF/ACRI was
seeking a quasi-African mercenary force limited southern and South
African support.

In addition, various South African security analysts had studied previous African peacekeeping missions and realized the difficulties
involved. South Africa's white paper on defence reflected these concerns: "In the short-term, such participation [peacekeeping and peace
enforcing] will be regarded with a fair measure of caution," and any
peace support operation must have "parliamentary approval and public
support . . . a clear mandate, mission and objectives . . . realistic criteria
for terminating the operation," and authorization by the UN Security
Council, OAU, and Southern African Development Community.[57]
South Africa lacked experience in international peace support operations: its most recent previous international involvement had been the
destabilization of southern Africa. In the end, South Africa fully realized that foreign military deployment would raise regional fears of
hegemonism and awaken memories of past SADF actions.

Does the lack of support by Nigeria and South Africa hurt ACRI?
To a degree, certainly, but perhaps not as much as some observers sug-

gest.[58] Some African states may welcome a strengthening of their military capabilities vis-à-vis the regional superpower, and, finally, neither Olusegun Obasanjo's Nigeria nor Thabo Mbeki's South Africa has publicly criticized ACRI.

Numerous African politicians and military officers feel that the U.S. role as the decisionmaker in ACRI's composition constitutes unwarranted Western influence. These critics want the OAU and regional organizations to select the recipients of assistance. The International Peace Academy's 1997 conference on African security concluded that a Ghanaian participant's sentiment represented the conference's consensus:

> We will point out in very plain words that we do not believe in selectivity. Whether the support is American, French, British, or joint, participants want Africans to have the final say in who benefits and where. This should be obvious if African problems are to have African solutions.[59]

The actual composition of ACRI battalions raises questions about the initiative's effectiveness. Only Uganda provided an extant battalion to the ACRI trainers—but after training, the members of that battalion were dispersed among the rest of the Ugandan People's Defence Force (UPDF). This policy may help spread the training throughout the entire military, but it eliminates a cohesive and well-trained unit for domestic or regional purposes. Such dispersal may also occur if leaders see a threat from an especially well-trained and equipped military unit.

Another factor related to the composition of ACRI battalions has been France's concern that the United States is covertly championing *anglophonie,* especially in central Africa. France has militarily supported some regimes that it sees as bulwarks against U.S., and U.S. surrogate, inroads. By mid-2000, ACRI had trained Senegalese, Malian, Beninois, and Ivoirian units, and hesitant cooperation by France had replaced competition; but whether this trend will continue remains unclear.

Questions about control and structure also remain unresolved. ACRI has not proposed a location for its headquarters, selected its African officials, or specified its criteria for entering or disengaging from a conflict. It has not resolved how to finance actual deployments—a crucial point considering that some peacekeeping missions have cost billions of dollars.

Specific questions abound. Could an ACRI-trained force, citing a "sovereignty-as-responsibility" argument, enter a sovereign state—even as a peacekeeper—without that state's permission? Who would call for, and then decide on, specific deployments of ACRI troops: the Western supporters, the UN, the OAU, regional African organizations, or the contributing nations? Would unanimous agreement from these five (at least) different official layers be necessary for deployment? Who would provide the necessary airlift?

ACRI may wisely be avoiding political pitfalls by not addressing these contentious issues. Decisions on ACRI's structure and composition, whether by Western or African governments, would necessarily offend those states not favored by the choices. The West's seeming indecision defuses the "Trojan horse" or "neocolonial" accusations and allows African states eventually to make their own decisions.[60] And in fact, ACRI's "bottom-up" approach of capacity building is increasing its political support in Africa.

But ACRI's insistence on determining the criteria for military assistance grates on long-standing African sensitivities about control of the continent's destiny. And there are Africans who wonder whether the United States has used ACRI to increase conflict in Africa, noting that some of the initiative's beneficiaries, most notably Uganda, have subsequently stepped up domestic or regional conflict.[61]

Some African military officers also seriously question the basic ACRI assumptions that African militaries need Western training and that U.S. methods can easily be transferred to Africa. These officers claim that their forces are already professional and that the West should provide only logistical support. As an ECOMOG commander said:

> We have been in Liberia for seven years, and within this duration we have gone through every aspect of what peacekeeping entails. We have conducted classical peacekeeping operations . . . and peace enforcement, involving low intensity group operations, sea operations, and air operations. . . . What we lack is not training. We lack the logistic requirements. . . . I think we should be asking for logistic support and not training.[62]

Conclusions

Analysis of ACRI must be tentative, given its work-in-progress nature. By mid-2000 ACRI was still recruiting nations for training; training had occurred only at the battalion level within (rather than between) countries; and only about half of ACRI's envisioned manpower had received any training or equipment. Although ACRI-trained units had served in peacekeeping missions in Guinea-Bissau, Sierra Leone, and the Central African Republic, U.S. officials felt that they could not adequately evaluate how these units had performed, in part because most of the ACRI-trained personnel had been scattered among different units following their training.

Yet ACRI deserves credit for addressing the major objections to military assistance. It has singled out military professionalism as a sine qua non of African security; it has wrestled with the difficulties posed by several security dilemmas; and it has trained troops from countries whose reforms may warrant such aid.

ACRI has achieved some limited progress in helping to professionalize African forces. Its emphasis on interoperability, follow-up sustainment, and responsible state behavior addresses three major deficiencies of most previous aid programs: differently skilled militaries in a multinational force, militaries receiving "one-shot" temporary training, and repressive militaries that do not represent their nations' needs. ACRI displays an anticipatory, rather than reactive, motivation, and this allows for more systematic planning than that of ad hoc groups such as ECOMOG. ACRI noted the major operational flaws of ECOMOG and other hastily assembled interventions and has tried to correct them; for example, it has provided radios that can communicate within and between national units. It also has dispensed assistance that the national militaries and their foreign patrons should have previously provided (ACRI's optometrists found significant vision problems in about 20 percent of the trainees and then supplied them with free glasses).

ACRI has advanced several conceptual innovations in security assistance "double-multilateralism," interoperability, and prior planning. Some of these key points may become the templates of future military assistance, regardless of ACRI's overall performance. Notably, ACRI reflects and encourages the trend toward multiple Western donors and both Francophone and Anglophone African recipients; this double-multilateralism could provide greater political legitimacy to future interventions while allowing the pooling of resources.

ACRI is not a silver bullet for Africa's security problems. It fails to combine ECOMOG's appeal of an African-generated solution with Executive Outcome's effective offensive operations. Despite the significant publicity about ACRI, the initiative is, as Col. Karen Kwiatkowski notes, "only a small part of all peacekeeping and humanitarian readiness activities on the continent."[63] Some observers worry that ACRI could inadvertently fuel African conflicts. James Woods, although a supporter of ACRI, acknowledges that "elements of the ACRI may respond or be used in a wide range of different crises. This will by no means be limited to peacekeeping. Indeed, once ACRI component capabilities are created we have very little idea and very little influence as to where and how they may be used."[64]

ACRI's limited purpose of peacekeeping seems largely irrelevant and wasteful to many Western and African observers. A senior U.S. official on African military matters predicted in August 2000 that ACRI could be an early political fatality of any post-Clinton administration and that Washington intended to emphasize such peace enforcement-related programs as JCETS as being more pertinent than peacekeeping.[65]

Some ACRI critics automatically see a contradiction between military assistance and conflict resolution. *Africa News* commented on Secretary of State Christopher's ACRF: "The promotion and facilitation of peaceful negotiations for the settlement of Africa's violent crises should be a major anchor of US military involvement in Africa. Military engagement which leads to further armament in the continent is undesirable."[66] Critics also worry that increased military skills could discourage peaceful diplomacy.

Dan Volman notes that Senegal and Uganda both have domestic insurgencies and that "much of the [ACRI] training and equipment provided can also enhance their capability to engage in counterinsurgency operations."[67] Government opponents have claimed that ACRI-trained battalions have engaged rebels in the Casamance area of southern Senegal and in the Kabarole district of western Uganda. As more ACRI units from more countries receive training, the chances increase of ACRI training being used in combat—either to repress domestic opposition or to engage in interstate conflict. ACRI-supplied radios and even such mundane items as canteens and backpacks upgrade present force projection capability. Gerry Cleaver notes that these latter items "are apparently not frequently encountered among the inventories of African armies as they are generally configured to operate within their own borders and food and water are generally supplied by the local populace."[68]

But does the use of ACRI training and equipment necessarily destabilize Africa? The answer appears to be mixed. The United States trains those African countries that have a purported reputation for encouraging democracy and good governance—major criteria for ACRI assistance. Increasing the stability of these governments, whether through economic, political, or military means, accords with U.S. national interests. This certainly is true in Uganda, where much of the insurgent threat comes from the Lord's Resistance Army, which has committed numerous human rights abuses. Destabilization of some especially repressive regimes may usher in more responsive governments.

ACRI tries to restrict how states use its training and equipment. It selects nonpretorian militaries and hopes to "shape the environment by promoting apolitical militaries, respect for human rights, and the role of the military in a democracy."[69] It insists that all ACRI nations sign end-use and nontransfer agreements that, in theory, will prevent equipment from being used for activities other than humanitarian and peacekeeping work. Additionally, ACRI's refusal to provide direct-fighting skills, weaponry, and other offensive equipment lessens the chance of heightened interstate conflict.

Yet, these safeguards may prove insufficient. Much of Africa's recent cross-border fighting has featured competing armies, such as elements of the former Rwandan Armed Forces against the UPDF, both of which have received Western assistance. And despite its willingness to stop the training of militaries that commit objectionable actions (as discussed in the next chapter), ACRI's training and materiel is insufficient for a threatened pullback of this assistance to act as a significant deterrent.

ACRI, following the embarrassment of the ACRF of 1996, anticipated many of the possible limitations on its attempts to upgrade African military professionalism. But its limited successes and uncertain future indicate the difficulties of obtaining a joint Western-African consensus on security issues, especially in an era when African nations are increasingly willing to pursue their national and regional interests by military means.

A Footnote

In late 1999, the United States began a parallel program to ACRI: the Africa Center for Strategic Studies (ACSS). The ACSS is important because it reflects both the West's increasing emphasis on military professionalism and the bringing together of both officers and civilians to discuss common areas of interest. The center "supports democratic governance in Africa" by stressing "the notion of civil-military boundaries"[70] while offering seminars in civil-military relations, national security strategy, and defense economics.[71] Among other things it explores how democratizing states define national interests and how, in conjunction with military planners, these states in transition can accommodate a mix of civilian and security needs. The center plans to focus on how to overcome some of the operational limitations of African militaries, including systems procurement and regularized pay disbursement. The U.S. Department of Defense has budgeted $42 million over five years. The center held its first conference in Senegal in September 1999 and its second in Botswana in July 2000.

The ACSS differs from ACRI in several ways, largely by emphasizing the need for political democratization. The center will not offer any tactical or operational military training, but will convene a roughly equal number of civilians and military officials in multinational seminars and conferences to discuss civil-military relations.[72] Because it does not deal directly with training military forces, it can operate with less restrictive criteria for selecting participating countries. ACRI trains soldiers only from stable and democratizing states, but the ACSS hopes to draw "from as many African states as possible, except Sudan, Libya, and Somalia."[73]

Notes

1. The initial title was the African Crisis Response Force. The change to "Initiative" occurred in early 1997 and reflected several changes in the U.S. proposal.

2. Its original mandate was for five years, but by the end of 1999 some ACRI planners were suggesting that the initiative might last for a longer period. The countries, in order of training, are Senegal, Uganda, Malawi, Mali, Ghana, Benin, and Côte d'Ivoire. Kenya and Nigeria are future possible participants.

3. ACRI initially had "sustainment" exercises that were refresher courses. Follow-on training includes computer-assisted exercises that add to, rather than repeat, the initial training.

4. Logicon provides computer simulation exercises for command post exercises and Military Professional Resources, Inc. (MPRI) supplies senior leadership training.

5. Speech by Ambassador Marshall F. McCallie, "The African Crisis Response Initiative (ACRI), America's Engagement for Peace in Africa," Camp Pendleton, California, April 8, 1998.

6 . Chapter 2 has detailed much of this involvement. France, when compared with Britain, has worked more actively with African militaries since independence. French troops have been based in Djibouti, the Central African Republic, Gabon, Côte d'Ivoire, and Senegal, and they, along with French trainers, have assisted African militaries. Equally important, French security personnel in Africa have greatly assisted regime stability. See Shaun Gregory, "The French Military in Africa: Past and Present," *African Affairs,* July 2000.

British military presence is far more modest and has focused on training rather than on furnishing troops to guard against coups. Two Centres of

Excellence, in Ghana and Zimbabwe, have helped train African officers, and British Military Advisory and Training Teams have gained wide praise.

7. U.S. trainers write post-training intelligence reports and develop personal relations with potentially politically important officers. Trainers with the JCET program "learn about a country's edible and poisonous plants, insects, and animals, about water currents and prevailing winds, about what twigs in a forest crack under a human footfall. They improve their language skills and knowledge of foreign cultures and can evaluate the readiness of foreign troops, special operations officers say." "Free of Oversight, U.S. Military Trains Foreign Troops," *Washington Post,* July 12, 1998.

8. Ibid.

9. The United States has locked horns with Equatorial Guinea's repressive governments since the mid-1980s (Equatorial Guinea once expelled the U.S. ambassador, and in 1998 the United States opposed IMF funding for this country–only one of five such nations in the world.) Despite such diplomatic acrimony, the *Washington Post* notes that U.S. Army Special Forces "[continues] to train scores of local troops . . . in light infantry skills, including operations planning, [and] small unit tactics." *Washington Post,* July 12, 1998.

10. U.S. Special Forces trained the same Liberian units in the late 1970s that then overthrew President William Tolbert a year later. French troops trained the same Central African Republic troops in 1996 that then quickly carried out several mutinies and then attempted to overthrow President Patassé in 1997.

11. "Demilitarization for Democracy," *Fighting Retreat* (Washington, July 1997), pp. ii, 20. John Marks, president of Search for Common Ground, argues that "putting more weapons in the hands of the military in Africa is like putting more gasoline on the fire." "U.S. Deepens African Military Contacts," *Washington Post,* December 13, 1998.

12. Colonel Henk continues, however, that ample evidence exists of IMET's "value in promoting professional ethics." Henk, *Uncharted Paths, Uncertain Vision.*

13. NGOs helped to sell the U.S. government on supporting the creation of an all-African force, in part by raising the specter of mass slaughter in Burundi.

14. European and African skepticism subsequently persuaded George Moose, assistant secretary of state for African affairs, to propose designated national battalions rather than a standing force.

15. "News Hour with Jim Lehrer," Public Broadcasting System, October 15, 1996.

16. Peter Schraeder maintains that "U.S. policymakers have tended to ignore the African continent until some sort of politico-military crisis grabs their attention," and that this leads to "policy that often becomes driven by events, as opposed to the more desirable outcome of policy shaping events." Peter J. Schraeder, *United States Foreign Policy Toward Africa,* p. 2.

17. "None of our European allies would touch it." Interview with a U.S. Defense official, September 1998.

18. Jeffrey Herbst, *Securing Peace in Africa,* p. 21. Many French advisors, according to Herbst, felt that "the victories by English-speaking Tutsi in Rwanda and their allies in Congo-Kinshasa as part of an ambitious Anglo-Saxon plot to take over the African continent."

19. "France Looks for Ways to Keep Its African Influence Intact," *Jane's Defence Weekly,* October 23, 1996, p. 17.

20. Cited in Daniel Volman, "The Clinton Administration and the African Crisis Response Force," Africa News Service, March 24, 1997.

21. "Mr. Christopher Visits the Dark Continent," *The Independent,* October 19, 1996.

22. Among the favorable points were the absence of Western ground troops. The promised transfer of Western technology and skills was a definite incentive, as was the apparent absence of Western control: the United Nations would provide the sanction and the OAU and regional organizations would play some, albeit unspecified, role. The limited mandate of peacekeeping and the option of ACRI-trained and equipped states declining involvement in specific conflicts proved attractive.

23. William Foltz, "The Organization and the Resolution of Africa's Conflict," in Deng and Zartman, *Conflict Resolution in Africa,* p. 360.

24. "Clinton Administration Revamps Plans for Trouble-Shooting All-African Force," *Washington Post,* February 9, 1997.

25. These included Kofi Annan, then the UN's under secretary for peace-keeping operations, and Salim Salim, OAU secretary general.

26. T. A. Imoghibie, "An African High Command," *African Affairs* (April 1980).

27. "Lagos Not Impressed by US Proposal for an African Force," Panafrican News Agency, October 16, 1996.

28. "It must not come from one country, it should be the initiative of the U.N. In such a case it would receive wide support. Africans would like to feel that they are handling things themselves . . . not acting in response to suggestions that come from outside the continent." "U.S. Gives Details of African Force," Reuters, October 10, 1996, quoted in Gerry Cleaver, "The African Crisis Response Initiative," paper presented at the African Studies Association of the United Kingdom, University of London, September 1998.

29. "US Presses for All-Africa Crisis Force," *Washington Post,* September 28, 1996.

30. Interviews, June and July 1997.

31. Mindful of the ambiguous mandates in Somalia, U.S. officials even argued among themselves what "peacekeeping" might mean within an African context. Few planners advocated a peace-enforcing group but they widely disagreed about the peacekeeping role. Some argued that only safe havens for refugees should receive protection.

32. A point underlined by Chester Crocker, former assistant secretary of state for Africa: "There's a lot of unanswered questions. If we don't do it right, we'll wind up with a good initiative being undercut both at home and overseas." "All Things Considered," National Public Radio, October 7, 1996. Transcript #2359-11. NPR.

33. "U.S. Ready to Train African Peacekeepers," *Washington Post,* June 30, 1997.

34. McCallie's previous African experience includes serving as ambassador to Namibia in the early-mid 1990s and as the deputy chief of mission in South Africa and Zambia.

35. Dan Henk writes about U.S.-African security relationships that "the

importance of partnership cannot be overstressed. In fact, any semblance of patronization or neocolonialism affronts African sensitivities, diminishes U.S. influence, and must be strenuously avoided." Dan Henk, *Unchartered Paths, Uncertain Vision.*

36. EUCOM, "African Crisis Response Initiative (ACRI) Concept and Training Update," p. 5. Http://www/eucom.mil./programs/acri/ppgrafix/acriupdt.sld001.htm undated.

37. EUCOM, "African Crisis Response Initiative Concept and Training Update," p. 13.

38. Statement by Col. David McCracken, U.S. Department of Defense Briefing, July 29, 1997.

39. Follow-on training sessions 1, 3, and 5 would have about 40 soldiers, session 2 would have about 200, and session 4 would include a full battalion (approximately 750 soldiers).

40. The Green Berets are among the pre-eminent U.S. military trainers, despite their public association with counterinsurgency warfare.

41. Speech by Ambassador McCallie before the 19th Annual Forum of Parliamentarians for Global Action, October 7, 1997, p. 1.

42. "We think it is sensible for peacekeeping operations to be conducted with the approval of the Security Council of the United Nations, whether or not the peacekeeping operation is conducted by the UN." "ACRI Does Not Aim to Create an Army in Africa, McCallie Says." USIS Washington File, September 3, 1997, p. 2. Http://www.usia.gov/current/news/geog/af...af.html.

43. McCallie, 19th Annual Forum of Parliamentarians, October 7, 1997, cited in Levitt.

44. "Clinton, Diouf Discuss Bilateral Matters," Africa News Online, April 2, 1998. Http://www.africanews.org/west/senegal/stories

45. "US Troops Teach Peacekeeping to Africans," *The Washington Post,* September 26, 1997.

46. Robert Rotberg, preface to Jeffrey Herbst, *Securing Peace in Africa,* p. 5.

47. "Amb. Cohen Favors All-African Response Force," USIS Washington File, September 29, 1997, p. 1. Http://www.usia.gov./current/news/geog/af...

48. Rotberg, preface to Herbst, *Securing Peace in Africa,* p. 6

49. EUCOM, "African Crisis Response Initiative Concept and Training Update," p. 3.

50. "Joint US-African Peacekeeping Training Kicks off in Mali," USIS Washington File, February 26, 1998.

51. Khareen Pech, "The Hand of War: Mercenaries in the Former Zaire, 1996–97," in Musah and Fayemi, eds., *Mercenaries,* p. 147.

52. "Kampala Has Itself to Blame," *Monitor,* September 21, 1999.

53. "No Impunity in Uganda," *New Vision,* September 22, 1999.

54. Foreign Minister Tom Ikimi stated that "we are [however] very concerned at the . . . initiatives designed to divide us into Anglophone or Francophone Peacekeepers. We believe that this will result in a re-partitioning of Africa into spheres of influence." "Intervention by the Honorable Minister of Foreign Affairs Chief Tom Ikimi on the Various Initiatives from Outside Africa to Enhance Africa's Capacity for Peace Support Operations." Undated.

55. Military experts state that the SANDF's operational capabilities are

notably less than the apartheid era's SADF. Yet these same experts agree that the SANDF is still a remarkably professional force in Africa.

56. Some white officers and defense planners from the apartheid era question Washington's reliability, given its precipitous pullout from Angola in 1975. Interviews, 1997, 1998.

57. South African Government, White Paper on Defence, *Defence in a Democracy,* p. 15.

58. Col. Godwin Ugbo, Nigerian defense spokesman, states about ACRI "I do not know if it is feasible without Nigeria." "Lagos not Impressed by US Proposal," Panafrican News Agency, October 16, 1996.

59. International Peace Academy, p. 21. A Southern African participant stated, "We [in SADC] are not averse to this initiative. . . . But we are saying that all the efforts should be channeled through the OAU and that nothing should be done to try to undermine the cohesion and unity of the region and of Africa." International Peace Academy Conference, p. 22.

60. "While we can work with African partners to support sub-regional and regional training exercises, we recognize that it is for Africans themselves to determine what the appropriate command and control structures will be." McCallie "The African Crisis Response Initiative," p. 4.

61. Interview, New York City, November 1998.

62. International Peace Academy Conference, pp. 22–23. Well-respected African security experts forcefully stated this point at Akosombo, Ghana, July 1999.

63. Col. Karen U. Kwiatkowski, "African Crisis Response Initiative (ACRI): Past, Present and Future?" Directorate for EAF Implementation, DCS/A&SO Headquarters Air Force, August 1999, p. 2.

64. James Woods, "The African Crisis Response Initiative," Presentation to the World Peace Foundation Conference on African Peacekeeping, Cambridge, Mass., September 1997.

65. Interview, U.S. Department of Defense, August 2000.

66. *Africa News.*

67. "The Development of the Africa Crisis Response Initiative," *Africa Policy Report* (8, 31), March 1998, p. 3.

68. Gerry Cleaver, "The African Crisis Response Initiative," paper presented at the African Studies Association of the UK meeting, University of London, September 14–16, 1998, pp. 5–6.

69. EUCOM, "Africa Crisis Response Initiative Concept and Training Update," p. 2.

70. "The Africa Center for Strategic Studies (ACSS)," undated, p. 3.

71. "Mission Statement," African Center for Strategic Studies, undated.

72. The African Center for Strategic Studies has started a rotating series of seminars in Africa, beginning with Dakar, Senegal, in November 1999. The two-week Dakar conference had 120 participants and demonstrated how the West is moving away from its previous bilateralism. The participants came from forty-three Anglophone and Francophone countries, the OAU, ECOWAS, the East African Community, and SADC.

73. "Participants, " African Center for Strategic Studies, undated.

7

CONCLUSION:
TOWARD RESTORING THE
CIVIL-MILITARY DIVIDE

D amaging the political-military divide has debilitated Africa's security capabilities and its hopes for peaceful development. The three
possibilities for external security enhancements offered by regional
groupings, private security firms, and Western upgrades of national militaries can provide some military relief, but each carries significant
shortcomings, many of which are related to their being foreign.

Individual African states carry the major responsibility for their
own security. They should concentrate on restoring the damaged divide
between their political and military spheres and professionalize their
national militaries. Capable local forces, when compared to foreign
interveners, can reduce the chances of a potential conflict from occurring, possess military and political knowledge before the conflict's outset, legitimize the regime by displaying domestic backing (rather than
having it hire foreigners), and remain committed to resolving the struggle (without supporting potential "Frankenstein" militias). Competent
national militaries could form the building blocks for regional forces in
Africa and also assist UN interventions worldwide. Finally, militaries
sometimes determine Africa's movement toward democratization;
Bratton and van de Walle underline this point with "as went the military, so went the transition."[1]

But how to accomplish the professionalization? A state's political
ethos strongly determines the extent of its military's professionalism.
Africa's major security dilemma—the inverse relationship between military capabilities and political loyalty—will continue to undermine
Africa's security as long as personal rule continues. Unaccountable
rulers will cross the political-military divide and discourage military
capabilities. In contrast, democracy's separation of powers and its

potential transparency and accountability could upgrade national militaries, as argued below.

Yet, even assuming a transition to democracy, how does a new government persuade previously privileged officers to accept the new status quo? And does democratization, sometimes uncritically championed by Western countries, pose its own risks to Africa? For example, could the competitive domestic politics of new democracies encourage regional conflict (the third security dilemma), as Mansfield and Snyder suggest?[2]

In this chapter, after concluding remarks on ECOMOG, EO, and ACRI, I appraise the possible democratization-professionalization linkage: Will a state's political democratization likely aid military professionalism, and how might increased democratization and professionalism affect regional conflict?

The Limitations of ECOMOG, Executive Outcomes, and ACRI

ECOMOG

ECOMOG demonstrates the problems of ad hoc multilateralism and of relying on militaries created by personal-rule regimes. ECOMOG was formed in 1990 as the ECOWAS membership was dividing over the conflict in Liberia. ECOMOG began and then remained as a collection rather than a unity of separate national forces. It entered Liberia with no combined training, with insufficient knowledge of the conflict and its complexities, and with inadequate military capabilities. These initial deficiencies were excusable, given the speed of the intervention and West Africa's inexperience in such operations. But the foreign, that is, regional, ECOMOG did not markedly improve over nine years, as the 1999 Freetown fiasco in Sierra Leone demonstrated.[3]

ECOWAS's organizational weakness partially explains ECOMOG's failures. This voluntary economic grouping has never been a command organization buttressed by any supranational loyalty of its members, sufficient finances, or enforcement capability. A weak tree does not produce strong branches: any ECOWAS security offshoot would face challenges when trying to develop a strong central authority as well as common training, equipment, and selection criteria.

But the military unprofessionalism of ECOMOG's members—and Nigeria, in particular—proved the far more important reason for

ECOMOG's weaknesses. Personal rule was the biggest cause of military unprofessionalism. Rulers, fearful of effective but possibly disloyal forces, had blurred the civil-military divide and deliberately undermined professional military capabilities before 1990. Personal rule in Nigeria and elsewhere had allowed state presidents to privatize their forces by creating and supporting parallel forces that lowered the budgets and morale of the state militaries, by "buying off" active-duty officers in allowing them to enter business and politics concurrently, by purchasing irrelevant but costly equipment while not obtaining appropriate counterinsurgency equipment and training, and by diminishing the militaries' leadership capabilities when transferring or retiring officers (sometimes because of their superior military capabilities).

Personal rule strongly weakened most of the national ECOMOG contingents. In 1990, General Babangida's authoritarian government did not encourage public debate about the hastily announced intervention, and the country lacked a legislature or independent political parties that would focus public debate about the imminent deployment. Personal reasons influenced Nigeria's initial role: many observers have cited Babangida's close friendship with Doe to explain Nigeria's involvement. The sovereignty versus legitimacy dilemma arose. Doe's personal-rule regime was sovereign (although barely by 1990) but its demonstrable illegitimacy weakened ECOMOG's moral rationale. A possible desire by Babangida to exile potentially dissident officers as well as have personal access to Liberia's resources constitute other personal explanations.

Following 1990, Babangida and then Abacha harnessed Nigeria's dominance of ECOMOG to dampen international criticism of their domestic repression (a variant of the domestic-regional dilemma). They hoped that ECOMOG's crucial role in defending Liberia's stability would counter international criticism of Nigeria and, specifically, the possibility of oil sanctions. There is an intriguing but impossible to prove chance that Nigeria initially was content not to resolve the Liberian conflict because ECOMOG's presence served the political purposes of defusing international opposition, keeping possibly disloyal officers out of Nigeria, and financially rewarding numerous Nigerians and other West Africans.

Nigeria's authoritarian rulers consciously continued to undermine Nigerian force capabilities, despite the increasingly clear lessons of ECOMOG, and their fear of an improved military appears the most likely explanation. U.S. intelligence officials contend that Abacha did not permit any field exercises of any Nigerian units above company level between 1996 and mid-1998, and that during this time Abacha removed many of Nigeria's more professional officers and replaced them with relative sycophants.

Nigeria's authoritarian rule hurt ECOMOG in other ways. The hypocrisy of a decidedly undemocratic state seeking credit for defending democracy abroad undoubtedly undermined ECOMOG's legitimacy (Nigeria, of course, was not the only undemocratic state in ECOMOG in 1990). The Nigerian government's domestic repression and its apparent complicity in the international drug trade compelled the U.S. government to "decertify" Nigeria and to exclude it from U.S. military equipment and training. Nigerian defense experts state that the U.S. policy restricted Nigeria's military capabilities, especially in the repair of its C-130 transport planes.[4]

ECOMOG can claim some limited achievements. It did enter the Liberian conflict, which more powerful nations had largely ignored, and in Monrovia it prevented probable bloodbaths in 1990 and 1992. Its military presence, and its support of Liberian anti-NPFL factions, undoubtedly convinced Charles Taylor to accept a ceasefire and elections. But ECOMOG also prolonged the conflict and its suffering and refused to learn from its mistakes.

Executive Outcomes and Other Private Security Companies

Executive Outcomes demonstrated in Angola and Sierra Leone the advantages of an established and professional intervention force. It proved that a military force can achieve a breathing space for peaceful negotiations and elections. EO had two advantages over ECOMOG: it came from a political system that had encouraged military professionalism, and it was already a capable and unified force when it intervened in Angola and Sierra Leone. Despite the South Africans' odoriferous apartheid baggage, EO acted in a more politically responsible way than had ECOMOG. EO's generally nonabusive treatment of civilians assisted its intelligence-gathering capabilities and diluted public suspicion. EO was a profit-seeking force, but it did not engage in the blatant theft so often associated with those ECOMOG units that won the "everything covered or movable or gone" epithet. Some observers have oversold EO's battlefield successes, but its Angolan and Sierra Leonean successes, albeit strongly aided by local forces, remain impressive in the African context and offer some valuable lessons.

But EO also demonstrated the costs of relying on private security companies (PSCs) for a state's primary security. "Mercenaries" may increase a regime's hold over its sovereignty but lessen its political legitimacy: for-profit companies can gain long-term economic concessions at a price that weakens a country's long-term development. They can anger a national military by garnering superior resources, by attracting more attention, and by earning larger salaries. A foreign force can achieve only a fragile military victory, rather than a long-lasting political solution. Most PSCs have noted EO's passing and offer their services as a complement to, rather than a replacement of, national militaries.

The African Crisis Response Initiative

The initiative breaks new ground by addressing Africa's needs for both national professional militaries and regional intervention capability. It has some success in addressing the dilemmas of capabilities versus loyalty and sovereignty versus legitimacy but has difficulty when dealing with the security dilemmas of domestic versus regional stabilizing and democratization versus destabilization.

ACRI stresses professionalism by (1) training only those militaries that have a nonpraetorian history and that come from purportedly democratizing states, (2) emphasizing the need for both civilian and military officials to respect the civil-military divide, and (3) upgrading some glaring military needs, including national logistics and communications capability and regional interoperability. As with other current African and non-African programs, ACRI works to lessen the ad hocism that plagued ECOMOG. ACRI's peacekeeping emphasis deals with the efficiency-loyalty dilemma by not offering enough offensive training and equipment to worry insecure rulers. And, ACRI does not operate in situ. France's RECAMP and Britain's Centres of Excellence provide similar or complementary training and equipment.

ACRI has significant problems. ACRI's peacekeeping emphasis and its limited number of trained troops sprinkled throughout the national militaries will also curtail ACRI's overall contribution to African security. Personal rule in some of the ACRI countries (Uganda being a primary example) will blunt the initiative's effectiveness. The often unpredictable regional expansionism of some of the domestically reformist regimes will likely undercut the effectiveness of ACRI, either by forcing ACRI to postpone training of specific forces or by discouraging congressional funding. ACRI training may also aid regional conflict should political pressures in democratizing states prompt cross-border military adventurism. Unpopular regional expansionism or human rights abuses by an ACRI-trained force could pose political problems for the United States.

The Foreign Factor

Their foreign origins ultimately hindered ECOMOG, EO, and ACRI/ACSS. External forces find that African states and factions judge these forces by their members' political baggage. Politically, EO's often noted apartheid provenance and its association with multinational mining companies immediately cast suspicion on its intentions. Nigeria, since independence, has raised regional fears of possible hegemony, and its dominance of ECOMOG encouraged such worries and probably reduced international support for ECOMOG. Also, Nigeria's domestic political and human rights record morally undercut ECOMOG's claim of defending regional democracy and its ability to attract foreign support. Militarily, the outside forces' ignorance about the operational areas hampered operations, especially those of ECOMOG.

Foreign intervention forces' missions are temporary, and unforeseen disasters may speed the forces' departure before they complete their task. This occurred with the UN in Somalia following the 1993 Olympic Hotel firefight and almost happened with ECOMOG in Sierra Leone following the RUF's entry into Freetown in early 1999. Outside forces' impermanent stay may further prolong the conflict by exacerbating existing local differences, militarizing local personnel, and leaving behind military supplies.

Even when foreign interveners complete the primary task, this is often insufficient for continued security. International forces often fail to train local personnel to assume control following the former's departure. In Sierra Leone, the vicious AFRC easily overthrew the Kabbah government, which lacked a competent army, a few months after EO's departure. ECOMOG, at best, provided limited training in both Liberia and Sierra Leone.

Several factors account for this absence of training: the interveners' focus on their primary task, limitations in qualified manpower, and a desire (by either the intervener, the local government, or foreign governments and lending agencies) that the force leave following a ceasefire. Charles Taylor forbade ECOMOG training of a new Liberian military, despite a common understanding that this would happen. Liberia and Sierra Leone by early 2000 each had perhaps a 5,000-man "army," which displayed little conventional training or discipline. The aura of illegitimacy suggested by relying on foreign soldiers, particularly "mercenaries," is another disadvantage of an outside force.

The foreign origin and funding of ACRI and ACSS cast suspicion on their intent. The political baggage of the United States includes accusations of historically not supporting liberation struggles in black Africa as well as skepticism about self-serving motives, arrogance, and political interference. Many African security experts dispute the general Western assumption that African forces need more training. ACRI's dependence upon year-by-year budgeting by an easily distracted Congress has made some Africans question, at least initially, whether to participate in the temporary program.

Yet each of these foreign innovations—ECOMOG, EO, and ACRI/ACSS—has broken new ground. ECOMOG created a precedent for regional forces, and its continuing nature has encouraged African and Western policymakers to support it and other regional force concepts. EO vividly demonstrated the effectiveness of a small but capable force. ACRI has shone the spotlight on the need for professional national militaries and interoperable regional forces. Yet each of these innovations offers only limited answers, largely because of their foreign roots: in the final analysis, African states must largely rely on themselves to create their own capable militaries.

The continuing personal rule by many of Africa's "new leaders" suggests that they will not act against what they perceive as their own political and financial interests. The tension between the two major components of military professionalism—technical capabilities and political responsibility—as well as widespread corruption within militaries, argue strongly that many African states will not quickly obtain professional forces to rectify the shifting balance of military power (Museveni's Uganda, where Salim Saleh and others undermine military professionalism, is a notable example). Without the democratic qualities of transparency, accountability, and meritocracy, many African militaries will remain corrupt and usually ineffective, regardless of whatever image they can create in Western eyes.

Political Democratization and the Civil-Military Divide

Professionalism and democratization are often closely linked. Military professionalism benefits from accountable and institutionalized governments that agree not to cross the civil-military divide but whose oversight may often benefit the armed forces' operational effectiveness.

Equally, democracy depends on nonpretorian security forces to protect the unfettered discussion of issues.

An inept selling of democratization to the military can bungle a democratic transition from authoritarianism. Huntington warns that reform and political change "may contribute not to political stability but to greater instability . . . [and] encourage demands for still more changes which can easily snowball."[5] A professional military with loyalty toward a constitutional state may aid this reform process, by either checking vengeful actions by those previously persecuted or any final violent convulsions by the old order.

A first glance suggests a positive link between democratization and professionalism in Africa.[6] Botswana and Senegal, for example, are among those countries with relatively high levels of political accountability and military professionalism; both their governments and militaries respect the civil-military divide. On the other hand, Africa's more despotic rulers generally have produced notably unprofessional security forces, the armed forces of Mobutu's Zaire and Amin's Uganda being two of the more obvious examples. Whereas some militaries have not needed democracies to build their operational capabilities—Nazi Germany is an obvious example—competent armed forces that also display political loyalty to the state are usually found in democracies.

A nascent democratization-professionalism linkage characterizes the recent Central and Latin American departures from authoritarianism. Juan Rial notes that "during the 1980's all of Latin America's military governments gave way to freely elected successors . . . [and] military subordination to elected civilian authority is becoming the regional norm."[7] The military and civilian sectors increasingly assert that functional autonomy serves their separate interests, as well as those of the state. Various officers state that political intrusions typical of authoritarianism increased military factionalization and indiscipline. At the same time, Huntington claims, civilians have come to see the dangers of crossing the political-military divide. They realize "that playing politics with the military is playing with a two-edged sword and that a politically neutral professional establishment is most congruent with their interests."[8] Concomitant with this process, the militaries' share of national budgets has declined in most Latin American countries.[9]

Analogies to Latin America are dangerous, in part because democratization is proving much harder to implement in Africa. Bratton and van de Walle believe that "the democratic gains of 1990 to 1994 . . . are eroding" and that personal rule, often with the formal trappings of democracy, is reasserting itself.[10] Specific problems include an underdeveloped national political culture ("democracy...is not possible without democrats"),[11] the lack of economic reform and development,[12] the continuing weaknesses of governing institutions and civic society,[13] and the increased possibility of military intervention during democratization. This last point is especially threatening because, as Bratton and van de Walle note, "the risk of military intervention is most likely to increase when elected governments attempt to wean senior officers from the patrimonial benefits to which they have become accustomed."[14]

Yet Africa is far more democratic now than during the Cold War. Several important individual states have achieved remarkable progress, notably South Africa and Nigeria, and the continent has moved away from de jure one-party states. Over half of Africa's heads of state by 1999 had acquired power from truly contested elections, whereas only three rulers had gained office that way by 1975. Whether Africa manages to institutionalize lasting democracy remains uncertain and will require both time and considerable effort.[15] Should African states backslide on democratization, the chances for professional militaries will recede.

Will the Military Accept Political Democratization?

The military sometimes supports democratic transitions. Bratton and van de Walle note thirteen cases of an independent military intercession during the early-mid 1990s, of which seven "were supportive of democratic initiatives."[16] African pretorianism sometimes assists democratization. Military abstinence from civilian politics is an integral aspect of armed forces professionalism in Western countries, but these states have well-established methods for preventing government tyranny. Few African countries have effective checks and balances against despotism other than the military. Therefore, military coups may sometimes aid, rather than oppose, democratization—but only if the intervention is temporary and encourages wider political participation. Officers who overthrew autocratic presidents and then encouraged democratic processes leading to elections include the exemplary Amadou Toumani Touré of Mali in 1991[17] and the coup leaders in Mali in 1999.[18]

Yet, the military may worry about the "messiness" of the transition—heated criticism of the government and military, public strikes, and possible violence—and feel a patriotic duty to stage a "guardian" coup against the transition. Ethnically based factions within militaries have been known to intervene when they find fault with the election results. And, individual officers may resent the threatened loss of financial and political privileges threatened by a more transparent and accountable government.

Negative Incentives.   Both negative and positive incentives can encourage military loyalty to civilian authority. For one, international and domestic pressure may persuade the military to accept a transition to democracy. Bratton and van de Walle maintain that the West has generally proven intolerant of coups against democracies in this post-Cold War era.[19] Diplomatic nonrecognition, unavailability of foreign (including military) assistance, and restrictions upon international travel (official invitations or issuing of visas, for example) are some possible sanctions. The world's refusal to recognize Sierra Leone's AFRC junta in 1997 was an encouraging first step, as was the OAU's pronouncement in Harare in 1997 that it would not tolerate coups against elected governments (however, such statements did not serve as lasting precedents).

Countervailing domestic institutions can discourage military pretorianism following the initial transition.[20] That a government is popularly elected will offer less justification and often more domestic and international opposition to possible pretorianism. Dissidents will usually prefer to work peacefully within a representative political system rather than support violence.

Specific governmental offices can exert some influence. A ministry of defense staffed by civil servants can provide effective oversight of budget, procurement, training, and pay. Democratically elected legislatures, especially through their defense and finance committees, acquire considerable influence when they decide about military budgets, publicly question officers, examine specific security policies, and authorize declarations of war or foreign deployment.[21] State investigations into past security malfeasance might discourage future misbehavior. Examples include South Africa's Truth and Reconciliation Commission and Nigeria's Human Rights Violations Investigation Panel. Finally, the elimination of ethnically homogeneous security units should lessen pretorianism; culturally pluralistic units might prove self-checking and be less likely to overthrow governments.

Well-publicized and enforceable military codes of conduct establish appropriate behavior. Forbidding of conflicts of interest should lessen political or economic motives for military enlistment and focus a soldier's attention on defense needs. Specific strictures could include forbidding active duty officers from holding political (or business) office and wearing uniforms when off duty or publicly supporting a specific party or candidate. Senegal goes so far as to prohibit its soldiers from voting, and the South African Defence Force Act of 1970 barred soldiers from partisan political activity.[22] Mali's 1997 military code has won accolades for its inclusiveness and enforcement capabilities.

Yet these negative influences usually lack teeth, owing to a lack of commitment and knowledge. International and African sanctions, even against military overthrows of democratically elected governments, usually prove ineffective. Even though the world refused to recognize Sierra Leone's AFRC junta, the UN arms embargo forbade military shipments to the ousted Kabbah government and other West African countries reportedly continued to aid the despotic junta. Few countries took measures against Angola in 1997 when it supplied military forces to help dissidents in Congo-Brazzaville overthrow the elected government of Pascal Lissouba, even though Angola's intervention occurred after the OAU's Harare declaration against military takeovers.

How to explain the ineffectiveness? Bratton and van de Walle note that the West views stability as more important than incipient democratization. Neither the West nor the UN will use combat troops against despotic rulers and only rarely will impose far-reaching sanctions. Availability of weapons on the private market undercuts official arms embargoes. In Africa, some African states support neighboring movements, many governments cannot patrol their own borders, and state investigations into military abuses are often ineffective because they can trigger a painful reaction.

Lack of knowledge restricts oversight; civilians must be able to understand the military to oversee its activities. Yet few African parliamentarians, reporters, and civic groups have specialized knowledge of military doctrine, strategy, tactics, and equipment.[23] Even African officers sometimes lament what a Guinean commander describes as "civilian incomprehension" of military matters.[24] This ignorance about the military has limited the development of national security strategies and has hurt the effectiveness of parliamentary defense committees. For example, Ghana's Parliamentary Select Committee on Defence has few well-informed critics of the military: in one informal conversation, two of the committee's members could not recall how many battalions (six) composed the national military.[25]

Independent expertise is crucial. Military officers, given their special status and expert understanding of often arcane weapons systems, can become what Claude Welch terms "the most skillful practitioners of budgetary politics."[26] Several retired officers sit on Ghana's defense committee, ostensibly to offer their expertise, but their detractors believe that they strongly lobby for military interests. Establishing free-dom-of-information access while restricting the extent of document classification, encouraging public legislative hearings, training media defense specialists, and sometimes summoning the expertise of retired military officers can increase public knowledge.[27] Conscription could provide the civilian sector with military knowledge gained during sol-diers' usually short service of several years before they reenter the civil-ian sector. Yet few African countries have national military service.[28]

Overzealous classification on grounds of "national security" will limit public understanding as well as prolong a directive, rather than a consultative, budget process. Hutchful relates a conversation with two senior parliamentarians from a purportedly democratizing nation. One of the legislators recalls how the defense committee had passed its first defense budget: "On the day in question the Minister of Defense came to the National Assembly. He explained that as this was a confidential security document, it could not be discussed by the Assembly. In accor-dance with tradition therefore we passed it [the military budget] without debate."[29]

Civilian authority must be willing to enforce penalties against mili-tary malfeasance. Security oversight must extend beyond the military and include the intelligence services and parallel forces, for example, presidential guards, which often hold deep allegiances to the ancien régime. But few African countries have an accepted tradition of civilian oversight, whereas many African militaries have a history of overthrow-ing civilian rule and of sometimes bullying government officials. Enforcement of oversight may require individual courage.[30] And, even though strong budgetary oversight might improve military capabilities, it could also trigger political disloyalty if generals use their monopoly of military power against reformist civilians.

Positive Incentives.   Negative incentives alone will not suffice, and any assertion that the military simply must accept democracy may violently backfire. The armed forces wield inordinate power in political systems that lack other powerful national institutions. Democratization advo-cates sometimes overlook a powerful selling point of democratization: that politically accountable systems can augment military effectiveness, and that such upgrading can legitimize the democratizing government for much of the officer corps.

Specific advantages offered by democratization include structural autonomy, transparency and accountability, and foreign military assistance. Civilian respect for the civil-military divide, which occurs more often in democratizing states, permits officers to control strictly military affairs. "Civil-military conflict can be controlled and confidence enhanced," writes Larry Diamond, "if civilian leaders always accord the military a position of high status, honor, and income."[31] South Africa's White Paper on Defence notes that "civil-military relations will be stable only [with] the fulfilment of certain responsibilities towards the SANDF . . . [including] not interfer[ing] in the military chain of command, the application of the Military Discipline Code or operational matters which are the authority of military commanders."[32] In other words, African militaries should not suffer from such presidentially mandated indignities of one bullet per soldier or political prohibitions against training.

Accountable governments try to refrain from employing their militaries domestically, a point that officers appreciate.[33] Internal policing can politicize a military and create internal fissures. The development of a competent national police force relieves the military from having to intervene in its own country.

Democracy's inherent transparency can abet operational capability. Militaries answerable to budget-controlling and publicity-creating legislatures may improve their procurement practices (e.g., fewer procurement kickbacks). Personal rule has often encouraged kleptocratic officers to gain valuable contracts for themselves, rather than to enhance operational capability. In the late 1990s, the Nigerian government allocated almost $1 billion for "defence spending"; no other public explanation was forthcoming.[34] Publishing government tenders and governmental scrutiny encourage competition: multiple bids that can be scrutinized for possible favoritism or conflict of interest, in effect, providing "more bang for the buck."

A more transparent and accountable government is likely to address the military's standard-of-living concerns that, while often regarded as mundane by outside observers, have precipitated some coups. Financial matters are especially important; the National Democratic Institute (NDI) notes that "many of the military uprisings that occurred in [African] transitioning countries . . . were over the nonpayment of salaries."[35] Unpaid soldiers delegitimize their government and military when they resort to stealing from civilians (Mobutu's Forces Armées Zaïroises and elements of ECOMOG in Liberia are two examples

among many). Regular payments to soldiers on active duty and assured
retirement benefits, as well as adequate housing, medical treatment,
home leave, and educational benefits, can help secure military loyalty.

Downsizing the militaries, a desire of many post-authoritarian governments, will usually increase technical capabilities. Purported manpower size in African armies often offers little correlation to military
strength. Personnel costs sometimes account for 80 percent of African
military budgets and leave few resources for training and procurement.
"Ghost soldiers," nonexistent individuals created by officers who pock-
et the extra pay, plague many African forces's operational effectiveness.
Computerized photo-identification cards, by quantifying exact force
numbers, can eliminate superfluous payments and assist strategic planners by providing more accurate knowledge of unit size. Downsizing
does pose problems, however. It may not release more funds for civilian
purposes, and the government may have to offer civilian employment to
the former soldiers.[36]

Changes such as improved procurement initially will aid operational effectiveness and can secure other future benefits from a publicly accountable government. The NDI states that "if the population is
cognizant of reforms within the military, they are more likely to support an increase in salaries, as was the case in Mali where the population supported a three-fold increase for soldiers between 1992 and
1994."[37]

Public accountability should discourage parallel militaries and
domestic military deployment, two hallmarks of personal rule and
unprofessional militaries. Demobilization of the often ethnicized presidential guards, state-sponsored militias, and party-dominated intelligence units should provide more resources and pride to the national
military as well as symbolize the government's more inclusive nature.
Civilian control should spread to the state's intelligence apparatus.

Democratization can encourage military cooperation when the
reformist government attracts foreign military aid. For example, ACRI
has a requirement that it assist only nonauthoritarian governments;
alternatively, U.S. legislation mandates the suspension of military assistance to governments created by coups against democratizing governments. A state's democratizing reputation aids in its military being
selected for international peacekeeping missions. Such peacekeeping
can provide the country and its military with significant foreign
exchange and heightened international status. Service with internation-
ally respected militaries also imparts specialized knowledge and training opportunities.

President Obasanjo and the Nigerian Military: A Case Study

Previously authoritarian states will encounter obstacles that hinder military reform. Nigeria by mid-2000 clearly saw the need for professional militaries. But President Obasanjo faced immediate security needs while also worrying about a backlash from some officers opposed to security reforms.

Obasanjo wisely cited potential military gains when justifying democratization to the officer corps. His 1999 inaugural address linked past authoritarianism to weakened professionalism and noted that "a great deal of re-orientation has to be undertaken and a redefinition of roles, retraining, and re-education will have to be done to ensure that the military submits to civil authority and regains its pride, professionalism, and tradition."[38]

Some benefits from democratization did quickly accrue to the military following Obasanjo's democratic election in February 1999. Foreign states began aiding the Nigerian military. The United States, for example, provided spare parts and restarted its International Military Education and Training program for Nigeria and assisted in rebuilding Nigeria's C-130 fleet. President Clinton signed a presidential decision directive that allows the United States to provide military support to ECOMOG (of which Nigeria had been the biggest funder). The U.S. government also sponsored MPRI, a private security company, to advise the ministry of defence on civil-military relations and, specifically, how to design budgets for legislative review and update such administrative procedures as payroll management.

By April 2000, the U.S. government had formulated a $10 million military assistance plan to help Nigeria develop a civilian-controlled Ministry of Defence and a better administrative and maintenance program. It included "a transparent budget process, control over personnel and promotion systems, military pay, all the things we take for granted in our own system that are not taken for granted in Nigeria," observes a senior U.S. military official.[39] The United States also hopes to help Nigeria's maintenance capabilities ("They have a lot of tanks, they have a lot of fighters," comments a U.S. official. "Actually they have a lot of stationary tanks and a lot of stationary fighters.")[40] Washington also will help fund a retraining center for demobilized soldiers and will spend $20 million on combat training of five Nigerian (and one Ghanaian) battalions for combat operations in Sierra Leone. Britain, Nigeria's former colonial ruler, also has offered training and equipment to Nigeria's military.

The United States has guarded hopes of success. Despite successive Nigerian presidents having reduced the military's professionalism, the force still retains some highly-regarded officers who support Obasanjo's reprofessionalism philosophy. Peter Lewis writes that "declining national stability, growing external isolation, and eroding unit and *esprit* within the armed forces had evidently convinced a segment of the military leadership that genuine political reform was necessary."[41] That Nigeria paid $3 million, to supplement the $10 million provided by the United States, demonstrated to U.S. planners an apparent commitment by the Obasanjo government.

But Nigeria's slow pace (as of August 2000) of military reform underlined several difficulties. The government's only major reform was its retiring of some 200 senior and mid-level military and police officers of questionable loyalty or effectiveness.

Domestic threats along with ethnic, regional, and personal interests discouraged such improvements. Rising armed violence in the Niger Delta and in western and northern Nigeria claimed some 500 lives during Obasanjo's first year. As a new ruler, Obasanjo needed a loyal security force to deal with immediate threats to stability before attempting long-term reforms.

Minorities in the oil-rich delta had long contended that successive governments had not compensated them in the exploitation of this natural resource.[42] Militant groups, often armed, had occupied some oil installations by mid-1999, held hostages for ransom, and fought against government security units (as well as among themselves). Religious, ethnic, and regional divisions have asserted themselves as mostly Hausa Muslims from the north fought Yoruba Christians from the west.

Regional-ethnic worries have restricted military reorganization. The north has virtually monopolized Nigeria's state house since independence, and some northerners, already angry that a Yoruba was in power, apparently believed that Obasanjo was demonstrating deliberate regional bias in his forced retirement of military and police officers, many of whom were northerners. Several Western analysts believe that the government fears that further reductions in the officer corps could provoke ethnic conflict.

The military understands, but does not appreciate, the government's need to deploy it domestically. The 1999 insertion of troops into Odi, Bayelsa State, underlined the military's limitations as domestic policemen. The 2,000 soldiers responded to some limited attacks by indiscriminately killing several hundred residents and razing Odi to the ground.[43] Chief of Army Staff Victor Malu emphasized that the present military lacked policing abilities: "We do not feel too comfortable being asked to go in to assist the police in the type of situation like what happened in Odi. When we go in, we do not act in a police role . . . if you are firing at me, by my training and my professionalism I do not fire to injure you, I fire to take off your head."[44]

An effective police force would greatly assist Nigerian stability and eliminate the government's need to employ its military inside the country. But the Nigerian police force is woefully understaffed, suffers from reportedly systemic corruption, and often mistreats the citizenry.[45] The government has announced an ambitious five-year program to upgrade the police force in quality and quantity.

The personal interests of some officers and enlisted men have hampered Obasanjo's proposed reforms. Peter Lewis writes that for contemporary Nigeria to "rein in a recalcitrant military elite . . . [is] perhaps the most sensitive and difficult challenge to constitutional government."[46] Western observers believe that some lower ranking officers (captains and majors), who during the Abacha period had assumed that they would eventually tap into government largesse, opposed being excluded from such privileges. Officers worried that their existing patronage networks, based partly on extended-family connections, would disappear. The continuation of corruption in the civilian sector has added to the officers' anger. As one colonel remarked, "We want to resist corruption but we see civilians getting the goodies and so we have asked ourselves, 'why should we be left behind?' It's just human nature."[47]

Demobilizing 5,000–10,000 soldiers had been a major goal, and Defense Minister Theophilus Danjuma has argued that downsizing would raise effectiveness. "If we keep a smaller and better trained army, it would do a better job rather than a larger and less equipped army."[48] Yet several fears, especially a possible negative reaction from newly unemployed soldiers and the inability of the Nigerian economy to absorb them, forced Obasanjo in late 1999 to state that the Nigerian military would remain at its present size.

Investigations into past malfeasance, while serving, it is hoped, as an object lesson for current officers, may trigger additional difficulties. "General Babangida may not stand idly by while he is accused," London's *Guardian* writes about Nigeria's investigative panel. "The general commands a small fortune and still has many friends in the army."[49]

President Obasanjo has been clearly saddened by the woeful state of Nigeria's military, but several pressing domestic security threats and the difficulty in weaning officers from a privileged existence illustrate the difficulties faced by a democratizing state when trying to reform its military.

Domestic Democratization and Regional Stabilization

Democratization could well assist national military professionalism, but its effect on regional conflict is less clear. Mansfield and Snyder suggest a possibility for destabilization. They accept that "mature democratic states have virtually never fought wars against each other," yet they also argue that "promoting democracy may not promote peace because states are especially war-prone during the *transition* toward democracy [emphasis added]."[50] Chauvinistic nationalism can easily accompany democratization as "newly ambitious elites and the embattled old ruling groups often use appeals to nationalism to stay astride their unmanageable political coalitions."[51] Gilbert Khadiagala writing about postcolonial Africa suggests that "elites in search of respite from mounting internal conflicts often find solace in border wars."[52]

Although this has rarely happened in Africa, one possible example is the conflict between Ethiopia and Eritrea (Ethiopia being the more democratic of the two states). Popular pressure in both countries encouraged the continution of major conventional fighting, which began in May 1998, between the two previously friendly states. Patrick Gilkes notes that "a central point of this crisis is that neither Prime Minister Meles Zenawi nor President Issaias Afeworki can afford to be seen to back down. Both are rather weak[er] politically than they have been and both have seen this crisis as a valuable way to tap into national feeling and regain support slipping away."[53]

The major counterargument to Snyder and Mansfield is that democratization's accountability, as shown in unfettered public debate, increased access to information, and future elections, will compel regimes to focus on the needs of their constituents and reject expensive foreign interventions—especially if they involve peace enforcement. Indeed the constitutions of some African countries restrict their executives' ability to deploy forces abroad.[54]

Such restraints were not always in place in early 2000. The presidents of Zimbabwe, Namibia, Angola, and Uganda had neither advised nor sought permission from their parliaments before sending troops into the Congo conflict. Despite little overt public support—and, indeed, growing opposition—most of the governments that dispatched units in 1997 and 1998 were still keeping forces in Congo in late 2000. The absence of long-standing institutions, including a strong civil society, parliament, and judiciary, had facilitated the regional adventurism.

But the Congo conflict could prove a watershed, demonstrating the political and economic dangers to African states of using their troops in foreign upheavals. The continued toll on domestic economies, the growing reticence of international lenders, and an unknown amount of internal military bitterness about rising losses could polarize opposition and eventually force troop withdrawals. Most of the countries engaging in intervention reportedly were searching for ways to gracefully leave the unresolved Congo conflict. Chad withdrew its 2,000 troops in 1999 following two "friendly-fire" exchanges with incompetent Congolese units, and press reports suggested that experienced Congolese associated with Osleg, the joint mineral-marketing company, had taken Zimbabwe for an embarrassing economic ride.[55]

Conversely, authoritarian rulers probably have significant power to deploy their militaries with inpunity, given the absence of institutional restraints. As of mid-1998, the Abacha government had not released documentation about the financial costs or the number of Nigerian casualties resulting from its eight-year ECOMOG involvement. Opponents of the regime in Ghana told this author of the difficulty in rallying public sentiment without any figures detailing ECOMOG's costs to Ghana.

Africa faces a worrisome security future. The restraints of the Cold War have largely disappeared, as insurgencies and invading militaries threaten state stability and as Africa possesses no silver security bullet to repulse these threats. Regional military groupings, private security assistance, and Western upgrading of African military professionalism offer some benefits but provide, at best, only partial hope to Africa. Military professionalism can be achieved only when national governments no longer see competent militaries as a domestic political threat. Yet many personal-rule regimes continue to prevent greater accountability, and well-intentioned reformist regimes encounter immediate needs as well as entrenched elites who will oppose heightened military professionalism. Political democratization may well hold the key to Africa's security, but such reform will be slow in coming.

Notes

1. Bratton and van de Walle, *Democratic Experiments in Africa,* p. 217.
2. Mansfield and Snyder, "Democratization and War."

3. This point is arguable. A U.S. expert on African militaries notes that "Freetown was [also] a really hard test. It would be hard to find any conventionally trained and armed military that could do well against a motivated guerrilla force." Personal correspondence, December 1998.

4. Interviews with Nigerian defense attachés, Embassy of Nigeria, Washington, D.C., February and March 2000.

5. Samuel P. Huntington, *Political Order in Changing Societies,* p. 363.

6. Civilian control is usually, although not always, a result of democratic control. Ghana, which has not had a coup since late 1981, has achieved self-imposed restraint from its military. Institutional mechanisms remain weak. The U.S. Institute of Peace notes that "public accountability and parliamentary restraint remain weak" as does legal force in maintaining constitutional and legal rights. David R. Smock, ed., "Creative Approaches to Managing Conflict in Africa." U.S. Institute of Peace, April 1997, p. 13.

7. Juan Rial, "Armies and Civil Society in Latin America," in Diamond and Plattner, *Civil-Military Relations and Democracy,* pp. 51, 57.

8. Samuel P. Huntington, "Reforming Civil-Military Relations," in Diamond and Plattner, *Civil-Military Relations and Democracy,* p. 7

9. Rial, "Armies and Civil Society," in Diamond and Plattner, *Civil-Military Relations and Democracy,* p. 57.

10. Bratton and van de Walle, *Democratic Experiments in Africa,* p. 233.

11. Ibid., p. 235.

12. "A wide range of socioeconomic attainments that increase with national income correlate well with consolidated democracy." Ibid., p. 237. They also note that governments' playing a major political role increases the "control of the state and its resources [as] the primary end of politics," p. 239.

13. Ibid., pp. 246–255.

14. Ibid., p. 245.

15. John Harbeson and Donald Rothchild write that "a critical and relatively unexamined question [is] to what extent and under what circumstances may democratic initiatives not just represent ends in themselves but display instrumental importance in either furthering or undermining the strengthening of states?" "The African State and State System in Flux," *Africa in World Politics,* p. 9.

16. Bratton and van de Walle, *Democratic Experiments in Africa,* p. 211. The seven were Benin, Congo, Lesotho, Madagascar, Malawi, Mali, and South Africa.

17. Col. Amadou Toumani Touré, a paratroop commander, supported Mali's democratic transition. Touré balked at the government's brutal quelling of public protests and thereupon installed a transitional government, apologized for past military crimes, and oversaw the convening of a national conference, a constitutional referendum, and elections. Touré then departed public life when a democratically elected government took office.

18. Following the shooting of Gen. Ibrahim Baré Mainassara, Niger's military ruler, in April 1999, Maj. Daouda Mallam Wanke quickly implemented a timetable that led to an accepted October election of the new president.

19. They do caution, however, that international opposition has its limits. Bratton and van de Walle, *Democratic Experiments in Africa,* p. 241.

20. Ghana is one country that seemingly has civilian control of the mili-

tary: the civilian president as commander in chief can remove disloyal officers, the parliament votes on the nominee for minister of defence, an auditor-general inspects military finances, and both the cabinet and parliament (which includes a Select Committee on Defence), can publicly discuss and then vote on the defense budget.

21. South Africa's Joint Standing Committee on Defence "shall be competent to investigate and make recommendations on the budget, functioning, organisation, armaments, policy, morale and state of preparedness of the SANDF." South African Government, White Paper on Defence, *Defence in a Democracy* (Pretoria: Ministry of Defence, 1998), p. 7.

22. Furthermore, "no member of the Regular Force shall hold office in any political party or political organisation. Military personnel shall not attend political meetings in uniform save where they are on official duty." Ibid., p. 11.

23. Rial notes that the same problem confronts Latin American countries. "Achieving military subordination to civilian authority is made even more difficult by the frequent absence of a civilian elite knowledgeable about military issues and capable of exercising effective oversight." Rial, "Armies and Civil Society in Latin America," in Diamond and Plattner, *Civil-Military Relations and Democracy*, p. 58.

24. "The Role of the Legislature in Defense and National Security Issues," Seminar, National Democratic Institute, Dakar, April 19–22, 1999, p. 3.

25. Conversation in Ghana, July 1999.

26. Claude Welch, "Civilian Control of the Military: Myth and Reality," in Claude Welch, ed., *Civilian Control of the Military*, p. 9.

27. Ghana's proposed Right to Information Bill of 1999 is one such example. See Justice P. D. Anin, "The Right to Information Bill, 1999 (draft), Institute of Economic Affairs, Accra, Ghana, 1999.

28. Financial costs and a lower force readiness are two reasons. Ongoing basic training of entering soldiers incurs considerable expense and may detract from developing more specialized capabilities.

29. Hutchful, "Military Policy and Reform," *Journal of Modern African Studies* (June 1997), p. 52.

30. Again, Rial notes the similarity with Latin America. "In Latin America as in other developing regions, the task of overseeing the armed forces is a thankless one that creates powerful enemies and rarely enhances political careers." Rial, "Armies and Civil Society in Latin America," p. 58.

31. Larry Diamond, "Introduction," in Diamond and Plattner, *Civil-Military Relations and Democracy*, p. xxxii.

32. South African Government, White Paper on Defence, *Defence in a Democracy*, p. 10.

33. Harsh realities may dampen such hopes, however. Annette Seegers notes that South Africa's military has deployed more troops inside South Africa than did the previous, apartheid, government. Annette Seegers, "SADC's Political and Security Dimensions (circa 2000): South Africa's Experience." Paper prepared for the U.S. State Department Conference on New Directions in the Southern African Development Community, Washington, D.C., December 10, 1999.

34. "Military Left Nigerian Coffers Dry," *Daily Mail & Guardian*, May 25, 1999.

35. "The Role of the Legislature," National Democratic Institute, p. 17.

36. The military may request spending on additional logistics and communications for its currently smaller force.

37. "The Role of the Legislature," National Democratic Institute, p. 17.

38. President Obasanjo's inauguration speech reprinted as an advertising supplement in the *Washington Times,* September 30, 1999, p. 3.

39. "U.S., Nigeria Discuss Defense Cooperation," Armed Forces Press Service, April 3, 2000. Http:www.afisnews_sender@DTIC.MIL

40. Ibid.

41. Peter Lewis, "From Despair to Expectation," *Current History,* May 1999, p. 224.

42. Groups in the delta note that their region receives only 3 percent of the revenue from oil sales, despite being the major petroleum source. These groups have also protested environmental damage, including the contamination of fishing areas. Princeton Lyman and Linda Cotton note that "these conflicts . . . cost the companies and the country enormously. They also reflect a breakdown of control not only by government but by traditional leaders in the region." Princeton Lyman and Linda Cotton, "Reviewing U.S.–Nigeria Relations: New Links to Reinforce Democracy," *ODC Viewpoint,* March 2000, p. 1.

43. See "Nigeria: Lousy Legacies," *Africa Confidential,* December 3, 1999.

44. Malu quoted by "Network Africa," British Broadcasting Corporation World Service, January 25, 2000. Unclassified U.S. State Department Cable, INA7943.

45. Peter Lewis writes that the Nigerian police of the late 1990s "appeared as a virtually occupying force, especially in the country's southern states, extorting money from citizens and sometimes colluding with criminal gangs." Lewis, "From Despair to Expectation," *Current History* (May 1999), p. 224.

46. Ibid., p. 227.

47. Interview, March 2000.

48. "30,000 Soldiers to Go, Says Danjuma," *Vanguard,* August 18,1999. Http://www.afbis.com/vanguard/fp1889.html

49. "Nigeria Army Called to Account," the *Guardian,* November 4–10, 1999.

50. Mansfield and Snyder, "Democratization and War," *Foreign Affairs,* May-June 1995, p. 94.

51. Ibid., p. 88.

52. Gilbert M. Khadiagala, "Reflections on the Ethiopia-Eritrea Border Conflict," *The Fletcher Forum of World Affairs* (Fall 1999), pp. 43–44.

53. Gilkes quote. Ibid., p. 47.

54. Nigeria's 1999 constitution, for example, restricts the president's personal power to dispatch troops to foreign countries: "Except with the prior approval of the Senate, no member of the armed forces of the Federation shall be deployed on combat duty outside Nigeria." The constitution does provide an exception for "limited combat duty" if Nigeria's security "is under imminent threat or danger." Constitution of the Federal Republic of Nigeria 1999. Http://www.ngrguardiannews.com/features/R749101.html

55. The *Zimbabwe Independent* stated in March 2000 that Zimbabwe,

which was apparently spending $3.5 million per month on the project, "has yet to reap any benefits from the project [and that] Zimbabwe was being cheated by the more experienced Congolese in the diamond-buying business." "No Diamond Cheques for Zimbabwe in the DRC," *Zimbabwean Independent,* March 10, 2000.

François Misser wrote in December 1999 about the Zimbabwean-owned Gecamines that it "has not been by any means the 'cash cow' that some Harare officials expected." "The Carpet-Bag Generals," *Africa Business,* December 1999, p. 31.

ACRONYMS AND ABBREVIATIONS

ACRF	African Crisis Response Force (United States)
ACRI	African Crisis Response Initiative (United States)
ACSS	Africa Center for Strategic Studies (United States)
ADF	Allied Democratic Forces (Uganda)
ADFL/CZ	Alliance des Forces Démocratiques de Libération du Congo-Zaïre
AFL	Armed Forces of Liberia
AFRC	Armed Forces Revolutionary Council (Sierra Leone)
AOF	Afrique Occidentale Française (French West Africa)
APC	All People's Congress (Sierra Leone)
ARMSCOR	Armaments Development and Manufacturing Corporation (South Africa)
BMATT	British Military Advisory and Training Team
BRA	Bougainville Revolutionary Army (Papua New Guinea)
CDF	Civil Defense Forces (Sierra Leone)
CNN	Cable News Network
COIN	counterinsurgency
DFI	Defense Forecasts International (United States)
DFID	Department for International Development (Great Britain)
DROC	Democratic Republic of the Congo (Congo)
DSL	Defense Systems, Limited (Great Britain)
DSP	Division Spéciale Présidentielle (Zaire)
DST	Direction de la Surveillance du Territoire (France)
ECOMOG	ECOWAS Cease-fire Monitoring Group
ECOWAS	Economic Community of West African States
EDA	Excess defense articles (United States)

EO	Executive Outcomes (South Africa)
FAA	Forças Armadas de Angola
FAR	Forces Armées Rwandaises
FAZ	Forces Armées Zaïroises
FRELIMO	Front for the Liberation of Mozambique
GSU	General Services Unit (Kenya)
HALO	High altitude, low opening
ILO	International lending organization
IMET	International Military Education and Training (United States)
INPFL	Independent National Patriotic Front of Liberia
ISDSC	Interstate Defense and Security Committee (Southern Africa)
JCET	Joint Combined Exercises and Training (United States)
KANU	Kenya African National Union
KAR	King's African Rifles (East Africa)
LPC	Liberian Peace Council
LRA	Lord's Resistence Army (Uganda)
MISAB	Inter-African Mission to Monitor the Implementation of the Bangui Agreements (Central African Republic)
MPLA	Popular Movement for the Liberation of Angola
MPRI	Military Professional Resources, Incorporated (United States)
MTT	Mobile Training Team (United States)
NATO	North Atlantic Treaty Organization
NCO	noncommissioned officer
NGO	nongovernmental organization
NIF	National Islamic Front (Sudan)
NPFL	National Patriotic Front of Liberia
NPRC	National Provisional Ruling Council (Sierra Leone)
NRA	National Resistence Army
NRM	National Resistence Movement
OAU	Organization of African Unity
OB	order of battle
O.B.E.	Order of the British Empire
PDF	Peoples' Defense Force (Sudan)
POGR	President's Own Guard Regiment (Ghana)
PSC	private security company
RCD	Rassemblement Congolais pour la Démocratie (Congo)
RECAMP	Reinforcement of African Capabilities for Peacekeeping
RENAMO	Mozambique National Resistance Movement

RGF	Rwandan Government Forces
ROE	rules of engagement
RPA	Rwandan Patriotic Army
RPF	Rwandan Patriotic Front
RSLMF	Republic of Sierra Leone Military Force
RUF	Revolutionary United Front (Sierra Leone)
RWAFF	Royal West African Frontier Force (West Africa)
SADC	Southern African Development Community
SADF	South African Defense Force
SAM	surface-to-air missile
SANDF	South African National Defense Force (successor to SADF)
SAS	Special Air Service (Great Britain and Rhodesia)
SBS	Special Bodyguard Service (Nigeria)/Special Boat Service (Great Britain)
SFF	Special Field Force (Namibia)
SMC	Standing Mediation Committee (ECOWAS/Liberia)
SOFA	status of forces agreement
SPLA	Sudanese People's Liberation Army
SSD	Special Security Division (Sierra Leone)
SWAPO	South West African People's Organization
ULIMO-J	United Liberation Movement of Liberians for Democracy-Johnson
ULIMO-K	United Liberation Movement of Liberians for Democracy-Kromah
UNAMIR	UN Assistance Mission in Rwanda
UNITA	National Union for the Total Independence of Angola
UNITAF	United Task Force (United States-UN, Somalia)
UNOMIL	UN Observer Mission in Liberia
UNOSOM	United Nations Operations Somalia
UPDF	Ugandan People's Defense Force
USAID	U.S. Agency for International Development
ZANU	Zimbabwe African National Union
ZAPU	Zimbabwe African People's Union
ZDI	Zimbabwe Defense Industries

BIBLIOGRAPHY

Abdullah, Ibrahim. "Bush Path to Destruction: The Origin and Character of the Revolutionary United Front." *Journal of Modern African Studies* 36, 2.

Africa Watch. *Kenya: Taking Liberties.* New York: Africa Watch, 1991.

Afrifa, A. A. *The Ghana Coup.* London: Frank Cass, 1966.

Annan, Kofi. "Two Concepts of Sovereignty." *The Economist,* September 18, 1999.

Arlinghaus, Bruce E. *Military Development in Africa: The Political and Economic Risks of Arms Transfers.* Boulder, Colo.: Westview, 1984.

Arlinghaus, Bruce E., and Pauline J. Baker. *African Armies: Evolution and Capabilities.* Boulder, Colo.: Westview, 1986.

Austin, Kathi. "The Illicit Gun Trade, Fanning Flames of Conflict." *Washington Post,* January 24, 1999.

Azarya, Victor, and Naomi Chazan. "Disengagement from the State in Africa: Reflections on the Experience of Ghana and Guinea." *Studies in Society and History,* January 1987.

Bakwesegha, C. J. "The Role of the Organization of African Unity in Conflict Prevention, Management and Resolution in the Context of the Political Evolution of Africa." *African Journal on Conflict Prevention, Management and Resolution* 1, 1 (January–April 1997).

Ball, Nicole. *Security and Economy in the Third World.* London: Adamantine Press, 1989.

Bayart, Jean-François, Stephen Ellis, and Béatrice Hibou. *The Criminalization of the State in Africa.* Bloomington: Indiana University Press, 1999.

Bayham, Simon. *Military Power and Politics in Black Africa.* London: Croom Helm, 1986.

Berry, LaVerle, ed. *Ghana: Area Handbook.* Washington, D.C.: U.S. Library of Congress, 1995.

Bienen, Henry S. *Armed Forces, Conflict, and Change in Africa.* Boulder, Colo.: Westview, 1989.

Boutros-Ghali, Boutros. *Agenda for Peace.* New York: United Nations, 1995.

Bratton, Michael, and Nicholas van de Walle. *Democratic Experiments in*

Africa: Regime Transitions in Comparative Perspective. Cambridge: Cambridge University Press, 1997.

Brown, Michael, ed. *The International Dimensions of Internal Conflict.* Cambridge, Mass.: Massachusetts Institute of Technology Press, 1996.

Bryans, Michael, Bruce D. Jones, and Janice Gross Stein. "Mean Times, Humanitarian Action in Complex Political Emergencies—Stark Choices, Cruel Dilemmas." Centre for International Studies, University of Toronto, 1999.

Burchett, Wilfred, and Derek Roebuck. *The Whores of War: Mercenaries Today.* Hammondsworth, U.K.: Penguin, 1977.

Bureau of Intelligence and Research. "Arms and Conflict in Africa." U.S. Department of State, 1999.

Burnett, Archie, ed. *The Poems of A. E. Houseman.* Oxford: Clarendon Press, 1977.

Butts, Kent Hughes, and Steven Metz. "Armies and Democracy in the New Africa: Lessons from Nigeria and South Africa." Carlisle Barracks, Pa.: U.S. Army War College Strategic Studies Institute, 1996.

Byrnes, Rita, ed. *Uganda: Area Handbook.* Washington, D.C.: U.S. Library of Congress, 1992.

Campbell, Guy. *The Charging Buffalo.* London: Leo Cooper, 1986.

Carter, Gwendolyn, and Patrick O'Meara. *African Independence: The First Twenty-five Years.* Bloomington: Indiana University Press, 1985.

Cawthra, Gavin. *Brutal Force: The Apartheid War Machine.* London: International Defence and Aid Fund, 1986.

Chabal, Patrick, and Jean-Pascal Daloz. *Africa Works: Disorder as a Political Instrument.* Oxford: James Currey, 1998.

Chazan, Naomi, Peter Lewis, Robert Mortimer, Donald Rothchild, and Stephen Stedman. *Politics and Society in Contemporary Africa.* 3rd ed. Boulder, Colo.: Lynne Rienner Publishers, 1999.

Cilliers, Jakkie, ed. *Peacekeeping to Complex Emergency: Peace Support Missions in Africa.* Johannesburg and Pretoria: South African Institute of International Affairs and the Institute of Strategic Studies, 1999.

Cilliers, Jakkie, and Christian Dietrich. "Editorial Comment: Privatising Peace Enforcement." *African Security Review* 5, 6 (1996).

Cilliers, Jakkie, and Peggy Mason, eds. *Peace, Profit or Plunder? The Privatization of Security in War-Torn Societies.* Halfway House, South Africa: Institute for Security Studies, 1999.

Cimbala, Stephen J. "Military Persuasion and the American Way of Life." *Strategic Review* (Fall 1997).

Clapham, Christopher. *Liberia and Sierra Leone: An Essay in Comparative Politics.* Cambridge: Cambridge University Press, 1976.

———. ed. *African Guerrillas.* Oxford: James Currey, 1998.

Clapham, Christopher, and George Philip. *The Political Dilemmas of Military Regimes.* Totowa, N.J.: Barnes and Noble, 1985.

Clark, John F. "Foreign Intervention in the Civil War of the Congo Republic." *Issue* 26, 1 (1998).

Clayton, Anthony. *Frontiersmen: Warfare in Africa Since 1950.* London: University College of London Press, 1999.

Collins, Alan. *The Security Dilemma and the End of the Cold War.* New York: St. Martin's Press, 1997.

Constitution of the Federal Republic of Nigeria, 1999. http://www/ngrguardiannews.com.features/R749101.htm

Cox, Thomas S. *Civil-Military Relations in Sierra Leone: A Case Study of African Soldiers in Politics.* Cambridge, Mass.: Harvard University Press, 1976.

Cranna, Michael, ed. *The True Cost of Conflict.* New York: The New Press, 1994.

Crocker, Chester. "Military Dependence: The Colonial Legacy in Africa." *Journal of Modern African Studies* 12, 2 (1974).

Crocker, Chester, and Fen Osler Hampson, eds. *Managing Global Chaos: Sources of and Responsibilities to International Conflict.* Washington, D.C.: U.S. Institute of Peace, 1996.

Crowder, Michael, ed. *The Cambridge History of Africa, vol. 8, 1940–1975.* Cambridge: Cambridge University Press, 1984.

Damrosch, Lori Fisler. *Enforcing Restraint.* New York: Council on Foreign Relations, 1993.

David, Stephen. "Internal War: Causes and Cures." *World Politics* 49 (July 1997).

Decalo, Samuel, "Modalities of Civil-Military Stability in Africa." *Journal of Modern African Studies* 27, 4 (1989).

———. *Coups and Army Rule in Africa: Motivations and Constraints.* New Haven, Conn.: Yale University Press, 1990.

———. *The Stable Minority: Civilian Rule in Africa.* Gainesville: Florida Academic Press, 1998.

Demilitarization for Democracy (DFD), *Fighting Retreat.* Washington, D.C.: DFD, 1997.

Deng, Frances, and I. William Zartman. *Conflict Resolution in Africa.* Washington, D.C.: Brookings Institution Press, 1991.

Deng, Frances, Sadikiel Kimaro, Terrence Lyons, Donald Rothchild, and I. William Zartman. *Sovereignty as Responsibility.* Washington, D.C.: Brookings Institution Press, 1996.

Des Forges, Alison. *Leave None to Tell the Story.* New York: Human Rights Watch, 1999.

Diamond, Larry, and Marc F. Plattner, eds., *Civil-Military Relations and Democracy.* Baltimore: Johns Hopkins University Press, 1996.

Donahue, John D. *The Privatization Decision: Public Ends, Private Means.* New York: Basic Books, 1989.

Du Toit, André. "The White Body Politic: What Has de Klerk Wrought?" *The Southern Africa Policy Forum Report.* Queenstown, Md.: Aspen Institute, 1991.

Duignan, Peter, and Lewis Gann. *Burden of Empire.* London: Pall Mall Press, 1968.

Durch, William, ed. *UN Peacekeeping, American Politics, and the Uncivil Wars of the 1990s.* New York: St. Martin's Press, 1996.

Echenberg, Myron. *Colonial Conscripts: The Tirailleurs Sénégalais in French West Africa, 1857–1960.* Portsmouth, N.H.: Heinemann, 1991.

Edgerton, Robert. *Mau Mau: An African Crucible*. New York: Free Press, 1989.
Eisenstadt, S. N., ed. *Max Weber on Charisma and Nation-Building*. Chicago: University of Chicago Press, 1968.
Ergas, Zaki. *The African State in Transition*. London: Macmillan, 1987.
Fayemi, J. 'Kayode. "Threats, Military Expenditure and National Security: Analysis of Trends in Post-Civil War Defence Planning in Nigeria— 1970–1990." Ph.D. diss., University of London, 1993.
Feil, Scott. *Could Five Thousand Peacekeepers Have Saved 500,000 Rwandans?* Washington, D.C.: Institute for the Study of Diplomacy, Georgetown University, April 1997.
Finer, S. E. *The Man on Horseback*. London: Pall Mall, 1962.
First, Ruth. *Power in Africa*. New York: Pantheon, 1970.
Fleischman, Janet, and Lois Whitman. *Easy Prey: Child Soldiers in Liberia*. New York: Human Rights Watch, 1994.
Foltz, William J., and Henry S. Bienen. *Arms and the African: Military Influences on Africa's International Relations*. New Haven, Conn.: Yale University Press, 1985.
Francis, Dana. "Peacekeeping or Peace Enforcement? Conflict Intervention in Africa." World Peace Foundation, 1998.
Frankel, Philip H. *Pretoria's Praetorians: Civil-Military Relations in South Africa*. Cambridge: Cambridge University Press, 1984.
Fukayama, Francis. "Against the New Pessimism." *Commentary* (February 1994).
Furley, Oliver, ed. *Conflict In Africa*. London: Tauris, 1995.
Glynn, Patrick. "The Age of Balkanization." *Commentary* (July 1993).
Gourevitch, Philip, *We Wish to Inform You that Tomorrow We Will Be Killed with Our Families*. New York: Farrar, Straus and Giroux, 1998.
Grundy, Kenneth W., *Conflicting Images of the Military in Africa*. Nairobi: East African Publishing House, 1968.
———. *The Militarization of South African Politics*. Bloomington: Indiana University Press, 1986.
Gutteridge, William F. *Military Regimes in Africa*. London: Methuen, 1975.
Handloff, Robert E., ed. *Côte d'Ivoire: Country Handbook*. Washington, D.C.: U.S. Library of Congress, 1991.
Harbeson, John W., and Donald Rothchild, eds. *Africa in World Politics: The African State System in Flux*. Boulder, Colo.: Westview, 1991.
Hartung, William D. "Mercenaries, Inc." *Progressive* (April 1996).
Henderson, Ian, and Philip Goodhart. *Manhunt in Kenya*. Toronto: Bantam, 1958.
Henk, Daniel. *Uncharted Paths, Uncertain Vision: U.S. Military Involvements in Sub-Saharan Africa in the Wake of the Cold War*. Colorado Springs: Institute for National Security Studies, Occasional Paper 18, U.S. Air Force Academy, 1998.
Herbst, Jeffrey. "The Regulation of Private Military Forces." Paper prepared for The Privatization of Security in Africa conference, South African Institute of International Affairs, December 10, 1998.
———. *Securing Peace in Africa*. Cambridge, Mass.: World Peace Foundation, 1998.

Herskovits, Jean. "Africans Solving African Problems: Militaries, Democracies, and Security in West and Southern Africa." Report of a conference convened by Ambassador J. N. Garba, International Peace Academy, 1998.

Hochschild, Adam. *King Leopold's Ghost: A Story of Greed, Terror, and Heroism in Colonial Africa.* Boston: Houghton Mifflin, 1998.

Howe, Herbert M. "The South African Defence Force and Political Reform." *Journal of Modern African Studies* 32, 1 (1994).

———. "South Africa's 911 Force." *Armed Forces Journal International* (November 1996).

———. "Lessons of Liberia: ECOMOG and Regional Peacekeeping." *International Security* (Winter 1996/1997).

———. "Private Security and African Stability: The Case of Executive Outcomes." *Journal of Modern African Studies* 36, 2 (1998).

Huband, Mark. *The Liberian Civil War.* London: Frank Cass, 1998.

Human Rights Watch. "Sierra Leone: Sowing Terror: Atrocities Against Civilians in Sierra Leone." July 1998.

———. "Global Trade, Local Impact: Arms Transfers to All Sides in the Civil War in Sudan." August 1998.

———. "Bulgaria. Money Talks: Arms Dealing with Human Rights Abusers." April 1999.

———. "Getting Away with Murder, Mutilation, and Rape." June 1999.

———. "Angola Unravels." October 1999.

Huntington, Samuel P. *The Soldier and the State: The Theory and Politics of Civil-Military Relations.* New York: Vintage, 1964.

———. "Political Modernization: America vs. Europe." *World Politics* 18 (1996).

———. *Political Order in Changing Societies.* New Haven, Conn.: Yale University Press, 1968.

Hutchful, Eboe. "Military Policy and Reform." *Journal of Modern African Studies* 35, 3 (June 1997).

Ignatieff, Michael. "The Gods of War." *New York Review of Books,* October 9, 1997.

———. *The Warrior's Honor.* Vintage: London, 1999.

Imobighe, T. A. "An African High Command: The Search for a Feasible Strategy of Continental Defence." *African Affairs* (April 1980).

———, ed. *Nigerian Defence and Security: Issues and Options For Policy.* Jos, Nigeria: Macmillan, 1987.

International Institute of Strategic Studies, *Military Balance.* London: International Institute of Strategic Studies (various years).

Iroh, George. *48 Guns for the General.* London: Heinemann, 1976.

Isenberg, David. "Soldiers of Fortune, Ltd." Center for Defense Information Monograph, November 1997.

———. "The New Mercenaries: Corporate Warriors Market Combat Expertise." *Christian Science Monitor,* October 13, 1998.

Jackson, Robert, and Carl Rosberg. *Personal Rule in Black Africa: Prince, Autocrat, Prophet, Tyrant.* Berkeley: University of California Press, 1982.

Johnson, J. J., ed. *The Role of the Military in Underdeveloped Countries.* Princeton, N.J.: Princeton University Press, 1962.

Kamanu, Onyeonoro S. "Security and the Right to Self-Determination: An OAU Dilemma." *Journal of Modern African Studies* 12, 3 (1974).

Kaplan, Robert. "The Coming Anarchy." *Atlantic,* February 1994.

Khadiagala, Gilbert M. "Reflections on the Ethiopia-Eritrea Border Conflict." *The Fletcher Forum of World Affairs* 32, 2 (Fall 1999).

Kilson, Martin, and Wildred Cartey, eds. *The Africa Reader.* New York: Random House, 1970.

Kramer, Reid. "Liberia: A Casualty of the Cold War's End?" *CSIS Africa Notes* 174 (July 1995).

Lamb, David. *The Africans.* Vintage: New York, 1985.

Lewis, Peter. "From Despair to Expectation." *Current History* (May 1999).

Liebenow, J. Gus. *Liberia: The Evolution of Privilege.* Ithaca, N.Y.: Cornell University Press, 1969.

———. *Liberia: The Quest for Democracy.* Bloomington: Indiana University Press, 1987.

Luckham, Robin. *The Nigerian Military: A Sociological Analysis of Authority and Revolt.* Cambridge: Cambridge University Press, 1971.

Luttwak, Edward. "Toward Post-Heroic Warfare." *Foreign Affairs* 74, 3 (May–June 1995).

———. "Give War a Chance." *Foreign Affairs* 78, 4 (August 1999).

Lyman, Princeton, and Linda Cotton, "Reviewing U.S.-Nigerian Relations: New Links to Reinforce Democracy." *ODC Viewpoint* (March 2000).

Machiavelli, Niccolò. *The Prince.* New Haven, Conn.: Yale University Press, 1997.

Magyar, Karl, and Earl Conteh-Morgan. *Peacekeeping in Africa.* New York: St. Martin's Press, 1997.

Malan, Mark, ed. *Resolute Partners: Building Peacekeeping Capacity in Southern Africa.* Halfway House. South Africa: Institute for Security Studies Monograph, 21 (February 1998).

———, ed. *Whither Peacekeeping in Africa?* Halfway House, South Africa: Institute for Security Studies, 1999.

Mansfield, Edward, and Jack Snyder. "Democratization and War." *Foreign Affairs* (May–June 1996).

Mazrui, Ali. *The Warrior Tradition in Modern Africa.* Leiden: E. J. Brill, 1977.

Meditz, Sandra, and Tim Merrill, eds. *Zaire: Country Handbook.* Washington, D.C.: U.S. Library of Congress, 1994.

Migdal, Joel. *Strong Societies and Weak States: State-Society Relations and State Capabilities in the Third World.* Princeton, N.J.: Princeton University Press, 1988.

Miner, N. J. *The Nigerian Military, 1956–66.* London: Methuen, 1971.

Misser, François. "The Carpet-Bag Generals." *Africa Business* (December 1999).

Mommsen, Wolfgang, and Jurgen Osterhammel. *Imperialism and After: Discontinuities.* Boston: Allen and Unwin, 1986.

Mueller, John. *Retreat from Doomsday: The Obsolescence of Major War.* New York: Basic Books, 1988.

Musah, Abdel-Fatua, and J. 'Kayode Fayemi. *Mercenaries: An African Security Dilemma.* London: Pluto Press, 1999.

Naidi, Geno J., ed. *Documents of the Organization of African Unity.* New York: Mansell, 1992.

Nelson, Harold D., ed. *Kenya: A Country Study.* Washington, D.C.: American University Press, 1984.

———. *Liberia: A Country Study.* Washington, D.C.: American University Press, 1984.

Ottaway, Marina. "Keep out of Africa." *Financial Times,* February 25, 1999.

———. "Post-Imperial Africa at War." *Current History* (May 1999).

Peters, Jimi. *The Nigerian Military and the State.* London: Tauris, 1997.

Prunier, Gerald. *The Rwanda Crisis.* New York: Columbia University Press, 1995.

Reno, William. "The Business of War in Liberia." *Current History* (May 1996).

———. "Privatizing War in Sierra Leone." *Current History* (May 1997).

———. *Warlord Politics and African States.* Boulder, Colo.: Lynne Rienner Publishers, 1998.

———. "Mines, Money, and the Problem of State-Building in Congo." *Issue* 26, 1 (1998).

Rice, Susan. "Central African Conflict and Its Implications for Africa and for the Future of U.S. Policy Goals and Strategies." Statement before the U.S. Senate Foreign Relations Committee, Subcommittee on African Affairs, June 8, 1999.

Richards, Paul. *Fighting for the Rainforest: War, Youth, and Resources in Sierra Leone.* Portsmouth, N.H.: Heinemann, 1996.

Roberts, A. D. *The Cambridge History of Africa, vol. 7, 1905–1940.* Cambridge: Cambridge University Press, 1986.

Rodney, Walter. *How Europe Underdeveloped Africa.* Dar-es-Salaam: Tanzania Publishing House, 1972.

Rouvez, Alain. *Disconsolate Empires. French, British, and Belgium Military Involvement in Post-Colonial Sub-Saharan Africa.* Lanham, Md.: University Press of America, 1994.

Rubin, Elizabeth. "An Army of Their Own." *Harper's,* February 1997.

Ruggie, John. *Multilateralism Matters: The Theory and Praxis of an International Forum.* New York: Cambridge University Press, 1993.

———. *Winning the Peace: America and World Order in the New Era.* New York: Columbia University Press, 1996.

Sandline. "Private Military Companies–Independent or Regulated." March 28, 1998. Http:///www.sandline.com.site/index.html

Schatzberg, Michael. *The Dialectics of Oppression in Zaire.* Bloomington: Indiana University Press, 1988.

Schraeder, Peter J. *United States Foreign Policy Toward Africa: Incrementalism, Crisis, and Change.* Cambridge: Cambridge University Press, 1994.

Science Applications International Corporation. "Analytical Study of Irregular Warfare in Sierra Leone and Liberia." September 30, 1998.

Scully, Will. *Once a Pilgrim.* Headline: London, 1998.

Sesay, Max Ahmadu. "Collective Security or Collective Disaster? Regional Peacekeeping In West Africa." *Security Dialogue* (1995).

Shearer, David. "Outsourcing War." *Foreign Policy* 112 (Fall 1998).

———. "Private Armies and Military Intervention." International Institute for Strategic Studies, Adelphi Paper 316, 1.

Sills, David L. *International Encyclopedia of the Social Sciences.* New York: Macmillan, 1968.

Silverstein, Ken. "Privatizing War: How Affairs of State Are Farmed out to Corporations Beyond Public Control." *Nation,* July 2, 1997.

Smock, David, ed. *Making War and Waging Peace: Foreign Intervention in Africa.* Washington, D.C.: U.S. Institute of Peace, 1993.

Smock, David, and Chester Crocker. *African Conflict Resolution.* Washington, D.C.: U.S. Institute of Peace, 1995.

Snow, Donald M. *Uncivil Wars: International Security and the New Internal Conflicts.* Boulder, Colo.: Lynne Rienner Publishers, 1996.

Snyder, Jack. "Nationalism and the Crisis of the Post-Soviet State." *Survival* 35, 1 (Spring 1993).

South African Government. *Defence in a Democracy.* Pretoria: Ministry of Defence, 1998.

St. Jorre, John de. *The Brothers' War: Biafra and Nigeria.* Boston: Houghton Mifflin, 1972.

Stock, Robert. *Africa South of the Sahara.* New York: Guilford, 1995.

Thompson, Janice. "State Practices, International Norms, and the Decline of Mercenaries." *International Studies Quarterly* 34, 1 (March 1990).

Tilly, Charles. *The Formation of National States in Western Europe.* Princeton, N.J.: Princeton University Press, 1975.

Tocqueville, Alexis de. *The Old Regime and the French Revolution.* Garden City, N.J.: Doubleday, 1955.

Toffler, Alvin and Heidi. *War and Anti-War: Survival at the Dawn of the 21st Century.* Boston: Little, Brown, 1993.

Tucker, David. "Fighting Barbarians." *Parameters* 27, 2 (Summer 1998).

United Kingdom. Department for International Development-WNAD. "Sierra Leone Security Sector Programme (SISEP): Project Memorandum and Framework." May 1999.

Van Creveld, Martin. *The Transformation of War.* New York: Free Press, 1991.

Vogt, Margaret, ed. *The Liberian Crisis and ECOMOG: A Bold Attempt at Regional Peacekeeping.* Lagos: Gabumo Publishing Company Limited, 1992.

Weber, Max. *The Theory of Social and Economic Organization.* Translated by A. M. Henderson and Talcott Parsons. New York: Free Press, 1964.

Welch, Claude. *Soldier and State in Africa: A Comparative Analysis of Military Intervention and Political Change.* Evanston, Ill.: Northwestern University Press, 1970.

———, ed. *Civilian Control of the Military.* Albany: State University of New York Press, 1976.

———, ed. "Praetorianism in West Africa." *Journal of Modern African Studies* 10, 2 (July 1992).

Weller, Mark, ed. *Regional Peace-Keeping and International Enforcement: The*

Liberian Crisis. Cambridge International Document Series, vol. 6. Cambridge: Cambridge University Press, 1994.

Welsh, David. "Ethnicity in Sub-Saharan Africa." *International Affairs* 72, 3 (July 1996).

Woronoff, Jon. *Organizing African Unity.* Metuchen, N.J.: Scarecrow Press, 1970.

Xenophon. *Anabasis.* New York: Harper and Bros., 1847.

Young, Crawford. *The African State in Comparative Perspective.* New Haven, Conn.: Yale University Press, 1994.

Zarate, Juan Carlos. "The Emergence of a New Dog of War: Private International Security Companies, International Law, and the New World Disorder." *Stanford Journal of International Law* 34, 1 (Winter 1998).

Zartman, I. William, ed. *Collapsed States: The Disintegration and Restoration of Legitimate Authority.* Boulder, Colo.: Lynne Rienner Publishers, 1995.

INDEX

Abacha, Sani, 145, 250–251, 271–272, 287
Abuja accords, 145
Africa Center for Strategic Studies (ACSS), 263
Africa Crisis Response Initiative (ACRI), 18–19, 173, 174, 243–264, 282; achievements, 260–261; anticipatory motivation of, 244–245; command and control structure, 254, 259–260; composition, 253, 255–259; control of, 253–254; double multilateralism of, 248, 261; financing, 259; foreign origins of, 274–275; and interoperability, 244; limitations, 273–274; and logistic support, 260; parallel program, 263–264; peace enforcement, 254–255; peacekeeping mission, 252, 255, 262, 273; personal rule and, 256–257; professionalism, 273; purpose and goals, 244, 252–253; and regional conflicts, 256–257, 261–263; and sovereignty-as-responsibility argument, 259–260; training, 244, 252–253; U.S. decisionmaker role in, 259
African Crisis Response Force (ACRF), 247–251, 274
African renaissance states, 15, 74
Afrifa, A. A., 45
Ahmadu, Abu, 172
AIDS, 6, 21n.15

Albert, Carl, 204–205
All Peoples Congress (APC) party, 36
Alliance des Forces Démocratiques de Libéation du Congo-Zaïre (ADFL), 93, 98
Amin, Idi, 33, 40, 46, 48, 56, 92, 276
Angola: Congo intervention of, 99; defense spending, 205; and preemptive self-defense, 95–96; state development, Executive Outcomes and, 205–212; Western intercession in, 48
Angolan conflict, 198–200, 202–203
Annan, Kofi, 1–2
Armed Forces of Liberia (AFL), 138, 140–41, 161; ethnicization of, 129; military unprofessionalism of, 132, 133
Arms trade: African, 82; international, 91–92

Babangida, Ibrahim, 43, 133, 136, 137, 271. See also Nigeria
Barlow, Eeben, 195
Barre, Siad, 38, 88
Belgium, African military involvement of, 249–250
Berlin conference, 32
Biafra, mercenaries in, 193
Boer War, 34
Bokassa, Jean-Bedel, 10
Boley, George, 141
Bongo, Omar, 45
Borders, national: arbitrary creation of,

76; concept of *uti possidetis* and, 95; inviolability of, 48
Bosnian intervention, 105, 108
Botswana, military professionalism in, 276
Bout, Victor, 81
Boutros-Ghali, Boutros, 248
Branch Group, 196, 199, 200; diamond concessions and, 206; Executive Outcomes connections, 205–208, 213; Sandline operations, 190, 212–213, 236n.102
Brazzaville Accords, 198
Britain: African militaries of, 33, 34; Department for International Development (DFID), 15; mercenaries and, 191; and Sandline's "Arms to Africa" controversy, 220; and U.S. initiatives, 249
Bulgarian arm sales, 80–81
Burkina Faso, 221; Liberian conflict and, 133, 137, 140, 147, 148, 150

Cameroon, 39
Campaore, Blaise, 97, 103, 137
Caprivi Liberation Army, 6
Carter, Jimmy, 143
Chad, 45, 60, 287
Chan, Julius, 236n.102
Child soldiers, insurgents' use of, 82, 83–84, 130, 141, 146
Christopher, Warren, 248, 249, 262
Civilian military oversight, 280
Civil-military divide, 13; colonial military forces and, 27, 28–29; democratization and, 269–270, 275–287; domestic versus external deployment and, 30–31; institutionalized agreements and, 35–36; military professionalism and, 9–10; personal rule and, 21
Clinton, Bill, 15, 111, 213, 249, 251, 283
Cohen, Herman, 255
Cold War demise: African security and, 77–79; Liberian conflict and, 130; nature of African conflict and, 77–78, 92–93
Collapsed states, 7; defined, 22n.22
Colonialism, 28–35; and domestic deployment, 30–31; ethnic recruit-

ment under, 29–30; indigenous officer class development and, 30, 32–34; and military professionalism/unprofessionalism, 28–35; military politicization and, 27; postindependence conflicts, 76; regional military organizations under, 29; security impacts and legacies, 27, 76
Conflict resolution, wars as means of, 16–17
Conflicts, African: brutality and human rights abuses in, 1, 4, 5–6; child soldiers in, 82, 83–84, 130, 141, 146; Cold War demise and, 78–79; colonialism and, 76; democratization and, 78–79; insurgency activity in, 1, 3, 4, 75–76; interstate, 6, 75, 79; economic impacts of, 5, 7–8; ethnicity and, 76; military solutions to, 13–17; patterns and causes, 1–8, 73–77; political impacts of, 6–7; organized crime involvement in, 4. *See also* Domestic conflicts; Regional conflicts
Congo: conflict, 94, 97–98, 286–287; Katanga's attempted secession in, 47–48, 189
"Congo effect," 99
Congo-Brazzaville, 79, 83; Angolan invasion of, 95–96, 279
Côte d'Ivoire, Liberian conflict and, 40, 133, 135, 137, 147, 148, 150
Cotonou agreement, 144, 161
Counterinsurgencies, 32; economic motivations for, 88–92; low-intensity conflict and, 74–76; order of battle in, 153–154; urban, 75–76
Coups: civil-military divide and, 46–47; ethnic, 39–40
Crime and banditry, military, 85, 86

Dallaire, Roméo, 109
De Klerk, F. W., 52
Defence Systems Ltd. (DSL), 188, 191
Democratization: conflict and, 78–79; and donor demands, 4; military professionalism and, 275–286
D'Estaing, Valery Giscard, 49
Diamond(s): embargo, 103; Executive Outcomes and, 206, 208; insurgencies financed by, 97, 102–103; mili-

tary mercantilism and, 89–90, 97–100; smuggling, 210, 221
Disease, conflict and, 5–6
Doe, Samuel, 10, 38, 130, 139, 161; personal rule of, 132–134, 135, 146. *See also* Armed Forces of Liberia (AFL); National Patriotic Front of Liberia (NPFL)
Dogonyaro, Joshua, 139
Domestic conflict, 79–94; civilian targets of, 90, 92–94; economic motivations for, 88–92; ethnicity and, 87–88; increased number of combatants in, 83–87; unprincipled politics and, 89–92; weapon availability and, 79–83. *See also* Insurgencies
Domestic deployment, 46–47
Domestic institutions, and military loyalty, 278
Dos Santos, José, 91, 102, 213
Drug smuggling, 89, 92, 251

ECOMOG. *See* ECOWAS Cease-fire Monitoring Group
Economic Community of West African States (ECOWAS), 43, 57, 141–142
Economy, African: impact of conflicts on, 5, 7–8; reform, 4, 7
ECOWAS Cease-fire Monitoring Group (ECOMOG), 15, 16, 17, 43, 57, 81, 82, 83, 135, 136–139; administration, 155–156; contributing members, 129–130, 137; corruption and criminal activities, 156, 158, 168; costs and funding, 138, 171, 173; equipment and personnel problems, 156–157; factions in, 85, 86, 134 140–142, 144, 145, 146, 158–159, 161, 163; future of, 169–173; geographical and logistical difficulties, 157; human rights record, 168; intelligence, 147–148, 157, 167; internal discipline, 168; Liberian commitment, 159–162; Liberian deployment, 138–145; limitations and failures, 146–165, 177n.18; manpower, 155; military capabilities, 137–138, 153–159; Nigerian dominance in, 133, 158; order of battle, 153–154; peace enforcement actions, 139–140,

143–144; mandate, peacekeeping versus peace enforcement as, 136, 139, 142, 148, 168, 180n.55; political legitimacy and responsibility, 149–153, 167–168, 169; praise for, 169, 176n.3; regional attitudes toward, 170–171, 173; regional cleavages and, 149; in Sierra Leonean conflict, 165–169; strategy, 138–139; training, 156–157, 167; UN partnership, 131; and urban counterinsurgencies, 75–76
Emigré armies, 6
Entente Agreement, 49
Equipment purchasing and maintenance, 42–43, 49, 154
Ethiopia: parallel forces in, 45; Western intercession in, 48
Ethiopian-Etritean conflict, 101, 286
Ethnic conflict, 76, 87–88
Ethnicization, military: colonial, 29–30; negative effects of, 29; under personal-rule systems, 37–40
Etritean-Ethiopian conflict, 101, 286
Executive Outcomes (EO), 18, 52, 165, 195–229; accountability concerns and, 213; in Angolan conflict, 198–200, 202–203; African influence of, 202; apartheid connections, 213; civilian treatment and human rights record, 203–204; commercial ties, 196; diamond concessions to, 206, 208; as force multiplier, 199, 201, 202; forces, elite background of, 195–196; intelligence capabilities, 202–203; loyalty, 204, 205; military effectiveness, 202–204, 214; national militaries and, 209–211; order of battle, 198; payments to, 205, 206; and political responsibility, 204–205; professionalism, 197–198; and racist/neocolonialist concerns, 213–214; Sandline's Papau New Guinea operations and, 212, 213, 236n.102; in Sierra Leonean conflict, 165–166, 200–204; state development and, 205–212; termination of, 212; "white knight" status, 214–215
Exercise Natural Fire, 174
Eyadema, Gnassingbe, 103

Forças Armadas de Angola (FAA), Executive Outcomes and, 205, 209–210, 214
Force Publique (Congo), 31, 33–34, 38–39
Forces Armé Zaïroises (FAZ), 31, 49
Forces Armées Rwandaises, 57
France: colonial militaries of, 34; Francophone states' defense links with, 60–61; interventionist stance, 105; mercenaries and, 191; military interventions of, 49, 78; Rwanda intervention of, 111; and U.S. initiatives, 249, 259
Front for the Liberation of Mozambique (FRELIMO), 11

Gabon, parallel forces in, 38, 45
Gambia, military coup, 145
Genda, Ambrose, 36
Genocide Convention, 111
Ghana, 42, 279–280; Liberian conflict and, 138, 139, 161
Globalization: insurgencies and, 3–4
Government irregular forces, 84–86; and child soldiers, 83–84; civilian abuse by, 86
Great Trek, 34
Green Berets, 253

Habyarimana, Juvénal, 79
HIV/AIDS incidence rates, 59–60
Human rights abuses: civilian suffering and deaths, 5–6: insurgents' terrorism and violence against, 90; Liberian conflict, 141; military solutions to, 16
Humanitarian intervention, 104–111. *See* Western humanitarian intervention
Huntington, Samuel, 9, 11, 23n.28, 27–30

Ideology, African military professionalism and, 50–51
Independent National Patriotic Front of Liberia (INPFL), 134, 138, 139, 140, 142, 153
Innih, George, 42
INPFL. *See* Independent National Patriotic Front of Liberia

Institutionalization, stability and, 11
Insurgencies: brutality and human rights abuses of, 1, 90, 92–94; diamond-financed, 97, 102–103; low-intensity, and counterinsurgency planning, 75–76; political agenda of, 88–89; weapon availability and, 81–83
Intelligence, tactical, 147–148, 157
International Charter Incorporated (ICI), 189–190
International Convention Against the Recruitment, Use, Financing, and Training of Mercenaries, 228
International Monetary Fund, (IMF), 201, 224
International Rescue Committee, 6
Interstate conflict. *See* Regional conflict
Iroha, Joshua, 140

Johnson, Yourmie, 134. *See also* INPFL

Kabbah, Ahmed, 17, 201, 274
Kabila, Laurent, 93, 193
Kaunda, Kenneth, 40
Kenya, 174; ethnically based parallel security forces in, 44; military ethnicization in, 38, 39
Kenya African National Union Party, 46
Kenyatta, Jomo, 39, 40
King's African Rifles (KAR), 32, 33
Kony, Joseph, 82

Leigh, John, 202
Liberia: Americo-Liberian rule, 131–132; ethnic groups, 131; military ethnicization, 38; relief aid theft in, 191; True Whig Party rule, 132; U.S. and, 130, 131, 132–133, 145. *See also* Doe, Samuel; Johnson, Yourmie; Taylor, Charles
Liberian conflict: child soldiers in, 84; factions in, 83, 85, 86, 90, 134, 140–142, 144, 145, 146, 158–159, 161, 163; child soldiers in, 84, 141, 146, 157; costs, 145, 160; historical background, 131–133; human rights abuses in, 141, 161; military unprofessionalism in, 141; Operation Octopus, 143, 149, 154, 157; peace negotiations/settlement, 140–143, 144, 145; private security forces in,

189–190; significance of, 145–146. *See also* ECOMOG
Liberian Frontier Force, 31
Liberian military. *See* Armed Forces of Liberia (AFL); National Patriotic Front of Liberia (NPFL)
Liberian Peace Council (LPC), 141
Lissouba, Pascal, 79, 96
Lord's Resistance Army (Uganda), 82, 91, 92, 262–263
Luitingh, Laffras, 195

Machiavelli, Niccolo, 193
Mali, 277, 279
Mandela, Nelson, 97, 102, 251
Margai, Albert, 36
Mau-Mau rebellions, 32
Mbeki, Thabo, 259
McCallie, Marshall, 252
Mengistu, Haile Mariam, 14, 45, 88
Mercenary, defined, 187, 228–229. *See also* Private security forces
Militaries, African: brutality of, 5; counterinsurgency activities of, 75–76; HIV/AIDS incidence rates in, 59–60; and political party loyalty, 11; politicization of, colonial rule and, 27; size and strength of, 74–75; and state stability, 8–17; and urban fighting, 75–76; Western-sponsored upgrades of, 2
Military capabilities, 58–61; economic gain and, 91; interstate cooperation and, 60–61; mobility in combat and, 58–59; multilateral capability and, 60; patron-client structures and, 12; political responsibility and, 2–3; procurement and, 43; relativity of, 3; states' lack of, 4;
Military codes of conduct, 278–279
Military corruption: irregular pay and, 59; of officer corps, 54–56; procurement and, 40–44
Military ethnicization: colonial, 29–30; negative effects of, 29; under personal-rule systems, 37–40
Military interventions: acceptance of, 149; ad hoc versus permanent, 108; foreign origins of, 274–275; OAU and, 131, 135; peacekeeping versus peace enforcing mandate, 147, 148.

See also Regional intervention forces; Western humanitarian intervention
Military mercantilism, 92, 97–100, 102–103; institutionalization of, 100; mineral-military symbiosis and, 221–226, 228; as motive for conflict, 5, 97
Military politicization: colonial rule and, 27; internal policing and, 281; unprofessionalism and, 53–58
Military Professional Resources, Inc. (MPRI), 191, 220–222, 228
Military professionalism: concept, 2; democratization and, 275–286; development and, 15; and military requirements and responsibilities, 9–10, 27; relativity of, 15–16; and Western initiatives, 17, 18–19
Military unprofessionalism, 9–13; colonial roots of, 28–35; domestic deployment and, 46–47; ethnicization of militaries and, 37–40; and foreign patronage and intervention, 48–49; ideology and, 50–51; infrequent interstate conflict and, 47–48; military politicization and, 53–58; military rulers' role in, 13; operational capabilities and, 42–43, 49, 50; and parallel security forces, 44–45; peripheralization and privatization and, 12–13; of postindependence personal rule, 35–58; procurement corruption and, 41–43, 50; professional officers and, 3
Militias, 84–85
Mineral-military symbiosis, 221–222, 224
Mobutu Sese Seko, 10, 35, 38, 43, 49, 50, 56, 78, 96, 276
Moi, Daniel Arap, 39, 40, 46
Momoh, Joseph, 129, 143, 200–203
Mozambique, 51
MPLA. *See* Popular Movement for the Liberation of Angola
Mugabe, Robert, 38, 102
Multilateral intervention, 107–109
Museveni, Yoweri, 55, 102

National Islamic Front government (Sudan), 85

National Patriotic Front of Liberia (NPFL), 97, 129, 130, 138–139, 141–143, 146, 147, 148, 153, 162

National Union for the Total Independence of Angola (UNITA), 6, 83, 89, 96, 103; diamond smuggling of, 89; Executive Outcomes and, 195, 198–199, 203, 205, 214

Nationalism, civic versus ethnic, 9, 23n.31

Natural resources. *See* Diamonds; Mineral-military symbiosis; Military mercantilism

Nigeria: ACRF/ACRI and, 250–251, 257; combat capabilities in, 56; officer corps of, 53–55; Operation Seadog, 43; procurement corruption in, 41–43; support of ECOMOG, 171–173; Liberian ties with, 133

Nigerian military, 160, 162, 169; ECOMOG dominance, 133, 158; domestic deployment, 284–285; foreign aid to, 283; mediocrity of, 129; and personal rule, 129–130; reform proposals, 284–286. *See also* ECOMOG

Nkrumah, Kwame, 35, 39, 48, 50, 60. *See also* Ghana

Nongovernmental organizations: attacks on, 93–94; sovereignty and, 105

Nujoma, Sam, 102

Nyerere, Julius, 38

Obasanjo, Olusegun, 3, 48, 54, 172; ACRI and, 257, 259; Nigerian military and, 283, 285–286

Obote, Milton, 46, 50. *See also* Uganda

Officer corps: Africanization of, 38–39; colonialism and, 30; corruption of, under military rule, 53–56; independence and, 35;

Operation Desert Storm, 104–05

Operational weakness, 56–57

Operations other than war" (OOTW), 8

Order of battle (OB), 153–154

Organization of African Unity (OAU), 8, 14, 47, 48, 111–112, 248; Convention for the Elimination of Mercenarism in Africa, 228; external intervention and, 60, 131, 164; peacekeeping force, 174–175; pri-

vate security and, 209; sovereignty and, 95

Osleg Private Ltd., 224

Papau New Guinea, private security operations in, 212, 213, 220, 236n.102

Parallel militaries, 12, 44–45, 282

Paramilitaries, 84–85

Patron-client structures, military capability and, 12

Peacekeeping forces, 15, 18–19; training, 173–174; Western involvement in, 8. *See also* Economic Community of West African States Ceasefire Monitoring Group (ECOMOG)

Personal rule, 10–13; in ACRI recipient states, 256–257; expanded activities of, 86–87; civil-military divide and, 2; and ethnicization of militaries, 37–40; independence and, 35; and political loyalty versus military competency, 11–12, 28; parallel forces and privatization under, 12–13; political systems, 10–11; postindependence, 35–58; and private profiteering, 35–37; structural adjustment demands and, 78; survival tactics, 28

Political decolonization, 196

Political discourse, militarization of, 4

Political modernization, 23n.30

Political responsibility, military capabilities and, 2–3

Popular Movement for the Liberation of Angola (MPLA), 222; Executive Outcomes and, 198–200, 209–210

Private security forces, 2, 18, 187–229; accountability, 194–195, 213, 227; advantages and disadvantages, 192–195; confidentiality, 227; demobilization and, 86–87; expanded activities of, 86–87; as force multiplier, 215–216; and foreign-imposed victory, 216; financing, 216–217; as foreign policy tool, 222–224; and government-company relationships, 219–221; history of, 188–189; and human rights, 216, 227; industry growth, 188, 217; legitimacy, 229; local control of, 222–226; loyalty of, 193; military mercantilism and,

221–226, 228; mineral-military linkages, 221–222, 228; national military and, 216; neocolonialism and, 194; and combat versus nonlethal support, 219–221; post-Cold War demobilization, 189, 192; post-independence operations, 188–189; professionalism and respectability of, 49, 190–192; regulation and future of, 226–229; relief agencies and, 191–192; size implications, 218–219; supply and demand, 217–218; training costs, 193; Western governments and, 190–191. *See also* Executive Outcomes
Privatization of security, 12–13; 84–85. *See also* Government irregular forces; Private security forces
Procurement corruption, 41–43, 50

Quainoo, Arnold, 138, 139

Reagan, Ronald, 130
Reagan Doctrine, 77
Reconciliation policies, 21n.19
Recruitment: and combat capabilities, 57; subnational/ethnic, 29–30, 37–40
Refugees, 21n.11; and political problems, 6
Regional conflict, 6, 75, 79, 94–103; causes and consequences, 94; democratization and, 286–287; military mercantilism and, 97–100; international nonintervention in, 96; long-range weaponry's impact on, 101; and personal rule, 102–103; and preemptive self-defense, 95–97
Regional intervention forces, 2, 17–18; acceptance of, 149–153; ad hoc versus designated, 156, 163–164, 243; commitment of, 159; democracy and, 161–162; human rights adherence and, 164; possible advantages of, 130–131, 146–165; as peacekeeping versus peace enforcing mandate, 147, 148, 160–161, 163; military capabilities of, 153–159; national values and, 159, 160; peacekeeping iniatives, 173–175; politics and, 149–153, 164; and regional identity, 174; structure and support

system, 164; tactical intelligence, 157. *See also* African Crisis Response Initiative (ACRI); ECOMOG
Regulation of Foreign Military Assistance Act (South Africa), 212
Relief agencies, 253; attacks on, 93–94; private security forces and, 191–192, 218; sovereignty and, 105
Rentier concept, 44
Republic of Sierra Leone Military Force (RSLMF), 36–37, 37, 165; Executive Outcomes and, 210; unprofessionalism of, 56–57, 200–201, 202;
Revolutionary United Front (RUF) (Sierra Leone), 37, 81, 89, 90–91, 92, 130, 140, 165–169, 172, 221; brutality of, 5, 17, 56, 57; Executive Outcomes and, 205, 211, 214
RSLMF. *See* Republic of Sierra Leone Military Force
Rubin, James, 169
RUF. *See* Revolutionary United Front
Rules of engagement (ROE), 156
Rwanda: anti-Tutsi genocide, 79, 83; ethnicization of military in, 39; failure to intervene in, 109, 111; genocide in, 16, 79, 85–86, 247, 255; parallel forces in, 44; paramilitary groups, 85–86
Rwandan Patriotic Front (RPF), 25n.53, 81–82

SADF. *See* South African Defense Force
Saleh, Salim, 100, 222, 256
Salim, Salim Ahmed, 8, 55
Sanctions, 279
Sandline International military advisory group, 190, 228; "Arms to Africa" controversy, 220; Papau New Guinea operations, 212, 213, 236n.102
Sankoh, Foday, 130
Sassou-Nguesso, Denis, 79
Savimbi, Jonas, 7, 79, 195, 198, 203
Sawyer, Amos, 139
Secessionist attempts, 47–48
Security, definitions of, 74
Security, African, 2–3, 73–112; charac-

teristics of, 75–77; Cold War policies
and, 77–78; and foreign intervention,
78; foreign internal approaches to,
17–19; growth of nonstate forces
and, 193; military ethnicization and,
29–30; military mercantilism and,
225–226; post–Cold War, 77–79,
145–146; privatization and peripheralization of, 12–13, 84–85; state
legitimacy and, 76–77; state strategies, 2; state weakness and, 76–77;
and superpower support and influence, 77–78. *See also* Conflict,
African
Self-determination, 95
Senegal: ECOMOG and, 155; Senegal,
military professionalism in, 276,
279
Shelpidi, Timothy, 75
Sierra Leone: diamond smuggling in,
221; insurgency in, 165; Liberian
conflict and, 142; military budget,
205; mineral industry in, 200; security crises in, 74; state development,
Executive Outcomes and, 205–212.
See also Republic of Sierra Leonean
Military Force (RSLMF);
Revolutionary United Front (RUF)
Sierra Leonean conflict, 165–169; child
soldiers in, 84; ECOMOG forces in,
166–169; Executive Outcomes
forces in, 165–166, 200–204; private
security forces in, 189–190;
Singirok, Jerry, 236n.102
Somalia, 75; civil war, 255; military
ethnicization in, 38; Operation
Restore Hope in, 105, 106, 107, 108,
110; relief aid theft in, 191
South Africa: ACRF/ACRI and,
250–251, 257–259; and regional
peacekeeping, 174
South African Defence Force (SADF),
34, 45, 195, 196, 203, 215; profes-
sionalism of, 51–53, 197–198. *See
also* Executive Outcomes
South African National Defence Force
(SANDF), 60, 258
South Sudan Independence
Movement/Army, 88
South West African People's
Organization (SWAPO), 11

Southern African Development
Community countries, 174
Sovereignty: disregard for, 4; economic
aggrandizement and, 97–100;
humanitarian interventions and, 104,
105; mercenary groups and, 196;
versus state legitimacy, 14
Sovereignty-as-responsibility argument,
95, 97, 104, 259–260
Soviet Union, 77, 77, 246
Special Field Force (Namibia), 86
State, African: collapsed, 8, 77; criminalization of, 14; democracy and,
78–79; ethnic nationalism and,
87–88; stability, African militaries
and, 8–17; weakening of, 2–5,
76–77, 87–88, 96–97
State legitimacy: conflict and, 76–77;
government irregular forces' impact
on, 85; growth of nonstate forces
and, 193; impact of conflict on, 6–7;
militia crimes and, 85; and state sov-
ereignty, 14
Stevens, Siaka, 10, 36, 38, 50, 129, 200.
See also Sierra Leone
Strasser, Valentine, 201
Subnational groups, ethnic nationalism
of, 9
Sudan: military ethnicization in, 39;
National Islamic Front government,
85
Sudanese National Islamic Front gov-
ernment (NIF), 45
Sudanese Peoples' Defense Force
(PDF), 45
Sudanese Peoples' Liberation Army
(SPLA), 88
Superpower support, 77–78

Tanzania, 174; ECOMOG and, 155;
military ethnicization in, 38
Taylor, Charles, 40, 82, 133–134, 137,
139–140, 142–145, 146, 147,
148–149, 153, 161, 165, 221. *See
also* National Patriotic Front of
Liberia (NPFL)
Tirailleurs Sénégalais, 33
Tocqueville, Alexis de, 17
Togo, 39
Touré, Amadou Toumani, 277
Training exercises, 59

Ugandan military: ECOMOG experience of, 155; ethnicization in, 40; of Amin, 56, 276. *See also* Lord's Resistance Army

Ugandan People's Defence Force (UPDF): corruption and incompetence of, 55–56, 256, 259

ULIMO. *See* United Liberation Movement of Liberians for Democracy

UN Assistance Mission in Rwanda (UNAMIR), 109

UN Mission in Sierra Leone (UNAMSIL), 168–169, 254

UN Observer Mission in Liberia (UNOMIL), 144, 153

UN peacekeeping, 104, 163; force size, 105; peace enforcement operations, 103, 104, 106–107, 110; and self-determination, 95

UNITA. *See* National Union for the Total Independence of Angola

United Liberation Movement of Liberians for Democracy (ULIMO), 140–143; ethnic split in, 140–141

United Nations: African Crisis Response Force and, 248; ECOWAS partnership with, 131; Liberian conflict and, 135–136, 177n.19; mercenaries and, 228–229; and regional forces, 164

United States: Executive Outcomes and, 214; Liberian relations, 130, 131, 132–133, 145; military reductions, 110

United States military assistance: Cold War policies and, 77–78; costs, 8; ECOMOG and, 169; history of, 245–246; MPRI and, 220–221, 222; Somalia intervention, 8; Somalia syndrome and, 247. *See also* African Crisis Response Force (ACRF); Africa Crisis Response Initiative (ACRI)

UPDF. *See* Ugandan People's Defence Force

Urban fighting, 75–76

U.S. Agency for International Development, 220

U.S. Central Command, 174

U.S. Demilitarization for Democracy project, 245–246

U.S. European Command (EUCOM), 252

U.S. Joint Combined Exercises and Training Program (JCET), 245–246

Uti posidetis, concept of, 48

Van den Bergh, Nic, 195–196

Weapon(s): advances, 101; availability, 7, 79–83; financing, 101; profiteering, 91–92; trade and embargoes, 80–81; technology, 82; transport routes, 83

Weber, Max, 2, 9, 11, 193

West African states, regional peacekeeping and, 171, 173–174. *See also* ECOWAS

Western humanitarian intervention: failures of, 110; moral arguments for, 104; multilateral, 107–109; neutrality in, 106; peacekeeping versus peace enforcement mandate of, 106–107; reactions against, 105–111; sovereignty and, 104, 105

Wilson, Joseph, 254

World Bank, 81–82, 201, 224

Yamoussoukro accords, 142, 143, 161

Zaire: military corruption in, 43–44; military ethnicization in, 38; Western intercession in, 48

Zimbabwe: Congo intervention, 97–99, 100; economy of, 99; military ethnicization in, 38

Zimbabwean African National Union (ZANU), 11

ABOUT THE BOOK

F aced with a growing crisis of military insecurity, some African states have actually collapsed while others are threatened by ongoing insurgencies. This original work examines three potential options for increasing state security in contemporary Africa: regional military groupings, private security companies, and a continent-wide, professional peacekeeping force.

A case study of ECOMOG in Liberia and Sierra Leone examines the possibilities for regional military cooperation. Analysis of the infamous Executive Outcomes' operations in Angola and Sierra Leone raises the provocative question of whether mercenaries contribute to national security in the long run. The book also includes an assessment of the developing Africa Crisis Response Initiative, the first continental and rapidly deployable peacekeeping capability in Africa.

Howe explores these alternatives within the larger context of why African militaries have proven incapable of handling new types of insurgency; how the failed intervention in Somalia has limited Western efforts to act in subsequent crises, such as the genocide in Rwanda; and how African attempts to redefine "sovereignty" provide philosophical justification for armed intervention in the internal affairs of other states. Based on extensive travel in African war zones, his findings provide an important contribution to the growing field of African security.

Herbert M. Howe is assistant professor of African politics at Georgetown University.